PAUL'S DIVINE CHRISTOLOGY

Paul's Divine Christology

Chris Tilling

WILLIAM B. EERDMANS PUBLISHING COMPANY
GRAND RAPIDS, MICHIGAN / CAMBRIDGE, U.K.

First published 2012 in Germany by
Mohr Siebeck, Tübingen
This edition published 2015 in the United States of America by
Wm. B. Eerdmans Publishing Co.
2140 Oak Industrial Drive N.E., Grand Rapids, Michigan 49505 /
P.O. Box 163, Cambridge CB3 9PU U.K.

Printed in the United States of America

21 20 19 18 17 16 15   7 6 5 4 3 2 1

ISBN 978-0-8028-7295-1

www.eerdmans.com

Contents

Foreword

In order to appreciate the full significance of Chris Tilling's study, I will need to sketch out the basic contours of the Christology debate in the modern period in relation to Paul. This sketch will of course be quick and highly oversimplified. Tilling's survey is far more comprehensive, and I recommend reading it carefully. But there is value in identifying just the key figures and arguments within a more complex picture. This should make apparent Eerdmans' wisdom in republishing Tilling's work, making it more widely accessible. There is a sense in which Tilling's book really does chart the way forward for this fascinating and important debate. Whether Paul thought that Jesus was divine – however we conceive of that epithet exactly at the outset of our discussion – matters, and Tilling's intervention into this debate now matters as well. Things have now taken a new and profoundly constructive turn.

Our sketch can begin with Wilhelm Bousset.[1] It will be uncontroversial to suggest that the work of Bousset has cast a long shadow over the analysis of Paul's Christology in the modern period. He had predecessors, to be sure, not to mention comrades, and many later followers, some of whom populate our current discussions. But he is a key representative as well as a seminal figure. In Bousset we can observe three important analytic trends that have massively affected the discussion of Paul's Christology down to the present day.

First, Bousset is not merely historical but histori*cizing* in his approach. That is, history is treated as a closed process possessing only immanent causality. This metaphysical view is not, strictly speaking, derivative from the historical method itself. Discussion is restricted to the evidence left behind by "observables." Further, results are assumed to unfold historically out of their observable antecedents. Hence figures, texts, and notions embedded in particular cultures, which Bousset can analyze, generate further historical events. These he can consequently supply a responsible, objective, rational account for – objective

---

1. Bousset's most famous treatment was first published in 1913. It is available to English-speaking readers as *Kyrios Christos: A History of the Belief in Christ from the Beginnings of Christianity to Irenaeus,* 4th German ed., trans. J. E. Steely (Nashville: Abingdon, 1970).

and rational in the foregoing terms. Paul's Christology is therefore susceptible primarily to the analysis of its observable cultural antecedents. Those antecedents, internal to observable history, generate the apostle's position. Bousset is of course not alone in adopting this posture; it has characterized much work in the academy through the modern period.

Second – however – Bousset traces a consistent upward arc in his historical account on the assumption that history evolves, develops, and *progresses*. Much as we see in Darwin's famous theory – and this is no coincidence – reality evolves inexorably from lower to higher forms.[2] Within the church, then, the interpretation of Christ is held to rise steadily from lower notions like "prophet," to higher notions like Messiah, and ultimately to full divinity. To be early is to be low, one might say, and to be late is to be high. To be low is necessarily to be early and to be high is necessarily to be late. A historical map of the New Testament's internal development can consequently be traced in terms of these assumptions, and Paul will be placed on it at the appropriate point.

Third, Bousset matches this evolution from lower to higher with a centrifugal expansion by the early church through different cultural layers. Primitive Palestinian milieux give way to more sophisticated, urban, Greco-Roman environments. And it is precisely this expansion that provides the cultural engine for the evolution of Christology. As the early church expanded into these new contexts, the new thought forms it encountered, and the new needs of its missions, generated new Christological positions that ascended ever higher. (An underlying assumption here is really that ancient Greco-Roman culture was intrinsically superior to ancient Judaism.)

Paul operates at a critical, although arguably somewhat ambiguous, juncture in this process. As the missionary to the pagans, he bursts across the threshold of Judaism into Greco-Roman territory – Bousset thinks, precisely and quite possibly correctly, at Syrian Antioch[3] – and his Christology ascends under the impress of the new culture's enthusiasm for divine figures. He is consequently somewhat late in the developmental process, being preceded by key stages. But he is clearly the earliest extant witness in the New Testament. So these earlier layers must be painstakingly reconstructed largely from fragmentary evidence embedded in his letters.

Paul's contribution was not the ultimate Christological stage in the New Testament's development – an auspicious position usually reserved for the Fourth Gospel. Nevertheless, Bousset was happy to view Paul's Christology in fairly

2. Charles Darwin's *On the Origin of Species* was published in 1859. Developmental and evolutionary theories were in vogue well in advance of this date, however. A key philosophical contribution by G. W. F. Hegel was published from 1807–30, and he was drawing on earlier advocates.

3. See the telltale remark of Acts 11:26c – "the disciples were first named 'Christians' at Antioch."

elevated terms, at least in a Greco-Roman sense. Paul developed a view of Christ as a cult figure of Greco-Roman devotion, similar to a figure like Alexander the Great, and arguably under the pressure of Greco-Roman cults like Mithraism, where the central figure was overtly mythical. The result of this critical development then was a view of Jesus as a god in a delimited sense, which made him the basis of a highly comprehensible, effective missionary gospel for pagans.

Of course, this view of Jesus as a Greco-Roman cult figure, and its related view of the New Testament, by no means accords with the church's later understanding of Christ and expectations of the New Testament witness, as evidenced by the Nicene-Chalcedonian creeds. The notion of divinity in play in the creeds is of a single, monotheistic, transcendent deity more recognizable within Judaism than against Bousset's pagan backdrop. Jesus combines that divinity and his humanity fully within his one person, the creeds affirm. But this is – for Bousset – a fully evolved account of Jesus as God far removed from the early church, the New Testament, its Pauline witness, and of course from Jesus himself (referring here to "the historical Jesus" who actually walked the dusty roads of Palestine).

Bousset's analysis obviously issues a profound challenge to Christian scholars who hope that the New Testament bears a stronger relation to Christian orthodoxy than this. Indeed, they see in this type of argument – correctly – the re-emergence of two key heresies that the church battled in its first centuries: Ebionitism[4], although this could easily be supplemented by other related heresies like Nestorianism[5] and Adoptionism[6]; and Marcionism[7] – a deadly double challenge. Ebionitism denies the full divinity of Christ as the church later defined this – in relation to a universal, transcendent monotheism. Jesus was just a human figure and this alone. This understanding of Jesus wedges apart the interpretation of Jesus from its antecedents in Judaism and the Old Testament, and even in creation. Marcion went on to attribute them to another god. Of course neither of these alternatives is particularly desirable. So the stakes could not really be higher in relation to the historical claims made by Bousset and those like him.

Despite these stakes, however, it is probably fair to say that an evolutionary account of Christology has largely dominated scholarly reconstruction of the New Testament more broadly and Paul more narrowly until relatively re-

---

4. A heretical movement that reputedly emphasized the Jewish law, rejected the teachings of the Apostle Paul, and held Jesus to be merely a human and not God.

5. This is the view that Jesus existed as two persons rather than as a unified person, the human person, Jesus, being assumed by the divine Son of God. It was ascribed primarily to Nestorius (386–450 C.E.), Patriarch of Constantinople from 428–431 C.E.

6. This is the view that Jesus was adopted as God's Son either at his baptism, his resurrection, or his ascension.

7. Marcion of Sinope argued in the middle of the second century that Jesus was a savior sent by a benevolent God, and Paul was his chief Apostle, but argued as well that the vengeful God of Israel and of creation was not the same god, and that the Hebrew Scriptures were therefore to be abandoned.

cently. As Tilling notes in his own more detailed summary, an important shift in the conversation in relation to Paul took place after 1970. Moreover, it has been associated in particular with the subsequent work of two scholars, Richard Bauckham and Larry Hurtado, to whose contributions we now turn. (Other important figures are noted by Tilling's survey as well.) Both scholars made largely historical but powerful cases repudiating the principal suggestions of Bousset and his descendants.

Bauckham's case is largely – to put matters very summarily – an argument from predication.[8] He assembles data from Jewish sources to argue that certain predications were strictly reserved by Jews for their single, transcendent deity, for example, his name, along with fundamental creative, redemptive, and eschatological judging activities. He then argues that some of these predications are attributed to Jesus by Paul, from which it follows that Jesus was included by Paul within the divine identity. We can reproduce the basic structure of his argument with the following syllogism:

> For all Jews, activities A, B, and C, are only predicated of God.
> The early Christians, who were Jews, predicated activities A, B, and C of Jesus.
> Therefore (other things being equal), the early Jewish Christians held Jesus to be God.[9]

Hurtado's approach is a little different. In a sense he simply inverts Bousset's case.[10] Like Bauckham, he argues first for the importance of Jewish resources for Paul over against Greco-Roman notions, but he goes on to observe that Paul's account of devotional activities by the early Christians in relation to Jesus paralleled Jewish devotional activities in relation to God. The conclusion to this argument is then again that Jesus was divine for Paul in the full Jewish transcendent monotheistic sense, although the syllogism has been constructed in slightly different terms:

8. Now most accessible in his *Jesus and the God of Israel: God Crucified and Other Studies on the New Testament's Christology of Divine Identity* (Grand Rapids: Eerdmans, 2008). The first important essay within this collection, "God Crucified," appeared initially in 1998 as *God Crucified: Monotheism and Christology in the New Testament* (Carlisle: Paternoster), but Bauckham's advocacy of this position predates these publications considerably – see, e.g., "The Worship of Jesus in Apocalyptic Christianity," *NTS* 27 (1980/81): 322–41.

9. Note: Bauckham defines this "equation" very carefully. He argues on the basis of this material that the early Christians included Jesus within the divine identity. Moreover, Bauckham did also briefly advance the argument later developed at length by Hurtado in terms of worship and devotion, which functions differently, as we will see momentarily.

10. *One God, One Lord: Early Christian Devotion and Ancient Jewish Monotheism* (Philadelphia: Augsburg Fortress, 1988); a second edition appeared in 1998 (Edinburgh: T&T Clark). See also *Lord Jesus Christ: Devotion to Jesus in Earliest Christianity* (Grand Rapids: Eerdmans, 2003).

All Jews believed only God was to be worshiped.
The early Christians, who were Jews, worshiped Jesus.
Therefore (all other things being equal), the early Jewish Christians
    believed Jesus was God.[11]

Both these arguments have met with successes and problems.

On the one hand, many have found their basic claims fundamentally plausible. Certainly those advocating a high (Jewish) Christology in Paul have regained some confidence. On the other hand, both arguments suffer from counter-evidence, and this is at least in part because both accept Bousset's initial historicizing challenge. They argue forward from historical and cultural antecedents and so become vulnerable to the messy complexities of history.

Much of Bauckham's case rests on the initial demonstration that all Jews maintained strict semantic boundaries in relation to their God-talk. They always reserved certain predications for God and never, under any circumstances, allowed the same predications for non-divine agents. But historians informed by a dash of postmodernism will suspect that it is very unlikely that this position is sustainable. People are simply a lot sloppier than this thesis suggests. History is complex and untidy, as is language. And so, sure enough, occasional instances can be found in Jewish sources that use the predications Bauckham strictly reserves for God in relation to non-divine, intermediary figures. Arguably, such counter-examples falsify his case, or, at least, reduce it to probabilistic status. For the case to hold entirely – for the underlying syllogism to be valid – the initial premise must be universally true. Certainly the vast preponderance of evidence is on Bauckham's side, but – at least arguably – not all of it is.

Hurtado may well have similar difficulties (as do arguments in relation to *Yahweh* texts and pre-existent entities).[12] Evidence can be found of worship – or at least of arguably devotional activities – being performed by Jews in relation to non-divine figures and entities. And so Hurtado's underlying syllogism could be falsified as well. The preponderance of evidence is on his side, as it is on Bauckham's. But his underlying syllogism is, strictly speaking, invalid. We do not know *for sure* that the early Christians could not, in the exceptional circumstances created by Jesus' resurrection and presumed ascension, have resorted to these practices in their tradition. If parallel devotion or veneration might be shown within Judaism to extremely important but non-divine figures like angels or the High Priest or Enoch's Son of Man, then veneration to Jesus would not

---

11. Again, this "equation" is not to be taken strictly literally as a summary of Hurtado's case, which is clearly more complex and extended than this. Also, Hurtado phrases his conclusion slightly differently from this – and from Bauckham. The early Christian evidence suggests for him "a novel devotional pattern that is genuinely 'binitarian' " ("Preface to the Second Edition," *One God, One Lord*, 2003, xv).

12. Tilling canvasses this material helpfully in what follows.

necessarily entail that Jesus was divine in the sense of being included alongside the God of Israel in a fully "binitarian" pattern of devotion per Hurtado. I think this is unlikely, as does Hurtado, but his argument nevertheless, like Bauckham's, can be reduced to merely probabilistic status.

It is at this point that Tilling enters the lists. He has learned a great deal from both Bauckham and Hurtado – nothing he says invalidates their conclusions. However, his case for divine Christology is, at bottom, fundamentally different in its approach, and in a manner that seems to avoid their vulnerabilities.

As we have just seen, both Bauckham and Hurtado work "forward." They argue for a universal set of practices in the Judaism of Paul's day, and for the importance of his Jewish background. This creates weaknesses on the front end of their argumentation, so to speak. It is difficult to make the case for a pristine set of practices within the Judaism of Paul's day given the complexity and sheer messiness of history. However, both Bauckham and Hurtado then turn to Paul and make a further case in relation to a rather slim slice of the relevant evidence, whether in terms of certain divine predications or particular devotional practices as evident in Paul's letters. And this creates a weakness at the back end of their analyses as well. The result of this procedure is a *narrowness* in relation to Paul himself. Even if these scholars succeed in their initial case, Christ's putative divinity plays no obvious role in most of Paul's writing! And this feels like a Pyrrhic victory, not to mention one that invites a riposte in relation to all the evidence in Paul that remains unexplained. (Tilling repeatedly notes Casey's objection that this evidence is simply "sparse," and it is a fair point.[13])

Tilling's argumentative strategy – and it might be worth noting here in passing that he is a chess player of some sophistication – is designed to get around these two weaknesses. There are – I suggest – four key steps in it.[14]

13. "Monotheism, Worship and Christological Developments in the Pauline Churches," in *The Jewish Roots of Christological Monotheism,* ed. C. Newman, J. Davila, and G. Lewis (Leiden: Brill, 1999), 214–33, quoting from 222.

14. Strictly speaking, another argumentative issue is raised that I am reluctantly not going to introduce here. At the end of his book, especially in an important Appendix, Tilling starts to investigate first-order questions of epistemology in relation to historicism. This opens up a critical conversation. Moreover, his work here can be well positioned within what I would want to suggest is the most constructive side of this very important debate that ultimately has extremely serious implications for Christology – the "revelational" or "apocalyptic" side. But this material moves the entire conversation to a different plane; different issues and figures are in view. So I am going to regretfully pass over the opportunity to comment on all this and simply sketch his basic *historical* case here for Paul's divine Christology. This will, I suspect, be sufficient trouble for the day.

An incisive introduction to an apocalyptic view of history and its modern historicizing detractors is Nathan R. Kerr, "Ernst Troeltsch: The Triumph of Ideology and the Eclipse of Apocalyptic," in *Christ, History and Apocalyptic: The Politics of Christian Mission* (London: SCM, 2008), 23–62. The key epistemological questions for Christology are treated superbly in two essays by Alan J. Torrance: "The Trinity," in *The Cambridge Companion to Barth,* ed. John Web-

Unlike Bauckham and Hurtado, Tilling begins internally to Paul, in one of the happy hunting grounds for a divine Christology, namely, 1 Corinthians 8 and 10. Paul's conspicuous use of the *Shema* in 1 Corinthians 8:6 in particular allows Tilling to demonstrate exegetically that Jesus is functioning through much of Paul's argument in this passage in the location of Israel's God. In this, then, key aspects of both Bauckham's and Hurtado's positions are apparent, not to mention those of Gordon Fee, another major recent contributor.[15] The predications or activities ascribed to God here and elsewhere are important, as is the relationship between the Corinthian believers Paul here addresses and Christ. The result is a confident – and persuasive – judgment by Tilling that Jesus is being treated by Paul in this argument in a way that is divine in the full, Jewish sense. However, by starting here, the shifting sands of prior general historical reconstruction have been avoided. Tilling does not have to prove that Jewish sources were critical for Paul all the time; they simply are here and overtly so. And he doesn't have to prove that all Jews thought about God in a certain way all the time; he just has to observe that some did for much of the time and that thought is plainly apparent in this passage as well.

In his second key argumentative step Tilling drills down into this passage to uncover the way Christ's divinity is actually functioning rhetorically and pastorally for Paul. Tilling's word for this function is "pattern," and he discovers in due course that the key pattern in play is "relational." The meaning of this might be a little opaque at first glance, but when he develops it, we see that Tilling's contention is that Paul's divine Christology is operating at one end of a relationship between Christ and his people, the church. But this relationship is being articulated constantly – we might also say "mapped" – by the relationship between God and his people, Israel, in the Old Testament. So the *pattern* that emerges from 1 Corinthians 8 and 10 in relation to Paul's divine Christology is *relational* and *in this particular sense,* namely, the relationship between God and his followers. Moreover, this is a relational pattern with rich potential.

It is not limited to devotional practices, *although it includes them.* Neither is it limited to predications in relation to creation or eschatology, *although it includes them.* The basic relationship between the Christian person and Christ is, Tilling observes, simply being mapped by Paul constantly in terms of the relationship between God and Israel evident in both the OT and in the Jewish sources of Paul's day. As such, it includes all the many important aspects of that relationship – prayer, revelations, zeal and desire, obedience, ethics, praise,

ster (Cambridge: Cambridge University Press, 2000), 72–91; and "Jesus in Christian Doctrine," in *The Cambridge Companion to Jesus,* ed. M. Bockmuehl (Edinburgh: Cambridge University Press, 2001), 200–219.

15. Fee's important contribution in many respects prefigures Tilling's work: *Pauline Christology: An Exegetical-Theological Study* (Peabody, Mass.: Hendrickson, 2007). But Tilling's case is effected with greater clarity and precision.

thankfulness, service, and so on. (It does not *reproduce* that pattern exactly; but the relational pattern in Paul is articulated by material drawn almost exclusively from that earlier God-and-Israel pattern, and a great deal is being drawn from it.) So Tilling's Christological syllogism looks more like this:

> God ← practices of his[16] people in this relationship
> Christ ← practices of the Corinthians and Paul in this relationship
> Therefore, Christ is functioning as God did (and does)
> (and the text directly corroborates this location as well).

The importance of this step – not to mention its derivation – can hardly be overstated. Tilling's judgments emerge from his consideration of Paul's texts in 1 Corinthians 8 and 10, so his conclusions concerning Paul's Christology are rooted in inductive work. He thereby locates Paul's divine Christology where it is actually operating for Paul, doing the work that the apostle wants it to do in relation to his Corinthian community and hence, by implication, everywhere else. Paul's Christology is thereby married to his epistolary rhetoric. With these theories in place, where does Tilling then find this relational pattern operating in Paul elsewhere?

Everywhere.

In his third step, Tilling quickly demonstrates – and the claim need not be labored – that the relationship between Christians and Christ developed in terms of the relationship between God and Israel is evident in all of Paul's letters, and does most of the key argumentative work within them. It explains almost everything he says and urges, from praise to admonition and from prayer to exhortation and calling. So Tilling succeeds in building a bridge where others seem to have failed, and it is a highly strategic one.

Paul's divine Christology is in effect operationalized through all his texts so those writings now attest constantly to this Christology. But the heart of Paul's relationship with Christ has now also been illuminated. Paul's devotional and *participatory* aspects are threaded with Christology and, beyond this, basic Jewish notions about relating to God. Hence the long tradition that understands the heart of Paul's gospel in participatory terms, but that has arguably for an equally long time struggled to explain this precisely, has had a critical explanatory dimension added to it – a profoundly constructive, even orthodox one.[17] Moreover,

---

16. The use of the male pronoun here should be taken advisedly.

17. In most recent Pauline discussion, the advocacy of this important motif would be associated most strongly with Michael Gorman; see especially his *Inhabiting the Cruciform God: Kenosis, Justification, and Theosis in Paul's Narrative Theology* (Grand Rapids: Eerdmans, 2009). Robert C. Tannehill supplies a useful summary in "Participation in Christ: A Central Theme in Pauline Soteriology," in *The Shape of the Gospel: New Testament Essays* (Eugene, Ore.: Cascade [Wipf and Stock], 2007), 223–37. The origin of an emphasis on the importance

this considerable broadening of the case's evidential base has also neatly avoided the second major weakness that was apparent earlier on in the contributions of Bauckham and Hurtado, namely, the narrowness of their evidence when they turned to Paul. Tilling's account of Paul's divine Christology possesses real explanatory power in relation to Paul himself.

In his final step – at least for the purposes of this introduction – Tilling turns back to the qualifications that scholars have offered to the cases of Bauckham and Hurtado, and shows how his approach overcomes them, thereby revalidating the conclusions to their syllogisms within his broader argument. Once Tilling's larger construct is seen in play in the writings of Paul – and it has been established internally and exegetically, not in broad historical terms that ultimately prove somewhat fragile – then the argument in terms of exceptions is easily negated.

In a little more detail: both Bauckham and Hurtado in effect lay out a spectrum of semantic options. The preponderance of the data they adduce relates to *Yahweh*'s divinity, but occasionally, as their critics have pointed out, predications and cultic and devotional practices stray toward intermediary figures, as do even *Yahweh* scriptural texts on occasion. It was these exceptions that weakened the syllogisms of both Bauckham and Hurtado.[18] We could not tell, when initially interpreting Paul's text in terms of these prior options, which option ought to be in play – a divine Christology or an exalted intermediary figure as sometimes attested in the literature. But everything becomes clearer when these possibilities are reintroduced within the relational pattern Tilling has detected widely in Paul. As Christ and Paul's communities relate very much as God and Israel, the specific options Bauckham and Hurtado advocated earlier on, in terms essentially of full divinity, are confirmed and activated as overwhelmingly likely. Then the exceptional data is more readily excluded as an overwhelmingly unlikely interpretative map for what is happening in Paul's letters. It is clear in this setting that the "high" reading of the data is *in fact* in play. Contextual markers in Paul activate it obviously and comprehensively. Tilling's construct therefore allows us to see that Bauckham's and Hurtado's advocacies are the correct ones, and affirms their analyses, although in the foregoing, largely reframed terms. But Tilling's analysis does rather more than this as well. His construct also allows us to see that in the very sources quoted to generate the exceptions, the God-Israel

---

of this motif for Paul within the modern period is usually held to be G. Adolf Deissmann; see his *St. Paul: A Study in Social and Religious History,* 2nd ed., trans. L. R. M. Strachan (London: Hodder & Stoughton, 1912).

18. It is only fair to acknowledge that both Bauckham and Hurtado would deny this. They are well aware of these objections and have done a great deal to respond to them. Tilling is not convinced, however, that enough has yet been done; the debate here in his view has reached something of a stalemate. Moreover, he thinks the entire case for a divine Christology in Paul can be significantly strengthened if it is reoriented methodologically.

relation in them explains the Pauline material better than the exceptions! Not only are the exceptions to the work of Bauckham and Hurtado defused then, but the evidence marshalled by those arguing for a lower Christology is now turned back on their own heads (a masterful stroke, one has to admit).

It should be plainly apparent then by this stage in our sketch that Tilling's study enacts a significant new phase in the divine Christology debate in relation to Paul, and has indeed taken things to a new level. It deftly overcomes the weaknesses arguably apparent in the earlier seminal contributions of Bauckham and Hurtado, affirming both the fact of Paul's divine Christology and its ubiquitous and vital function within his letters – significant contributions to scholarship indeed. To say then in closing that Tilling's work is required reading for Pauline scholars is something of an understatement. Its arguments need to pass into the warp and woof of our analyses, very much as Tilling has articulated the way Paul's divine Christology was part of the warp and woof of his.

DOUGLAS CAMPBELL
The Divinity School,
Duke University

Preface to the Eerdmans Edition

Three years have passed since the publication of the Mohr Siebeck edition of *Paul's Divine Christology,* and I have enjoyed following its reception in different communities. A book like this, you see, is written primarily for the academic community, so I'm naturally happy that I seem to have persuaded most readers in the academy of its central contention, or at least further substantiated previously held views. That said, the subject matter of this book, namely the earliest Christian understanding of Jesus in terms of God's "transcendent uniqueness" (to use Richard Bauckham's phrase), is of inestimable importance for many other people. In this respect I have particularly enjoyed correspondence with several church pastors and undergraduate level students who have benefited from grappling with my arguments. Indeed, I claim in the appendix of this book that to attend to the dynamics of Paul's own christological rhetoric is ultimately to find ourselves wrestling with the challenge of living in communal relationship with the risen Christ *today.* And so I am delighted that Eerdmans is making this book available to a wider audience.

I remain as confident as ever about the case I make here for Paul's divine Christology, yet I was not quite aware of just how many typos, split infinitives, and other such "grammar crimes" there were in the Mohr Siebeck version until a chat with Tom Wright at SBL one year. He kindly showed me a list of my blunders, all of which he had compiled while reading it in preparation for his epic *Paul and the Faithfulness of God.* Not only is this man something of a living legend in New Testament scholarship; I also learnt that he has a very sharp eye! Tom was kind enough to find time to type up that list and send it my way in preparation for this edition, and his efforts have surely improved the book. My sincere thanks to Tom for this and for his encouraging words about *Paul's Divine Christology.* It would seem that there is an extremely promising future for him in proofreading if the writing career doesn't work out!

Admittedly, I have left some things unchanged. Three are worth mentioning. First, please forgive the slightly indiscriminate and often inappropriate use of the hyphen between "divine" and "Christology" throughout. Second, I occasionally refer to dissertations that have been published. I think, for example, of Suzanne

Beth Nicholson's "Dynamic Oneness," now published by Pickwick (a Wipf and Stock imprint), and of Volker Rabens' superbly researched "The Holy Spirit and Religious-Ethical Life in Paul," published by Mohr and then in revised form by Mohr and Fortress. Third, my musings in the appendix have since developed considerably, and my thoughts are taking me in a direction that will warrant another book. Rather than anticipate those changes, however, it seemed best to leave the original arguments intact for now.

I must reserve a special thanks to those who have kindly endorsed this book for Eerdmans. I remain particularly grateful to Steve Fowl, Max Turner, Nick Norelli, and Richard Bauckham for their encouragement and scholarly insight over the years. Thanks also to Michael Thomson of Eerdmans, for his friendship as well as his determination to make this new edition a reality. I must also record my sincere thanks to Douglas Campbell for the Foreword. I consider him to be not only a friend, but also the most brilliant scholar in the world of Pauline studies, and I'm honored by his words.

Since the 2012 printing, my beautiful wife gave birth to our first child, a son. With all my love I dedicate this new edition both to Anja and to Karl Lucas Benjamin Tilling.

CHRIS TILLING
St Mellitus College, 2015

Preface to the Mohr Siebeck Edition

Writing the Preface to a monograph is a daunting task, especially when so many people have contributed to the final product. As this work is only a slightly revised version of my Ph.D. thesis, to start off I would like to thank my *Doktorvater*, Max Turner, for his friendly, wise and insightful comments at key points, for his faith in this project and his encouragement. I am very thankful to my examiners, Professors Steve Walton and Larry Hurtado. I considered myself honoured to be examined by you. I would also like to thank the Laing Foundation for a number of generous scholarship awards, all of which helped to make my research a financial possibility. I am very grateful to Professor Jörg Frey for accepting this thesis for publication, and to Doctor Henning Ziebritzki and the not only helpful but also friendly team at Mohr Siebeck. For their assistance, particularly that of Frau Dominika Zgolik, my appreciation. Thanks also to Katie Law for her superb work in producing the indices.

I must also acknowledge the constructive feedback from participants of the New Testament research seminars of Professor Hans-Joachim Eckstein, and the New Testament research conferences at London School of Theology. Most of all, however, I must warmly thank the members of the bilingual Colloquium for Graduates of Professor Hermann Lichtenberger and Doctor Scott Caulley. Since my move to London I have missed our weekly gatherings, the valuable learned input and discussions, not to mention friends left behind.

But moving to London also has had its benefits, not least life at a most remarkable church, Holy Trinity Brompton. Inspiration, encouragement and, most important of all, new friends and colleagues have helped smooth the last few months of this project. I would like to thank my colleagues at St Mellitus College, especially Andrew Emerton and Graham Tomlin, for their kindness and support. I consider it an honour to work with you and the rest of the team.

I would like to thank a number of people who have made an effort to help me in the proofreading process. Doctor Michael Gorman, in particular, made numerous helpful comments, and I was most grateful for his expert input. I remain grateful also to Doctor Stephen Fowl for his encouragement. Thanks to Nick Norelli for his numerous insightful observations – I await his own academic contributions with great anticipation. My sincere thanks also to Volker Rabens and David Vinson, who gave of their time to read through earlier drafts of my thesis. Your help was both valuable and appreciated! Special mention must go to my good friend Jim West, who has not only made valuable suggestions to improve my argument at various points, but has been a constant source of encouragement. His friendship is the best thing to have come out of my adventures as a 'biblioblogger'. Of course, I want to also acknowledge the wider, growing, diverse and evolving community of biblio- and theo- bloggers. You know who you are. Our discussions have sometimes enriched my work tremendously.

My warmest thanks to my dear parents, Roger and Rosalind Tilling, for financial support, proofreading help, and most of all, more love and encouragement than I can ever repay. This project would not have been possible without you.

My deepest thanks are reserved for my beautiful wife, Anja, who not only financially supported me through the last few years of the Ph.D., but also proofread every page of my work with a fine-tooth comb, spotted more mistakes than I care to remember and helped correct my grammar at various points (and that even though she is German!). Her precious love and support throughout this project could never be summarised with mere words, and the end product is, at many levels, as much her work as it is mine. I dedicate this thesis to her with every ounce of my affection and love.

It was during a season of prayer that the idea behind this thesis developed. During the entire research process, I felt sustained, animated and inspired by my Heavenly Father. I hasten to add, of course, that all mistakes and shortcomings in the following argument remain mine! Indeed, having begun life as a New Testament lecturer, I am not surprised that aspects of my thinking have subsequently sharpened, but as one of Leo Tolstoy's characters said in *Anna Karenina:* 'If you look for perfection, you'll never be content'. Nor would one ever publish! I look forward to continued interaction with the academic community in the coming years, together with the inevitable correction of my own proposals that this will entail, over the truly fascinating subject of the nature and development of early Christology.

Soli Deo honor et gloria!

CHRIS TILLING
St Paul's Onslow Square, 2012

Abbreviations

The abbreviations in this thesis adopt those in P. H. Alexander et al. (eds.), *The SBL Handbook of Style for Ancient Near Eastern, Biblical, and Early Christian Studies* (Peabody, Mass.: Hendrickson, 1999). Only abbreviations not found in the *SBL Handbook of Style* are noted below.

General Abbreviations:

EMSM	Boccaccini, G., ed. *Enoch and the Messiah Son of Man.* Cambridge: Eerdmans, 2007
ESV	English Standard Version
ETS	Evangelical Theological Society
LJC	Hurtado, Larry W. *Lord Jesus Christ: Devotion to Jesus in Earliest Christianity.* Grand Rapids: Eerdmans, 2003
NET	New English Translation
NLT	New Living Translation
NT	New Testament
OG	Hurtado, Larry W. *One God, One Lord.* London: SCM, 1988
OG²	Hurtado, Larry W. *One God, One Lord.* Edinburgh: T&T Clark, 1998² (second edition)
OT	Old Testament

Abbreviations for journals not noted in the *SBL Handbook of Style:*

ED	*Euntes Docete*
FzB	*Forschung zur Bibel* (Würzburg)
JHeS	*Journal of Hebrew Scriptures*

Chapter 1

Paul's divine-Christology. An introduction

1. Framing the debate

The question concerning the identity and divinity of Christ is one born and raised in controversy. Ever since it has been asked it has generated a wide mixture of responses, ranging from physical violence and vicious debate to worship and praise, with not just a little painfully subtle metaphysical theorising on the way. Debate continues in many quarters, especially within the world of Pauline scholarship which, for the last few decades, has witnessed a resurgence of dispute as to whether Paul's Christology should be properly understood as 'divine'. And these are not peripheral concerns for if those who deny a Pauline divine-Christology are correct, perhaps some difficult questions need to be fearlessly pursued and not sidestepped in the name of unthinking orthodoxy. This is all the more true as Paul has traditionally been understood to have authored over half of what became the canon of the New Testament. What is more, it is also arguably fair to claim that without an understanding of what Paul thought about Christ, one is not likely to understand much about Paul at all. Indeed, it can be maintained that a clearer grasp of Paul's Christology will speak into contemporary debates concerning justification. On top of this, given that the (at least, undisputed) Pauline corpus is the earliest layer of NT literature, the question of whether Pauline Christology is divine is of great significance for one's understanding of the development of early Christology generally, and thus the history of early Christianity.[1]

So this is not a minor topic, and one must, therefore, immediately address matters of definition, even if only in a preliminary fashion. This is necessary because what one scholar means, by cheerfully affirming particularly a Pauline *divine*-Christology, means something very different when the same language is used by other scholars - even to the point of contradiction. To give this discussion focus, the following provisional and working definition of 'divine-Christology' will thus be adopted. To cite Bauckham, a divine-Christology is one that places Christ, 'on the divine side of the line which

---

[1] For the range of views, cf. Carey C. Newman, "From (Wright's) Jesus to (the Church's) Christ: Can We Get There from Here?" in *Jesus and the Restoration of Israel. A Critical Assessment of N.T. Wright's Jesus and the Victory of God* (ed. Carey C. Newman; Carlisle: IVP, 1999), 281–87.

monotheism must draw between God and creatures'.[2] It will be possible, in light of this thesis, to critically return to this definition in chapter 10.

But first, an important question can be anticipated. As shall be seen in the next chapter, mid-20th century scholarship exhaustively analysed the various Pauline christological titles, and Larry Hurtado's work in particular has already proficiently analysed the importance of Pauline Christ-devotion. On top of this, in 2007, Gordon Fee published a massive tome addressing precisely the sort of questions we wish to analyse here.[3] Some may wonder, then, what more needs to be said. Can another book on Paul's Christology offer any new insight or will it simply be doomed to a matter of 'moving the furniture'?

What is more, modern scholarship has arguably reached something of an impasse on the precise question to be tackled in this volume, namely Is Paul's Christology divine? On the one hand, scholars such as Gordon Fee, Richard Bauckham and Larry Hurtado have variously answered in the affirmative. Yet others remain profoundly unpersuaded. So James Dunn, while maintaining an early 'high-Christology',[4] surrounds his affirmations with all manner of qualifications, and ultimately denies the kind of divine-Christology affirmed by Bauckham and others. After all, Christ is, for Paul, unambiguously *subordinate* to God (e.g. 1 Cor. 15:27–28) and the Father is Christ the Lord's 'God' (e.g. 2 Cor. 1:3). Maurice Casey, too, opines that Paul's Christology cannot properly be called 'divine'. Such a decisive break with Jewish monotheism could only come later, with the influx of Gentiles into the population of those professing Christian-faith. Indeed, some could suggest there is, in some very recent scholarship, a turning of the tide away from affirmations of a Pauline divine-Christology to its denial, as is evidenced in the publications of, for example, James McGrath, James Crossley and Pamela Eisenbaum.[5] This is consistent with the fact that not only can a case be made for a less-than-fully divine-Christology in Paul, some observe weaknesses in the arguments used by scholars to affirm a divine-Christology. For example, Bauckham's divine-identity categories do not, when examined against the literature of second Temple Judaism, appear as clear-cut as he seems to maintain, and one won-

---

[2] Richard J. Bauckham, "The Worship of Jesus in Apocalyptic Christianity," *NTS* 27 (1981): 335.

[3] Gordon D. Fee, *Pauline Christology: An Exegetical-Theological Study* (Peabody: Hendrickson, 2007).

[4] James D.G. Dunn, *The Theology of Paul the Apostle* (Grand Rapids: Eerdmans, 1998), 258.

[5] James F. McGrath, *The Only True God: Early Christian Monotheism in Its Jewish Context* (Urbana: University of Illinois Press, 2009); Pamela Eisenbaum, *Paul Was not a Christian: The Original Message of a Misunderstood Apostle* (New York: HarperOne, 2009); Michael F. Bird and Crossley James G., *How Did Christianity Begin? A Believer and Non-Believer Examine the Evidence* (London: SPCK, 2008); James G. Crossley, *Reading the New Testament: Contemporary Approaches* (London: Routledge, 2010), 75–98.

ders to what extent his approach really gets to the heart of Paul's language. Hurtado's approach, too, must be critiqued at important points, and it can be maintained that the weaknesses in his own arguments have indeed provoked some of the Pauline-divine-Christology-denial now entering the field of NT studies. Likewise, Fee's contributions, while extensive, are problematic at numerous levels, as will be explored below.

This volume enters the debate by offering a fresh way of approaching the question of Pauline Christology, in terms of the 'divinity debate'. This, it will be argued, is demanded by a number of factors, ranging from Paul's monotheism, his epistemology, and most importantly, the shape and content of his major concerns in his letters. Building on the works of Hurtado, Bauckham and Fee, it is the contention of this volume that affirmation of a Pauline divine-Christology is necessary. In a nutshell, it will be argued that the whole Pauline divine-Christology debate has yet to grasp sufficiently the most obvious, namely Paul's own language and the most appropriate pattern of Pauline themes relevant to this debate. By analysing the data in Paul which concerns the relation between the risen Lord and believers, it will be maintained that relational data concerning Christ in Paul's letters corresponds, as a pattern, only to the language concerning YHWH in second Temple Judaism. It is concluded that the Christ-relation is Paul's divine-Christology expressed as relationship. Before overviewing how this argument will unfold in the following chapters, two points will be made about wider concerns addressed by the approach of this thesis.

2. Two wider concerns

The first matter tangentially engaged in the following thesis concerns the present debate about the legitimacy of theological readings of the NT, and the propriety of the 'great ugly ditch' in academic theological research between NT studies, on the one hand, and theology or dogmatics, on the other. To what extent should the NT be read from within the concerns of a faith community, as a supposedly God-inspired text, or to what extent should the text be better analysed via recourse to 'independent' scholarship using historical-critical tools employed in other disciplines concerned with historical research? For many this sets up a false alternative, but some will insist that the only properly academic route must resist the commitments and concerns of faith communities, which more often that not project anachronistic concerns on to ancient texts. Some, on the other hand, will argue that to engage with the NT texts correctly, one must necessarily speak of God, thus theologically, while others will further add that to appreciate the context, substance, purpose, and origin of these texts correctly, one must allow one's rhetoric to be determined by the content of God's triune self-revelation in the gospel.[6]

This study certainly begins with what some could consider a rather special-ised New Testament academia-insider matter, namely the debate concerning whether or not, to what extent or in what sense, Paul's own Christology should be considered 'divine'. Certainly the main dialogue partners in what follows are NT scholars. And this thesis likewise engages this question using the usual tools of NT exegesis, those which would be employed by my aca-demic colleagues without any personal association with a faith community. Yet what may be most surprising for some, as it certainly was for me, is that the following exegetical argument, by its very nature, arguably cannot end where it begins. It shall be maintained that to correctly engage this debate in a Pauline fashion, the scholar must ultimately end up making statements about communal and contemporary Christian life. To speak correctly of Paul's divine-Christology is to speak both the languages of NT studies and the *ecclesia*, where Christians believe the risen Lord is present and active through his Spirit. Paul's Christology, understood in terms of the divine-Christology debate, is a vital instance of Church dogmatics. In other words, while the larger debate concerning theological exegesis cannot be directly engaged here, arguably the shape of this thesis contributes to it as it is an illustration of engagement with the NT that is theological *because* it is critically exegetical.

A second aspect of the following study needs comment. This thesis aims to make, again albeit indirectly, a methodological point concerning how NT study is best undertaken. Many NT studies now seek to refract Pauline text through a variety of hermeneutical models,[7] and they often do so by engaging with his letters in an atomised fashion (with in-depth exegesis of a few texts declared to be 'key'). In such a context, not only must one spend a few chap-ters detailing the specific model of interpretation before one engages with the primary literature, but also broader NT patterns simply *cannot* be examined due to space and time limitations.[8]

---

[6] This is not the place to list all of the relevant literature, but cf. the different positions represented in, e.g., H. Räisänen, *Beyond New Testament Theology* (London: SCM, 1990) on the one hand, and Stephen E. Fowl, *Engaging Scripture: A Model for Theological Interpretation* (Oxford: Blackwell, 1998) and John Webster, *Holy Scripture: A Dogmatic Sketch*, Current Issues in Theology, vol. 1 (Cambridge: Cambridge University Press, 2003), on the other.

[7] This can be coupled with the questionable research method of analysing (usually) second Temple Jewish literature for the majority of a work, before, at the end, spending a few words on the NT texts to demonstrate a 'new' reading.

[8] Although this is anecdotal evidence, I am not surprised that I was chided by one reviewer of an earlier version of this work – my unpublished PhD thesis – for attempting to analyse too much Pauline material. I needed, it was urged, to rather focus on a few key passages. As understandable as this comment was, my method was deliberate. I leave it for the reader to judge if it is successful.

Long ago, Adolf Schlatter contended that for NT theology and exegesis 'the hardest thing to observe is often right in front of our eyes'.[9] The present volume thus seeks to refocus the Pauline divine-Christology debate by re-engaging the sweep of themes in Paul's letters, while avoiding the construction of an interpretative lens that is uninformed by those same Pauline themes. This is certainly not to capitulate once again, as some could misunderstand Schlatter to mean, to a supposedly 'objective' simple reading of the NT. Rather, it can be understood to counterbalance some unhealthy trends in the approach of some NT studies, which neglect broader Pauline themes and construct various reading models without sufficiently intense engagement with Paul's letters.[10] Nor is this to suggest, of course, that detailed exegesis be sidelined.

A few examples of these problems from the following study can be cited. First, Fee attempts a 'primarily exegetical' approach,[11] but neglects to consider how an arguably unrecognised Aristotelian, and unPauline, metaphysics shapes his own questions and claims. His results, as we shall seek to demonstrate, are thus slightly out of step with Paul's letters. Larry Hurtado's works have sought to analyse early Christian devotion,[12] but one wonders, however, to what extent his understanding of devotion is something Paul would recognise. It is to suggest that his key interpretive angle has been under-informed by Paul's own texts (cf. chapters 3 and 4 below). One could also mention the learned contributions of William Horbury and Andrew Chester's, in which they opine that to understand Pauline Christology correctly, one must precisely not 'set Pauline Christology as the central point'.[13] We shall argue later that this counterintuitive claim is also counterproductive.

Naturally, any thesis faces the problem of circularity, of reading the texts from a particular perspective while hoping that one's exegetical approach is

---

[9] Cited in Thomas R. Schreiner, *Paul: Apostle of God's Glory in Christ. A Pauline Theology* (Leicester: IVP, 2001), 16.

[10] In a compatible manner, Douglas Campbell has also, in his magisterial book *The Deliverance of God*, rejected an atomistic preoccupation with Pauline pericopae, analysed one after another, and sought to cultivate what he calls a 'horizontal' approach, namely one which keeps overarching themes close to mind, which appreciates how individual texts work as 'semantic and rhetorical events' within that broader sweep of concerns. See Douglas A. Campbell, *The Deliverance of God: An Apocalyptic Rereading of Justification in Paul* (Grand Rapids, Mich.: Eerdmans, 2009), xxviii-xxix.

[11] Fee, *Christology*, 4.

[12] Larry W. Hurtado, *One God, One Lord*, reprint, 1988 (Edinburgh: T&T Clark, 1998[2]); Larry W. Hurtado, *Lord Jesus Christ: Devotion to Jesus in Earliest Christianity* (Grand Rapids: Eerdmans, 2003); Larry W. Hurtado, *How on Earth Did Jesus Become a God?* (Grand Rapids: Eerdmans, 2005).

[13] Andrew Chester, *Messiah and Exaltation: Jewish Messianic and Visionary Traditions and New Testament Christology*, Wissenschaftliche Untersuchungen Zum Neuen Testament (Tübingen: Mohr Siebeck, 2007), 329.

shaped by, or at least not entirely alien to, those texts. And if there is no one objective perspective to clear up all debates, how can one judge the value of different interpretive proposals? This thesis, without claiming any kind of naive realism, or even critical realism, simply wants to return as a point of method, again and again, to Paul's own texts, both in the shaping of its reading method and in the scope of its engagement with Paul's letters. That is, it refuses the *cul-de-sac* methodological 'professionalism' of the in-depth exegesis of a few 'key' texts – an approach that, in terms of the Pauline divine-Christology debate, has arguably not delivered on its claims – for a broader analysis of Paul's letters. To understand Paul's Christology, to Paul's letters we will repeatedly go. What all of this will look like in this thesis of course remains to be detailed, and much ground will be covered before these claims can be sufficiently justified. It will prove useful to now offer a short reconnaissance of the upcoming ground to be covered.

3. An overview of the argument

Chapters 2–4 will open up an argumentative space for this thesis. Chapter 2 offers a 'history of scholarship', and will examine how particularly post 1970s NT experts have sought to determine whether, or not, Paul's Christology is divine. After a demonstration of the reasons for the scholarly shift in the 70s, it orders the various scholarly proposals according to two questions: a) How does Paul's Jewish-style faith in God affect our understanding of his Christology? and b) Where, if at all, is there evidence in the Pauline corpus for (or against) a divine-Christology? Chapter 3 will critically examine the works of three key scholars overviewed in the previous chapter, namely Gordon Fee, Larry Hurtado and Richard Bauckham.

Criticisms of their works will begin to point the way to a fresh approach which will be discussed in more depth in chapter 4. Having already argued that post 1970s academic discourse about the Pauline divine-Christology debate proceeds by engaging two overlapping questions, this chapter makes observations about the first. Through engagement particularly with the proposals of Bauckham and Hurtado, it is maintained that one should still speak of Paul's monotheism, even a strict monotheism, and Bauckham's language of God's transcendent uniqueness is employed to this end. Importantly, while agreeing with the thrust of Hurtado's response to scholars such as Fletcher-Louis and Barker, that no one has yet demonstrated 'an actual *devotional pattern* involving public and corporate worship offered to any figure other than the God of Israel' in Second Temple Judaism,[14] it is noted that to reduce "'the

---

[14] Hurtado, *LJC*, 34, italics his.

decisive criterion" by which Jews maintained the uniqueness of God'[15] to such worship does not appear particularly appropriate in light of the fact that true Jewish worship of God was meant to involve the entire life of the Second Temple Jew, that by its very nature and content, it reached beyond the cultus into the life, habits, goals and desires of the faithful (cf. the *Shema*), and that if it did not, it induced the scorn of the Prophets. This suggests a broader pattern needs to be found, into which cultic worship finds significance. Before this pattern is elucidated, the relational nature of both OT and Pauline monotheism is detailed, and in light of this three points are maintained. First, the more comprehensive context, one in which cultic worship belongs, is the God-*relation* pattern of data. Second, as God was understood, and faith in him expressed, in a thoroughly relational manner, then God's *uniqueness* is like-wise expressed, i.e. relationally. Third, this chapter argues that the YHWH-relation pattern of data, not just cultic worship, is the appropriate context in which to understand the emergence of early Christology.

All of this paves the way for a new suggestion concerning the second question, namely, Where, if at all, is there evidence in the Pauline corpus for (or against) a divine-Christology? It proposes to analyse the data in Paul's undisputed letters concerning the relation between the risen Lord and believers. Just as Paul's faith in God is relational, so this thesis will examine the relation between the risen Lord and believers in Paul's letters, with a view to the divine-Christology debate. In the following exegetical section (chapters 5–8), an attempt is made to map the contours of this Christ-relation.

Chapter 5, while it begins the exegetical study of Paul's letters, also functions as a frame for the following 4 chapters. It does this because it pursues two main propositions, one concerning the nature of Paul's monotheistic strategy in 1 Corinthians 8:1–3, and another concerning the relation between risen Lord and believers, thus bringing together the two questions posed above. It is argued that Paul, having opened his argument in a way that expresses true faith in the one God as the relational commitment of believers to this God over against idolatry, goes on to explicitly and continually speak of the relation between risen Lord and believers over against idolatry. Furthermore, he details this Christ-relation with the terms and categories drawn from the complex of themes and concepts that, in the Jewish scriptures, describe the relation between Israel and YHWH over against idolatry.

Having established that Paul spoke of the Christ-relation in terms of the God-relation, chapter 6 examines the Christ-relation throughout the undisputed letters. This chapter, the longest in the thesis for the methodological reasons noted above, examines the broad pattern of data concerning the Christ-relation. It refuses to be tied to one or two key passages and instead works through the entire undisputed corpus, which leads to mixed exegetical depth.

---

[15] Hurtado, *Earth*, 129.

But the goal is reached: in particular, the general shape of this Christ-relation is uncovered, seen in Paul's ultimate goals and motivations, in the variety of his explicit Christ-devotion language, in the passionate nature of this Christ-devotion, in the language Paul contrasted with this devotion, in the presence and activity of the risen Lord, yet also in the absence of Christ, and thus the Lord's presence through the Spirit, in the communications between the risen Lord and believers, and finally in the various ways Christ was characterised and the depiction of the scope of his lordship. At various points it is shown that the relation between the risen Lord and believers is explicitly expressed, as in 1 Corinthians 8–10, with the language used to describe relation to YHWH in the scriptures of Second Temple Judaism. With all of this data gathered together, chapter 7 argues that it is a pattern of material that Paul would recognise, hence it functions as the best perspective from which to assess christological significance. The final chapter of this extensive engagement with Paul's letters ends with an examination of 1 Corinthians 16:22, a text full of christological significance once relational factors are kept in focus.

Some have considered it good methodology to start with second Temple texts before engaging with Paul. Unfortunately, in terms of the divine-Christology debate, scholars have combed the dense and complex texts for various intermediary figures before really grasping the significance of Christ in Paul, and the meaning and extent of Paul's interrelated language, and so necessarily draw faulty conclusions. Here we started with Paul, making sure we clearly grasp some of the key contours of his Christ-relation, and only having done this do we, in chapter 9, look at Jewish devotion to figures other than God, particularly as evidenced in Sirach 44–50, Adam in the *Life of Adam and Eve* and the 'Son of Man' in the Similitudes of Enoch. These texts are often used by detractors of Hurtado and Bauckham to assert that beings other than God could be worshipped, that blur God's transcendent uniqueness. It is argued, however, that precisely in these texts the Pauline Christ-relation finds very little correspondence with the language concerning 'worshipped' figures other than God (whether Adam in *L.A.E*, the praised Ancestors in Sir., or the Son of Man in *1 En.*). Rather, the pattern of data concerning Paul's Christ-relation is, with remarkable consistency, reflected in the *God*-relation in these texts (whether the deity be called Lord of Spirits, YHWH or God). Indeed, aspects of Paul's language suggest Paul did know of Enochic traditions, and sought in some important ways to associate Christ with the Lord of Spirits, and the Son of Man with Christians.

At this stage of the argument, in chapter 10, it is possible to propose some conclusions regarding the divine-Christology debate. Four points lead to the conclusion that Paul's Christ-relation *is* a divine-Christology. First, it is argued that Jewish God-relation data, including Paul's own, overlaps considerably, in general shape and in detail, with Paul's Christ-relation. Second, it is noted that the pattern of God-relation data constitutes the way God was conceived as unique. Third, the correspondence between Paul's Christ-relation and the Jewish God-relation is expounded. It is argued that because of Paul's deliberate link between God-language and certain Christ-relation elements, the use of the title κύριος, the relational monotheistic context with which Paul framed his rhetoric concerning the Christ-relation, and the important overlap of the general shape and contours of the Christ-relation with the Jewish God-relation pattern, the way Second Temple Judaism understood God as unique, through the God-relation pattern, was used to express the pattern of data concerning the Christ-relation. But fourth, the argument of Boers is engaged, in which he asserts that to write a Pauline Christology is merely a 'scholarly abstraction'. In light of recent studies of Paul's epistemology, it is noted that this epistemology was *relational*. On this basis it is maintained that, by analysing the Christ-*relation* in Paul, and by noting the Apostle's relational epistemology, one can claim that to speak of Paul's divine-Christology is actually to present Paul's own conceptions, and in a mode that the Apostle likely employed. In a study of Paul's epistemology it has been argued that knowledge, for Paul, can be expressed as relationship.[16] In light of the previous chapters it is argued that the Christ-relation *is* Paul's divine-Christology – knowledge expressed as relationship. The Christ-relation was Paul's way of expressing a divine-Christology. With this way of constructing a Pauline divine-Christology, nine important arguments proffered by those denying such a Christology are reengaged.

Having summarised the central arguments of this thesis in chapter 11, a final appendix makes a point which, as noted above, surprised even its author. The conclusions of the exegetical work of this thesis facilitate fresh engagement with various broader ecclesial questions. Building on the work of Bauckham, the problem of Lessing's ditch – in terms of the 'Jesus of history' and the 'Christ of faith' – is broached, followed by an extended meditation on the new avenues of conversation opened up between Pauline Christology, as presented in this thesis, and the concerns of theologians such as Jürgen Moltmann, Catherine LaCugna, John Zizioulas and others. This all suggests, in ways that remain beyond the scope of this thesis to fully justify, that it is in this relationship with Christ that not only theology and history meet, but also ethics, epistemology and doxology.

Admittedly, summaries of entire arguments, like the one above, can often seem a little unintelligible, and only truly make sense *after* the book is read from cover to cover – even when the reader is a fellow specialist (the same could be said about Paul's so-called 'thesis statements' in Romans 1:16–17!). Nevertheless, it will provide a road map for navigating the upcoming

---

[16] Mary Healy, "Knowledge of the Mystery: A Study of Pauline Epistemology," in *The Bible and Epistemology*, eds Mary Healy, Robin Parry (Milton Keynes: Paternoster, 2007), 142.

Sehenswürdigkeiten. It only remains for me to hope, especially if my summary appeared a little opaque, that you, my reader, will press on to the end of this book and continue the important task of wrestling with the question of 'what to make of Jesus'.[17]

---

[17] Hurtado, *LJC*, 652–53.

Chapter 2

A Pauline divine-Christology? A history of research

1. Introduction

Given the contemporary Pauline divine-Christology debate, it is perhaps somewhat surprising that a detailed history-of-research concerning the specific question of *Pauline* divine-Christology has not been written.[1] And while this chapter partly attempts to make up for this lacuna, it will nevertheless do so selectively. First, pre-1970s scholarship is examined. This division of material is based on the judgment that the 1970s involved a revolution in approach and focus concerning the divine-Christology debate. Scholarly questions and strategies, which had until then largely focused on chronological schemes of development, the background of Paul's Christology (Jewish or Hellenistic) and the study of titles and their etymology, were creatively developed and expanded in various new directions which deserve more detailed examination and classification, under the heading 'Post-1970s scholarship'.

2. Pre-1970s scholarship and Pauline divine-Christology

During the Reformation and the so-called 'Period of Orthodoxy', Paul's Christology was not seen as a self-contained subject of study. And so while christological discussion referred to Pauline texts, the specific question of whether Paul's Christ was divine was not a matter of debate.[2]

However, the developing dogma of the early enlightenment era posed a fundamental challenge to the theological notions of incarnation and divine-

---

[1] However, see the helpful but limited and/or indirect treatments in Timo Eskola, *Messiah and the Throne: Jewish Merkabah Mysticism and Early Christian Exaltation Discourse* (Tübingen: Mohr Siebeck, 2001), 1–15; Carl Judson Davis, *The Name and Way of the Lord: Old Testament Themes, New Testament Christology* (Sheffield: Sheffield Academic Press, 1996), 13–27; L.J. Kreitzer, *Jesus and God in Paul's Eschatology* (Sheffield: Sheffield Academic Press, 1987), 15–27; Fee, *Christology*, 10–15.

[2] Cf. e.g. the approach in John Calvin, *The Institutes of the Christian Religion* (Philadelphia: Westminster John Knox, 1960), 1:2:14, which is representative of others.

Christology.[3] To oversimplify the complexities of the range of argumentation then used, it was seen as *a priori* unacceptable to assert a 'new' and historically bound, but nevertheless 'universal' revelation of truth, such as the incarnation.[4] Furthermore, the 'Gospel miracles', which were traditionally used as a defence of the divinity of Christ, were also unacceptable on philosophical grounds. And while most efforts were not specifically focused on *Pauline* Christology, the matters raised set the frame for almost all proceeding debate.

And what were these raised matters? First, it became clear that Paul had to be treated on his own terms. Early English Deists (e.g. Thomas Morgan[5]), proposed that behind the apparent unity of the NT, there was evidence of theological development. This line of reasoning was picked up somewhat later in Germany, particularly by J. S. Semler (1725–91), F. C. Baur (1792–1860) and A. Harnack (1851–1930). Philosophical 'wind in the sails' was provided by Hegel (1770–1831) and his dialectical model of history. Thus a fundamental challenge against those who assumed that Paul's divine-Christology must be substantially the same as that in the Johannine material was developed. Christology was no longer seen as a static formulation within the NT. The dogmas themselves developed, and Paul must be plotted on the line of this development. And in the light of this, many were to start doubting that Paul's Christology was divine at all, that the earliest Christology was 'low' (i.e. not divine), and only later developed into a divine-Christology.[6]

Second, and hand in hand with the above, was the division posited, especially by Harnack, between Jewish and Greek/Hellenistic thought forms.[7] He argued that Christology proper was to be associated with abstract Greek thinking, while soteriology was more fundamentally Jewish. Harnack himself was to situate Paul somewhere in-between these two 'worlds'. Thus Paul, he argued, while nevertheless not going as far as the later church Creeds in his Christology, started to introduce into it the influences of Greek categories of thinking.[8]

These two foundational matters were to change the shape of christological debate entirely. Key assumptions concerning the theological unity of the NT

---

[3] Cf. Alister E. McGrath, *The Making of Modern German Christology 1750–1990*, reprint, 1987 (Leicester: Apollos, 1994[2]), 13–35; Werner G. Kümmel, *The New Testament: The History of the Investigation of Its Problems* (London: SCM, 1973), e.g., 55; Anthony C. Thiselton, "New Testament Interpretation in Historical Perspective," in *Hearing the New Testament. Strategies for Interpretation*, ed. Joel B. Green (Carlisle: Paternoster, 1995), 10–36; and J.C. O'Neill, *Who Did Jesus Think He Was?* (Leiden: Brill, 1995), 7–14.

[4] Cf. esp. Alister E. McGrath, *Making*, 20–35, and the literature cited there.

[5] Cf. the citations in Kümmel, *History*, 56–57. For the following cf. O'Neill, *Jesus*, 7–8.

[6] On the introduction of an 'adoptionist' reading of Rom. 1:4 and Acts 2:3 by Julius Wellhausen cf. O'Neill, *Jesus*.

[7] Adolf Harnack, *Lehrbuch der Dogmengeschichte*, reprint, 1909 (Tübingen: Mohr, 1990[4]).

[8] Harnack suggests that this is to be seen especially in Paul's thinking about the risen Lord in terms of 'spirit' (Harnack, *Dogmengeschichte*, 103, 105–6, 803).

and in it the place of Paul, were forever overturned. In one way or another they were to appear in and guide the discussions that were to follow.

Also important in these early days of critical engagement with Pauline Christology is the reaction of conservative scholars to the sort of reasoning outlined above. Conservatives within Germany,[9] England[10] and America[11] sought to reaffirm more traditional christological claims on the basis of Paul. Although some of them worked with an arguably naive hermeneutic for understanding Paul,[12] it would only be a slight exaggeration to claim that their creative and learned engagement with the Pauline-corpus anticipated almost all modern debate in a small way.[13]

The development of (especially German) critical scholarship in regards to Christology through the 19th century is a story of reaction, absorption and counter-reaction. The rise of the Ritschlian school, while seemingly absorbing an apparent 'Kantian agenda'[14] reacted to the eroding confidence in Hegelianism and the 'feeling' emphasis of Schleiermacher. And Christology was read through these lenses. Likewise, in reaction to the German Ritschlian school and the so-called 'Paulinism' of much (largely German) scholarship, the *Religionsgeschichtliche Schule* developed. Thus, instead of focusing on moralism, or abstract doctrines or liberal understandings of the religious significance of the personality of the historical Jesus etc., scholars such as Hermann Gunkel (1862–1932) and Adolf Deissmann (1866–1937) emphasised the experiential aspects in Paul.[15] However, the most significant contribution from this *Schule* to be made in relation to the question of Christology was that of W. Bousset. In his famous *Kyrios Christos* he focused on Paul's personal Christ piety and devotion which, he maintained, was the Apostle's unique

---

[9] E.g. A. Schlatter, *Die Theologie der Apostel* (1922; repr., Stuttgart: Calwer, 1977), cf. e.g. 336–37; and Paul Feine, *Jesus Christus und Paulus* (Leipzig: Hinrichs, 1902), 14, 25, 50, etc.

[10] E.g. H.P. Liddon, *The Divinity of Our Lord and Saviour Jesus Christ. Eight Lectures Preached Before the University of Oxford in 1866* (London: Rivingtons, 1875[7]), 306–59, and Joseph B. Lightfoot, *Biblical Essays* (London: Macmillan, 1893), 232, including his commentaries (on, e.g., Phil. and Rom.).

[11] Benjamin B. Warfield, *The Lord of Glory: A Study of the Designations of Our Lord in the New Testament with Especial Reference to His Deity* (1907; repr., Grand Rapids: Baker, 1974), 229–32.

[12] It appears, however, that Schlatter's hermeneutic was more sophisticated (cf. the discussion in Peter Stuhlmacher, *Vom Verstehen des Neuen Testaments: eine Hermeneutik* [Göttingen: Vandenhoeck & Ruprecht, 1986], 169–74, 'Adolf Schlatters Hermeneutik der Wahrnehmung').

[13] Cf. e.g., the scope of material covered in Liddon, *Divinity*, 306–59.

[14] Cf. Alister E. McGrath, *Making*, 82.

[15] H. Gunkel, *Die Wirkungen des heiligen Geistes nach der populären Anschauung der apostolischen Zeit und der Lehre des Apostels Paulus* (Göttingen: Vandenhoeck & Ruprecht, 1888), 62–110; A. Deissmann, *Saint Paul: A Study in Social and Religious History* (London: Hodder & Stoughton, 1912), xi.

adaptation of the Christ-cult mysticism of the Hellenistic Gentile Christian communities. Bousset was well aware of the christological implications of such Christ-devotion. Indeed, it suggested that the simple God-human relationship would appear to be complicated by 'a peculiar thoroughgoing duplication' of the object of religious faith and veneration.[16] As Bousset admitted, this would all seem to suggest a Pauline divine-Christology.[17] However, in the light of certain theological and titular considerations, which Bousset felt spoke against this (particularly the absence of θεός applied to Christ[18]), he concluded that 'one still may not actually speak of a deity of Christ in the view of Paul'.[19] Bousset has thus also helped to steer the focus of study onto the importance of christological titles which, as shall shortly be seen, is a matter of no small significance.

The dovetailing of the *Religionsgeschichtliche Schule* with the 'consistent eschatological' reaction to Ritschlian liberalism manifests most formidably in the writings of Bultmann whose contributions to NT scholarship in the mid 20th century are, in terms of influence, without equal. Indeed, Bultmann's basic acceptance of Bousset's thesis served to confirm the latter's influence. Of particular importance was Bultmann's agreement with the division postulated between Palestinian Jewish and Hellenistic Gentile, so fundamental to Bousset's chronological scheme.[20] And it was this very scheme, tied as it was to the study of individual titles, that was to dominate NT christological discussion from the middle of the 20th century up to the beginning of the era of the modern debates.[21]

Indeed, these were precisely the problems caused by this historical scheme, as it was used to understand the history of certain christological titles, that stimulated much academic discussion. One of the first historical critiques of

---

[16] W. Bousset, *Kyrios Christos: Geschichte des Christusglaubens von den Anfängen des Christentums bis Irenaeus* (New York: Abingdon, 1970), 205.

[17] Ibid., 209 n.150.

[18] Cf. his comments on the disputed Rom. 9:5 (Bousset, *Kyrios*, 210).

[19] Bousset, *Kyrios*, 210. It is for this reason that Schrage is hardly correct to speak of 'the one sided preference of the cult over the teaching [of Paul] ..., as practised in the *Religionsgeschichtliche Schule and especially in relation to the topic "monotheism"*, now, e.g., brought back into the debate by L. W. Hurtado' (Wolfgang Schrage, *Unterwegs zur Einzigkeit und Einheit Gottes: zum "Monotheismus" des Paulus und seiner alttestamentlich-frühjüdischen Tradition* [Neukirchen-Vluyn: Neukirchener Verlag, 2002], 159, italics and translation mine). In reality it was precisely these theological considerations that stopped Bousset from pushing the significance of the Christ-cult to what he felt were its natural theological consequences.

[20] Though it appears that Bousset himself derived this scheme from W. Heitmüller (cf. Hurtado, *LJC*, 15).

[21] Most, however, did not consider Christology a subject that deserved separate treatment (cf. e.g. Conzelmann, Eichholz, Goppelt, Ridderbos etc. See the useful, if rather lopsidedly German focused, analysis in H. Hübner, "Paulusforschung seit 1945. Ein kritischer Literaturbericht," in *ANRW* II.25.4 [1987], 2649–2840).

Bousset's scheme was Oscar Cullmann's important monograph, *The Christology of the New Testament*.[22] Apart from the fact that it was for its titular emphasis a model that many were then encouraged to follow,[23] it provided a strong case against Bousset's argument that the 'Christ cult' emerged only on Hellenistic Gentile soil, not earlier. Particularly telling was Cullmann's recourse to the Aramaic prayer, μαράνα θά, preserved in 1 Corinthians 16:22.[24] Furthermore, based on his understanding of certain titles, Cullmann, contrary to Bousset, did not have the same hesitations in concluding that Paul's Christology was indeed divine.[25]

Such was the lot of Pauline scholarship for the decades until the 1970s: major emphasis on chronological schemes of development, the background of Paul's Christology (Jewish or Hellenistic), and the study of titles, especially their etymology. By the 1970s the scholarly questions, strategies and historical schemes were about to experience a process of significant change.

3. Post-1970s scholarship and Pauline divine-Christology

What happened in the 1970s to create such a change in the scholarly landscape? In 1979 Hurtado insisted on the need for fresh analysis of the question of NT Christology.[26] In 1985 he published an article describing the forces that he saw as creating this need. He argued that because of the discovery of new material (the Nag Hammadi material,[27] revision and further publication of pseudepigraphal material, the publication of Qumran manuscripts), a better appreciation of how to handle some of that material (particularly a reconsideration of the importance placed on rabbinic material for understanding Paul)

---

[22] O. Cullmann, *The Christology of the New Testament* (London: SCM, 1963²).

[23] Cf. Werner Kramer, *Christ, Lord, Son of God*, reprint, 1963 (London: SCM, 1966); F. Hahn, *The Titles of Jesus in Christology: Their History in Early Christianity*, reprint, 1963 (New York: World Publishing, 1969); and R.H. Fuller, *The Foundations of New Testament Christology* (New York: Scribner's, 1965).

[24] Cullmann, *Christology*, 208–9.

[25] This difference of opinion comes about primarily through an alternative understanding of Rom. 9:5, as well as the christological use of the title 'Lord'. It appears that the christological implications of Christ-devotion were thus allowed full expression, for Cullmann, as Bousset's theological objection had been removed (cf. Cullmann, *Christology*, 312–13, 320–21). However, Cullmann makes this affirmation as a primarily (though *not* exclusively, as some have misunderstood him) functional rather than ontological Christology (3–4). Hahn and Fuller also affirmed a Pauline divine-Christology (Hahn, *Titles*, e.g. 110; Fuller, *The Foundations of New Testament Christology*, 230).

[26] Larry W. Hurtado, "New Testament Christology: A Critique of Bousset's Influence," *TS* 40 (1979): 306–17.

[27] In relation to the general scholarly change, Stuckenbruck highlights, in addition, documents found in Oxyrhynchus, Cairo Geniza and the Elephantine papyri (Loren T. Stuckenbruck, *Angel Veneration and Christology: A Study in Early Judaism and in the Christology of the Apocalypse of John* [Tübingen: Mohr Siebeck, 1995], 7 n.7).

and the publication of important monographs, especially by Schillebeeckx and Dunn (which attempted to interact with this wider range of material in constructing the development of NT Christology), it was possible to claim that 'the origin and development of christology remains an engaging and unsettled topic'.[28] One could also mention Hengel's learned and important contributions as another force of change. During the 1970s he, in a number of publications, developed some telling arguments against the titular and chronological schemes, particularly of Hahn and Kramer. Against Hahn's distinctions between Palestinian Jewish Christianity, Hellenistic Jewish Christianity and Hellenistic gentile Christianity, Hengel simply pointed out how difficult distinctions of this kind are to maintain in reality. Historical analysis shows that such boundaries did not exist in a strict sense, and certainly not when chronologically understood.[29] Already in the late 1960s, Hengel had influentially argued that, since approximately the middle of the 3rd century B.C., Judaism should best be called a 'hellenistic Judaism'.[30] This is a fact that placed a large question mark against the neatly defined stages of historical development and Paul's supposed place within it.

Furthermore, against Kramer, Hengel was to stress that the attempt to study in an isolated manner 'individual christological ciphers [i.e., titles, formulae and phrases]' misses the point.[31] The ultimate goal of understanding the development of early Christology must attempt to see matters more holistically. This important critique fed the growing dissatisfaction with the christological studies of the years following Bousset and meant that scholars were ready to experiment with new approaches. What is more, Hengel also maintained that a high Christology was very early.[32]

The 1970s thus marked a change in Pauline scholarship. In fact, probably one could even speak of the beginnings of a veritable explosion of scholarly interest and publications on Pauline Christology in this period.[33] Although it will be the individual arguments that will concern us, the new proposals mostly grew out of a more intense and judicious engagement with the literature and nature of Second Temple Judaism. This, in turn, has led to the mod-

---

[28] Larry W. Hurtado, "New Testament Christology: Retrospect and Prospect," *Semeia* 30 (1985): 19.

[29] M. Hengel, *Between Jesus and Paul: Studies in the Earliest History of Christianity* (London: SCM, 1983), 35–38.

[30] M. Hengel, *Judaism and Hellenism: Studies in Their Encounter in Palestine During the Early Hellenistic Period* (London: SCM, 1974), 1:104. Cf. the commentary in Hübner, "Paulusforschung," 2737.

[31] Hengel, *Jesus*, 38.

[32] M. Hengel, *The Son of God: The Origin of Christology and the History of Jewish-Hellenistic Religion* (London: SCM, 1976), sections 6.3 and 6.4.

[33] In this light, Berger's claim 'that Paul, in the last 25 years has disappeared from the centre of NT scholarship' (Klaus Berger, *Paulus* [Munich: C. H. Beck, 2002], 7, translation mine), is inexplicable.

ern more self-conscious divide on the question of whether Paul's Christology should be called 'divine'. Although scholarly opinion concerning the question of whether Pauline Christology should be called 'divine' has always, since the enlightenment, been divided (e.g., Harnack more-or-less denied it, while Liddon and Lightfoot affirmed it; Bousset denied it, while Cullmann, Fuller and Hahn affirmed it), up until the 1970s there was less consensus concerning other important related questions (such as regarding the appropriate religious and cultural milieu in which to situate Paul's Christology, the best chronological scheme for understanding the historical development of early Christology etc.), and thus this line in scholarship was not as sharply defined. There is now an intensification of definite sides being taken specifically with regard to this question. Yet despite their differences, it appears that scholars on both sides of this dispute have all been trying to answer two fundamental questions: a) How does Paul's Jewish-style faith in God[34] affect our understanding of his Christology?[35] and b) Where, if at all, is there evidence in the Pauline corpus for (or against) a divine-Christology? In the following we shall overview how post-1970s scholarship, in both affirming and denying a Pauline divine-Christology, has reacted to these two questions.

3.1. The post-1970s engagement with the first question

If Paul was a Jewish monotheist, how can he treat or think of a recently cruci-fied Jew as divine? How can Jewish "monotheists" worship him? This is, as M. Barker has put it, indeed a 'problem'.[36]

Four basic proposals exist. The first maintains that because Jews were monotheists, it would be impossible for Paul to accommodate a divine-Christology as this would blur the strict line of distinction monotheism draws around God. On this basis some deny a Pauline divine-Christology.[37] Others

---

[34] This way of formulating the question leaves open, for the time being, whether 'monotheism' is an appropriate term. In chapters 4 and 5 it will be necessary to examine the term 'monotheism'. For now, the meaning of the word, when used, will be understood according to its usage in the scholarly literature analysed.

[35] Indeed, Bauckham categorises approaches to the question of NT Christology by its relation to the question of monotheism (cf. Richard J. Bauckham, *God Crucified: Monotheism and Christology in the New Testament* [Carlisle: Paternoster, 1998], 2–4, and the critique in S. Vollenweider, *Horizonte neutestamentlicher Christologie: Studien zu Paulus und zur frühchristlichen Theologie* [Tübingen: Mohr Siebeck, 2002], 4, 24).

[36] Margaret Barker, "The High Priest and the Worship of Jesus," in *The Jewish Roots of Christological Monotheism*, eds C.C. Newman, J.R. Davila, and G.S. Lewis (Leiden: Brill, 1999), 93.

[37] So, e.g., A.E. Harvey, *Jesus and the Constraints of History* (London: Duckworth, 1982), 154, 157–58; James D.G. Dunn, "How Controversial Was Paul's Christology?" in *The Christ and the Spirit: Christology*, reprint, originally published in 1993 (Edinburgh: T&T Clark, 1998), 225–26; Maurice Casey, *From Jewish Prophet to Gentile God: The Origins and Development of New Testament Christology* (Cambridge: James Clarke, 1991), 116.

object, however, that this does not do justice to the evidence for a Pauline divine-Christology, to be surveyed below.

Second, some deny that first century Jewish faith in God was really 'monotheistic' in a strict sense. Hence, Barker, for example, denies not the divine-Christology, but Jewish monotheism, claiming that a popular less official religion forms the backdrop to Paul, one which maintained belief in two deities: the 'High God' and YHWH, Israel's god, the son of the High God.[38] However, not many have followed her in this reasoning.[39]

Representative of a third approach is William Horbury who can solve Barker's problem, not by abandoning the category 'monotheism', but by maintaining a rather different understanding of it.[40] He argues that:

> [T]he interpretation of Judaism as a rigorous monotheism, "exclusive" in the sense that the existence of other divine beings is denied, does less than justice to the importance of mystical and messianic tendencies in the Herodian age - for these were often bound up with an "inclusive" monotheism, whereby the supreme deity was envisaged above but in association with other spirits and powers. Christianity would then have perpetuated some features of Jewish monotheism that were characteristically Herodian.[41]

Horbury's words will also make it obvious why this 'problem' question has also helped energise the large number of publications dealing with so-called 'intermediary figures'.[42] Can one of the many intermediary figures in the literature of Second Temple Judaism provide the conceptual 'missing link' for understanding the exalted status of Christ in Paul? Is there a conceptual background in the language surrounding intermediary figures which explains how the monotheistic Paul could speak in such exalted terms of Christ without threatening the uniqueness of Israel's God? If Christ can be associated with a divine intermediary then naturally one could use such material to deny a Pau-

---

[38] Cf. Margaret Barker, *The Great Angel: A Study of Israel's Second God* (London: SPCK, 1992); Barker, "Priest". Cf. also Peter Hayman, "Monotheism—a Misused Word in Jewish Studies?" *JJS* 42 (1991): 1–15.

[39] Cf. the discussions in Hurtado, *LJC*, 33–4; Richard J. Bauckham, *Jesus and the God of Israel* (Milton Keynes: Paternoster, 2008), 112–14, and the short but pointed comments in Richard J. Bauckham, "Biblical Theology and the Problems of Monotheism," in *Out of Egypt: Biblical Theology and Biblical Interpretation*, eds Craig Bartholomew, et al. (Milton Keynes: Paternoster, 2004), 218.

[40] Note also O'Neill, *Jesus*, who attempts to argue that Christianity adopted a Jewish trinitarian theology. But see the incisive critique in Maurice Casey, "Monotheism, Worship and Christological Developments in the Pauline Churches," in *The Jewish Roots of Christological Monotheism*, eds C.C. Newman, J.R. Davila, and G.S. Lewis (Leiden: Brill, 1999), 218.

[41] William Horbury, "Jewish and Christian Monotheism in the Herodian Age," in *Early Jewish and Christian Monotheism*, eds Loren T. Stuckenbruck and Wendy E. S. North (London: T&T Clark, 2004), 17.

[42] For the extensive history-of-scholarship on this matter see especially Charles A. Gieschen, *Angelomorphic Christology: Antecedents and Early Evidence* (Leiden: Brill, 1998); Eskola, *Messiah*, 1–15; and most recently Chester, *Messiah*, 329–96.

line divine-Christology. However, many have affirmed, in various ways, a Pauline divine-Christology through a study of intermediary figures.[43]

Others have critiqued this line of reasoning by insisting that a clear line was drawn between God and all creatures in Jewish monotheism, all intermediary figures being excluded from the divine.[44] But rather than simply affirming the first position, some maintain a 'strict' monotheism *and* a divine-Christology, hence presenting an important fourth approach. A crucial voice for this approach is that of Bauckham who affirms both by drawing attention to the ways in which Second Temple Judaism commonly distinguished the divine identity.[45] He then maintains that Christ was included in this 'identity', a term used to thus offer conceptual space to affirm what those in position one consider mutually exclusive. While God, for Bauckham, is identified in his relationship *to Israel* as the one who reveals the divine name, YHWH, known through 'the consistency of his acts and character',[46] this is not where his emphasis lies. More importantly God is identified in his relationship *to all reality* 'most especially [in] that he is Creator of all things and sovereign Ruler of all things'.[47] Bauckham then seeks to show how Christ is included in the divine identity so defined, as agent in creation, sitting upon the divine throne, exercising divine sovereignty etc. Hence, Bauckham writes:

> The essential element in what I have called Jewish monotheism, the element that makes it a kind of monotheism, is not the denial of the existence of other 'gods', but an understanding of the uniqueness of YHWH that puts him in a class of his own, a wholly different class from any other heavenly or supernatural beings, even if they are called 'gods'. I call this YHWH's transcendent uniqueness.[48]

---

[43] E.g. Alan F. Segal, *Two Powers in Heaven: Early Rabbinic Reports About Christianity and Gnosticism* (Leiden: Brill, 1977); Alan F. Segal, "Heavenly Ascent in Hellenistic Judaism, Early Christianity and Their Environment," in *ANRW II.23/2* (1980), 1333–94; Alan F. Segal, *Paul the Convert: The Apostolate and Apostasy of Saul the Pharisee* (London: Yale University Press, 1990), 62; Nils Alstrup Dahl, *Jesus the Christ: The Historical Origins of Christological Doctrine* (Minneapolis: Fortress, 1991), chap. 6; Andrew Chester, "Jewish Messianic Expectations and Mediatorial Figures in Pauline Christology," in *Paulus und das antike Judentum*, eds. M. Hengel and Ulrich Heckel (Tübingen: Mohr Siebeck, 1991), 17–89, esp. 74; Stuckenbruck, *Angel Veneration*; Loren T. Stuckenbruck, "'Angels' and 'God': Exploring the Limits of Early Jewish Monotheism," in *Early Jewish and Christian Monotheism*, eds Loren T. Stuckenbruck and Wendy E.S. North (London: T&T Clark, 2004), 45–70; Gieschen, *Angelomorphic Christology*, e.g. 350; and importantly, Hurtado, *OG²*, 115, 123.

[44] Cf. Eskola, *Messiah*, 324. Likewise, Fatehi also maintains that a 'divine agency model cannot give a full account of the Pauline communities' perception of the risen Lord' (Mehrdad Fatehi, *The Spirit's Relation to the Risen Lord in Paul: An Examination of Its Christological Implications* [Tübingen: Mohr Siebeck, 2000], 18–22, esp. 19).

[45] Bauckham, *God*, vii, 6–7, 16–22.

[46] Ibid., 9.

[47] Ibid., 10.

[48] Bauckham, "Monotheism," 210–11.

However, Andrew Chester has raised important criticisms of Bauckham's proposal, maintaining that it does not do justice to the actual evidence.[49] Bauckham is well aware that the Son of Man in the Similitudes of Enoch does not fit his scheme, yet he insists it is the 'one exception which proves the rule'.[50] Chester protests this logic,[51] as well as Bauckham's 'neatly compartmentalized and absolutely differentiated categories' used to distinguish the divine identity.[52] Not just 1 Enoch but also Philonic material blurs Bauckham's boundaries between what is in and outside the divine identity. The neat edifice Bauckham constructs around God's unique identity is, he argues, an arbitrary move that surely not all original readers could have anticipated. The only way Bauckham can claim Word and Wisdom were known to be associated with the divine identity is through his own rhetorical construct, yet this puts Bauckham's hermeneutical divisions in danger of circular reasoning.[53] Indeed, Philo can speak of the Logos 'as the "archangel" and chief of the angels"' which 'implies that Logos and angels could be seen as very much overlapping categories', making it impossible to assert 'an absolute distinction between them'.[54]

In identifying this one God, Bauckham also (as in his earlier publications) emphasises the exclusive worship of the one God, but Hurtado claims Bauckham has unhelpfully backed away from 'worship as the crucial criterion and manifestation of Jewish monotheism' to erroneously attempting to find certain conceptual/doctrinal themes decisive in determining the divine identity.[55]

Indeed, Hurtado offers a second important voice to be associated with this fourth approach. He likewise affirms a 'strict' monotheism *and* a divine-Christology but instead of focusing on the divine identity as Bauckham does, he sees the divine distinguished more decisively in 'the giving and withholding of worship'.[56] However, while Bauckham has appropriated the term 'identity' to bring together two seemingly mutually contradictory claims, i.e., that Jewish monotheism was 'strict' *and* that Christ is divine, Hurtado appeals to an inductive reading of the term 'monotheism'. One must understand Second Temple Jewish monotheism in the light of its own attestation. The significance of the worship of Christ should not be negated by monotheism, as in the first approach above, nor should it negate that 'strict' monotheism. If it is what the self-consciously monotheistic literature maintains, then both divine-Christology and monotheism must be affirmed, and the question then put to

---

[49] Chester, *Messiah*, 20–27.
[50] Bauckham, *God*, 19.
[51] Chester, *Messiah*, 22–23.
[52] Ibid., 24.
[53] Ibid., 24–25.
[54] Ibid., 23.
[55] Hurtado, *LJC*, 47 n.66.
[56] Ibid.

the appropriateness of the modern definitions of monotheism. On this basis he can argue that divine-Christology can be understood as part of a Jewish faith albeit as a variant form of their monotheism.[57]

However, the sceptic may respond that an inductive reading simply sweeps the problems under a rhetorical carpet and refuses to deal with the question of how a first century Jewish 'strict' monotheist like Paul, if that is what he was, could accommodate a divine-Christ. How can this be imagined as possible? Further, others argue that the criterion of 'worship' is not so decisive after all, as certain figures other than God could also be pictured as worshipped. In chapter 4 a solution to these problems will be introduced.

3.2. The post-1970s engagement with the second question

Hurtado's application of inductive logic obviously assumes that there is clear evidence in Paul for a divine-Christology. Thus, it is now necessary to turn to the second of the questions mentioned on page 17: Where, if at all, is there evidence in the Pauline corpus for (or against) a divine-Christology?

In reaction to the restricted focus of many pre-1970s titular studies, scholarship has become broader in its approach.[58] In the following it will be attempted to introduce the main lines of argumentation used in affirming and denying a divine-Christology in today's scholarship. While oversimplifying a little the complexities and interrelatedness of the modern proposals, it is nevertheless possible to discern four principal approaches in modern scholarship to the question of Pauline divine-Christology: 1. The arguments involving theological language and titles, 2. those emphasising Paul's christological hermeneutic, 3. those stressing the significance of Paul's experience of the risen Lord, and 4. those concerning the alleged 'worship' of Jesus in Paul. It will also be noticed that those denying a Pauline divine-Christology are, apart from their involvement with 'subordinationist' language in Paul and intermediary figures, less creative and rather more reactionary in their proposals compared to those affirming it. This will be reflected in the structure of the following as the arguments of those affirming a divine-Christology will be mentioned followed by the critical reaction, where available, of those denying it.

3.2.1. Arguments involving theological language and titles

Angelology traditions. Gieschen affirms a Pauline divine-Christology through an analysis of angelology traditions. Specifically, while proposing that the confession Κύριος Ἰησοῦς can be read as 'Jesus is YHWH', he argues that this enabled the early church 'to link one or more of the unnamed

---

[57] Larry W. Hurtado, "What Do We Mean by 'First Century Jewish Monotheism'?" *SBLSP* (1993): 348–68. Cf. also and Fatehi, *Relation*, 326–30.

[58] Though note that this is not to claim that all mid-20th century NT scholarship only produced titular studies (cf. e.g. A.W. Wainwright, *The Trinity in the New Testament* [London: SPCK, 1962]).

angelomorphic figures intimately identified with YHWH (i.e., the Angel, the Glory, the Name, the Word, Wisdom) to the fleshly Jesus'. Thus the Pauline appropriation of angelology traditions goes hand-in-hand with a divine-Christology.[59] Others, however, deny the divine-christological significance of the asserted worship of Christ in Paul based on a study of intermediary figures, as shall be seen below.

Wisdom-Christology. The potential parallels between Paul and the Wisdom literature have long been recognised.[60] However, E.J. Schnabel and B. Witherington have taken scholarship, on this matter, further. Schnabel concludes that the identification of Christ with the Wisdom of God leads to a Christology in which one cannot merely speak of the risen Lord 'in a functional manner but rather in ontological respects'.[61] Noteworthy also is S. Kim's claim that 'the element of Wisdom-christology in the εἰκών-christology basically affirms the divinity of Christ'.[62] Furthermore, if Bauckham is correct in his assertion that Wisdom belongs unambiguously within the divine identity,[63] then the argument that a Wisdom-Christology is a divine-Christology is strengthened. However, Fee's recent monograph on Pauline Christology, which shall be examined below, makes a case against perceiving any 'Wisdom Christology' in Paul.[64]

Eschatology. The christological consequences of Paul's eschatology have been analysed by Kreitzer. The aim of his monograph, *Jesus and God in Paul's Eschatology,* is to examine the question: 'Do any of the New Testament writers call Jesus "God" or identify Jesus with God ontologically?'[65] His attempt to answer this through a study of Paul's eschatology leads him to suggest that the 'remarkable degree of conceptual overlap between God and Christ' in Paul, means that 'Christ is specifically identified with God'.[66]

---

[59] Gieschen, *Angelomorphic Christology,* 350, but cf. also 345–46.

[60] Liddon, *Divinity,* 62, 322. It was discussed at the beginning of the 20th century by Hans Windisch, *Die göttliche Weisheit der Juden und die paulinische Christologie* (Leipzig: Hinrich, 1914).

[61] Eckhard J. Schnabel, *Law and Wisdom from Ben Sira to Paul: A Tradition Historical Enquiry Into the Relation of Law, Wisdom, and Ethics* (Tübingen: Mohr Siebeck, 1985), 262. Thus Schnabel takes issue with Dunn's claim that 'to understand the Wisdom passages as ontological affirmations about "Christ's eternal being" is most probably to misunderstand them' (James D.G. Dunn, *Christology in the Making: A New Testament Inquiry Into the Origins of the Doctrine of the Incarnation* (London: SCM, 1989[2]), 195).

[62] Seyoon Kim, *Paul and the New Perspective: Second Thoughts on the Origin of Paul's Gospel* (Grand Rapids: Eerdmans, 2002), 172; Seyoon Kim, *The Origin of Paul's Gospel* (Tübingen: Mohr Siebeck, 1984[2]), 258–60.

[63] Bauckham, *God,* 20–22.

[64] Fee, *Christology,* esp. 595–619.

[65] Kreitzer, *Jesus,* 15.

[66] Ibid., 165.

In a rather different way, Bauckham has also highlighted important christological implications of Paul's eschatology. His case, based on an exegesis of Philippians 2:6–11, aims to demonstrate that the Pauline christological reading of Deutero-Isaianic prophecy in vv. 9–11 evidences a reworking of Jewish eschatological monotheism such that it becomes christological monotheism.[67]

The divine identity and early Christology. However, this eschatological argument is only a part of Bauckham's wider approach to the question of Pauline divine-Christology. His main contribution to the debate has been succinctly summarised in his small but influential monograph, *God Crucified.* His approach to the question of monotheism was overviewed above. Bauckham maintains that Jews focused on certain matters to identify the uniqueness of God.[68] He then proceeds to argue that NT Christology, when read in the light of these identifying categories, 'included Jesus, precisely and unambiguously, within the unique identity of the one God of Israel'.[69]

Other theological themes. Additionally, there are a number of other publications dealing with certain theological language in Paul that have made notable divine-christological claims:

Murray J. Harris, in his study of 'slave' language in the NT argues that:

The very existence of the phrase "the slave of Christ" alongside "slave of God" in New Testament usage testifies to the early Christian belief in Christ's deity. Knowing the expression "slave of the Lord" from the Septuagint, several New Testament writers ... [including Paul] ... quietly substitute "Christ" for "the Lord", a substitution that would be been [sic.] unthinkable for a Jew unless Christ was seen as having parity of status with Yahweh.[70]

Raymond C. Ortlund Jr has provided a study of biblical 'whoredom' language, and in light of 2 Corinthians 11:1–3 argues for the 'deity and ultimacy' of Christ.[71] Instead of the familiar OT theme of the jealousy of God in this passage we find a divine jealousy concerning the relationship between *Christ and his Bride.*[72]

---

[67] Richard J. Bauckham, "The Worship of Jesus in Philippians 2:9–11," in *Where Christology Began: Essays on Philippians 2*, eds Ralph P. Martin and Brian J. Dodd (Louisville: Westminster John Knox, 1998), 128–39.

[68] God is identified in his relationship *to Israel* as the one who reveals the divine name, YHWH, and as one who is known through 'the consistency of his acts and character' (Bauckham, *God*, 9). He is identified in his relationship *to all reality* 'most especially [in] that he is Creator of all things and sovereign Ruler of all things' (10). However, in identifying this one God, he also (as in earlier publications) emphasises the exclusive worship of the one God (see below).

[69] Bauckham, *God*, vii.

[70] Murray J. Harris, *Slave of Christ: A New Testament Metaphor for Total Devotion to Christ* (Leicester: Apollos, 1999), 134.

[71] Raymond C. Ortlund Jr., *Whoredom: God's Unfaithful Wife in Biblical Theology* (Leicester: Apollos, 1996), 150–51.

[72] In light of his approach, he oddly does not discuss 1 Cor. 10:22 which explicitly mentions the jealousy of the (risen) Lord.

V. Koperski's, *The Knowledge of Christ Jesus My Lord. The High Christology of Philippians 3:7–11*, maintains that 'the christological force of Phil 3:7–11 is just as strong [as Phil. 2:6–11], if not stronger, and is expressed more straightforwardly'.[73] She continues: 'This confession [in 3:7–11] is so strong that though Paul does not literally use the words "Christ is God", his depiction of the utter incomparability of Christ can lead to no other conclusion'.[74]

It will be noticed that these (quite independent) studies all involve language that describes, in one way or another, the relation between Christ and believers. This point shall be elaborated later.

Christological titles. Despite the modern reaction to the excesses of the mid 20th century titular studies,[75] and Schnelle's recent but overly pessimistic claim: 'Titles are, at present, part of a neglected area in Pauline Christology',[76] they have continued to remain a focus of important monographs, even if this approach is usually complemented by others (i.e., the significance of the 'worship' of Jesus and so on).[77]

Θεός. Harris has studied the christological use of the title θεός in the NT and concludes that it is 'very probable' that the term θεός is applied to Jesus in Romans 9:5.[78] However, Bauckham writes that:

If Paul had applied scriptural statements about "god" to Jesus, we could have understood him to be doing what 11QMelchizedek does with reference to Jesus [sic! he means 'Melchizedek'], that is, interpreting the "god" to whom the scriptural texts refer in these

---

[73] V. Koperski, *The Knowledge of Christ Jesus My Lord: The High Christology of Philippians 3:7–11* (Kampen, Netherlands: Kok Pharos, 1996), 323–4.

[74] Ibid., 323.

[75] L. E. Keck asserted that '[p]robably no other factor has contributed more to the current aridity of the discipline [of NT Christology] than this fascination with the palaeontology of christological titles' (L.E. Keck, "Toward the Renewal of New Testament Christology," *NTS* 32 [1986]: 368). In reality, however, it appears that his assertion concerning the 'current aridity' comes about 10 years too late.

[76] Udo Schnelle, "Heilsgegenwart. Christologische Hoheitstitel bei Paulus," in *Paulinische Christologie*, eds Udo Schnelle, Thomas Söding, and M. Labahn (Göttingen: Vandenhoeck & Ruprecht, 2000), 178, translation mine.

[77] This is not least the case in Fee, *Christology.* Cf. e.g. also Christopher Tuckett, *Christology and the New Testament: Jesus and His Earliest Followers* (Edinburgh: Edinburgh University Press, 2001); Schreiner, *Paul*, chap. 7; Dunn, *Theology*, esp. 182–293, 390–412.

[78] Murray J. Harris, *Jesus as God: The New Testament Use of Theos in Reference to Jesus* (Grand Rapids: Baker, 1992), 271, 171. Cf. also 'the probabilities are nicely balanced, but the scales seem to turn in favour of recognising *theos* here [in Rom. 9:5] as a title of Christ' (William Horbury, *Jewish Messianism and the Cult of Christ* [London: SCM, 1998], 148). Indeed, with impressive exegetical honesty, Casey also affirms θεός as a christological title in Rom. 9:5, even though it can be taken to speak against his general thesis (e.g. Casey, *Prophet*, 135).

particular instances to be not YHWH, the unique Creator and Lord of all things, but an angelic being created and ruled by YHWH.[79]

Indeed, the occurrence of ὁ θεός in 2 Corinthians 4:4 in reference to Satan should be a warning not only to Jehovah Witnesses and their fixation with the anarthrous θεός in John 1:1,[80] but also to the large number of scholars, among those both affirming and denying a Pauline divine-Christology, who place such weight on the shoulders of Romans 9:5. Recently, though Fee maintains a divine-Christology, he does so by explicitly arguing Christ is never called 'God' by Paul. θεός was the title for the Father, whereas Christ was called κύριος.[81]

Κύριος. The christological import of the title κύριος has also remained a focus of many modern publications.[82] However there is some suggestion that the study of the christological implications of this title have yet to be fully recognised as they have not taken seriously enough the experiential dimensions of the issues involved.[83] To date, G.D. Fee's study of the christological implications of this title are the most developed (to be examined below).[84]

The title 'Son of God', unlike in the *Religionsgeschichtliche Schule*, is now used far less to affirm a Pauline divine-Christology.[85] However, Fee has recently thrust divine-christological attention back onto this title, primarily by associating with it the notion of pre-existence.[86]

Theological and titular concerns in denying a Pauline divine-Christology.[87] Most of the theological and titular reasoning outlined above is,

---

[79] Bauckham, *God of Israel*, 224.

[80] But cf. Donald E. Hartley's ETS paper, '2 Corinthians 4:4: A Case for Yahweh as the "God of this Age"'.

[81] Fee, *Christology*, cf. e.g. 16–17, 272–77, 564 etc.

[82] Cf. the various publications of Hurtado in this regard (Hurtado, *LJC*, 108–18; Larry W. Hurtado, "Lord," in *DPL*, eds G.F. Hawthorne, R.P. Martin, and D.G. Reid (Leicester: IVP, 1993), 560–69). For a study of the divine-christological significance of the overlap of the titles θεός and κύριος in Paul, see Neil Richardson, *Paul's Language About God* (Sheffield: Sheffield Academic Press, 1994). He concludes his study with the claim that 'the later doctrines of the Incarnation and Trinity were the logical consequences of his [Paul's] theological grammar' (315).

[83] Fatehi, *Relation*, 324–26.

[84] Fee, *Christology*, esp. 558–85.

[85] Larry W. Hurtado, "Son of God," in *DPL*, eds G.F. Hawthorne, R.P. Martin, and D.G. Reid (Leicester: IVP, 1993), 900.

[86] Fee, *Christology*, esp. 530–54.

[87] It should be pointed out that those denying of Pauline divine-Christology nevertheless maintain that Paul's Christology is very 'high' (Richard is an exception when he claims that 'Paul has a low christology', E. Richard, *Jesus: One and Many. The Christological Concept of New Testament Authors* [Delaware: Michael Glazier, 1988], 328). Dunn's understanding of Paul's Christology is somewhat more nuanced and 'higher' than is often recognised (cf. e.g. James D.G. Dunn, "Was Christianity a Monotheistic Faith from the Beginning?" in *The Christ and the Spirit: Christology*, reprint, originally published in 1982 (Edinburgh: T&T

of course, read in a rather different way by those denying a Pauline divine-Christology. The titular considerations, especially those concerning κύριος and θεός, are understood in the light of other Pauline themes, particularly Adamic and subordinationist[88] language. Thus, in relation to the exegesis of Romans 9:5, subordinationist language is often used to justify a rejection that the passage could be christological in reference.[89] Dunn argues that even if Paul did mean this passage to refer to Christ, it would only be because 'Paul's own [christological] reserve ... slipped at this point ... [and should thus not be taken] as a considered expression of his theology'.[90]

Those who deny a Pauline divine-Christology tend to understand the title κύριος as a way of *distinguishing* Christ from God, and they emphasise subordinationist language in Paul and stress the Adam-Christology of certain passages (e.g. Rom. 15:6; 1 Cor. 15:24–28; 2 Cor. 1:3; 11:31).[91] In this way, the high christological claims associated with the title κύριος are relativised. Indeed, Dunn even goes as far as to claim that 'Paul's fullest statement of Christ's lordship' is found in 1 Corinthians 15:24–28, a passage emphasising Christ's subordination to God.[92]

More elaboration is required concerning Dunn's developing understanding of Adam-Christology. He first introduced his interpretation of it in *Christology in the Making* (particularly with respect to Rom. 8:3; 2 Cor. 4:4;[93] 8:9; Gal. 4:4; and Phil. 2:6–11[94]). However, in 1993 he was to develop these arguments by claiming that 'the lordship of Christ is the completion of the lordship of Adam ... [and] the "in Christ" language is a natural outworking of

---

Clark, 1998), 339–40). Yet, at the end of the day, he still cannot speak of a Pauline divine-Christology in the way Bauckham defines above.

[88] The use of such language in this thesis is simply meant to indicate the subordination of Christ under God (cf. Schrage, *Unterwegs*, 158 n.361).

[89] E.g. Schrage, *Unterwegs*, 138; M. Jonge, de, *Christology in Context. The Earliest Christian Response to Jesus* (Philadelphia: Westminster John Knox, 1988), 122–23.

[90] Dunn, *Theology*, 257.

[91] Cf. Dunn, "Faith," 337–38.

[92] Dunn, *Theology*, 249.

[93] Dunn further developed his arguments concerning the Adamic interpretation of this verse in James D.G. Dunn, "'A Light to the Gentiles': The Significance of the Damascus Road Christophany for Paul," in *The Glory of Christ in the New Testament: Studies in Christology*, eds L.D. Hurst and N.T. Wright (Oxford: Clarendon, 1987), 251–66, especially in response to Kim's thesis (see above).

[94] In relation to this hymn, Dunn drew on and developed the earlier work of Murphy-O'Connor (J. Murphy-O'Connor, "Christological Anthropology in Phil., II, 6–11," *RB* 83 [1976]: esp. 38–9, 48–50 and J. Murphy-O'Connor, *Becoming Human Together* [Dublin: Veritas Publications, 1978], 51. This position has been affirmed in his more recent publications: J. Murphy-O'Connor, *Paul: A Critical Life* [Oxford: Oxford University Press, 1996], 227; J. Murphy-O'Connor, "The Origins of Paul's Christology: From Thessalonians to Galatians," in *Christian Origins: Worship, Belief and Society*, ed. Kieran J. O'Mahony [London: Sheffield Academic Press, 2003], 130).

Adam christology'. Furthermore, even the 'idea of Christ as in some sense a "corporate"[95] person is part and parcel of Adam christology'.[96]

That Christ is subordinate to God in Paul (the language of subordination) is a major emphasis among those denying a Pauline divine-Christology. Apart from noting the particular subordinationist texts (e.g. 1 Cor. 15:24–28, etc.), these scholars most often stress the primary nature of Theology over Christology in Paul. Thus, Dunn can write that 'Pauline christology again and again in its "highest" moments shows itself to be in essence an aspect of theology'.[97] This emphasis has been justified by various scholars pointing out i) the different prepositions typically used in Paul in relation to God (ἐκ) and Christ (διά), ii) the fact that, for Paul, Christ lives for God (cf. Rom. 6:10; 2 Cor. 13:4),[98] iii) that Christ is the subject of God's activities and belongs to God,[99] and iv) that Christ is seen only as 'the *mediator* of creation and salvation ..., not its initiator and not its end'.[100] In the light of these subordinationist elements, Schrage can claim: 'Such expressions *en passant* make clear the obviousness of the "subordinationist" thinking in Paul, and exclude ... an equality [*Gleichstellung*] between God and Christ'.[101]

Importantly, it appears that modern publications affirming a Pauline divine-Christology have not engaged with such material and scholarly arguments, as overviewed here, thoroughly enough. Thus Dunn justifiably complains that both Capes and Kreitzer entirely omitted to engage with the subordinationist emphasising work of W. Thüsing.[102]

---

[95] For the meaning of 'corporate' here, cf. the discussion concerning Moule's proposals below, on p. 29.

[96] James D.G. Dunn, "Pauline Christology: Shaping the Fundamental Structures," in *The Christ and the Spirit: Christology*, reprint, originally published in 1993 (Edinburgh: T&T Clark, 1998), 232–33.

[97] James D.G. Dunn, "Christology as an Aspect of Theology," in *The Christ and the Spirit: Christology*, reprint, originally published in 1993 (Edinburgh: T&T Clark, 1998), 382. Cf. also Schrage, *Unterwegs*, 141.

[98] Cf. Schrage, *Unterwegs*, 148, 152, 155; Dunn, "Aspect," 378–79.

[99] Schrage, *Unterwegs*, 142–43, but cf. 157.

[100] Ibid., 170, italics mine.

[101] Schrage, *Unterwegs*, 158, translation mine. Note, however, that Schrage contrasts his position with Bultmann's less nuanced understanding of Christ's subordination to God. He argues (while citing Conzelmann) that it is 'probably even more adequate to speak of a "dialectic of *subordination* and *coordination*"' (150, translation mine). However, his discussion concerning Christ as the 'middle' and not 'end' in Paul (cf. 182–83), arguably demonstrates that he does not manage to maintain this dialectical tension in practice, preferring rather to emphasise subordinationist aspects.

[102] James D.G. Dunn, "Why 'Incarnation'? A Review of Recent New Testament Scholarship," in *The Christ and the Spirit: Christology*, reprint, originally published in 1994 (Edinburgh: T&T Clark, 1998), 414. Fee at least attempts to explain away subordinationist language in Paul, but his reasoning is problematic (Fee, *Christology*, 113, 142–43. Cf. also 179), as shall be explored in the next chapter.

3.2.2. Arguments through Paul's christological hermeneutic or exegesis

Important for this theme are the publications of D. Capes. He argues that Paul 'occasionally applied to Jesus texts originally referring to Yahweh. Given his high regard for scripture, this exegetical practice means that Paul considered Jesus to be a manifestation of Yahweh'.[103]

Recently, Bauckham, Eskola and Wright have also forcibly argued for the christological significance of Paul's hermeneutic in relation to scripture and his traditions. Bauckham, while noting that Second Temple Jewish and early Christian[104] theology 'was primarily a tradition of exegesis, not a tradition of ideas passed on independently of exegesis', he points out the 'foundational importance of Psalm 110:1 for early Christology'.[105] The significance of this must be seen in the light of Bauckham's wider approach as discussed above. Briefly put, he refers to the early Christian exegesis of Psalm 110 and its association with Psalm 8:6[106] (as in, e.g., 1 Cor. 15:25–28) in order to demonstrate that Jesus was included in God's unique sovereignty over all things, and thus also in the divine identity.

Wright's scheme is a little different in that he emphasises the importance of the theme of Messiahship. In the light of contemporary Jewish understanding of Psalm 2, Daniel 7 etc., the very fact that Jesus is understood as the Messiah means that he must also be '*the world's true lord*. He is the *kyrios* at whose name every knee shall bow'. Furthermore, 'the biblical texts which speak in this way are harder and harder to separate from the texts which, when they say *kyrios*, refer to Israel's god, YHWH himself'.[107] Wright thus seems to be suggesting in this passage that a certain amount of exegetical confusion was an important part in the development of early Christology. Along with Bauckham, Wright also wants to affirm that the early church handling of

---

[103] David B. Capes, *Old Testament Yahweh Texts in Paul's Christology* (Tübingen: Mohr Siebeck, 1992), 185. Cf. also David B. Capes, "YHWH Texts and Monotheism in Paul's Christology," in *Early Jewish and Christian Monotheism*, eds Loren T. Stuckenbruck and Wendy E.S. North (London: T&T Clark, 2004), 120–37. While Davis qualifies Capes's arguments by pointing out 'numerous examples of passages where a writer applies an earlier passage about God to a second figure' (Davis, *Name*, 179), he nevertheless still affirms a divine-Christology (154–55).

[104] Many object to the usage of the word 'Christian' to describe the early Pauline Christ-believers on the grounds that it is anachronistic and encourages false associations. However, while these points are accepted, this thesis will continue to use the word 'Christian', and means to simply indicates Christ-believers.

[105] Richard J. Bauckham, "The Throne of God and the Worship of Jesus," in *The Jewish Roots of Christological Monotheism*, eds C.C. Newman, J.R. Davila, and G.S. Lewis (Leiden: Brill, 1999), 62.

[106] Cf. also M. Hengel, *Studies in Early Christology* (Edinburgh: T&T Clark, 1995), 119–225.

[107] N.T. Wright, *The Resurrection of the Son of God* (London: SPCK, 2003), 395, italics his.

Psalm 110 'seems to mean that the one true God has exalted him to share the divine throne itself'.[108]

Eskola has also recently affirmed a Pauline divine-Christology as 'grounded on Christian merkabah speculation working on subtexts such as Psalm 110'.[109] His sophisticated discussion, including treatment of modern linguistics and the complexities of Jewish mysticism, leads him to conclude that the 'enthronement story based on exaltation discourse as such implies the idea of the deity of Christ ... Christology has appeared to be a radical intertextual transformation where tradition is completely in the service of the new message'.[110]

However, Dunn, in response to Capes, wants to still emphasise a measure of christological ambiguity in the light of such reasoning because of what he perceives to be the force of Paul's subordinationist language.[111] He argues that Capes simply has not attended to the variety of christological language in Paul, and thus 'oversimplifies Paul's hermeneutics'.[112]

3.2.3. The christological significance of Paul's experience of the risen Lord

The most popular way of engaging with the christological significance of Paul's experience of the risen Lord has been through painstaking analysis of Paul's Damascus Christophany.[113] However, another line of reasoning has been pursued by C. F. D. Moule who attempted to flesh out the christological consequences of the early Christian 'understanding and experience of Christ as corporate'.[114] The apparently locative sense of some 'in Christ' passages in Paul is, Moule maintains, 'Christological datum of great significance'. It suggests that the risen Lord is 'an inclusive, all-embracing presence'. Indeed, 'such a person is beginning to be described in terms appropriate to nothing less than God himself'.[115] Thus Moule suggests that 'Paul was led to conceive of Christ as any theist conceives of God: personal, indeed, but transcending the individual category'.[116] Arguably, these are lines of thought that NT scholarship involved in the question of Pauline divine-Christology has yet to fully appreciate.[117] Dunn, while at least appreciating the christological

---

[108] Ibid., 395.

[109] Eskola, *Messiah*, 388.

[110] Ibid., 389–90.

[111] Cf. Dunn, "Incarnation," 414.

[112] Dunn, *Theology*, 250 n.82.

[113] Cf. Carey C. Newman, *Paul's Glory-Christology: Tradition and Rhetoric* (Köln: Brill, 1992), 164–212; Segal, *Paul the Convert*, 60–61; the thesis of Kim, mentioned above, and recently Timothy William Ralph Churchill, *Divine Initiative and the Christology of the Damascus Road Encounter*, PhD thesis (Brunel University, 2008).

[114] C.F.D. Moule, *The Origin of Christology* (Cambridge: Cambridge University Press, 1977), 47.

[115] Moule, *Origin*, 53 and cf. also 62.

[116] Ibid., 95.

[117] Cf. the comments in Dunn, *Theology*, 409.

potential of this reasoning, nevertheless asserts that 'it refuses conceptual clarity' and will thus remain 'confusing' when considered in christological categories.[118]

Another crucial approach to the question of Pauline divine-Christology in the light of Paul's experiences of the risen Lord has been proposed by Max Turner (first in the early 1980s), and, particularly with regard to Paul, by his doctoral student Mehrdad Fatehi. Based on the Apostle's experience of the risen Christ and his lordship through the Spirit, Turner argues that:

Paul believes that the Spirit relates the presence and actions of the exalted Christ to the believer in ways that immediately evoke the analogy of the Spirit's extension of *God's* person and activity to humankind. It is difficult to see how such a claim would stop short of some form of "divine" Christology.[119]

Fatehi, while dissenting from his *Doktorvater* in certain details, essentially affirms the correctness of Turner's reasoning and develops it in more detail.[120] Dunn's criticism of Turner's argumentation, i.e., that Turner fails to consider that, in Paul, 'it is always God who is described as the one who gives the Spirit',[121] misses the point – Christ's 'lordship of the Spirit' in Paul was not understood to refer to Christ as giver of the Spirit. Furthermore, Dunn's response to Fatehi's monograph betrays an uncritical rehash of his 'argument from silence',[122] and fails to dialogue with even Fatehi's own comments on this matter.[123] Thus the force of Turner's and Fatehi's arguments are yet to be fully acknowledged, a point that will need further exploration as this thesis unfolds.

3.2.4. The alleged 'worship' of Jesus in Paul

As early as 1972, David Aune claimed: 'Perhaps the single most important historical development within the early church was the rise of the cultic worship of the exalted Jesus within the primitive Palestinian church',[124] and in 1980 R. T. France called the 'worship' of Jesus a neglected factor in

---

[118] Dunn, *Theology*, 410 and 409. Indeed, Moule himself seems to acknowledge this (Moule, *Origin*, 47–54).

[119] Max Turner, "The Spirit of Christ and 'Divine' Christology," in *Jesus of Nazareth: Lord and Christ. Essays on the Historical Jesus and New Testament Christology*, eds Joel B. Green and Max Turner (Carlisle: Paternoster, 1994), 434, italics his. Cf. also Max Turner, "'Trinitarian' Pneumatology in the New Testament? – Towards an Explanation of the Worship of Jesus," *AsTJ* 58, no. 1 (2003): 167–86.

[120] Fatehi, *Relation*.

[121] Dunn, *Theology*, 254 n.105.

[122] James D.G. Dunn, "Review: The Spirit's Relation to the Risen Lord in Paul," *JTS* 55 (2004): 285.

[123] Fatehi, *Relation*, 326–30.

[124] D.E. Aune, *The Cultic Setting of Realised Eschatology in Early Christianity* (Leiden: Brill, 1972), 5, also quoted in Hurtado, *LJC*, 135.

christological inquiry.[125] It is not surprising, then, that this alleged 'cultic worship' and its christological significance has been at the centre of academic debate for the last couple of decades.[126] Indeed, Barker's 'problem', as noted above, is precisely 'how Jesus came to be worshipped'.[127] Furthermore, as will be seen in the early Bauckham, but also later in Hurtado,[128] the criterion for identifying the one God of Jewish monotheistic faith and practice has often been singled down to the question of 'worship' (cf. the scholarly use of the term 'monolatry').

Bauckham first argued for the divine-christological significance of the worship of Jesus in certain significant NT contexts. It is this worship, he maintained, which was 'the real test of monotheistic faith in religious practice'.[129] Bauckham's work inspired the publications of Hurtado whose works in this respect are the most significant. Hurtado's major contributions are found in two monographs published in 1988 (*OG*) and 2003 (*LJC*). *OG* has been at the centre of the developing debate concerning the christological significance of the alleged 'worship' of Jesus in Pauline Christianity. The focus of this small volume was, as Hurtado himself summarised ten years later, 'the religious devotion to the figure of Christ in first-century Christianity, especially the reverencing of Christ in ways that connote a view of him as in some way divine'.[130] He sought to explain the origins of the 'worship' of Christ by analysing its history-of-religions context (although unlike the *Religionsgeschichtliche Schule*, with a greater emphasis on 'the importance of the rich and varied Jewish religious background'[131]). To do this, he studied Second Temple Jewish 'divine-agents' and, for example with regard to Philippians 2:6–11, concludes that 'the fundamental category by which Christ's status is interpreted here is the divine agency category'.[132] However, the worship of the risen Lord in early Christianity signifies a

---

[125] This argument was presented at the 1980 Laing Lecture at London School of Theology (then, London Bible College), later published in R. T. France, "The Worship of Jesus: A Neglected Factor in the Christological Debate," in *Christ the Lord: Studies in Christology Presented to Donald Guthrie*, ed. Harold H. Rowdon (Leicester: IVP, 1982), 17–36.

[126] C.C. Newman, J.R. Davila, and G.S. Lewis, eds, *The Jewish Roots of Christological Monotheism* (Leiden: Brill, 1999), was published as a result of *The International Conference on the Origins of the Worship of Jesus* (1998).

[127] Barker, "Priest," 93. Cf. also the introductory remarks in J.R. Davila, "Of Methodology, Monotheism and Metatron: Introductory Reflections on Divine Mediators and the Origins of the Worship of Jesus," in *The Jewish Roots of Christological Monotheism*, eds C.C. Newman, J.R. Davila, and G.S. Lewis (Leiden: Brill, 1999), 3.

[128] Hurtado, *OG*[2], 38; Hurtado, *LJC*, 37, 51.

[129] Bauckham, "Apocalyptic," 322. Cf. also Hengel, *Jesus*, chap. 5.

[130] Hurtado, *OG*[2], vii. Observable is Hurtado's dependence on the older *Religionsgeschichtliche Schule* emphasis on Paul's experience of Christ.

[131] Hurtado, *OG*[2], ix.

[132] Ibid., 97.

fundamental break with Second Temple Judaism, driving the early church's religious devotion in a binitarian direction.[133] He suggests:

...six features of the religious devotion of early Christianity that indicate a significant mutation in the Jewish monotheistic tradition: (1) hymnic practices, (2) prayer and related practices, (3) use of the name of Christ, (4) the Lord's Supper, (5) confession of faith in Jesus, and (6) prophetic pronouncements of the risen Christ.[134]

He argues that Paul 'wrote of the exalted Christ and reverenced him in ways that seem to require us to conclude that Paul treated him as divine'.[135] The contribution of *LJC* to Hurtado's thesis, and critical responses to his project, shall be explored in the next chapter.

3.2.5. Gordon Fee's Pauline Christology

In 2007 Fee published the most important work to date on Pauline Christology.[136] This is the first monograph dedicated to Pauline Christology in modern scholarship, and at over 600 pages it makes a massive contribution to the divine-Christology debate. Significantly, he draws together a number of the threads analysed above, and so is best analysed on its own terms. For example, Fee is concerned with what Capes called 'Yahweh texts', he examines Christ-devotion like Hurtado, he attempts to build on Bauckham's notion of 'identity', and he responds to some of Dunn's arguments etc. Not only is his scope broad, but his exegetical depth on the many relevant verses is the most thorough to date. Indeed, the importance of Fee's monograph is such that it will be necessary to justify the argumentation of the present thesis at some length in the following chapter.

What does Fee argue? In his introduction, Fee explains that his twofold purpose is first to perform a detailed exegesis of 'those texts deemed to have or, in some cases, not to have christological significance'.[137] Second, Fee will provide a thematic analysis with the goal of 'determining how we might best speak *theologically* about Paul's Christology'.[138] In particular, this will involve examining the relationship between Christ and God in Paul's thinking – while affirming a strict monotheism in Paul.[139] In contradistinction from a narrative or titular method, Fee's is (what he calls) 'primarily exegetical'.[140] Corresponding to this approach, the book is divided into two parts, an exegetical analysis (part 1), and a thematic synthesis (part 2).

His definition of 'Christology' focuses upon the 'person', not 'work' of Christ. Indeed, given that Paul, Fee maintains, does not write about

---

[133] Ibid., chap. 5.
[134] Ibid., 100.
[135] Ibid., 4.
[136] Fee, *Christology*.
[137] Ibid., 10.
[138] Ibid., 10, italics his.
[139] Ibid., 9.
[140] Ibid., 4.

Christology as such, Fee's task is formulated thus: 'to try to tease out what Paul himself understood *presuppositionally* about Christ, and to do so on the basis of his explicit and incidental references to Christ'.[141] While 'Paul nowhere tries to establish a Christology as such', Fee argues that 'Paul drops the curtain just often enough so that we can basically reconstruct what he and his churches believed about Christ'.[142]

The exegetical section tends to examine the Pauline material under titular subsections. Under Paul's supposed 'Son of God Christology', Fee spends time assessing to what extent this is meant messianically, and to what extent pre-existence is implied. Occasionally Fee associates this with Paul's Christ-devotion too. Fee's second major subdivision in his exegetical chapters involves examination of Paul's supposed Κύριος Christology. Here Fee spends most of his time examining the divine roles and prerogatives adopted by Christ, and notes the times Paul appears to deliberately apply 'Yahweh texts' to the risen Christ.

Fee, in the synthesis section of the work, concludes that:

> [T]wo primary christological emphases ... emerge regularly in the corpus and that arguably hold the keys to Paul's answer to the question "Who is Christ?" The suggested answer: Christ is, first of all, the messianic/eternal Son of God ...; and second, Christ is the messianic, now exalted "Lord" of Ps 110:1 ..., who for Paul has come to be identified with κύριος (*Lord*) = Yahweh.[143]

4. Conclusion and bridge

This history of research has argued that the modern debate concerning Pauline divine-Christology, coloured as it is by reaction to and dependence upon pre-1970s scholarship, is productively structured according to the various responses to the two questions noted above (p. 17). The various highways and byways of the controversies can be plotted on this basic map. Of course, this exercise in conceptual cartography is not an end in itself, and in the following chapters it will be shown that a different way of handling both of these questions presents itself, supporting the claims made in the first chapter, that Paul's own language and the most appropriate pattern of Pauline themes relevant to the divine-Christology debate has not yet been sufficiently grasped. A critique of key scholars will be pursued in the next chapter, which will serve as the launching pad for a new proposal, to be introduced in chapter 4. It will maintain that a different method exists, of both approaching the Pauline data, and assessing its christological significance in terms of the divine-Christology debate, both of understanding what counts as relevant data in Paul, and how one should understand his monotheism. In essence, this thesis seeks to

---

[141] Ibid., 3–4.
[142] Ibid., 523–24.
[143] Ibid., 482, italics his.

advance the divine-Christology debate through fresh examination of the pattern of data in the undisputed Pauline letters, concerning the relation between the risen Lord and believers. But this is to run ahead of the argument. First it is necessary to examine the key contributions of Fee, Hurtado and Bauckham.

Chapter 3

Preparing the stage. Reflections on the works of Gordon Fee, Larry Hurtado and Richard Bauckham

1. Introduction

The previous chapter suggests that the prominent proponents of a Pauline divine-Christology are Fee, Hurtado and Bauckham. This thesis hopes to build on their many insights and strengths. Nevertheless, critique of their proposals is necessary, not least because it will arguably demonstrate the need for an altogether different approach to the debate surrounding Pauline divine-Christology. Further, given the scope and ambition of Fee's work in particular, as noted in the previous chapter, it will be necessary to justify this thesis in clear contradistinction from his monograph, *Pauline Christology*. Hence, numerous arguments shall be presented in criticism of various aspects of particularly Fee's project, mainly as they relate to the undisputed Pauline letters engaged in this thesis. It will also be argued that undeveloped insights and omissions in Fee's work suggest a better way of handling the subject of Pauline divine-Christology. We then turn to critically examine the relevant arguments of both Hurtado and Bauckham.

2. The focus of Fee's *Pauline Christology*

2.1. Fee's definition of 'Christology'

It will first be noticed how traditional is Fee's definition of Christology. The question to be asked is if it is appropriate. He takes the word 'Christology' 'to refer to the *person* of Christ – Paul's understanding of who Christ was/is, *in distinction* to the *work* of Christ – what Christ is for us as Savior' (1, italics changed).[1] Fee himself notes problems with this definition, namely that one cannot really divorce Paul's soteriology from his Christology, and that only Colossians 1:15–17 is actually Christology in Paul according to his definition (though it is unclear why this should be Christology and, say, 1 Cor. 8:6 is not). This means, as noted in the previous chapter, that his study of Pauline Christology moves into Paul's christological *presuppositions*. However, while

---

[1] In this chapter, all such numbers in brackets following citations will refer to page numbers in Fee's work.

the question Fee wants to examine, according to his definition, is legitimate, one wonders whether this definition of Christology actually fits the Pauline material appropriately. Arguably, his definition struggles to deal with the Pauline material – a claim to be supported later. It will be suggested that Fee's definition neither coheres too well with the nature of Pauline monotheism, nor with Paul's understanding of Christ and the nature of Paul's letters, nor does it show adequate understanding of Bauckham's notion of 'identity'. These matters arguably demand a different handling of 'Christology', as shall be discussed in the following chapters. Furthermore, his understanding of Christology has been heavily challenged in modern theological writings, not least by Karl Barth,[2] Gerhard Ebeling and many others.[3] Fee would have benefited from dialoguing with such concerns. One must also question whether use of the slippery and theologically disputed word 'person', especially when employed without qualification, actually assists Fee's project.

2.2. Fee and Christ's pre-existence in Paul

When I first encountered Fee's strong emphasis on pre-existence, one which an initial reading of Paul's letters did not seem to warrant, I suspected it was evidence that he was letting his dialogue with James Dunn dictate his agenda, rather than the Pauline corpus (cf. 559 n.4 and Dunn's focus on pre-existence in his many publications), However, while this may certainly have played a part, I have since come to the conclusion that the key reason for this emphasis is to be understood in terms of likely ontological commitments. This would also cohere with his concerns in his definition of Christology above (i.e., it involves the person and *not* work of Christ). To be precise, Fee's understanding of Christology arguably reflects an Aristotelian ontology, something I will argue below powerfully shapes his project. This entails a consequent emphasis on the substance or essence of Christ, which explains the inordinate focus on pre-existence in his argument generally. Concurrently, this ontology involves a suppression of 'relation' as 'accidental' to a thing,[4] hence Fee tends to struggle to grasp the importance of relational language as part of his wider thematically synthesizing conclusions, as will be demonstrated below. Ontology is perhaps also a key reason why Fee's exegetical rigour seems to slip when engaging with subordination texts, as will be detailed below. If Christology is about static 'being',[5] subordination will be difficult to accommodate.

---

[2] Cf. e.g. Karl Barth, *Church Dogmatics* (London: Continuum, 2008), IV/1, §58.3.

[3] Gerhard Ebeling, *Word and Faith* (Philadelphia: Fortress, 1963), 202–3.

[4] Cf. explication of Aristotle, metaphysics, ontology and relations in the various publications of Shults (e.g. F. LeRon Shults, *Reforming Theological Anthropology: After the Philosophical Turn to Relationality* [Grand Rapids: Eerdmans, 2003]; F. LeRon Shults, *Reforming the Doctrine of God* [Grand Rapids: Eerdmans, 2005]; F. LeRon Shults, *Christology and Science* [Aldershot: Ashgate, 2008]).

[5] Cf. his telling recourse to the language of 'being' in, e.g., Fee, *Christology*, 142–43, 267, 269. But cf. his opaque comments on 'ontology' and 'choice' in 503 n.8.

If ontology pushes Fee to emphasise pre-existence, one must likewise question whether his specific reasoning in relation to pre-existence convinces. He questionably and directly associates the language of 'high' and 'low' Christology with pre-existence (9), rather than divinity.[6] Very important to Fee's central conclusions is the perception of Christ as the eternal Son of God (530). But he regularly, and arguably problematically, reasons 'pre-existence *thus* eternal' (Cf. 531, 35, 99, 209, 212, 213, 240, 246–47, 253, 521, 547, 553, 548). He also directly associates pre-existence with divinity (481, 500, 509, 511, 547, 584). But this is to mix categories. Pre-existent need not mean eternal. Reference can be made to the Son of Man in the Similitudes of Enoch who, while very exalted, is probably not to be understood as divine in the sense of God (in this document, the 'Lord of Spirits').[7] Yet the Son of Man is described in *1 Enoch* 48:6 as pre-existent, as shall be explored in chapter 9. One can also make mention of the apparently pre-existent Jacob-Israel in the *Prayer of Joseph*.[8] What is more, Fee's claims for the centrality of pre-existence in Paul's Christology are often bolstered by less convincing exegetical manoeuvres (cf. the claims on 508 compared with 213, his claims in relation to, e.g., Gal. 4:4–7 on 212–15; Rom. 9:5 on 243; Rom. 8:3 on 246 etc.) which problematically associate the notion of 'pre-existence' with specifically Paul's supposed 'Son of God Christology'. In particular, he reads pre-existence into texts when it is not mentioned and arguably not even implied (cf., e.g., his claims in relation to the implied pre-existence inherent in the phrase κατὰ σάρκα in Rom. 9:5). Without wanting to deny a pre-existent Christology in Paul, the central place Fee has given it appears forced onto the texts, which is arguably itself evidence of an ontological misstep.

3. Inner tensions in Fee's *Pauline Christology*

3.1. A Christology in Paul's letters?

Another question that this focus on Christ's pre-existence generates concerns Fee's claims regarding the presence or absence of Christology in Paul's letters. He regularly claims this or that passage asserts and explicitly states Christ's pre-existence (cf., e.g., 213, 500, 509). What is more, in his synthesis, Christ's pre-existence is one of the major categories involved in his portrayal of Paul's understanding of the person of Christ (cf., e.g. the logic at the top of 488). But if pre-existence is about Christology and it is explicit in Paul's letters at numerous points, then how can Fee claim that Christology never

---

[6] Cf. Raymond Edward Brown, *An introduction to New Testament Christology* (London: Chapman, 1994), 4–5.

[7] Cf. James A. Waddell, *The Messiah in the* Parables of Enoch *and the Letters of Paul: A Comparative Analysis* (University of Michigan: Phd Thesis, 2010), 124–25.

[8] As discussed in Chester, *Messiah*, 369–70.

directly surfaces in Paul, except in Colossians 1:15–17 (e.g. 370, 481)? This tension in Fee's approach surfaces at various points. For example, he can claim that 'the only intentionally christological moment in the corpus is Colossians 1:15–17. Otherwise, Paul's Christology is simply assumed' (370). Cf. also 481 and the instructive comment on 142 that '"being" is simply not part of Paul's epistolary discourse; his concern is always with the role or function of the Son in the divine plan of redemption'. Of Galatians he writes that it 'is specifically and *singularly* given over to the question of soteriology' (207, italics mine). However, he can also state, in relation to Christology in Galatians that 'we find much less in Galatians that is explicitly christological' (208). This implies that there is more explicit Christology in other letters, and that there is some, even if less, explicit Christology in Galatians. It is this inner tension in his argument at this point that arguably accounts for his claim that Galatians 4:4–7 involves *explicit* statements about pre-existence (e.g. 213), when a few pages later he goes on to claim that Paul is '*speaking presuppositionally* about Christ's preexistence' in Galatians (215, italics mine). But how can Fee claim that Paul *speaks* presuppositionally about preexistence here? Surely, speaking is an active matter, expressing something concrete. Likewise, in his exegesis of Romans he writes that 'even though the concern regarding Christ's role is *primarily* soteriological, in this letter especially, one can scarcely miss the *christological emphasis as well*' (238, italics mine). He claims that Romans 8:3 'both assumes *and expresses* an eternal Son of God Christology' (247, italics mine). In light of Philippians 4:13 Fee also writes that 'not everything that he [Paul] thinks about Christ is strictly soteriological' (412). This all makes it a little confusing to determine whether Fee actually thinks there is an explicit Christology in Paul's letters apart from Colossians 1:15–17.

3.2. The overlap between Christology and soteriology

An important passage in Fee's introduction, to which it will be necessary to return, is the following:

[T]he attempt to extract Christology from Paul's letters apart from soteriology is like asking a devout Jew of Paul's era to talk about God in the abstract, without mentioning his mighty deeds of creation and redemption. Although one theoretically may theologize on the character and "person" of God on the basis of the revelation to Moses on Sinai ..., a Jewish person of Paul's era would hardly imagine doing so. What can be known and said about God is embedded in the story in such a way that God's person *can never* be abstracted out of the story (8, italics mine. Cf., also e.g., 86.).

Fee's understanding of the relation between Christology and soteriology deserves more attention. In one passage he argues that Paul's soteriology – what Christ has done for us – can only be made sense of in light of his christological presuppositions – namely who Christ is. Christology makes sense of soteriology (cf. 86). Fee can also speak of certain statements in Paul that '*move us to think beyond* soteriology to ontology' (245, italics mine) and in other places of soteriology spilling over into Christology (413). Elsewhere it will be formulated differently: while adding the demurral 'that one can never truly disassociate Christology from soteriology' (106 n.62), Fee still develops what he calls a '*soteriological, and thus nonchristological*' understanding of 1 Corinthians 1:24 (106, italics mine). Then again, in comment on the themes of 'Re-creation into the Divine Image' (starting on 484), he argues that presupposed in all of this 'soteriological talk' 'are both the preexistence and incarnation of the Son' such that 'precisely here ... Christology and soteriology *intersect* in Paul's thinking' (488, italics mine). This variety of conceptions of the relationship between soteriology and Christology in Paul suggests that the matter has not been systematically considered, which is a problem magnified by the importance of these issues for the central claims of Fee's thesis.

3.3. Subordination and Fee's method

Fee's treatment of subordination texts has been noted above, referred to as a symptom of his arguable ontological commitments. Indeed, his analysis of these texts is particularly illuminating. Fee can regularly assert that God and Christ share in divine purposes and activities (e.g. 48–55) and that this is evidence of a high Christology (54). Such *roles* are of direct significance for Paul's Christology. Nevertheless, when Fee is confronted with subordinationist 'problem passages' his argumentative strategy changes. In response to certain verses in 1 Corinthians 15, Fee reasons:

Although it could easily be argued that this implies some form of "eternal subordination" of the Son to the Father, it is unlikely that Paul is thinking in terms of Christ's *person* here, but rather his *role* in salvation history (113, italics his).

In light of 1 Corinthians 3:23 Fee argues that:

[S]uch statements fall far short of speaking to his *essential being or eternal relationship with the Father*. That is, such statements as these reflect *functional* subordination and have to do with Christ's *function* as Savior, *not with his being* as such (142–43, italics mine. Cf. also 179).

The argumentative tension is perhaps clear. If Fee's earlier claims about the person of Christ only being in purview in Colossians 1:15–17 are correct, then his major christological claims about Paul are almost all based on Christ's roles and functions. Indeed, in a different context Fee has argued that one cannot stay satisfied with questions about function but insists that 'at some point one must wrestle with the "being" that underlies the function' (13). In this way he manages to claim Paul's Christology is very 'high' – the functions and prerogatives Christ shares with God are used in almost every chapter as evidence of a divine or high Christology. But now, when dealing with subordination texts, Fee strictly divides function and being, and one must ask whether this is consistent. Interestingly, Fee notes Dunn's argument which maintains that Paul's point in Romans 14:12–13 is not christological, but rather concerns salvation-history. In other words, Dunn uses much the same strategy as Fee only with texts that point in a different direction. But Fee's response to Dunn is that, though Paul does not assert a christological point, he assumes it (258 n.54). However, cannot Paul also assume a christological point in the subordinationist texts? And if we place this matter in the context of Fee's understanding of the christological task, it would have been important for Fee to explain how one distinguishes whether an *assumption* is more than a role or a salvation-history and about 'being' or 'person'. On what grounds can these distinctions be made? This arguably puts a question mark against the consistency of Fee's whole method of determining christological significance.

3.4. Fee, identity and being

Summarising Bauckham's arguments, Fee notes that he suggests one should use 'the language of "identity" instead of "being" ... Bauckham is concerned with *who* God is rather than *what* God is' (15, italics his). Fee immediately goes on to state that his study will hope to 'follow in the train' of Bauckham (and Hurtado – 15). However, it is a surprise that Fee then continues to use the language of ontology and being in his book, and essentially conflates these concepts with "identity". So, in relation to Romans 5:10, Fee states that these 'are the kind of statements that move us to think beyond soteriology to ontology: the Son is to be *fully identified* with God the Father' (245, italics mine). In light of 'the Spirit of Christ' language in Romans 8, Fee writes that at 'issue is whether Paul intends a *full identification* of the risen Christ with the Spirit, so that in effect the two are the same in terms of "being"' (269, italics mine). But this gives rise to further problems. In particular, Fee will later argue, in apparent tension with these remarks about the Spirit, that though Paul can completely include the Son in the divine identity, he does not absolutely identify the two (585). Further, if Paul's only purposeful Christology is in Colossians 1:15–17, and Fee's task involves teasing out Paul's presuppositions, one wonders if Fee is claiming to know too much when he adumbrates on the differences between the 'full identification' of Father and Son, on the one hand, and Son and Spirit, on the other, in ontological terms.

At other times, however, Fee details more of a logical relation between 'identity' and 'ontology'. Having discussed material in Romans 14, Fee argues that the evidence 'indicates that both [Father and Son] share alike in the divine identity and that there is *therefore* conceptual overlap as to their being' (267, italics mine). However, in an offhand remark in a footnote, Fee can also claim, while discussing the 'divine identity', that '"[i]dentity" leads one to think of the divine Triad as a matter of "choice", so that "ontology" as such is a derivative, not primary idea' (503 n.8). But it is doubtful if Fee is now following in Bauckham's train. For Bauckham, identity means 'the personal identity of self-continuity'.[9] Bauckham writes:

Reference to God's identity is by analogy with human personal identity, understood not as a mere ontological subject without characteristics, but as including both character and personal story (the latter entailing relationships). These are the ways in which we commonly specify "who someone is".[10]

It is doubtful to what extent Bauckham's notion can cohere with Fee's opening claim that Christology is about the 'person' and not 'work' of Christ. All of these factors arguably demonstrate a lack of precision in Fee's handling of the notion of identity. Furthermore, a major aspect that Fee misses is the relational import of identity, a matter to which it will be necessary to return in much more depth below.

3.5. Devotion to Christ, soteriology and Christology

We noted above the tensions involved in Fee's language concerning the relation between soteriology and Christology. But arguably more difficulties surface when the matter of devotion is added to the mix. To take an example: when commenting on Galatians 2:20 Fee claims that 'it is nearly impossible to explain Paul's Christology without taking seriously his utter devotion to Christ' (223). However, just a few pages later, and after examining the much debated πίστις Χριστοῦ, Fee concludes that an objective genitive reading is preferable, so that it indicates faith *in* Christ, not Christ's own faithfulness.[11] What is debatable is that Fee then reasons: 'Thus, given this high level of doubt that this phrase has to do with Christ's own faithfulness, it does not seem to add to our understanding of Paul's understanding of the *person* of Christ' (226, italics his). But in the same context Fee has asserted that devotion to Christ (of which faith in Christ is arguably a part) must be taken seriously to understand Paul's Christology.

It is to Fee's credit that he does examine Christ-devotion. However, some of his statements at this point lack engagement with various scholarly counterproposals. For example, he writes that '[w]hatever else one may think of this kind of pure devotion to Christ [in Philippians], it *must* be acknowledged as devotion toward one's deity, not toward a merely exalted human being' (413, italics mine). Yet Fee has not shown why this is the sort of devotion towards a deity in dialogue with others who would dispute this claim (to be noted below), who need only refer to the worship of the Son of Man in 1 Enoch.

In examining Paul's prayers to the risen Lord, Fee asserts that 'such devotion to Christ is in many ways more telling theologically than actual "theological statements" themselves' (494). He goes on to approvingly summarise Hurtado to the effect that such devotional matters 'precede any known

---

[9] Bauckham, *God*, 7 n.5, citing K.J. Vanhoozer.
[10] Ibid., 7 n.5.
[11] We would disagree with this conclusion, but that is beside the point here.

attempts to express theologically the implications of such devotion; and the latter surely arises out of the former' (494 n.29. Cf. also his later claim: 'Paul's devotion to Christ and his way of speaking about Christ are such that he, without argument, attributes to Christ Jesus his Lord many of what are strictly divine prerogatives' [585]). While I am inclined to partly disagree with both Hurtado and Fee on this,[12] that is beside the point. Rather, one must ask why, for Fee, these matters are more telling theologically than actual 'theological statements' and, if devotion was prior to theology, why then does he state that worship of Christ is 'both because of *what* he did for us and especially because of *who* he is as divine Savior' (494–95, italics his)? It could be claimed that Fee only speaks of *expressed* theology as later than devotion, but when he argues that devotion to Christ can only be explained and accounted for on the basis of the incarnation and in light of Christ's pre-existence (511–12, 547), it can be responded that it is better to say that worship would best presuppose Christ's divinity, rather than directly pre-existence.

Though Fee's exegesis is often extremely well informed, and his analysis of Philippians 2:6–11 is nothing short of brilliant, these tensions in Fee's argumentation need addressing. We turn now to arguable problems associated with Fee's synthesising method for determining christological significance.

4. Fee's synthesising method

4.1. Paul and the Septuagint

It is a matter of considerable importance for Fee's thesis that Paul knew and cited the Septuagint, not least because he will make much of the claim that Paul uses the replacement name for YHWH in these texts (κύριος) as a christological title, such that Christ is the κύριος = *Adonai* = YHWH. But did Paul really know and use the Septuagint that we know? Fee is well aware of the discussion surrounding this matter (cf. 20–21) yet as he admits, experts of the Septuagint will be very uncomfortable with some of his claims in this regard.[13] The issue at hand is whether Fee is placing too much christological weight on such debated foundations. One may also wonder if Fee's confidence in Paul's use of the Septuagint is legitimate when he has to explain some OT 'citations' as a collage from two or more OT Septuagint texts (cf. e.g. 257, 263). Fee notes that Paul himself is not always precise regarding his biblical citations (263 n.67), but arguably this Pauline data can be construed as evidence against Fee's thesis. That said, Fee has made a good case for Paul's usage of at least something very much like the Septuagint,[14] and this thesis,

---

[12] Cf. the comments in, e.g., Fatehi, *Relation*, 21.

[13] Cf. the summary of scholarly discussion in Melvin K. H. Peters, "Septuagint," in *ABD* (London: Doubleday, 1992), V, 1100–1101.

[14] Fee, *Christology*, 20–25.

too, will often make recourse to wording in the LXX to inform exegesis of Paul. However, it will do this in a manner that does not make final christological claims overly dependent on this point.

4.2. Fee's titular study and divisions

Crucial to Fee's project is the division of material under two major headings in Paul, the 'Son of God Christology' and the 'Κύριος Christology'. Fee indicated in his introduction that he appreciates the problems involved in mere titular analyses, and so he states he will (heeding L. Keck's advice) also attend to the grammar of theological discourse in Paul (5). Fee's synthesis section attempts to gather the exegetical conclusions and present 'Paul's primary categories for understanding the person of Christ' (530). So *who* is Christ for Paul?: 'The answer proposed here ... is twofold: (1) the risen Jesus was none other than the preexistent *Son of God*, who came present among us to redeem; and (2) the risen Jesus is the *exalted Lord*' (530, italics his). However, a number of questions must be raised. Namely, Does Paul really possess a 'Son of God' on the one hand, and a 'Κύριος' Christology on the other? And, Is Fee correct to associate abstract themes with these titles, for example 'preexistence' with Paul's supposed 'Son of God' Christology? It will be suggested in the following that the answers to these questions raise further problems for Fee's project.

Turning to the proposal concerning the 'Son of God' Christology and 'Κύριος' Christology, one could respond that this twofold division is not so much the result of Fee's analysis of the text. After all, it was with this basic division that Fee ordered his material in the analytical section. It could even be argued that these divisions are sometimes rather imposed upon the material. For example, 1 Corinthians 8:6 is strong proof, for Fee, that Paul's 'Son of God Christology' was a pre-existent Christology. But it could be objected that Fee simply imports this supposed type of 'Christology' into the material because of the presence of the word 'Father', hence implying the sonship of Christ. Is it not (more?) possible that Paul used this title of God not in accordance (conscious or otherwise) with some Son of God Christology, but simply because he needed to indicate God the Father twice in the passage to maintain the parallelism? Besides, Paul then goes on to speak of the 'Lord' Jesus Christ, and does so for much of the developing argument right through to 11:1. Nevertheless, Fee can claim that Paul's Son of God language is 'used to refer to him [Christ] in his prior existence as God' (544. Cf. also 538, 552). This conclusion is arguably not justified by the texts to which he makes reference.

Before this argument is continued, it is worth noting a small inconsistency in Fee's argument in light of the last citation. Fee insists that Paul never called Christ 'God' and that Christ, for Paul, was not YHWH as such (564, 570). However, Fee can also write, in relation to 2 Corinthians 5:21, that Christ was truly one of us, and 'in all of this he never ceased to be God as well' (529). Speaking of Paul's 'Son of God language', Fee asserts that it is 'used to refer to him [Christ] in his prior existence as God' (544). Fee may well maintain that Christ is God for Paul, too, even if Paul does not use this title, but Fee calls Christ 'God' without offering any such qualification. What is more, Fee can claim that Jesus is not YHWH as such (e.g. 570, 573) but by 'happy circumstance ... the Divine Name had been translated in the Septuagint by way of the Aramaic *Adonai*' (585). So Paul can call Christ Lord and include Jesus in the divine identity 'in a complete way', without implying 'absolute identification (merging the two into one)' (585) as would have happened had Paul simply called Christ YHWH. This is an ingenious proposal, but are these inner divine distinctions really implied by these translation matters? I submit that it is at least possible that Fee is claiming to know too much.

To continue the main argument, it is to be noted that this 'Son of God Christology' is, Fee argues, something of a conscious reality for Paul, as it has two poles within it that Paul holds in tension (545). But if this designated type of 'Christology' is simply Fee's own projection back onto Paul, then no tension exists within a certain subdivision of a Pauline Christology in the first place. Can Fee be sure that this christological presupposition is also a distinct entity that Paul holds in internal tension? That is perhaps saying a bit too much about something that is not actually in the text, but rather a presupposition.

And what about the claim that certain themes are to be associated with these distinct 'christologies'? It is not to be disputed that Fee has shown that some contours of Paul's thinking are loosely associated with certain titles, but he has arguably exaggerated his success in these proposals. For example, he speaks of the transformation of believers specifically in light of Paul's Son of God Christology. It is through *the Son* that 'we are ever being transformed' (548). But when Paul explicitly uses transformation language in 2 Corinthians 3:18, Paul indicates Christ with the title κύριος. His claims that κύριος is used 'exclusively of Christ and never as a reference to God' (561) is simply not true (cf. his own examples, 87 n.7). It was *mostly* used of Christ, granted, but not only, and his reference to explain the exceptions does not appear to answer the problem (561 n.8 citing 87 n.7). In the interests of delineating a Κύριος Christology, Fee can claim that the title 'Lord' is 'used predominantly of Christ's *present* reign and anticipated *coming*, rarely of his earthly life' (561, italics his). But this title can be used of Christ's earthly life, as Fee notes, and the fact that the title predominantly indicates Christ's present reign and eschatological coming is simply because Paul's letters as a whole are predominantly concerned with Christ's present reign and eschatological coming. It is unlikely that there is anything specific to a certain type of Pauline Christology here. It is further questionable if Paul associated with a 'Son of God' Christology the notion of pre-existence, something, as noted above, so central to his project. For example, some of the clearest expressions of Christ's pre-existence in Paul are found in 1 Corinthians 8:6; 10:4, 9. But neither of the latter two verses necessitate any kind of 'Son of God Christology' and, as noted above, it can be disputed that mention of 'Father' in 8:6 should be understood as implying a 'Son of God Christology' mode. Rather, Paul speaks of pre-existence in terms of Christ and the κύριος in these verses. One must also ask in this context why certain texts using the title κύριος (like 1 Cor. 8:6) in Paul must serve 'as the presuppositional basis for our understanding of Paul's consistent and regular use of (ὁ) κύριος' elsewhere in Paul (562).

It can be suggested that Fee is not entirely justified in pushing his divisions back into Paul's letters in the way he has done. Furthermore, to speak of Paul's 'theological enterprise' (554) in the context of such distinctions argu-ably promotes misunderstanding concerning the nature of Paul's theologising.[15]

Finally, on what grounds does Fee divide Paul's devotion into 'personal devotion' on the one hand, and 'object of worship' on the other (488–490)? Even more puzzling is that he deems Paul's prayers to Christ to be part of the worship category, not Paul's personal devotion. These are wooden categories that may have helped to structure his chapter, but it is doubtful to what extent they bring clarity to the subject matter.

4.3. Divine prerogatives and Fee's interpretative patterns

Fee occasionally makes appeal to the pattern of evidence of his lists of 'divine prerogatives' and 'purposes'. On the basis of the data he gathers under these headings, he draws christological conclusions. For example, reference can be made to his exegesis of 1 Corinthians (cf. 141–42).

One may, however, question why these lists tend to suppress or ignore important alternative readings of the data. To cite an example, he speaks of the role of Christ in Paul as eschatological judge in terms of its supposed divine-christological implications. But this is done without mention of the role of the Son of Man (or Enoch) in the *Similitudes of Enoch* who is also eschatological judge despite, as noted above, probably not being divine as God, the Lord of Spirits. He discusses the worship of Christ as direct evidence of Christ's divinity without mention of certain material in the *Life of Adam and Eve*, nor does he engage the evidence cited by Horbury, Fletcher-Louis, and others to be noted below.

A second issue is that he lists the material under headings which are often arguably not appropriate to his projected pattern. For example, in 1 Thessalonians Fee includes, under the major heading 'God and ὁ Κύριος Share in Divine Purposes and Activity' (48), such material as existing 'in

---

[15] Against this notion of abstract categories in Paul's Christology, cf. the discussion in chapter 10 in dialogue with Hendrikus Boers, *Christ in the Letters of Paul: In Place of a Christology* (Berlin: W. de Gruyter, 2006).

Christ' and 'in God' (48–50) and invoking Christ in prayer (51–55). But is
prayer to Christ best described as a divine purpose or activity? Prayer is the
activity *of a believer* not God, and its significance, as this thesis will show,
lies in its expressing part of the relation between the risen Lord and believers.
In his exegesis of Romans, Fee titles a section: 'Christ and the Divine Prerogatives' (268). He then goes on to list an attribute of Christ, namely his love
(270. Cf. Rom. 8:35), and mentions Paul's language of the 'assemblies of
Christ' (Rom. 16:16) as a 'divine prerogative' because the usual meaning of
'belonging to God' is here 'designated as belonging to Christ' (271). But is
'belonging to Christ' a divine prerogative or a relational concept that goes
beyond such language?[16] And is the love of Christ in Romans 8:35 best
termed a divine prerogative? In relation to Philippians, he gathers the following language under the subtitle 'Sharer of Divine Prerogatives' (410): 'with
the compassion of Christ Jesus (1:8)' (410), 'hope in the Lord Jesus (2:19)',
'confident in the Lord (1:14; 2:24)' (410–11) and 'the one who strengthens
(4:13)' (411–12). While the last may well be best described as a divine prerogative ascribed to Christ, the others say something more directly about the
nature of the believers in their relationship with the risen Lord. This continues
in his synthesis section. He gathers much material under the major heading
'Jesus the Lord: Sharer of Divine Prerogatives' (576), yet included under the
subheading 'Christ, the "Lord" of Septuagint Texts' (577) he adds such Pauline language as 'boast in the Lord', 'beloved of the Lord', 'the Lord be with
you' and 'the Lord is near' (577–78). In the longer section subtitled 'Κύριος
and Θεός Share Prerogatives' he lists such Pauline language as 'in Christ',
'the grace of the Lord', the presence of the Lord, the Lord of peace, 'walk
worthy of the Lord', the 'parousia of Christ', 'the Lord who strengthens
believers', 'the glory of the Lord', Christ 'sending/commissioning Paul',
'pleasing the Lord' and 'the fear of the Lord' (578–84). But arguably these are
better included in the pattern of language in Paul that describes the relation
between risen Lord and believers, not simply divine prerogatives. The fear of
the Lord, for example, is hardly directly a divine prerogative. It is relational
language, as is 'walking worthy of the Lord', 'boasting in the Lord', 'pleasing
the Lord' etc.

It is worth citing these examples at some length because it is clearly not
unimportant to Fee's thesis but right at the very heart of his understanding of
Paul's so-called 'Κύριος Christology' (cf. e.g. the claims in 559). If Fee has
allocated this material to be part of a pattern that is not the most appropriate,
one wonders if the full significance of the material will be appreciated. More
will be said about the crucial matter of these prerogatives and the relational
import of the language in the last section of this chapter.

---

[16] The language of 'relation' here and in the following will be explored below, in chapter
4.

4.4. Fee and the assessment of christological significance

The final point to be made here in terms of Fee's methodology is the manner in which he attempts to ascertain christological significance. This will serve as a helpful bridge into the last section of this critique. As noted above, he often draws attention to material (that should best be understood as part of the pattern of language in Paul that denotes the relation between risen Lord and believer) and simply states that this or that is christologically significant, noteworthy, carries its own christological weight etc. (e.g. 121). The question which this thesis hopes systematically to treat is why and how such material can be considered significant christologically. The point to make here is simply that Fee leaves such questions largely unanswered. He does seek to show christological significance in the cases where God and Christ share divine prerogatives, and this is helpful. But he does not make explicit why his reasoning about the sharing of prerogatives in Paul demonstrates the christological point he wants it to, especially in distinction from the (lack of) significance of the subordinationist texts.

5. Fee and relationality[17]

It was claimed above that Fee's project involves an ontological commitment that may not be the most helpful to analyse Paul. As noted above, an Aristotelian ontology involves a suppression of 'relation' as 'accidental' to a thing. Later we shall maintain that any approach to Pauline monotheism and Christology which would suppress 'relation' will lead to severe problems. Coherent with this, the present section attempts to justify two important claims: 1) Fee sometimes notices a relational emphasis in Paul but underestimates its significance. 2) Because Fee misses the importance of Paul's relational Christology, his exegesis and analysis overlooks material of significance and sometimes obscures some of what he does see.

5.1. On Fee affirming a relational emphasis, while underestimating its significance

This point arguably gets straight to the heart of the matter and is supported in three ways. First, Fee says he wishes to follow in the train of Bauckham, but arguably he does not. Had he really done so, he would have pursued a more relational approach. Second, Fee even starts to glimpse how soteriology and Christology can be seen to come together and be bridged. When he does this he uses relational language, but does not seem to notice its significance. Third, and most importantly, this underestimation of relationality is evidenced at numerous points in Fee's actual engagement with the Pauline letters, analysis of which follows in 5.2. These points will now be treated in turn.

---

[17] The precise import of the language of 'relation' will be explored below in chapter 4.

5.1.1. Does Fee really 'follow the train' (15) of Bauckham (or rightly evaluate Hurtado)?

Fee's problematic handling of Bauckham's use of 'identity' has already been noted above. Now more can be said in criticism of his reading of Bauckham, especially as he states at the start of his project that his study hopes to follow the train of both Bauckham and Hurtado.

Reference can first be made to the block citation from Fee (8) above on p. 38. As he writes: '*What can be known and said about God is embedded in the story in such a way that God's person can never be abstracted out of the story*' (8, italics mine). All that needs to be added here is that this story is one largely about the *relation* between YHWH and Israel (and sometimes the world). Yet if God's person cannot be abstracted from this relational story, then neither should Christ's person be abstracted from his relation to his people. This comes to the heart of Bauckham's use of the concept of identity, as noted above.[18] Yet Fee explicitly sets the christological task in terms of the relation between Son and Father only (cf. 9). But what of Christ's relation to believers? What is surprising is that Fee states these things while noting the importance of Bauckham's study. As Fee *himself* summarises Bauckham:

> Bauckham's first concern is to demonstrate that Israel's understanding of God was *always in terms of God's relationship to Israel and then to all other reality*. Thus Yahweh was never thought of in Greek abstractions. His character is always described in terms of *relationship to Israel* ... [and] [i]n terms of God's relation to all other reality (15, italics mine).

Bauckham sees the importance of relation to God's people, and Fee cites him to this effect. But still the only relation Fee pursues in any significant way is that between Christ and God, not believers, even though so much of the language he examines under titles and prerogatives is better understood as relational. And it can be asked if the task Fee sets himself is after all to abstract 'person' from relations and story. It can be doubted to what extent Fee follows the train of Bauckham.

At this point it is worthwhile noting that one may also question whether he understands Hurtado, the other scholar whose train he wishes to follow. In describing Hurtado, Fee argues that, in *Lord Jesus Christ*, 'his concern is less with what Paul *believes* than with what Paul's letters reflect about early Christian practices regarding *worship*, especially in their ways of expressing devotion to Jesus' (15, italics his). But even a casual flick through Hurtado's chapter on Paul will show that more of it is given over to an analysis of christological language and themes, and only a smaller section at the end to binitarian worship.[19] Hurtado defines 'devotion' in terms of beliefs *and* related religious actions.[20]

---

[18] Bauckham, *God*, 7 n.5.

[19] Hurtado, *LJC*, 98–134 = 'Christological language and Themes', 134–53 = 'Binitarian Worship'.

[20] Ibid., 3, italics mine.

5.1.2. Bridging the gap between soteriology and Christology with relational language

Fee's understanding of the relation between Christology and soteriology has been explored above. It can also be noted that, in brief moments, Fee appears to acknowledge a way beyond this, what he himself considers, unnatural and un-Pauline divide. While in one section Fee implies that the relational aspect of Paul's life is essentially synonymous with soteriological matters (161), he can also speak of the 'central place Christ has in Paul's entire worldview' that implies more than soteriology (412). In this context he even adds that Philippians 1:23 is not simply soteriological but *personal* (413). This is a thought left underdeveloped. To this can be added moments in Fee's work that appeal to the theological importance of Christ-devotion language. For example, he can state that 'it is *nearly* impossible to explain Paul's Christology without taking seriously his utter devotion to Christ' (223, italics mine). He then immediately goes on to state the very personal nature of this devotion in Galatians 2:20. However, it will be argued in this thesis that it is not *nearly* but *entirely* impossible to understand Paul's Christology without attending to Christ-devotion, as Christ-devotion itself is part of that wider pattern of language in Paul denoting the relation between risen Lord and believers. Finally, and perhaps most remarkably, in discussing Christ-devotion in his synthesis, Fee makes the following comment: 'the worship [of Christ] is both because of *what* he did for us and especially because of *who* he is as divine Savior' (494–95, italics his). The evidence of the worship of Christ, Fee states, brings together an appreciation of the work and person of Christ. These brilliant insights in Fee's thinking are left unattended to and do not yield the fruit they promise.

5.2. Fee, relationality and exegesis

First, a number of examples can be found in which Fee's exegesis shows that he notes the relational import of many verses, but likewise tends to fail to follow these thoughts through or develop the implications. For example, a relational emphasis is obvious in Paul's Christ-devotion. Indeed, it will later be argued that devotion is part of a larger relational pattern, a pattern, this thesis will maintain, Paul would recognise. So it is important that Fee opens the book with an emphasis on Christ-devotion (1). However, he appears to fail to link devotion with relation to Christ. He notes the relational significance of κοινωνία and other material in 1 Corinthians 1, but leaves the matter underdeveloped. He speaks of the devotional attitude towards the risen Lord expressed in 1 Corinthians 16:22, but does little with it. Perhaps most remarkably, he summarises the significance of language in Paul's argument in 1 Corinthians 8:1–11:1 in the following way:

Paul not only broadens the Corinthians' perspective on the Shema, but at the same time he anticipates the role that Christ is to play in the argument that follows (esp. 8:11–12; 10:4, 9, 16–22), *where everything hinges on their ongoing relationship to Christ* (92, italics mine).

However, rather than noting the significance of this in terms of the relational monotheism expounded in 1 Corinthians 8:1–6,[21] as will be argued in chapter 5, he instead immediately continues on a completely different angle about the title κύριος and the question of pre-existence (92), which he indeed considers to be the key that makes sense of Paul's argument here (98). Had he followed this point about the relationship to Christ through, Fee would arguably have been able to unlock this passage more convincingly and completely. This is arguably first to see yet then miss that which is of the utmost christological significance in this passage. It can even be argued that Fee's underestimation of relationality in the dynamic of this passage is a real weakness in his thesis, as it is one of the three main passages in which he sees his whole argument reflected. Further, 8:6 is the hermeneutical key for Fee at numerous points in his understanding of Paul's so-called 'Κύριος Christology' (cf. 88).

Fee also notes the language of 'personal relationship' in Galatians 2:20 (220), but ends up claiming that such language is 'rare' (223). This is, however, a questionable restriction of the scope of personal relationship language in Paul, as this thesis will attempt to show. He states that material in Romans 14:1–11 'has had only to do with the Romans' relationship to Christ as Lord' (263), but he does not spell this out in his exegesis nor show how it relates to other material in the context. In terms of Philippians, Fee notes as a main feature of the whole letter the 'absolute centrality of Christ to Paul's life and worldview' (370), but he does not link this with the wider pattern of relational language in Philippians. He can even note how 'day of Christ' language in Philippians is 'quite in keeping with his [Paul's] full-blown Christ devotion' (407), but he does not connect such language and Christ-devotion with any consistency, nor develop this key insight (cf. chapters 5–8 below). He does mention that Paul's eschatological language is 'personal', but again leaves matters undeveloped. If these insights were followed through, Fee would have arguably been able to uncover the christological significance of even more material in Philippians, and the pattern it evidences. Instead, Fee tends to divide his exegesis and analysis into patterns that sideline these insights.

Second, Fee arguably fails to see the relational import of numerous passages. As noted above, he also regularly underestimates the relational nature of his list of divine prerogatives. Mention can also be made of the lack of appreciation of the relational dynamic of, for example, 2 Corinthians 3:16–18

---

[21] 'Relational monotheism' will be explored in chapters 4 and 5, so it suffices here to simply state that it indicates an understanding of the uniqueness of God that cannot be detached from the believer's relationship to God.

(182 – where he focuses instead on pre-existence again);[22] the prayer detailed in 2 Corinthians 12:8–10 (576. Cf. also 194–5. Fee notes only that it involves a 'very personal matter'); 1 Corinthians 8:1–10:22 and 16:22; Philemon 3, 5, 6, 8, 16, 25 etc. Because Fee misses the relational import of material in Galatians, he can argue that the letter is 'singularly given over to the question of soteriology' (207) and states that Galatians 2:20 is a 'rare' example of 'personal relationship' language in Paul. Much is missed in Philippians, hence he can very questionably claim that the two major christological passages in Philippians are 2:6–11 and 3:20–21 (372) – a matter that simply corresponds to his pre-existence focus.[23]

Third, Fee arguably does not manage to see entire (relational) patterns of material in Paul. As shall be detailed in the exegetical section of this thesis, when one examines Paul's Christology in terms of the relation between believers and the risen Lord, other major themes come to light that Fee entirely misses. For example, part of the pattern of evidence analysed in this thesis includes Christ's presence and activity, and this in relation to his absence. There are the matters of Paul's Christ-shaped motivations, aims and goals which, though Fee touches upon every now and then, are not worked through at all. There are the many explicit descriptions of the character and communications of the risen Lord that are sidelined in Fee's arguments, as well as the importance of the type of passion involved in Paul's Christ-devotion. These, and other issues, will need chapters to examine in this thesis, matters Fee overlooks entirely or completely sidelines.

Fourth, as Fee tends to underestimate relational features, sometimes what he does attend to is obscured. For example, Fee claims that a christological crisis lies behind some of the material in the Corinthian correspondence. His confidence in this proposal grows as he repeats his points through the book such that he can later claim in relation to 2 Corinthians that 'what does emerge reflects something of the same undercurrent of *christological crisis* that marked much of 1 Corinthians, where *the significance of the person of Christ* is tending to be diminished in some way' (161, italics mine). Oddly, though he immediately goes on to speak of the relational aspect of Christian life in 2 Corinthians that 'continues to focus on one's relationship with Christ', he seems to read this relationship as synonymous with soteriology, as his argument there suggests, and does not link this to the supposed christological crisis (161) – he does this even though elsewhere soteriology is

---

[22] While on this subject, a rather big omission is Fee's failure to engage, in his discussions concerning Christ and the Spirit, with Fatehi, *Relation*, not only in terms of 2 Cor. 3:16–18, but also in his final chapter involving the Spirit.

[23] Astonishingly, Fee claims that, after Galatians, Ephesians has the least amount of christological data (363). While this thesis will not directly examine Ephesians, once the sort of themes that one needs to examine for a Pauline Christology are demonstrated on the basis of the undisputed letters, it will be easy to see why the truth is almost the opposite of Fee's claim here.

clearly distinguished from the personal (413). Yet another inconsistency. Earlier he suggests that behind 1 Corinthians 16:22 lies 'a faulty Christology', a
thesis supported by the 'another Jesus' of 2 Corinthians 11:4. Added to this is
Fee's reference to the material in 1 Corinthians 11:20. He notes in relation to
the Lord's Supper that 'the failures and differences within the community are
reflected in their dishonoring Christ himself at the meal in his honour' (85).
However, these texts in 1 Corinthians show that Paul is concerned that the
quality of *relationship* with the risen Lord is in jeopardy. Hence the language
in 1 Corinthians 10 focuses upon the nature of the believer's relation to Christ
against that with demons and idols, and 16:22 speaks of a curse on all those
who do not love Christ. This is not a christological problem in the sense of an
abstract notion of the person of Christ as opposed to his work. Paul's concern,
as in so many places in the Corinthian correspondence, has to do with the
quality of relationship between the risen Lord and believers (cf. e.g. Paul's
argument in 1 Cor. 7:32–35; 15:58 etc.). This crisis in the relation between
risen Lord and believers is not latent but explicitly dealt with by Paul in
numerous places in the Corinthian correspondence (cf. chapters 5 and 6
below).

   In other words, because Fee tends to miss the significance of relational
material, his exegesis and analysis overlooks much of significance and even
obscures some of what he does see. This arguably means that, despite Fee's
important and often brilliant contribution to Pauline christological studies,
there is need for more attention to questions of ontology, how christological
significance is conceptualised, and the issue of relationality.

6. Hurtado and Christ-devotion

Hurtado's important arguments which work in support of a Pauline divine-
Christology have been noted in chapter 2. It is now necessary to detail certain
scholarly criticisms of his position, his response to them and from this basis,
and in light of the critique of Fee above, point a different way forward for the
ongoing debate.

6.1. Four critical responses to Hurtado

1. The matter of 'discontinuity'. Hurtado emphasises a certain level of discontinuity between Second Temple Judaism and early Christianity. In particular,
Hurtado maintains that the sort of reverence rendered the risen Lord is the sort
denied other figures.[24] The 'cultic worship' of the risen Christ in the early
Christian communities is a decisive mutation of and break from the Jewish
religious tradition. However, a number of scholars have taken issue with this
matter, pointing out evidence of the worship of various figures in the Jewish

---

[24] Hurtado, *OG²*, 17–92.

literature.[25] For example, Barker analyses the reverence accorded the High Priest,[26] while Fletcher-Louis focuses upon the worship of the human being in Jewish tradition.[27] Likewise, Horbury associates the worship of Christ with Jewish messianism, and the praise of Jewish kings.[28] It is clear that, in one way or another, these scholars have brought into question the 'discontinuity' posited by Hurtado. By so doing, they put a question mark against drawing too firm a christological conclusion from the worship of Christ. So, Fletcher-Louis associates the worship of the 'image' of God in humanity with themes found in the Philippians hymn.[29] To speak of an early Christian break from Second Temple Judaism on the basis of the 'worship' of the risen Lord, is, they argue, to downplay evidence in this Judaism which speaks of the worship of various figures other than God.

2. Divine worship? Related to the previous, other scholars have questioned whether the evidence in Paul really amounts to full 'worship' as such, i.e., reverence rendered to a deity. For example, J. Lionel North has taken particular issue with the logic: Christ was worshipped, therefore he is divine. 'Worship', he argues, is a flexible word that can only connote worship in the sense of reverence rendered to God when it includes sacrifice.[30] Furthermore, he maintains that there is no evidence that sacrifice (either real or with a spiritualised understanding), was offered to Christ in the NT, unlike that found in association with worship and sacrifice offered to God.[31] Most importantly, Dunn has argued that the Pauline evidence amounts only to 'veneration' rather than 'worship'.[32] In support of his argument, Dunn stresses certain terminological distinctions, in Paul, in the devotional vocabulary associated with God and Christ.[33] He notes themes that qualify the place of Christ in the 'worship'

---

[25] Though note Adela Yarbro Collins, "The Worship of Jesus and the Imperial Cult," in *The Jewish Roots of Christological Monotheism*, eds C.C. Newman, J.R. Davila, and G.S. Lewis (Leiden: Brill, 1999), esp. 248, who argues that the strongest parallels for the early Christian worship of Jesus are not found in Judaism at all, but rather in Roman religion.

[26] Barker, "Priest."

[27] Crispin H.T. Fletcher-Louis, "The Worship of Divine Humanity as God's Image and the Worship of Jesus," in *The Jewish Roots of Christological Monotheism*, eds C.C. Newman, J.R. Davila, and G.S. Lewis (Leiden: Brill, 1999), 112–28; and Crispin H.T. Fletcher-Louis, "Alexander the Great's Worship of the High Priest," in *Early Jewish and Christian Monotheism*, eds Loren T. Stuckenbruck and Wendy E.S. North (London: T&T Clark, 2004), 71–102.

[28] Horbury, *Messianism*, esp. 109–52.

[29] Fletcher-Louis, "Worship," 128.

[30] J. Lionel North, "Jesus and Worship, God and Sacrifice," in *Early Jewish and Christian Monotheism*, eds Loren T. Stuckenbruck and Wendy E.S. North (London: T&T Clark, 2004), e.g. 198.

[31] Ibid., 199.

[32] Cf. James D.G. Dunn, *The Partings of the Ways: Between Christianity and Judaism and Their Significance for the Character of Christianity* (London: SCM, 1991), esp. 204–5; Dunn, *Theology*, 260.

[33] Dunn, *Theology*, 258–59.

language in Paul: the hymns are *about* Christ, not *to* him,[34] and Christ is mediator of worship, not its object.[35] Additionally, Dunn points out that the most extensive description of the early Christian worship service, as found in 1 Corinthians 14, does not mention Christ at all.[36] And thus, in the light of such reasoning, Dunn has concluded that Christ, in the NT, cannot be seen 'as an object *sufficient in himself* of Christian worship'.[37] Veneration, yes, but not worship in its fullest sense. Indeed, Dunn has recently expanded these points into a monograph in which he argues for recognition of christological ambiguity, rather than a simple divine-Christology.[38]

Casey also contributes to this protest by comparing, and noting the differences, in the way God the Father and the risen Lord were treated in the devotional life of the Pauline communities. In light of a discussion concerning the 1 Corinthians 16:22 μαράνα θά, he sums up his thinking in the following way:

[B]y the standards of the worship of any normal deity, the cultic veneration of Jesus was seriously lacking in the following ways. Firstly, there was no sacrificial cultus devoted to him. Secondly, no temple was built to him. Thirdly, to make prayers and hymns to him a serious matter, we have to generalise from this one prayer-like expression ..., one or two expressions (calling upon his name), and a small number of passages which do not particularly have the structure of hymns, and which are never said to have been sung.[39]

Thus he concludes that the '[e]vidence that Jesus was worshipped in the Pauline communities seems to me to be extremely sparse and not really convincing'[40] – a conclusion affirmed by Schrage.[41]

Finally, Schrage supports a similar position to Dunn's. After skilfully summarising much of the evidence, he concludes (in obvious response to Hurtado) that it 'cannot be said' how far 'these christologically filled phenomena and experiences actually effect a modification of "monotheistic" beliefs towards a "binitarian" devotion'.[42] Furthermore, against the suggestion that the early Christians worshipped Christ as God,[43] he writes that 'Paul cannot be said to confirm this'.[44]

3. Terminological imprecision. Hurtado has also been criticised for his lack of precision in the use of the words 'devotion', 'cultic' and 'worship'. In par-

---

[34] Cf. Dunn, *Partings*, 204.

[35] Cf. Dunn, *Theology*, 258, and the material on page 27 above.

[36] Dunn, *Theology*, 259.

[37] Dunn, "Aspect," 387, italics mine.

[38] James D.G. Dunn, *Did the First Christians Worship Jesus?: The New Testament Evidence* (London: SPCK, 2010).

[39] Casey, "Worship," 224–25.

[40] Ibid., 222.

[41] Schrage, *Unterwegs*, 166–67.

[42] Ibid., 165, translation mine.

[43] Here he cites Capes, *Yahweh Texts*, 169.

[44] Schrage, *Unterwegs*, 165, translation mine. For the whole discussion cf. 158–67.

ticular, Stuckenbruck takes issue with Hurtado's lack of clarity concerning the significance of 'cultic worship' over just 'worship'.[45]

4. Monotheism and worship. As noted above, Bauckham has recently developed arguments concerning the ways in which Second Temple Jews identified God as unique. Importantly, Bauckham has moved beyond the position he initially held in the early 1980s and which influenced Hurtado's 1988 monograph. Bauckham writes:

Some recent argument has tended to the position that the exclusive worship of the one God is really the factor that defines God as unique ... This, in my view, is a confusion, because the exclusive worship of the God of Israel is precisely *a recognition of and response to* his unique identity.[46]

Thus, in identifying God as unique, 'worship' should not be the sole consideration.

6.2. Hurtado's response to these criticisms

In relation to his claims that the risen Lord was worshipped (in a way that only God should be) in the Pauline communities, and that this devotion was an innovation in Second Temple Judaism (cf. 1 and 2 of the points above), Hurtado regularly refers to two main lines of reasoning. First, he insists that the evidence needs to be assessed as a pattern.[47] Second, he stresses the significance of the fact that the evidence he cites refers to the devotional practices of the corporate liturgical gatherings.[48] Thus he underscores, '[w]e are not talking about acts of private piety'.[49] Thus in relation to the challenge as to whether the NT evidence is really so discontinuous with Second Temple Judaism, he dismisses the material concerning the alleged precedent for the worship of Jesus in the worship of the Jewish High Priest by asserting that there, 'is hardly evidence of a *pattern of cultic devotion*'.[50] Likewise in his response to Barker (and Hayman) in *LJC*, he speaks of the lack of evidence of any 'actual *devotional pattern* involving public and corporate worship offered to any figure other than the God of Israel'[51]

Hurtado employs these reasons in defence of his thesis against those who question whether the Pauline evidence really amounts to worship in the fullest sense.[52] In reaffirming the fundamental importance of appreciating the pattern of cultic worship evidenced in the Pauline corpus, Hurtado, then, still main-

---

[45] Stuckenbruck, *Angel Veneration*, 13. In this respect one is reminded of the careful discussion and distinctions made in Aune, *Cultic Setting*, 9–11.

[46] Bauckham, *God*, 14, italics his.

[47] Larry W. Hurtado, *At the Origins of Christian Worship: The Context and Character of Earliest Christian Devotion* (Grand Rapids: Eerdmans, 2000), 72; Hurtado, *LJC*, 137.

[48] Hurtado, *LJC*, 137–38; Hurtado, *Origins*, 73.

[49] Hurtado, *LJC*, 138.

[50] Hurtado, *OG²*, xii, italics mine.

[51] Hurtado, *LJC*, 34, italics his.

[52] Cf. his 'several important points' in Hurtado, *LJC*, 137f.

tains that 'we can properly refer to the cultic worship of Jesus in Pauline Christianity'.[53]

While not in explicit response to those who have criticised his lack of precision in the use of key terms, in *LJC* he nevertheless carefully defines his use of the word 'devotion', which, he explains, 'is my portmanteau word for *the beliefs and related religious actions* that constituted the expressions of religious reverence of early Christians'.[54] Elsewhere, he defines 'worship' as 'the actions of reverence intended to express specifically religious devotion of the sort given to a deity ... That is, I use the term to designate "cultic" worship'.[55] In *LJC*, rather than clarify exactly the term 'worship', he insists 'that we have to consider the specific devotional actions attested in Paul's letters'.[56] This inductive approach to the question of what constitutes worship parallels his approach to the definition of monotheism (see chapter 2).

Lastly, while Hurtado does not respond to the development in Bauckham's thinking at any length, he briefly attempts to undermine any possible characterisation of Jewish monotheism from the perspective of the concepts Bauckham stresses indicate the divine identity.[57]

6.3. Remaining problems with Hurtado's thesis

Despite these responses, however, there remain problems with Hurtado's argumentation that must be addressed if the Pauline divine-Christology discussion is going to advance.

Hurtado correctly maintains that to 'do full justice to the way in which Jesus figures in early Christian circles',[58] it is not enough to examine the beliefs, concepts or doctrines about Jesus. To 'do full justice' to the subject, he argues, 'Christ-devotion' is a more preferable term than 'Christology' to refer to the 'range of phenomena' one must examine. Hence he writes that 'devotion' is 'my portmanteau word for the beliefs and related religious actions that constituted the expressions of religious reverence of early Christians'.[59] However, and first, though Hurtado's goal to do 'justice to the way in which Jesus figures' in Paul's letters is entirely commendable, his analysis of Paul misses not a little relevant material, as the next chapters will maintain. In other words, though his diagnosis of a key problem is quite correct, his prescription is inadequate. Assuming for a moment that this will successfully be

---

[53] Hurtado, *LJC*, 152.

[54] Hurtado, *LJC*, 3, italics mine. In a more recent work he defines 'devotion' as designating 'all that was involved in the place of Jesus in earliest Christian belief and religious life', though he continues: 'In particular, I emphasize the importance of the pattern of early Christian devotional *practice*' (Hurtado, *Earth*, 27, italics his).

[55] Hurtado, *Origins*, 69.

[56] Hurtado, *LJC*, 137; Hurtado, *Origins*, 70–71.

[57] Cf. only Hurtado, *LJC*, 47 n.66.

[58] Hurtado, *LJC*, 4.

[59] Ibid., 3.

demonstrated, there are two main reasons for doubting that Hurtado does 'full justice' in the way he proposes. i) It can be questioned whether Hurtado manages, in practice, to grasp the breadth of Christ-devotion in Paul's letters. In particular, Hurtado has likely not truly captured the 'spirit' of the older *Religionsgeschichtliche Schule*. Whereas Deissmann spoke of the 'yearning' in Paul's 'fellowship' with Christ, and Bousset of Paul's 'intense feeling of personal belonging and of spiritual relationship with the risen Lord',[60] in Hurtado the sparkle of such language has faded to an analysis of 'the beliefs and related religious actions' of Paul's Christ-devotion.[61] Noteworthy is that Dunn also, in his review of *LJC*, has questioned why 'Hurtado did not give more explicit attention to what might be called the "mystical" features of Paul's Christology, which seem to lie behind not simply his Christology but presumably also the devotional practices which he encouraged'.[62]

ii) Furthermore, it will be maintained in this thesis that to 'do full justice to the way in which Jesus figures in early Christian circles', Christ-devotion will not suitably cover the range of phenomena necessary to grasp. Indeed, Christ-devotion is itself best understood as part of a larger pattern of christologically relevant data, for which Hurtado has not sufficiently accounted. As will be maintained, this is the Christ-*relation* pattern of data. This includes devotion, but it also considers other matters already noted in response to Fee, such as the theme of Christ's presence and activity, and this in relation to his absence, Paul's Christ-shaped motivations and goals, the character and communications of the risen Lord, the type of passion involved in Paul's Christ-devotion,[63] certain non-cultic practices, that which Paul contrasted with Christ-devotion, and so on. What is more, this is a pattern of data which Paul would arguably recognise as such, as will be maintained in chapter 7. In sum, to grasp 'the way in which Jesus figures' in Paul's letters in terms of the divine-Christology debate, Hurtado's Christ-devotion will not allow 'full justice' to be done to the Pauline material. The scope of his analysis has not been

---

[60] Deissmann, *Paul*, 118,123, and Bousset, *Kyrios*, 153.

[61] Horbury is over optimistic about the range of material covered by Hurtado in *LJC*, at least in terms of Paul (William Horbury, "Review of Hurtado's *Lord Jesus Christ*," *JTS* 59, no. 2 [2005]: 531).

[62] James D.G. Dunn, "When Was Jesus First Worshipped? In Dialogue with Larry Hurtado's *Lord Jesus Christ: Devotion to Jesus in the Earliest Christianity*," *ExpTim* 116, no. 6 (2005): 194. Another reason explaining why Hurtado misses relevant Christ-devotional language in Paul could be linked, once again, to ontology. I cannot definitely confirm this hunch unambiguously from his own work but, there are signs that Hurtado subscribes to a theory-action dichotomy (Cf. telling statements found in, e.g., Larry W. Hurtado, *God in New Testament Theology* [Nashville: Abingdon Press, 2010], 35–36, 112.). This may explain why Hurtado seems often to overlook the import of Christ-devotion language in Paul that cannot be neatly categorised as either corporate *action* or simple stated belief.

[63] It should be noted that such material is not analysed even under the headings 'Fervour' and 'Intimacy' in Hurtado, *Origins*, 41–44, 46–49.

able to appreciate the significance of much material in the Pauline corpus. There is thus a necessity to revisit both Paul's Christ-devotion and its proper context, the Christ-relation, in order to advance the divine-Christology debate.

However, and second, this less-than-convincing embrace of the depth, context and breadth of Christ-devotion in Paul, means that Hurtado's constant recourse to his trump-card argument, namely to the *pattern* of material in justification of his own proposals, is seriously weakened.

Of course, Hurtado has suggested that, of the two points he refers his critics to (i.e., that the evidence is i. a pattern and ii. cultic), the *latter* is 'perhaps even more' important.[64] In justifying his reasoning he contrasts 'cultic' worship with that which is merely a literary phenomenon.[65] There is, quite obviously, a difference to be noted between the description of the exaltation or worship of a figure in a piece of imaginative literature, on the one hand, and the actual worship of a figure in a cultic setting, on the other. However, his reasoning is problematic. First, the most obvious correlate to worship that is a literary phenomenon, is not specifically 'cultic' worship, as he notes at least in the passage in the previous footnote, but rather something a little more broad, namely the worship of real people (which, of course, revolves around the cult).[66] This is a point of not just a little significance, as shall be explored later. Second, is not specification of worship as cultic to say something about the nature of the pattern of data involved? For example, if one seeks to answer whether the confession 'Jesus is Lord' in 1 Corinthians 12:3 is specifically 'cultic' (i.e. as part of the 'early Christian worship'[67]), one must address the question of the context of the text, the other themes in that setting which clarify the meaning – a procedure Hurtado himself undertakes with reference to this very verse.[68] Third, he admits that 'the biblical psalms include praises of the king ... which were intended to be sung in Jewish worship settings ... [They exist also] under the extracanonical writings ... and these may have been used liturgically in the circles where these writings originated'.[69] Thus he appears to admit some degree of *cultic* veneration of Jewish kings (cf. Horbury). However, Hurtado's counter-argument against the potential consequences of such reasoning involves emphasis on the pattern of evidence, thus demonstrating why this pattern is arguably the primary justification for his claims.[70] Thus, it seems that the *pattern* of evidence is Hurtado's major 'trump card'.

This matter of 'pattern' is consequently of considerable importance, as Hurtado's main response to the evidence, cited by critics such as Fletcher-

---

[64] Hurtado, *Origins*, 73.
[65] Ibid.
[66] Examples of non-cultic devotion will be examined in chapters 5–8.
[67] Cf. Hurtado, *LJC*, 113.
[68] Hurtado, *LJC*, 142, 198.
[69] Ibid., 149.
[70] Ibid., 149.

Louis and Horbury, is that the occasional apparent veneration of various figures other than God in the literature of Second Temple Judaism does not evidence the *pattern* one finds in relation to Jesus in the NT. Had he attended to the breadth of the material in Paul, he might have alighted on a broader, more Pauline, pattern and consequently provided stronger grounds for a divine-Christology. This is part of the task of this thesis.

Third, and again related to the above points, Hurtado's concentration on specifically *cultic* devotion needs re-examination. Indeed, one could claim that his focus on this question has led much scholarship, in reaction to his claims, into a christological *cul-de-sac*. Some (e.g., Dunn, Casey) examine Hurtado's claim that Paul 'wrote of the exalted Christ and reverenced him in ways that seem to require us to conclude that Paul treated him as divine',[71] by arguing that the data is more ambiguous (i.e. does not amount to the sort of cultic worship reserved for God alone), and *therefore* such divine-christological conclusions are likewise illegitimate. A good example of this is the learned and deeply intelligent work of Dunn. He contends that the evidence of the Lord's Supper, baptism in the name of Jesus etc. more accurately amounts to a picture of Christ as *central* to the cultic worship of the church without suggesting that Christ is thereby the *object* of cultic worship. Hurtado responds that such distinctions are anachronistic, and on the basis of Dunn's recourse to a distinction between 'worship' and 'veneration', in light of the later worship of the Virgin Mary and saints, he has a good point.[72] Yet the question remains whether such distinctions between 'centre' and 'object', 'veneration' and 'worship' actually help explain the Pauline evidence in terms of the (limited) data concerning the specific cultic 'worship' of Christ. Indeed, as seen above, in light of Pauline material cited by Dunn, Schrage and others, which clearly shows Christ as subordinate to God for Paul, the important question is whether such distinctions help the exegete to appreciate the variety of the Pauline data. The matter is not simply whether the analogies Dunn uses are anachronistic, which they surely are. It is therefore not surprising that Dunn's dissatisfaction with Hurtado's treatment of these matters remains, even in light of *LJC*.[73] Indeed, Dunn's recent monograph, responding to many of Hurtado's claims at this point, should be noted. He concludes that 'by and large, the first Christians did not worship Jesus as such'.[74] This, of course, coheres nicely with Dunn's claim that Paul's Christology, though 'high', evidences 'reserve'.[75] This is a situation compounded by another issue. Namely, it is questionable if Hurtado's recent response to critics has given ground for more confidence that Christ-devotion in the Pauline communities amounts to

---

[71] Hurtado, *OG²*, 4.
[72] E.g. Hurtado, *OG²*, xiv. Cf. in this respect also Stuckenbruck, *Angel Veneration*, 13–14.
[73] Dunn, "First Worshipped?" 193–94.
[74] Dunn, *Worship?* 150.
[75] Dunn, *Theology*, 257.

'worship'. Rather than detailing more evidence, he largely draws upon his earlier publications.[76] Continued scholarly dissatisfaction at this point is also reflected in the fact that Capes can recently insist that 'further scholarly attention to the language of worship is still needed'.[77]

Arguably, however, it is not simply more material that needs to be examined. A new analytical lens needs to be employed. Put another way, the question should be whether focus on the cultic worship of Christ is pertinent for the Pauline data. It is to be granted that worship, in the first century world, gained greater significance if undertaken in a cultic and corporate context (as Hurtado tirelessly reminds critics such as Barker and Fletcher-Louis). However, as Schrage recently pointed out: 'God's praise does not only have its place in the church service [Gottesdienst] ..., but the entire bodily existence should be for the glorification of God ... True monolatry mobilises and involves the whole'.[78] Käsemann writes in comment on Romans 12:1 ('present your bodies as a living sacrifice, holy and acceptable to God, which is your spiritual worship') that for Paul '[e]ither the whole of Christian life is worship ... or these [sacramental] gatherings and acts lead in fact to absurdity'.[79] Is Hurtado's focus perhaps a reason why he has not analysed this verse in any of his major publications?[80] It is arguably not implausible to claim that by its very nature and content, Jewish 'worship' reached beyond the cultus into the life, habits, goals and desires of the faithful, in their waking and sleeping, in their food habits, social interactions, business transactions etc. Indeed, confession of the uniqueness of God and the necessary response of consuming love for God, as in the words of the *Shema*, were to be recited at home and away, written on the doorposts of the people's homes (cf. Deut. 6:4–9). The Psalms expressed a desire and longing for God precisely when absent from the cultus (Ps. 84:1–2. Cf. also Ps. 63:6). Further, the realities of Diaspora life meant that the 'home and family replaced the temple and community as the focus of worship', and in this context prayer and acts of piety, among other matters, become central.[81] Indeed, worship that remained only in the cultus was often scorned by prophets (e.g. Isa. 58:1–14;[82] Amos 5:21–27; Zech. 7–8).

---

[76] E.g. Larry W. Hurtado, *One God, One Lord* (London: SCM, 1988), 100–114. However, in discussing theological language and themes, Hurtado does engage with more Pauline material in *LJC* than in *OG* (and he thereby invalidates the criticism of Schrage that he entirely forgets to deal with Paul's teaching on justification. Cf. Schrage, *Unterwegs*, 166, and Hurtado, *LJC*, 126–33).

[77] Capes, "Monotheism," 137.

[78] Schrage, *Unterwegs*, 159, 163, translation mine.

[79] E. Käsemann, *Commentary on Romans* (London: SCM, 1980), 327.

[80] It is not indexed as discussed in Hurtado, *OG*; Hurtado, *LJC*; Hurtado, *Origins*; or Hurtado, *Earth*.

[81] Lester L. Grabbe, *Judaic Religion in the Second Temple Period* (London: Routledge, 2000), 179.

[82] Cf. the commentary in John D. W. Watts, *Isaiah 34–66* (Waco: Word, 1987), 276–77.

Now, if true Jewish faith in God was meant to embrace and invade all of life, to what extent is it appropriate to reduce "'the decisive criterion" by which Jews maintained the uniqueness of God' to a 'worship' centred on the cultus? Does this not suggest that too strong a distinction between 'cultic' and 'non-cultic' could be problematic? Furthermore, is not cultic worship (an albeit important) part of something more comprehensive? Indeed, it will be maintained that both non-cultic and cultic devotion is a part of a larger, more Pauline pattern, one that needs to be grasped if we hope to do 'full justice' to Paul's letters.

In sum, Hurtado's understanding of the breadth of Paul's 'devotion' is problematic, and consequently his 'trump card' recourse to his 'pattern' of evidence is questionable. Further, the association of christological significance with 'cultic worship', while important, is not without problems. Indeed, this thesis will argue that for justice to be done to 'the way in which Jesus figures' in Paul, attention must be given to the broader pattern of evidence, that concerning the *Christ-relation*. But before that pattern is elucidated, it is necessary to note critical matters in relation to Bauckham's contributions.

7. Bauckham and the divine identity

As noted above, Bauckham's approach to divine identity helpfully emphasises *relations*. It will be remembered that he isolated 'two categories of identifying features of the God of Israel. There are those which identify God in his *relationship to Israel* and there are those which identify God in his *relation to all reality*'.[83]

While criticisms of Bauckham's proposals have already been noted in chapter 2, two particular problems should be stressed. First, Bauckham chose to focus on relation to 'all reality', because he maintains that 'these are the features of the divine identity on which Jews focused when they wished to identify God as unique'.[84] However, as noted, Chester in particular has highlighted weaknesses in Bauckham's thesis at this point.[85] It can indeed, be objected that Bauckham's own categories of identifying the unique divine identity are not always maintained in Second Temple literature, nor is it likely that a free-floating set of categories concerning God's relation to all reality was as decisive in the minds of these Jews as he maintains.[86] Nevertheless, arguably Bauckham is correct to associate the divine identity with relational themes. In the next chapter, an approach will be suggested which shows how

---

[83] Bauckham, *God*, 9, italics mine.

[84] Ibid., 10.

[85] Cf. the discussion in chapter 2 above.

[86] Cf. also Erik Waaler, *The Shema and the First Commandment in First Corinthians: An Intertextual Approach to Paul's Re-Reading of Deuteronomy* (Tübingen: Mohr Siebeck, 2008), 420; Hurtado, *LJC*, 47 n.66.

the uniqueness of God was likely maintained, though through a different understanding of the pattern of relational data.

Second, Bauckham's choice to focus on the 'all reality' relation (rather than relation to Israel), has the knock-on effect of restricting his focus on relevant Pauline material. Armed with his theological categories he has sought, with some success, to show how Christ relates to all reality in the way Jews identified the unique divinity of God.[87] However, he thereby misses a more prominent pattern of data in Paul, as shall be detailed in chapters 5–8 of this thesis. In the process his case for a Pauline divine-Christology is weakened. It will be maintained that the language involving YHWH's relationship with particularly Israel, as well as certain individuals, informs an understanding of Paul's Christology more adequately.

8. Conclusion

Hurtado, Bauckham and Fee all, in one way or another and despite different emphases, affirm a Pauline divine-Christology. However, the above critical examination of aspects of their arguments suggest that the present case for a divine-Christology is vulnerable. However, these same criticisms have arguably suggested a different, albeit related, way forward. Thus, in the next chapter the proposals of this thesis will be presented.

---

[87] Cf. esp. Bauckham, *God of Israel*, 182–232.

Chapter 4

The approach of this thesis. The relation between the risen Lord and believers

1. Introduction

This chapter outlines the proposals of this thesis in relation to the two questions detailed above on p. 17, namely the questions which, it was maintained, have concerned post-1970s academic discourse about the Pauline divine-Christology debate.

2. The first question about Paul's Jewish-style faith in God

The first question, as noted above, was 'how does Paul's Jewish-style faith in God affect our understanding of his Christology?' As then detailed, there is some disagreement among scholars as to both whether and how to use the word 'monotheism' in terms of Paul. Of course, any study seeking to examine Pauline Christology must say something about Paul's faith in God, for the two, by any reckoning, belong closely together. A faulty notion of Paul's faith in God will potentially obscure a christological study. On the other hand, a better appreciation of the nature of Paul's monotheism, if that is what it was, will potentially facilitate an analysis of Paul's Christology, especially in terms of whether or not it was divine. That said, space is limited and the focus of this study is not 'monotheism' but Paul's (divine-)Christology, so the following remarks about monotheism must remain provisional.[1]

At the start it is necessary to be clear that some associations with the word 'monotheism' do not best serve an understanding of Paul, especially those which smack of an Enlightenment and abstract conceptuality.[2] It is maintained by some that one can only speak of Paul's monotheism if by that one means the denial of the existence of all other heavenly or spiritual beings. Horbury, for example, defines an exclusive monotheism, as noted in chapter 2, as the denial of 'the *existence* of other divine beings' – beings which are for

---

[1] For a helpful recent summary of 'biblical monotheism' cf. Johannes Woyke, *Götter, "Götzen", Götterbilder: Aspekte einer paulinischen "Theologie der Religionen"* (Berlin: W. de Gruyter, 2005), 163–79.

[2] Examples are offered in Nathan MacDonald, *Deuteronomy and the Meaning of "Monotheism"* (Tübingen: Mohr Siebeck, 2003), 5–21.

Horbury, Bauckham rightly notes, equated with 'other spirits and powers'.[3] Hence, so the argument goes, one ought not to speak of a Pauline *strict* monotheism, or in some arguments a monotheism at all.[4]

But all of this is to import an unhelpful understanding of monotheism into the discussion and then to dismiss that 'monotheism' unfairly. While Woyke has argued that the rhetoric developed in Israel in the late Old Testament and in the Hellenistic-Jewish tradition reduces idols to the material of the human fashioned idol (e.g. Pss. 115; 135:15–18; Jer. 10:3–5, 8–9, 14; etc.), and that this entailed a denial of the existence of other 'gods',[5] Waaler details how such references are more complicated and do not easily, or at least straightforwardly, accommodate modern concerns with ontology.[6]

But if matters are not about modern concerns with ontology, what are they about? Here Bauckham's notion of identity has offered a way forward. As noted above, Bauckham emphasises the uniqueness of God, a 'strict' monotheism, through identifying the ways in which Second Temple Judaism generally expressed this uniqueness, in God's relation to all reality, on the one hand, and to Israel, on the other. On this basis Bauckham argues that Jewish monotheism explicitly did not mean 'the denial of the existence of other "gods"'. Rather, it was an understanding of the 'uniqueness of YHWH that puts him in a class of his own', in a way that understood YHWH as 'transcendently unique'.[7] In a different way Hurtado has maintained an 'exclusivist monotheism' in the Roman period, as noted above, by focusing more on the exclusive worship of Israel's God.[8] By 'worship' he means the '"cultic" wor-

---

[3] Bauckham, *God of Israel*, 108. This arguably unhelpful way of understanding 'monotheism' is also evident in, for example, Paula Fredriksen, "Mandatory Retirement: Ideas in the Study of Christian Origins Whose Time Has Come to Go," in *Israel's God and Rebecca's Children: Essays in Honor of Larry W. Hurtado and Alan F. Segal*, eds David B Capes, et al. (Waco: Baylor, 2007), 35–38.

[4] So Fredriksen, "Retirement". Her case that the term 'monotheism' should be dropped from use in scholarship on Christian origins is, however, arguably based on a variety of misunderstandings. Belief in the existence of other heavenly beings hardly makes ancient monotheists, as she claims (37), polytheists, and a more sophisticated handling of proper distinctions can be found in, for example, Woyke, *Götter*, 163–79. Furthermore, Fredriksen's language of 'tortured Chalcedonianism' (37) and 'austere and exclusive monotheism' (35) perhaps evidences an unexplored theological agenda in her claims, which have arguably led her to obscure more than she has clarified.

[5] For these references and his argumentation, cf. Woyke, *Götter*, 170–71.

[6] Waaler, *Shema*, 271–75, and cf. his argument that 'many first century Jews and Christians considered idols to be handmade pictures and vibrant evil spirits at the same time' (272).

[7] Bauckham, "Monotheism," 210–11.

[8] Hurtado, *LJC*, 28–48; Larry W. Hurtado, "First-Century Jewish Monotheism," *JSNT*, no. 71 (1998): 3–26, now published, with small changes, in Hurtado, *Earth*, chap. 5.

ship, especially devotion offered in a specifically worship (liturgical) setting'.[9] And only God is offered such worship.[10]

But both the arguments of Hurtado and Bauckham have been challenged. Against Bauckham it is pointed out that his categories are not as watertight as they would first appear.[11] Against Hurtado, as has been seen, it has been maintained that beings other than God were indeed worshipped, thus refuting his claim that it is 'in the area of worship that we find "the decisive criterion" by which Jews maintained the uniqueness of God over against both idols and God's own deputies'.[12] Hurtado's response and continuing weaknesses in his position were examined in the previous chapter. Nevertheless, his insistence that one must seek to grapple with the first century material inductively, is a point worth heeding.[13] Further, he also occasionally speaks about God, and knowledge of God, in more relational terms, even if he does not develop these claims significantly. So he asserts in a recent study:

[T]he God of the NT is not presented primarily as an *object* of intellectual reflection but instead is an acting *subject*, the knowledge of whom is gained by this deity acting toward people and establishing with them a *subject-subject* relationship. In keeping with this, the human knowledge of this God in the NT is to be exhibited primarily by participating in this relationship and not simply by ritual performance.[14]

It is a pity that these insights did not inform his study to a greater extent. Further, although Bauckham's arguments have been disputed, certain threads of his argument also need to be woven into this thesis. First, his notion of 'identity', despite potentially unhelpful ambiguity,[15] at least indicates that Jewish monotheism cannot be restricted to modern concerns about ontology. Related to this, his language of 'transcendent uniqueness' can be helpfully deployed. Bauckham argues that so long as Horbury's other divine beings are understood as 'created by and subject to God' then as such they are 'no more a qualification of monotheism than the existence of earthly creatures'.[16] Hence this language of 'transcendent uniqueness' distances Bauckham's understanding of Second Temple Jewish monotheism from Horbury's 'inclusive monotheism' on the basis that God's uniqueness is more considerable than if God were

---

[9] Hurtado, *LJC*, 31 n.10.

[10] Cf. now, in this regard, Hurtado, *God*, e.g. 5, 28–30.

[11] Cf. p. 20 above.

[12] Hurtado, *Earth*, 129.

[13] Hurtado, "Monotheism."

[14] Hurtado, *God*, 37. He even, in the next breath, claims that 'NT christological statements inescapably constitute at the same time *theological* statements' (Hurtado, *God*, 38). Sadly, however, and like Fee, he does not sufficiently attend to the christological implications of these insights.

[15] Cf. the comments of Robert W. Jenson and Markus Bockmuehl, concering the word 'identity', in their essays in Beverly Roberts Gaventa and Richard B. Hays, eds, *Seeking the Identity of Jesus: A Pilgrimage* (Cambridge: Eerdmans, 2008), 43–45, 60–61.

[16] Bauckham, *God of Israel*, 108.

understood merely as 'the highest member of a class of beings to which he belongs'.[17] Therefore he speaks of *transcendent* uniqueness.

But to return to Hurtado's thesis, the notion that this 'transcendent uniqueness' is expressed in terms of (cultic) worship may need adjusting. This thesis sets out a further option for understanding the data – even if only provisionally – in such a way that God's 'transcendent uniqueness' can be maintained albeit on different grounds to Bauckham (with his focus on the categories of divine identity) or Hurtado (with his focus on cultic and communal worship). To understand this proposal it will prove useful to examine how God and monotheism are detailed in the major OT Theologies, as well as in a number of important OT related monographs, before turning to Paul himself.

Important to notice first is a relational description of Jewish faith in God as elucidated in the major OT Theologies. This is evident not only in the titles they give significant chapters, but even in the way some have arranged their presentations. So Eichrodt, in his two volume *Theology of the Old Testament*,[18] has the following major subheadings: 'The Covenant Relationship' (Vol. 1, chap. 2), 'The Individual and the Community in the Old Testament God-man Relationship' (Vol 2, chap. 20), 'The Fundamental Forms of Man's Personal Relationship with God' (Vol 2, chap. 21), 'The Indestructibility of the Individual's Relationship with God (Immortality)' (Vol 2, chap. 24). As is well known, this covenant relationship was, for Eichrodt, 'the central concept, by which to illuminate the structural unity and the unchanging basic tendency of the message of the OT'.[19] Th. C. Vriezen's relational emphasis is also strong, as chapter 6 of his Old Testament Theology, 'The nature of the knowledge of God in the O.T. as an intimate relationship between the Holy God and man', shows most clearly.[20] Gerhard von Rad's section, 'Israel before Yahweh' must also be noted.[21] Reference can also be made to more recent OT Theologies, especially the repeated discussions concerning Israel, the individual human person, the nations etc. as 'Yahweh's Partner' in Brueggemann's *Theology of the Old Testament*.[22]

Then there are the numerous OT related studies which not only employ relational language but stress its importance. For example, noteworthy is Terence Fretheim's study, *God and the World in the Old Testament*, with the

---

[17] Ibid.

[18] Walther Eichrodt, *Theology of the Old Testament. Vol. 1*, trans. J. A. Baker (Philadelphia: Westminster John Knox, 1961).

[19] Ibid., 13.

[20] Th. C. Vriezen, *An Outline of Old Testament Theology*, revised edition no. 2 (Newton, Massachusetts: Charles T. Branford Company, 1970).

[21] Gerhard von Rad, *Old Testament Theology. Volume 1*, reprint, 1957 (London: SCM, 1975), 355–459.

[22] Walter Brueggemann, *Theology of the Old Testament: Testimony, Dispute, Advocacy* (Minneapolis: Fortress, 1998), Part 3.

important subtitle: 'A Relational Theology of Creation'.[23] Geller, who emphasises the different images of God found in the OT, argues that the 'prophetic tradition [which] pictures the covenant God, a personal covenant partner' is 'the dominant form of the presentation of divinity' in the OT'.[24] In discussing the nature of Jewish monotheism, the relational formulations of the renowned Old Testament Theologies, not to mention the various individual studies, should not go unnoticed, especially as these OT texts were those the Apostle Paul largely drew from and cited as Scripture.

Also important is MacDonald's monograph on 'monotheism' in Deuteronomy, especially as Paul draws from this text at key moments in his own rhetoric concerning faith in the one God of Israel (e.g. 1 Cor. 8–10, as discussed in the next chapter). He examines the manner of the text's 'monotheistic' rhetoric and carefully distinguishes this from Enlightenment monotheism.[25] While this work will be examined in more detail below, it suffices now to note that he seeks to show that biblical faith in the one God is fundamentally about the exclusive *relational* allegiance of Israel to this one God. It is not about denying the existence of other gods but a *loving commitment to God over against idolatry*.

At the end of his study he raises the question if 'what has been shown to be true of Deuteronomy may also be true of the rest of the Old Testament, including the priestly material and Isaiah 40–55'.[26] Bauckham, in a critical summary of MacDonald's work, confirms that this relational approach 'seem[s] to be broadly valid for much of the Old Testament',[27] though Bauckham also presses for more clarification on the way MacDonald precisely understands the uniqueness of God – a matter to which it will be necessary to return.[28] Sven Petry's recent study concerning monolatry and monotheism in Deuteronomy, Deutero-Isaiah and Ezekiel confirms the basic picture presented here.[29] MacDonald summarises and evaluates Petry's thesis concerning monolatry:

---

[23] Terence E. Fretheim, *God and World in the Old Testament: A Relational Theology of Creation* (Nashville: Abingdon, 2005), esp. chap. 1.

[24] Stephen A. Geller, "The God of the Covenant," in *One God or Many?: Concepts of Divinity in the Ancient World*, ed. Barbara N. Porter (Chebeague, Me.: Casco Bay Assyriological Institute, 2000), 280.

[25] MacDonald, *Monotheism*.

[26] Ibid., 209.

[27] Bauckham, *God of Israel*, 65.

[28] Ibid., 66–67.

[29] Sven Petry, *Die Entgrenzung JHWHs: Monolatrie, Bilderverbot und Monotheismus im Deuteronomium, in Deuterojesaja und im Ezechielbuch* (Tübingen: Mohr Siebeck, 2007). Cf. especially p. 6.

Monolatry is concerned most especially with YHWH's close relationship to his people, rather than primarily being about cultic worship. The centrality of the relationship between YHWH and Israel, so often overlooked in the discussion of monotheism, is to be welcomed.[30]

While it is beyond the scope of this thesis to justify, one could arguably also make the claim that practically all Second Temple texts operate within a similar relational framework for understanding their God. In chapter 9 below, three important pseudepigraphal and apocryphal texts will be examined in more detail, and a relational emphasis is once again seen. Yet even in texts evidencing the most abstract monotheism, for example the *Letter of Aristeas*, the *Sibylline Oracles* and Philo, arguably a relational impulse in some way remains important.[31] Indeed, Waaler's study of the reuse of the *Shema* and the First Commandment in first century culture confirms this proposal:

> Knowledge [of God] may sometimes have a theoretical content, but usually it is relational as well. Thus, to know that 'God is the only God' or that 'he is one' implies that one relates to one God only.[32]

Of course, Jewish faith in God in the first century was more than an accurate OT Theology, but was expressed in various religious practices and devotions, the most frequently practised of which was the confession of the *Shema*, something almost resembling a creed.[33] While the impact of the *Shema* on 1 Corinthians 8–10 will be examined below in more detail,[34] it suffices to note that the most common expression of faith in God was fundamentally about an understanding of the oneness of God in terms of loving commitment to this God.

While Paul's monotheism has not received the scholarly attention it deserves,[35] it should nevertheless cause no surprise that, turning to Paul, the

---

[30] Cf. MacDonald's online review of Petry, *JHeS* 9 (2009).

[31] This matter deserves more space, but a few comments can be made. *Let. Aris.* 16 and 139–140 speak of the *worship* of God in the context of describing religious convictions. It is not, in other words, about an '*abstract* monotheistic teaching', contra Woyke, *Götter*, 174, italics mine.

Certainly Philo could tend to the abstract (e.g. *Decalogue* 58–60), but even he did not do so in exclusion from the relational. See, for example, *Spec. Laws* 2:165 and the use of the verb δέω ('it was necessary for all people *to cling* to him [God]' – cf. C. D. Yonge, *The Works of Philo* [Peabody: Hendrickson, 1995³], 583, italics mine). See also *Spec. Laws* 1:5; 2:162; *Contempl. Life* 2, 4; *Drunkenness* 106 ('he who directs all the energies of his soul towards God, and who looks to him alone as the only source from which he can hope for advantage' – Yonge, *Philo*, 216); *Sacrifices* 77 etc.

Sib. Or. is even less evidence for an 'abstract' monotheism (again contra Woyke, *Götter*, 177). Cf. 3:29–31 where the text speaks of the reverence and fear of God (3:29), and the nature of idolatry as consisting in the *worship* of and *rejoicing* in the idols (3:30, 34).

[32] Waaler, *Shema*, 202.

[33] Cf. the detailed analysis in Waaler, *Shema*, 49–205.

[34] Cf. the discussion involving Waaler, *Shema* and MacDonald, *Monotheism* in the next chapter.

[35] So Dunn, *Theology*, 28.

same relational emphasis is generally found.[36] So Dunn notes that Paul's speech about God was 'Jewish through and through',[37] which means it is a relationally accented monotheism. In discussing the knowledge of God in Paul (in e.g. Rom. 1:19) Dunn notes that 'whereas in Greek thought the term characteristically denotes a rational perception, the Hebrew concept also embraced the knowing of personal relationship'.[38] He continues:

It is not merely a theoretical acknowledgement that theism is a viable intellectual position. To know God is to worship him ... to know God is to be known by him, a two-way relationship of acknowledgment and obligation (Gal. 4.9). As in the (Jewish) scriptures, the "knowledge of God" includes experience of God's dealings, the two-way knowing of personal relationship.[39]

What is more, Dunn notes that Paul's prayers to God indicate a 'relationship with God ... apprehended in personal terms'.[40] These general sentiments are uncontroversial in terms of Paul's God-language and are confirmed in numerous studies,[41] even sometimes despite their restricted focus.[42]

This case can be tested. As Wright has argued, Paul formulated his monotheistic convictions most sharply in his pagan idolatry polemic.[43] To cite a few concrete examples in the letters that focus on God and idols, notewor-

---

[36] Indeed, according to Bassler the same emphasis is found in the NT generally (cf. Jouette M. Bassler, "God in the NT," in *ABD* [New York: Doubleday, 1992], II, 1049).

[37] Dunn, *Theology*, 29, citing as examples: Rom. 1:25; 3:5; 4:17; 8:27 etc. Cf. also the material Dunn presents in pp. 29–50. Cf. the more nuanced discussion in Udo Schnelle, *Paulus: Leben und Denken* (Berlin: W. de Gruyter, 2003), 448–50.

[38] Dunn, *Theology*, 46. This distinction between 'Greek' and 'Hebrew' can, of course, be challenged (Ian W. Scott, *Implicit Epistemology in the Letters of Paul: Story, Experience and the Spirit* [Tübingen: Mohr Siebeck, 2006], 146–47). However, so long as claims are not exaggerated, there is arguably still truth in Dunn's statement.

[39] Dunn, *Theology*, 47.

[40] Ibid., 49.

[41] Cf. among others, the claims of Hurtado noted above, but also J. Neyrey, *Render to God: New Testament Understandings of the Divine* (Minneapolis: Fortress, 2004), 107–211, and the appendix, 'God-in-Relationship: Patron-Broker-Client' pp. 249–255; Hurtado, *LJC*, e.g. 48–50; Schnelle, *Paulus*, 441–61; Suzanne Beth Nicholson, "Dynamic Oneness: The Significance and Flexibility of Paul's One-God Language," PhD thesis (Durham, 2007), e.g. 12–14, 50, 54, 73; Charles H Giblin, "Three Monotheistic Texts in Paul," *CBQ* 37 (1975): 533–35, 537, 539, 542, 545–46; Ian W. Scott, *Epistemology*, 144–54; Fee, *Christology*, e.g. 8; Schrage, *Unterwegs*, e.g. 185; Halvor Moxnes, *Theology in Conflict: Studies in Paul's Understanding of God in Romans* (Leiden: Brill, 1980), e.g. 28–29; Regina Börschel, *Die Konstruktion einer christlichen Identität: Paulus und die Gemeinde von Thessalonich in ihrer hellenistisch-römischen Umwelt* (Berlin: Philo, 2001), 99; Healy, "Knowledge," 142–44.

[42] Arguably, neither Richardson, Hurtado nor Goodwin make nearly enough of the relational import of Paul's God-language, but they nevertheless cannot avoid mention of relational or experiential matters now and then (e.g. Richardson, *Paul's Language About God*, 298–99; and regularly in Mark Goodwin, *Paul, Apostle of the Living God : Kerygma and Conversion in 2 Corinthians* [Harrisburg, Pa.: Trinity Press International, 2001]).

[43] N.T. Wright, *The Climax of the Covenant: Christ and the Law in Pauline Theology* (Edinburgh: T&T Clark, 1991), 125–27.

thy, apart from 1 Corinthians 8–10 to be discussed in the next chapter, are 1 Thessalonians 1:9, 2 Corinthians 6:16,[44] Galatians 4:8–9, Romans 1:23, 25.[45] Turning to these, one will notice how a relational faith in God is emphasised. So in 1 Thessalonians 1:9, Paul writes of how the Thessalonian Christians '*turned to God* from idols, *to serve* a living and true God'. The rejection of idolatry was here not merely the intellectual conception that idols did not exist, but involved the life of the new believer, with 'turning' expressed in 'serving'.[46] In 2 Corinthians 6:16 Paul contrasts the 'temple of God with idols', claiming that 'we are the temple of the living God'. To make his point Paul refers to one of the most relationally accented promises in the scriptures: 'I will live in them and walk among them, and I will be their God, and they shall be my people' (cf. Lev. 26:11, 12 and Ezek. 37:27).[47] The phrase 'I will be their God' finds expression in numerous passages in Second Temple litera-ture, not least in Prophetic traditions that speak of a new or everlasting cove-nant and the giving of a new heart to love and obey God with single minded devotion coupled with the rejection of idolatry (Jer. 24:7; 31:33; 32:38–40; Ezek. 11:20; 14:11; 34:24; 37:23, 27; Zech. 8:8; Bar. 2:35). In Galatians 4:8–9 Paul employs the relational 'knowledge of God' language in contrasting God with 'beings that by nature are not gods'. So Dunn writes in comment on these verses: the 'conversion of Gentiles meant entering into that *relation* with God which was characteristic of Israel's covenant identity'.[48] In Romans 1:25 the 'truth of God' is exchanged for a lie precisely in that God is not wor-shipped and served, but rather[49] the creature.[50] In the next chapter it will be shown that 1 Corinthians 8–10 evidences the sort of relational monotheism over against idolatry as maintained here. But enough material has now been covered to propose that Paul's anti-idolatry-faith-in-God rhetoric emphasises the relational aspects of allegiance to and knowledge and worship of the true God.

Three important points follow from this overview of the relational nature of Jewish and Pauline God-language. First, it was argued in the previous chap-

---

[44] Admittedly, this passage may well constitute a non-Pauline interpolation. For an examination of this finely balanced debate, which ends up rejecting the interpolation thesis, cf. Murray J. Harris, *The Second Epistle to the Corinthians: A Commentary on the Greek Text* (Milton Keynes: Paternoster, 2005), 14–21.

[45] These are listed and examined in Woyke, *Götter*, albeit for different purposes.

[46] Cf. esp. Gene L. Green, *The Letters to the Thessalonians*, Pillar New Testament Commentary (Leicester: Apollos, 2002), 106–8.

[47] R.P. Martin, *2 Corinthians* (Waco: Word, 1986), 204; Harris, *Second Epistle*, 504–6.

[48] James D.G. Dunn, *The Epistle to the Galatians* (London: Black, 1993), 225, italics mine.

[49] For a discussion on this translation of παρά as 'rather than' or 'instead of', against the KJV 'more than', cf. Douglas J. Moo, *The Epistle to the Romans* (Grand Rapids: Eerdmans, 1996), 113 n.106.

[50] Charles E. B. Cranfield, *Romans 1–8*, reprint, 1975 (Edinburgh: T&T Clark, 2004[10]), 123–24.

ter that Hurtado's focus on cultic worship does not really correspond well with the way the texts portray faith and worship as encompassing the whole of life, not just the cultus. It is now clearer what the 'more comprehensive' context is, one in which cultic worship belongs as an important yet subsidiary part. That context is the God-relation pattern of data, of which worship is, of course, a part.

Second, building on Hurtado's thesis and drawing on important threads in Bauckham's proposals, a different way of conceiving the unique divine identity can be suggested. If God was understood, and faith in him expressed, in a thoroughly relational manner, then one would expect to find God's *uniqueness* likewise expressed, i.e., relationally. In other words, if Paul's faith in God emphasised the relational, it should not be expected that he would express the uniqueness of God in, say, Aristotelian terms, but rather relational ones.[51] Importantly, the *Shema* itself, the nearest thing to a creed in Second Temple Judaism, and probably repeated at least twice a day by devout Jews, implies an understanding of God's unique identity – YHWH's oneness – as intrinsically tied to the relationally accented notion of loving commitment to God. Of course, precisely how Deuteronomy 6:4–5 is to be translated and how the language was exactly understood in the first century remains disputed,[52] but it seems clear that to love God, as in Deuteronomy 6:5, is precisely an 'answer to a unique claim',[53] namely God's oneness as expressed in Deuteronomy 6:4. Paul similarly appears to understand God's oneness in terms of a commitment to God over against idolatry, and thus in some sense as also about the unique identity of God (cf. also Gal. 4:8).[54] In other words, the '"... decisive criterion" by which Jews maintained the uniqueness of God' was the unique YHWH-relation, of which an important yet subsidiary part was cultic worship of YHWH.

Indeed, chapter 9 will explore this claim with reference to important texts often cited as blurring the 'worship' boundary between God and creatures, namely the Similitudes of Enoch, the *Life of Adam and Eve* and Sirach 44–50. It will be claimed that these texts maintain the deity's 'transcendent uniqueness' through an absolutely unique pattern of relational language, associated only with the one God and not with any intermediary, however highly exalted or 'worshipped'. In these texts various figures are certainly worshipped, and the Son of Man is also described as pre-existent to creation, sitting on God's throne. Elsewhere, Melchizedek is called 'god' (11QMelch 2:10) and

---

[51] For a masterful study which highlights the close link between philosophical ('philosophy' here understood broadly to refer to the way faith was expressed relationally, with less emphasis on essence or ontology in such a way that a thing's relations are understood as incidental to its essence, as in Aristotelian metaphysics) presuppositions and the mode of theological expression, cf. Shults, *Christology*.

[52] Cf. the discussion in the next chapter.

[53] William Moran, as approvingly cited in Waaler, *Shema*, 115.

[54] Cf. Nicholson, "Oneness," e.g. 10; Waaler, *Shema*, 98–122.

Metatron the 'little YHWH' (*3 En.* 12:5), etc. Yet within just such texts which use exalted language of figures other than God, the God-relation *pattern* of data remains descriptive of the deity alone. An inductive study of these texts will detail the content of this God-relation, its shape and contours.

Third, Hurtado has urged that an exclusive monotheism, with God's unique identity maintained through corporate and liturgical worship, is the context in which one must understand early Christology.[55] With the adjustments to the theses of both Bauckham and Hurtado above, arguably the YHWH-relation pattern of data is the appropriate context in which to understand the emergence of early Christology, a point that will be born out in the exegetical section of this thesis, especially in terms of 1 Corinthians 8–10.

To what extent these proposals concerning monotheism are convincing needs to await further study, but a preliminary assessment of the explanatory power of these suggestions can be undertaken in light of the engagement with the Pauline material on the one hand, and the various Jewish texts analysed in chapter 9, on the other. With this God-relation context in mind as the response to the first question noted above on page 17, the stage is set for a description of the associated proposals of this thesis concerning the second question, the nature of the evidence in the Pauline corpus for a divine-Christology.

3. The second question: A new proposal

The second question is, Where, if at all, is there evidence in the Pauline corpus for (or against) a divine-Christology? Building on the undeveloped points in Fee and the relational emphasis of identity in Bauckham, as well as the Christ-devotion approach pursued with most rigour by Hurtado, this thesis will examine, as the most appropriate pattern of Pauline evidence, the relation between the risen Lord and believers with a view to the divine-Christology debate. In so doing it will provide a way of synergistically integrating many of the scattered proposals for a divine-Christology summarised in chapter 2 and suggest, as Moule claimed, that 'aspects of the relation between Christ and the believer' do indeed 'constitute evidence of a special status'.[56]

In the next chapter, in a study of 1 Corinthians 8–10, it will be maintained that in a context which frames the argument according to precisely the sort of relational monotheism discussed above, Paul goes on to speak about the relation between believers and the risen Lord, and he does so by using the sort of language and themes which Second Temple Judaism used to speak of the relation between Israel and YHWH. This paves the way for a more general analysis of the relation between the risen Lord and believers in the undisputed letters, one which aims to put a finger on the pulse of Paul's understanding of the

---

[55] Hurtado, *LJC*, 50–53.
[56] Moule, *Origin*, 47–48.

believer's relation to the risen Christ and to 'listen' to the variety of ways in which it reverberates throughout Paul's letters. Importantly, it will be maintained that the data concerning this Christ-relation was understood by Paul as a pattern, which means that it is not data jammed together under a heading (namely, the relation between the risen Lord and believers) inappropriately. With this Christ-relation in mind, the Similitudes of Enoch, the *Life of Adam and Eve* and Sirach 44–50 will be examined, for reasons that will become clear, as a way of assessing the christological significance of Paul's Christ-relation in terms of the divine-Christology debate. Remembering the proposal in relation to the first question above, *it will be maintained that this pattern of Christ-relation language in Paul is only that which a Jew used to express the relation between Israel / the individual Jew and YHWH. No other figure of any kind, apart from YHWH, was related to in the same way, with the same pattern of language, not even the various exalted human and angelic intermediary figures in the literature of Second Temple Judaism that occasionally receive worship and are described in very exalted terms.*

In other words, this thesis seeks to demonstrate a different method of both approaching the Pauline data and of assessing its christological significance in terms of the divine-Christology debate. In doing this it will affirm a Pauline divine-Christology and attend to the arguments of those who deny it, especially those employed against Hurtado and Bauckham.

4. A note on the language of 'relation to' and 'believers'

In the following chapters the language of 'relation to/between' means only to indicate '[t]he way in which one person or thing is related to another'.[57] This working definition is not used with necessary reference to 'personal relationship', nor to any ordered narrative plot that would situate this relation in terms of a diachronic temporality.[58] Within this broad conception, as will later be maintained, one may properly speak of the relation*ship* of believers *with* the risen Lord, and note an eschatological direction in such language – i.e., it is that which transcends a merely synchronic relatedness. That said, the language of 'relation*ship* (with or between)' will sometimes be used specifically to indicate an interpersonal dynamic analogous to one human's relationship with another, which may or may not be present when 'relation to/between' is

---

[57] Judy Pearsall and William R. Trumble, eds, *The Oxford English Reference Dictionary* (Oxford: Oxford University Press, 1995), 1216.

[58] For this language, cf. Anthony C. Thiselton, "Human Being, Relationality, and Time in Hebrews, 1 Corinthians, And Western Traditions," *ExAud* 13 (1997): 78–79, who draws on the work of Paul Ricoeur. This thesis examines the Christ-relation as it impinges on the divine-Christology debate, and so some issues are left undiscussed. For a more complete study of Paul's spirituality, cf. especially Michael J. Gorman, *Cruciformity: Paul's Narrative Spirituality of the Cross* (Cambridge: Eerdmans, 2001).

used.[59] While Wright is perhaps correct that the 'word "relationship" is responsible for too many fudged arguments in contemporary theology',[60] it will be argued that it is useful in approaching the question of Paul's Christology, reflecting Paul's own relational intuitions. Indeed, the point is not to over-define 'relation', and so generate a foreign construct to impose on the letters, but to fill out its shape and content as the study proceeds, much as Barth attempted in the *Church Dogmatics* in terms of the *analogia relationis*.[61] An inductive treatment of the term will hopefully avoid 'fudged arguments', and shed much light on Paul's thinking.[62]

On a few occasions in Paul's letters one may properly distinguish between the language that speaks of the relation between risen Lord and, on the one hand, believers generally, and, on the other, Paul specifically. Indeed, according to this distinction Boers has structured his recent monograph on Christ in the letters of Paul.[63] However, this distinction is as good as irrelevant to the project of this thesis, and by not attending to it neither the exegesis nor the general conclusions will suffer obfuscation.

5. Conclusion

In response to the question of how Paul's Jewish-style faith in God should affect our understanding of his Christology, it was contended that to speak of a Pauline 'strict' monotheism, of God's transcendent uniqueness, is not out of place. Further, this unique divine transcendence is expressed relationally, through a pattern of God-relation data unique to God alone. This proposal provides the frame for the suggested strategy concerning the approach to evidence in the Pauline corpus for a divine-Christology. Just as Paul's faith in God is relational, so this thesis will examine the relation between the risen Lord and believers in Paul's letters, with a view to the divine-Christology debate. In the following exegetical section (chapters 5–8), an attempt will be made to map the contours of this Christ-relation data.

---

[59] Cf. also Fatehi, *Relation*, 303 n.85.

[60] N.T. Wright, "The Letter to the Romans. Introduction, Commentary, and Reflections," in *The New Interpreter's Bible*, ed. L. E. Keck, et al. (Nashville: Abington, 2002), 446.

[61] Cf. Gary W. Deddo, *Karl Barth's Theology of Relations: Trinitarian, Christological, and Human: Towards an Ethic of the Family* (New York: Lang, 1999), 16–17.

[62] This approach is thus to be distinguished from a focus on just 'religious experience'. The attempt to treat Paul's letters as inductively as possible also distances this study from the procedures of both Theißen, with his developed 'typology of religious experiences' (Gerd Theißen, *Erleben und Verhalten der ersten Christen: Eine Psychologie des Urchristentums* [München: Gütersloher Verlagshaus, 2007], cf. e.g 116), and Johnson's phenomenological approach, which seeks to study religious experience in terms of matters of 'power' (Luke T. Johnson, *Religious Experience in Earliest Christianity: A Missing Dimension in New Testament Studies* [Minneapolis: Fortress, 1998], e.g. 46).

[63] Boers, *Christ*.

Chapter 5

1 Corinthians 8:1–10:22, and the relation between the risen Lord and believers

1. Introduction: framing and pursuing an exegetical study

1 Corinthians 8:1–10:22 is a complex passage full of hotly debated issues, yet it is rich in data relevant to the divine-Christology debate. Not only must the exegete negotiate difficult textual-critical and syntactical questions at important points, one must also be able to navigate further disagreement concerning the socio-religious background,[1] and even take a position on the disputed integrity of the text.[2] On top of this, numerous other matters evidence an astonishing plurality of scholarly perspectives. For example, did the 'weak' Christians actually exist (as most scholars believe), or were they invented for the sake of Paul's rhetoric?[3] Were they even Christians at all, or perhaps polytheist pagans?[4] Does Paul disagree with the propositions of the 'knowledgeable' or not?[5] And so on. The unenviable task of the exegete is to negotiate these choppy waters without being caught in the crossfire of one of the many exegetical skirmishes before leaving the harbour. Nevertheless, comment must be made at points about such wider matters or any argument will likely run against the rocks of superficiality.

---

[1] Cf. especially the analysis in John Fotopoulos, *Food Offered to Idols in Roman Corinth: A Social-Rhetorical Reconsideration of 1 Corinthians 8:1–11:1* (Tübingen: Mohr Siebeck, 2003) and Volker Gäckle, *Die Starken und die Schwachen in Korinth und in Rom: Zu Herkunft und Funktion der Antithese in 1 Kor 8,1–11,1 und Röm 14,1–15,13* (Tübingen: Mohr Siebeck, 2005).

[2] The integrity of the material has been challenged recently in Khiok-Khng Yeo, *Rhetorical Interaction in 1 Corinthians 8 and 10: A Formal Analysis with Preliminary Suggestions for a Chinese, Cross-Cultural Hermeneutic* (Leiden: Brill, 1995).

[3] John C. Hurd, *The Origin of 1 Corinthians* (London: SPCK, 1965).

[4] Mark D. Nanos, "The *Polytheist* Identity of the 'Weak', And Paul's Strategy to 'Gain' Them: A New Reading of 1 Corinthians 8:1–11:1," in *Paul: Jew, Greek and Roman*, ed. S. E. Porter (Leiden: Brill, 2008), 179–210.

[5] While many speak of the 'strong' and 'weak', the text does not actually mention 'strong'. The terminology adopted here, when not summarising the work of another, is 'knowledgeable' and 'weak', thus corresponding better with Paul's own language (cf. Nanos, "Polytheist").

The following analysis will consequently often be a little complex. But in a nutshell, it proposes an analysis of the relevant material in 8:1–10:22 (focusing on Paul's treatment, to use Eriksson's classifications, of the first finite question,[6] and excluding what he calls the *digressio* of 1 Cor. 9[7]) in terms of the believer's relation to the risen Lord, an approach which, it will be maintained, opens up the exegete to vistas of relevant material and interconnections otherwise left largely unnoticed in the divine-Christology debate.[8] In practice, this will mean pursuing two main propositions, one concerning the nature of Paul's monotheistic strategy in 1 Corinthians 8:1–3, and another concerning the relation between risen Lord and believers, thus bringing together the two questions posed above (p. 17). It will be argued that *Paul, having opened his argument in a way that expresses true faith in the one God as the relational commitment of believers to this God over against idolatry, goes on to speak explicitly and continually of the relation between risen Lord and believers over against idolatry. Furthermore, he details this Christ-relation with the terms and categories drawn from the complex of themes and concepts that, in the Jewish scriptures, describe the relation between Israel and YHWH over against idolatry.*

2. Framing Paul's argument: relational faith in God in 1 Corinthians 8

In the previous chapter it was suggested that one can properly speak of a Pauline *monotheism* so long as by this one means to indicate God's transcendent uniqueness through the unique pattern of relational data concerning commitment to the one God over against idols. Corresponding to this, it will now be argued that precisely such an understanding of monotheism frames Paul's entire argument concerning meat associated with offerings to pagan deities. To speak of his 'entire argument' however assumes the unity of the disputed literary integrity of the text. Happily, a growing majority of scholars today

---

[6] Anders Eriksson, *Traditions as Rhetorical Proof: Pauline Argumentation in 1 Corinthians* (Stockholm: Almqvist & Wiksell, 1998), 146, 152 (and cf. also n.79).

[7] Even if Eriksson's scheme is not accepted, it is uncontroversial to claim that the argument in 1 Cor. 8 is more directly continued in 1 Cor. 10 (Joseph A. Fitzmyer, *First Corinthians*, AB [London: Yale University Press, 2008], 332; Eckhard J. Schnabel, *Der erste Brief des Paulus an die Korinther* [Wuppertal: R. Brockhaus Verlag, 2006], 433; Fotopoulos, *Food*, 223–27. Reference can also be made to Ben Witherington, III, *Conflict and Community in Corinth: A Socio-Rhetorical Commentary on 1 and 2 Corinthians* [Grand Rapids: Eerdmans, 1995], 203–16; Wolfgang Schrage, *Der erste Brief an die Korinther [2]* [Zürich: Benziger, 1995], 213–14; Anthony C. Thiselton, *The First Epistle to the Corinthians. A Commentary on the Greek Text* [Carlisle: Paternoster/Eerdmans, 2000], 661–63; David E. Garland, *1 Corinthians* [Grand Rapids: Baker, 2003], 362; Waaler, *Shema*, 275–79; etc.).

[8] 1 Cor. 10:23–11:1 is not included in this analysis because of its restricted aims, but its absence from the discussion will not add or detract from the argument.

understand the text as a unity.[9] Not only does the unified textual transmission of the text speak against the various 'cut and paste' hypotheses, so does the complete lack of consensus among those denying literary integrity.[10] The various partition theories evidence considerable plurality of opinion as to which fragment belongs where – thereby reducing the plausibility, and certainly the clarity, of the general partition thesis. Gäckle notes how the parallelism with the text in Romans14:1–15:13 tends to affirm the literary integrity of the 1 Corinthians material, as do the numerous internal literary and lexical connections within the whole argument.[11] Exegesis emphasising rhetorical patterns, especially Mitchell's,[12] has further motivated much modern confidence in the literary unity of the text. The argument makes sense as a whole without necessary recourse to scissors.[13]

2.1. 1 Corinthians 8:1–3

Of key importance in the following argument is the role played by 8:1–3.[14] In it Paul circumscribes the extent of his concern, that it is about 'meat associated with offerings to pagan deities' (περὶ δὲ τῶν εἰδωλοθύτων).[15] As noted below, it is generally accepted that Paul, in 8:1a, cites the Corinthians,[16] introducing their voice with οἴδαμεν ὅτι.[17] 'We all', Paul probably cites the Corinthians as saying, 'have knowledge'.[18] Immediately Paul interjects a critical comment on the Corinthian γνῶσις, setting a pattern for what will follow:

---

[9] Cf. the helpful overviews of the debate in Gäckle, *Starken*, 112–15, and Waaler, *Shema*, 267–81.

[10] Cf. Thiselton, *Corinthians*, 610; Gordon D. Fee, *The First Epistle to the Corinthians* (Exeter: Paternoster, 1987), 15.

[11] Cf. Gäckle, *Starken*, 113–14; Waaler, *Shema*, 280.

[12] Margaret M Mitchell, *Paul and the Rhetoric of Reconciliation: An Exegetical Investigation of the Language and Composition of 1 Corinthians* (Tübingen: Mohr Siebeck, 1991). For a response to Yeo's critique of Mitchell, cf. Fotopoulos, *Food*, 26–30.

[13] Cf. also the discussion in Eriksson, *Traditions*, chap. 4; Garland, *1 Corinthians*, 347–504, esp. 347–62 and the critique of the partition theories in Thiselton, *Corinthians*, 607–12.

[14] Cf. Gäckle's claim that 8:1-3 create 'a fundamental theological ground work for the entire theme of 8:1–11:1' (Gäckle, *Starken*, 223).

[15] For this translation of εἰδωλόθυτα, cf. the discussion in Thiselton, *Corinthians*, 617–20, which, he argues, accommodates the complex social, socioeconomic and cultic dimens-ions associated with the term.

[16] Cf. n.80.

[17] Some consider these two words as themselves part of the citation. Cf. the discussion in Wendell Lee Willis, *Idol Meat in Corinth : The Pauline Argument in 1 Corinthians 8 and 10* (Chico, Calif.: Scholars Press, 1983), 67–70; Thiselton, *Corinthians*, 620–21; Schnabel, *Korinther*, 439.

[18] Schnabel speculates that the πάντες was added by Paul, but it is impossible to make a definite judgement (Schnabel, *Korinther*, 439).

'knowledge (ἡ γνῶσις) puffs up, up but love (ἡ ...ἀγάπη) builds up'. Instead of knowledge, Paul focuses upon ἀγάπη.

Before Paul develops his 'love critique' of the Corinthian γνῶσις, he continues his reaction to the Corinthian knowledge, this time in the form of a conditional sentence: 'If (εἰ) anyone thinks to have known anything, he has not yet known as it is necessary to know (δεῖ γνῶναι)'.[19] It thus becomes clear that Paul is not rejecting knowledge in and of itself.[20] There is a 'necessary knowing' which he will expound in the next conditional sentence: 'And if (εἰ) anyone loves God, he has been known by Him'. This is an important sentence for the developing argument, and needs to be justified given the presence of textual variations at this point.

The variant readings are in 𝔓[46] and Clement of Alexandria, which omit τὸν θεόν as well as ὑπ᾽ αὐτοῦ.[21] This shorter reading would yield the meaning that 'if anyone loves, he or she', to cite Thiselton's paraphrase 'has experienced true "knowing"'.[22] The omission of τὸν θεόν from the important and early textual witness 𝔓[46] leads some to think the two Greek words are a later addition to the autograph, which simply referred to an object free 'love' in the abstract. This could be taken to refute the argument that Paul, in this context, is addressing love for God at all. Three arguments can be used to support this claim. First, it can be argued that the context is precisely one of love for other humans, not God. So Fee writes that Paul 'is not dealing with loving (or knowing) *God*.[23] Rather, his concern is with their failure to act in love toward some in their midst who do not share their "knowledge"'.[24] Secondly, some may suggest that ἀγάπη language in Paul usually refers to God's own love, not human love for God. Thirdly, Johann Albrecht Bengel's textual critical dictum of *lectio brevior potior* (the shorter of two readings is to be preferred) could be cited as support for 𝔓[46]'s shorter reading, given the assumption that scribes were more likely to add than to delete as they copied a text.

However, none of these points convinces, and various arguments to prefer the longer reading make τὸν θεόν very likely authentic. First, the above arguments for the shorter reading are flawed for the following reasons. Fee's argument about context is actually support for the longer reading. Royse asks, if Fee is correct that the shorter reading is to be contextually preferred, why was

---

[19] But cf. Thiselton, *Corinthians*, 624, for a discussion concerning the significance of the use of the perfect and aorist infinitive of the verbs ἐγνωκέναι and γνῶναι respectively.

[20] This is why Torben Kjær's argument, that Paul could not identify 'knowledge' and 'love' (in 8:6 through supposed association with the *Shema*) because it is *in conflict with* 8:1–3, is amiss. There is a positive knowing – one which is, as shall be seen, characterised relationally (cf. the summary of Kjær's position in Waaler, *Shema*, 24).

[21] ℵ* and 33 leave out only ὑπ᾽ αὐτοῦ, which are probably best understood as the result of a copyist oversight (cf. Schnabel, *Korinther*, 435).

[22] Thiselton, *Corinthians*, 625.

[23] Cf., e.g., Thiselton, *Corinthians*, 607, 625–26; Fee, *Corinthians*, 367.

[24] Fee, *Corinthians*, 368.

it corrupted in virtually all witnesses?[25] Indeed, the context is emphatically not only about love toward other humans. The context deals with idolatry, and to this end alludes to the Deuteronomic themes and, importantly, the *Shema* in 8:3–6.[26] Furthermore, though the context is certainly concerned with love for the fellow believer, this is framed in such a way that emphasises the interrelated matter of relationship to the Lord.[27] This is a matter explicit in 8:12 ('when you thus sin against members of your family ... you sin against Christ'), and detailed in more depth as the argument develops in 1 Corinthians 10:1–22. Paul's argument actually reaches an important point in 8:12 when the behaviour of some believers means they 'sin against Christ'. But more of that below. What is more, as Nicholson has explored in depth, Paul tended to ground his ethical and interpersonal reasoning in theology.[28] She argues that the context suggests that Paul's love most likely deals with love *for God*, precisely because it is about love for one's neighbour. So she writes: 'if loving God means keeping his commandments and keeping his commandments necessarily involves loving others, then one loves God (at least in part) by loving others'.[29]

The argument concerning ἀγάπη language in Paul likewise supports not the shorter, but rather the longer, reading. Reference can be made to Romans 8:28, which has been cited by Zuntz, who supports the shorter reading, as explanation for how the longer reading was generated.[30] But on top of this verse, one can mention 1 Corinthians 2:9. Love for God is certainly not un-Pauline, and indeed, the allusion to the *Shema* should cause one to expect it here.

Finally, the argument that the shorter reading is principally to be preferred has recently been refuted by James Royse in his careful and important study of the scribal habits in early Greek New Testament papyri. His study demonstrates that 'the scribe of 𝔓⁴⁶ displays a very clear tendency to omit'.[31] Indeed, the scribal changes of 𝔓⁴⁶ adds 54 words in 52 additions, while it omits 298 or 299 words in 161 omissions.[32] As Royse argues: 'the tendency of 𝔓⁴⁶ is to produce a shorter text'.[33] Indeed, Aasgaard affirms Royse's thesis and even asserts that if 'we are to make a general principle, at least as far as the early

---

[25] James R. Royse, *Scribal Habits in Early Greek New Testament Papyri* (Leiden: Brill, 2008), 294.

[26] Waaler, *Shema*. Cf. also Richard B. Hays, *First Corinthians* (Louisville: John Knox Press, 1997), 140.

[27] This point has been stressed recently by Schnabel, *Korinther*, 436, 441.

[28] Nicholson, "Oneness."

[29] Nicholson, "Oneness," 75. Cf. also the recent remarks in Healy, "Knowledge," 157.

[30] Günther Zuntz, *The Text of the Epistles: A Disquisition Upon the Corpus Paulinum* (London: British Academy, 1953), 31–32.

[31] Royse, *Habits*, 297.

[32] Ibid.

[33] Royse, *Habits*, 298. Cf. also Peter M. Head, "The Habits of New Testament Copyists: Singular Readings in the Early Fragmentary Papyri of John," *Bib* 85, no. 3 (2004): esp. 408.

papyri is concerned, it even seems that the longer reading (*lectio longior*) is to be preferred'.[34] Hence, $\mathfrak{P}^{46}$ is 'to be viewed with considerable suspicion in the matter of addition and omission', a text which 'omits words and phrases far more often than any other of the central papyri'.[35]

Royse cannot discern a clear theological agenda in these changes,[36] so the question becomes, why did $\mathfrak{P}^{46}$ omit τὸν θεόν? If a cogent explanation can be given, then the authenticity of the longer reading is further strengthened. Royse notes numerous examples where $\mathfrak{P}^{46}$ made errors due to scribal 'leaps', where the copyist's eyes fell on the same letter at a later point in the text, thus omitting chunks of text. Royse identifies three such leaps' even only within 1 Corinthians 8.[37] The first of these is the most significant. In 8:2 the scribe has probably jumped from the iota at the end of ἐγνωκέναι, to the iota at the end of the next word, τι. In this way the knowing in 8:2a has become objectless. It is thus possible that the $\mathfrak{P}^{46}$ shorter reading was an attempt to harmonise the love of 8:3 with the objectless knowing of 8:2a, thus generating an object free love. Hoskier, who argues that in 1 Corinthians 8 '[w]e are therefore speaking of abstract knowledge, and of love in the abstract',[38] has perhaps hit upon the justification of $\mathfrak{P}^{46}$'s omission of τὸν θεόν. Indeed, Royse has shown that har-monisations in $\mathfrak{P}^{46}$ are most often motivated by immediate contextual con-cerns, as would be the case in 8:2–3.[39] Perhaps other factors can be adduced for $\mathfrak{P}^{46}$'s shorter reading. Royse notes that $\mathfrak{P}^{46}$ often errs when confronted by the *nomina sacra*.[40] 8:2 is likely another example of this trend.

These points also explain why the vast majority of textual traditions relat-ing to 8:3 all include τὸν θεόν and ὑπ᾽ αὐτοῦ,[41] an important factor that affirms the authenticity of the longer reading.[42] Wright is thus correct to argue that the context is not about 'love in general', but 'the Jewish-style allegiance to the one God'.[43]

Finally, even if $\mathfrak{P}^{46}$ does represent the autograph, one still cannot agree with Fee that Paul is 'not dealing with loving (or knowing) *God*'.[44] The love in 8:3 in $\mathfrak{P}^{46}$ is simply object free, and thus the context will clarify its mean-ing. As noted above, this context is indisputably about idolatry, with allusion to the *Shema* and the oneness of God. As will be argued below, there are rela-

---

[34] Reidar Aasgaard, "Brothers in Brackets?: A Plea for Rethinking the Use of '[]' in NA/UBS," *JSNT* 26, no. 3 (2004): 309.

[35] Ibid., 310.

[36] Royse, *Habits*, 356–57.

[37] Ibid., 284.

[38] Hoskier, cited in Royse, *Habits*, 292.

[39] Royse, *Habits*, 358; Head, "Habits," 400.

[40] Royse, *Habits*, 358.

[41] Gäckle, *Starken*, 224 n.549.

[42] For more reasons to accept the longer reading as authentic, cf. Waaler, *Shema*, 306–7.

[43] N.T. Wright, *Climax*, 127.

[44] Fee, *Corinthians*, 367.

tional aspects to Paul's language in 1 Corinthians 8:6, and there are further indisputable references to the commitment of believers to the risen Lord over against idolatry as this argument concerning idol food develops. So even if 𝔓⁴⁶ is accepted as the original reading, the abstract love in 8:2 would be clarified in the rest of Paul's argument as one concerning both love for God and fellow believers. Nevertheless, the longer reading is strongly to be preferred.

To return to the main argument, it is a fair suggestion that the two concessive sentences of 8:2 and 8:3, with the repetition of the verb γινώσκω, indicate that the 'necessary knowing' (ἔγνω καθὼς δεῖ γνῶναι) of the apodosis of 8:2 is the apodosis of 8:3, the state of 'being known by God' (ἔγνωσται ὑπ᾽ αὐτοῦ). This necessary knowing can thus be examined via reflection on the phrase 'being known by God'. Schnabel argues that the meaning of this formulation of γινώσκω (the passive perfect with God as subject) is to be understood in terms of the Hebrew word ידע. He continues:

> ידע with God as subject means "to attend to a person" and describes the special relationship between Jahwe and Israel or individual Israelites. In some verses ידי is used in the sense of בחר ("elect") (compare Num. 16:5).[45]

To speak of God's knowledge of humans is thus to speak in covenantal terms,[46] of *God's special relationship with his chosen people*, as clearly seen in, for example, Amos 3:2: 'You only have I known (ἔγνων) of all the families of the earth'. This is consistent with Paul's usage of the phrase 'knowledge of God' elsewhere (Gal. 4:9).[47] Likewise, Waaler concludes his study of this verse with the assertion that 'to love God and to be known by God (1Cor 8:3) describes the personal relationship between the believer and God'.[48] This theme of loving relationship with God will echo also in 8:6 where Paul draws on the language of the *Shema* (cf. Deut. 6:4–5).

In stating these matters *first* in his argument, and by tying them explicitly to the theme to be addressed (περὶ δὲ τῶν εἰδωλοθύτων – 8:1), Paul wants these comparisons to function as the foundation of all that will later be said. His use of the coordinating conjunction in 8:4 (οὖν) relates the next section directly to these verses. Hence his undermining of the Corinthian γνῶσις and his recasting of the 'necessary knowing' in terms of the relational, covenantal notion of God's knowledge of his people who love him, is of key hermeneutical importance for the following. One's understanding of 8:4–6 must be developed in light of 8:1–3. This is why the repetition of περί in 8:4 does not serve to distinguish a separate topic, the 'next subject' as Mitchell

---

[45] Schnabel, *Korinther*, 442–43, translation mine. For all of this, cf. also Schrage, *Korinther*, 234–35, and the comments in Thiselton, *Corinthians*, 626.

[46] Cf. Waaler, *Shema*, 50, who argues that covenantal themes are prominent in 1 Cor. 5:1–10:22.

[47] Cf. e.g. Gäckle, *Starken*, 225; J. Louis Martyn, *Galatians: A New Translation with Introduction and Commentary*, AB (London: Doubleday, 1997), 413; Dunn, *Galatians*, 225.

[48] Waaler, *Shema*, 351.

suggested.[49] Significantly, Paul repeats, in 8:4, his words in 8:1 (περὶ δὲ τῶν εἰδωλοθύτων) adding only that now the subject is *the eating* of this meat associated with offerings to pagan deities. 8:4 could thus be translated 'Consequently (οὖν), specifically concerning the *eating* of meat associated with offerings to pagan deities ...'. The subject of 8:4 is simply a subset of the larger topic noted in 8:1.[50] 8:1–3 provides the hermeneutic necessary to understand Paul's developing argument.

The upshot of this analysis of 8:1–3 is profound. Just as Paul typically made recourse to relationally accented language in his polemic against idolatry, just as his speech about God was, as Dunn put it, a 'two-way knowing of personal relationship',[51] so in discussing true faith in God over against idols in 1 Corinthians 8–10, Paul explicitly frames the whole matter at hand by emphasising a love-orientated relational monotheism.[52]

2.2. Relational monotheism in 1 Corinthians 8:6

First, some preliminary issues must be addressed. There is some debate about whether 1 Corinthians 8:6 actually constitutes Paul's own position. Some maintain that it is rather part of a statement from the Corinthian 'knowledgeable' against which Paul responds in 8:7 with 'it is not everyone, however, who has this knowledge'.[53] Most, on the other hand, understand 8:6 (and usually also 8:5[54]) as a response to the Corinthian position cited in 8:4,[55] while others deny that Paul's argument involves any citation of the Corinthians and that 8:4–6 is entirely reflective of the Pauline position.[56]

It is, however, difficult to know whether Paul is citing the Corinthians or not, and difficult to know precisely how his language should be understood on the basis of syntactical analysis alone. But perhaps a way forward in this discussion, and a way to cut through the complexity, is to recall the framing sig-

---

[49] Cited in Thiselton, *Corinthians*, 628.

[50] Cf. Thiselton, *Corinthians*, 628.

[51] Cf. p. 69 above.

[52] Cf. also Fitzmyer, *First Corinthians*, 340.

[53] Cf. in different ways, Willis, *Meat*, 83–87; Otfried Hofius, "'Einer ist Gott – Einer ist Herr'. Erwägungen zu Struktur und Aussage des Bekenntnisses 1.Kor 8,6," in *Eschatologie und Schöpfung: Festschrift für Erich Gräßer zum siebzigsten Geburtstag*, eds Martin Evang, et al. (Berlin: W. de Gruyter, 1997), 95–108; Woyke, *Götter*, 158–214; Johannes Woyke, "Das Bekenntnis zum einzig allwirksamen Gott und Herrn und die Dämonisierung von Fremdkulten: Monolatrischer und polylatrischer Monotheismus in 1. Korinther 8 und 10," in *Gruppenreligionen im römischen Reich. Sozialformen, Grenzziehungen und Leistungen*, ed. J Rüpke (Tübingen: Mohr Siebeck, 2007), 87–112.

[54] Fotopoulos think *only* 8:5b is Paul's corrective in 8:4b–6 (Fotopoulos, *Food*, 210–14).

[55] Cf. the references in Woyke, *Götter*, 180–88, and, e.g., Giblin, "Three," 529–37; Fee, *Corinthians*, 369–76; Garland, *1 Corinthians*, 371–77. Additionally, one can make reference to Thiselton, *Corinthians*, 607–45; Schnabel, *Korinther*, 443–50; Gäckle, *Starken*, e.g. 37–40, 227–36.

[56] Waaler, *Shema*, cf. e.g. 290–1, 358–438.

nificance of 8:1–3. By introducing his argument with 8:1–3 Paul likely wants to use the language of 8:4–6 for his own purpose. He wants it to be read in a certain way, one corresponding to relational monotheism. This is true whether Paul cites the Corinthians, to perhaps tease out significance in their own assertions that they had missed, or whether it is all new Pauline material to the Corinthians in contradiction of their statements. This suggestion will be revisited below.

Of course, scholarly preoccupation with 1 Corinthians 8, in terms of the Pauline divine-Christology debate, has focused upon 8:6. It has become widely accepted that in 8:6 Paul provides what can be called a christological reading of the first part of 'the *Shema*'.[57] In truth, 8:6 only constitutes a redeployment of the first part of the *Shema*, but more on that below. Briefly put, taking a Greek version of Deuteronomy 6:4, Paul has 'glossed "God" with "the Father", and "Lord" with "Jesus Christ"'.[58] Furthermore, as explored with most clarity by Bauckham, the prepositions are divided between the Father (ἐκ and εἰς) and the Lord (διά) in significant fashion. In Romans 11:36 Paul applies all three prepositions to God; in 8:6, they are significantly divided between the one God and the one Lord.[59]

Further Christ-relation significance of this passage will be examined below, but with these preliminary matters covered it is now time to attempt to understand the sort of monotheism implied by Paul's language. This will first be done by examining the text from which it draws, Deuteronomy. Second, it will involve an examination of the directly relational import of Paul's language.

Because Deuteronomy functions as a key text not only in 8:6 (and probably also 8:3[60]), but also in Paul's developing argument in 1 Corinthians 10, it will prove expedient to examine the monotheism of Deuteronomy in more depth. This move is justified for a number of reasons. Watson has recently argued that the Apostle is fundamentally an interpreter of Israel's scriptures. So he writes: 'In Paul, scripture is not overwhelmed by the light of an autonomous Christ-event needing no scriptural mediation. It is scripture that shapes the contours of the Christ-event'.[61] An analysis of the kind of 'monotheism' evidenced in Deuteronomy will thus potentially clarify Paul's point in drawing so

---

[57] Cf. the major study of Waaler, *Shema*, esp. 262 n.3. Cf. also the references in Bauckham, *God of Israel*, 211 n.69, and the recent study of Fee, *Christology*, 89–90. It is even affirmed by those whose general argument hardly lends to this conclusion: e.g. Schrage, *Unterwegs*, 168 n.385; Dunn, *Theology*, 253.

[58] That the word order in 8:6, which is different to that in Deut. 6:4, should not be taken as an argument against the textual link, contra Peterson, cf. Waaler, *Shema*, 202.

[59] Bauckham, *God of Israel*, 210–18.

[60] Cf. Waaler, *Shema*, 310–11, 348–51.

[61] Francis Watson, *Paul and the Hermeneutics of Faith* (London: T&T Clark, 2004), 17. But cf. the remarks in J. R. Daniel Kirk, *Unlocking Romans: Resurrection and the Justification of God* (Cambridge: Eerdmans, 2008), e.g. 12–13.

extensively from the Pentateuch in his argument, especially Deuteronomy. It may be objected that monotheism in Deuteronomy should not matter as much as how Deuteronomy was being read at the time of Paul. While there is some truth in this, Waaler's detailed study shows that the *Shema* continued to be used during the intertestamental period, in the relational manner found in Deuteronomy, as will be explicated in conversation with Nathan MacDonald's study of 'monotheism' in Deuteronomy.[62] The relevant points in MacDonald's thesis will be summarised.

First, MacDonald significantly argues that the word 'monotheism', in OT studies, tends to reflect an intellectualised and abstract notion, derived from the Enlightenment, that prioritises the question of the number of deities.[63] However, he makes a strong case that this notion of 'monotheism' hardly corresponds with what one finds in Deuteronomy. It is, he discovers, *relational*. In an analysis of the *Shema*, MacDonald argues that it is not a confession about the non-existence of other gods as the question of the existence of other deities is clearly alien to the context in Deuteronomy.[64] He maintains that the *Shema* (by which he means Deut. 6:4–9), is significant in how it emphasises the *personal and relational* in terms of the confession that YHWH is one. So, in a chapter entitled 'So Love Yahweh, Your God: "Monotheism" as Devoted Love', MacDonald notes that while in the modern intellectualised definitions '"Monotheism" is a truth to be comprehended', in Deuteronomy, it is 'a relationship in which to be committed'.[65] The 'monotheism' of Deuteronomy is relational in import, concerned with love and devotion to this one God.[66]

Second, MacDonald proceeds to show that the *Shema* is an address to a particular people, to God's covenanted people. So the 'primary significance of the *Shema* is the relationship between YHWH and Israel. YHWH is to be Israel's one and only'.[67] In terms of the *Bilderverbot*, as detailed in his sixth chapter, he notes that:

YHWH is unique, nevertheless this cannot be abstracted from the relationship between YHWH and Israel ... Thus, YHWH is seen to be unique through the relationship he has with Israel and, by implication, does not have with other nations. Thus, in both cases something is said about

---

[62] Waaler, *Shema*, 202.

[63] MacDonald, *Monotheism*, 15.

[64] Actually, matters may not be quite so simple. Since Martin Noth, *The Deuteronomistic History* (Sheffield: JSOT Press, 1981), it is widely accepted that the Deuteronomist also wrote a history, including 2 Kgs. And, as noted by Woyke, 2 Kgs 19:18 perhaps involves the denial of *the existence* of other gods (Woyke, *Götter*, 170).

[65] MacDonald, *Monotheism*, 97.

[66] So also Stephen Geller writes: 'Deuteronomy 6:4 may not be a statement of numerical monotheism at all, but the expression of a relationship between God and Israel, or humanity, and specifically with the individual' (Geller, "God," 293).

[67] MacDonald, *Monotheism*, 151.

the nature of YHWH, an ontological statement, so to speak, but a statement that cannot be divorced from the personal claim on Israel.[68]

As noted above, many scholars have spoken of a christological reworking of the *Shema* in 8:6. However, this is actually not an explicit reworking of the whole *Shema*. In the second century AD there is evidence that the *Shema* came to include Deuteronomy 11:13–21 and Numbers 15:37–41 in addition to Deuteronomy 6:4–9. It is not clear what the extent of the *Shema* was in Paul's day. Evidence in the NT suggests that it consisted of what Wyse has called the first two portions of 6:4–5 (cf. Mk. 12:28–34).[69] Either way, included in the *Shema* is 'You shall love the LORD your God with all your heart and with all your soul and with all your might' (Deut. 6:5).[70] Indeed, MacDonald notes that this connection is made explicit in the Hebrew, as the commandment to love YHWH is grammatically linked with the statement that YHWH is one.[71] In Deuteronomy, the *Shema* is about the confession that God is one *and at the same time* a love commitment to this God (as the *Shema* text, in Deut. 6:5 immediately goes on to state). In striking accord with this conclusion is the position of J. Gordon McConville in his study of Deuteronomic theology:

> The discussion whether Deuteronomy is monotheistic in the strict sense is arid. The book always thinks of God's oneness in relational terms, that is, in the context of his relationship with Israel. It is this God, Yahweh, and not another, who is supreme in the affairs of Israel and of the nations - a point made in dialogue, explicitly and implicitly, with the polytheism of Canaan.[72]

All of this not only directly corresponds to the type of monotheism explicated in the previous chapter, it is also arguably important for a proper understanding of Paul's argument. If Paul indeed repeated the *Shema* twice daily,[73] then in redeploying the words of Deuteronomy 6:4, Deuteronomy 6:5 is directly associated in Paul's mind. This is an observation made all the more likely given the 'love'/'knowledge' theme in 8:1–3 with which Paul framed his argument. After all, it was 'love for God' which ended Paul's comparisons (8:3). The 'knowledge' continued to be expressed in his argument in 8:4 ('we know'), and in 8:6 the love theme finds further expression via association

---

[68] Ibid., 207.

[69] Jackie A. Wyse, "Loving God as an Act of Obedience: The Shema in Context," in *Take This Word to Heart: The Shema in Torah and Gospel*, ed. Perry B. Yoder (Elkhart, Ind.: Institute of Mennonite Studies, 2005), 12–14.

[70] Cf. Birger Gerhardsson, *The Shema in the New Testament: Deut 6:4–5 in Significant Passages* (Lund: Novapress, 1996), 302, and MacDonald, *Monotheism*, 60 n.2.

[71] MacDonald, *Monotheism*, 98.

[72] J. Gordon McConville, *Grace in the End: A Study in Deuteronomic Theology* (Grand Rapids: Zondervan, 1993), 124.

[73] Cf. *m. Ber.* 1:1–9, and the discussion in David Instone-Brewer, *Traditions of the Rabbis in the Era of the New Testament, Vol. 1* (Grand Rapids: Eerdmans, 2004), 42–44, for evidence concerning the tradition's origin before AD 70. For a careful examination of the *Shema* in relation to *Tefillin, Mezuzot*, rituals and daily prayer in the first century AD, cf. Waaler, *Shema*, 124–33.

with the *Shema*. One of the few scholars to have seen something of this point expresses the matter as follows:

Paul responds to the claim to γνῶσις by insisting on the primacy of (not love in general, but) the Jewish-style allegiance to the one God ... The real *Gnosis*, Paul is saying, is not your *Gnosis* of God but God's *Gnosis* of you, and the sign of that being present is that one keeps the *Shema*: you shall love the Lord your God with all your heart.[74]

A relational understanding of Paul's monotheism in 8:6 is also affirmed by various features in the verse. First, it is suggested in the usage of the first person plural pronouns in 8:6. The threefold ἡμῖν—ἡμεῖς—ἡμεῖς arguably mirror the commitment and relationally accented understanding of the *Shema* faith within Deuteronomy.[75] Second, Giblin notes the argument of Sagnard, that 'the noun clauses [of 8:6] stress dynamic relationships to such an extent that supplying a form of the verb "to be" would petrify Paul's thought'.[76] Third, the very fact that Paul uses the language 'Father' and 'Lord', involves, for Paul, a relational tendency. For the special relational import of the title 'Father' in Paul, one need only refer to Galatians 4:6 and Romans 8:15 together with the analysis offered by Rabens.[77] The relational associations with Paul's use of 'Lord' will be explored in this and the next chapters. Finally, if 8:1–3 functions hermeneutically there are good grounds to understand the ἡμῖν in 8:6 as involving relational force.[78]

So, the faith in God which frames and begins Paul's developing argument in 1 Corinthians 8–10 is thoroughly relational. God's uniqueness, over against idols, is spoken of in terms of relational and loving commitment to this God, a uniqueness seen through the relationship he has with his people, as MacDonald also sees in Deuteronomy.[79]

---

[74] N.T. Wright, *Climax*, 127.

[75] The 'threefold ἡμῖν-ἡμεῖς-ἡμεῖς gives a strongly experiential note to the formula' (Richardson, *Paul's Language About God*, 298, and cf. also Schrage, *Unterwegs*, 75). We would say 'relational' given the Deuteronomic allusion.

[76] Giblin, "Three," 535. Thiselton affirms Sagnard's reasoning, adding that 'Rom 11:36 underlines this' (Thiselton, *Corinthians*, 638).

[77] For a study of the relational aspects of these verses, cf. Volker Rabens, *The Holy Spirit and Religious-Ethical Life in Paul: The Transforming and Empowering Work of the Spirit in Paul's Ethics* (Brunel University: PhD thesis, 2007), 196–215.

[78] So Waaler, *Shema*, 398 and his references. He understands it as *dative commodi*, 'making the issue relational rather than conceptual'. This, however, may be to frame the issue according to an inappropriate either/or.

[79] McGrath, in examining 1 Cor. 8:6, problematically argues that what distinguished God from all created reality was not just the worship of God, but rather 'sacrificial worship which took place in the Jerusalem temple' (cf. James F. McGrath, *God*, 50). The actual factors which distinguished God from all created reality will be examined below, but it suffices to say now that it is more complicated than simply 'sacrifice' in worship. As the examination above would lead one to expect, it rather involves relational factors that, as a pattern, was not ascribed to any figure other than God.

2.3. The Intellektualismus *of the 'knowledgeable': Gäckle's thesis*

Volker Gäckle, together with the scholarly majority, asserts that propositions of the Corinthian 'knowledgeable' are cited in 1 Corinthians 8.[80] Based upon an examination of these Corinthian slogans found in 1 Corinthians 8:1–11:1, the concepts and vocabulary found therein, and the semantic field of ἀσθεν-Gäckle proposes a portrait of the nature of the beliefs of the 'strong'.[81] The description of a group as 'weak' by another is, he maintains, based upon 'cognitive-rational educative and psycho-emotional categories'.[82] He thus argues that the 'strong' are notably concerned about *cognitive categories*.[83] Indeed, he shows that there are many examples in ancient literature in which the pejorative characterisation of another group as ἀσθενής is made by a cognitively focused group (cf. 1 Cor. 4:10; 8:7, 9, 10; 9:22; 12:22).[84] Gäckle writes:

> An aristocratic consciousness based on an intellectual perception of the world and God shines through this quotation, as is the case in almost all Corinthian quotations and terms ...The faith of the strong originated in the search for an intellectual understanding of God.[85]

Without wanting to claim this exhaustively describes the problem of these Corinthian Christians, it can be argued that their 'knowledge' involved elitist cognitive concerns, an *Intellektualismus*.[86] If Gäckle is correct, it is against this kind of intellectualisation that Paul responds in 1 Corinthians 8, a thesis that makes good sense of 8:1–3 and the relational hermeneutic.[87]

---

[80] That we are dealing with Corinthian citations is supported by the repetition of the ὅτι in 8:4b. This parallels the ὅτι in 8:1, which very probably evidences a Corinthian-citation-Pauline-correction structure. See Garland, *1 Corinthians*, 364, and the references in 366 n.6. Again, see also Schrage, *Korinther*, 220–21; Fotopoulos, *Food*, 209–11; and Gäckle, *Starken*, 37–41; Willis, *Meat*, 67–70, 83–84; Witherington, *Conflict*, 188; Fee, *Corinthians*, 362; Schnabel, *Korinther*, 439; Hofius, "Gott," 99. Once again, also see Woyke, *Götter*, 203–4; Thiselton, *Corinthians*, 630. Against the citation hypothesis, cf. Joop F. M. Smit, *"About the Idol Offerings": Rhetoric, Social Context, and Theology of Paul's Discourse in First Corinthians 8:1–11:1* (Leuven: Peeters, 2000), e.g. 73 n.25; and Waaler, *Shema*, 281–92.

[81] This thesis was received well even by Gäckle's 1 Cor. 8–10 'sparring partner', Woyke (cf. Woyke, "Bekenntnis," 101). Even Waaler allows the possibility that 8:1 and 4 are 'statements of the problem under discussion' (Waaler, *Shema*, 267), but cf. his cautions (371).

[82] Gäckle, *Starken*, 108, translation mine.

[83] 'Just as in 1 Cor. 8 the focus of the discussion in 1 Cor. 1–4 is on the issue of the significance of knowledge and understanding' (Gäckle, *Starken*, 200, translation mine).

[84] Gäckle, *Starken*, 189.

[85] Ibid., 190. Cf. also 189, 200–204, translation mine.

[86] Ibid., 201.

[87] Garland likewise maintains that Paul argues against a 'mere propositional knowledge about God' (Garland, *1 Corinthians*, 391, cited approvingly also in Fitzmyer, *First Corinthians*, 337).

While it is surely fair to assert, as Wright does, that the monotheism in this period 'was not a matter of theoretical belief',[88] the question remains: what sort of belief was it then? Fee concurs with Wright in contrasting 'abstract theology'[89] or 'philosophical theology' with the 'practical implications for the matter at hand'.[90] Nevertheless, Fee later maintains that 1 Corinthians 8:6 'is a clear example of Christian ethics being grounded in proper Christian theology'.[91] Again, the question is what sort of theology Fee refers to if he does not mean by it an abstract or philosophical theology. Furthermore, Garland claims that 'Paul's purpose', in 1 Corinthians 8, 'is not to reflect christologically on his monotheistic faith'.[92] However, he can write a few sentences later that Paul means to say: 'Consorting with the many other gods and lords ruptures the relationship with the one God and one Lord'.[93] But if there is no christological reflection on monotheistic *faith*, then how can the passage reflect a concern with *relationship* to this one God and one Lord? And if 8:6 is not 'christologically reflecting on monotheistic faith', what is it? Given the analysis of monotheism in 8:1–3, 6 above together with Gäckle's proposal an answer suggests itself: *Paul emphasises, partly in response to the intellectualised and cognitive knowledge of the 'knowledgeable', the relational nature of true knowing and faith in the one God.* As maintained above, one cannot be certain about whether Paul was really citing the Corinthians or not, but Gäckle's proposal would at least makes sense as the negative against which Paul contrasts his positive relational focus.

2.4. A suggested reading of 1 Corinthians 8:1–7. Relational monotheism as the key to the whole section

In light of the above suggestions, a reading of 8:1–7 can be outlined. Of course, it is probably fair to say that there are almost as many interpretive proposals concerning these few verses as there are monographs offering substantial examination of 1 Corinthians 8. Hence the following proposal is tentatively proffered. Yet it at least makes good sense of the flow of the argument as a whole and, crucially, takes seriously the presence of 8:1–3 in the reconstruction.

In 8:1–3 Paul, in contradistinction to the intellectualised position of the Corinthian 'knowledgeable', emphasises a relational understanding of true faith in God. These opening verses are meant to serve as the interpretive key for the following. Paul, likely citing the Corinthians in 8:4, does not want absolutely to contradict their position, hence no explicit correction is

---

[88] N.T. Wright, *Climax*, 125.
[89] Fee, *Corinthians*, 376.
[90] Ibid., 375.
[91] Ibid., 376.
[92] Garland, *1 Corinthians*, 375.
[93] Ibid., 376.

present,[94] or at least obvious. The disagreement, it can be suggested now, is one of hermeneutics rather than propositional content.[95] Paul, in linking 8:4–6 with 8:1–3 in the way he does, wants these monotheistic negations to be understood in light of a relational understanding of faith in God. In 8:6 the relational emphasis is developed more explicitly than in the (what Paul would likely consider correct) assertions in 8:4. Perhaps Paul wanted the close association of the *Shema*-love to be heard more clearly, and make the Corinthians feel the force of the first person plural pronouns and thus acknowledge the adversative nature of the ἀλλά in 8:6.[96] Paul is leading them toward the kind of relational monotheistic understanding explicated in 8:1–3. In this way Paul is attempting at this point 'by "dissimulation and indirection" unobtrusively to "steal into the mind of the auditor"'.[97]

In further support of this thesis, this proposed reading helps to make sense of the following conundrum: in 8:1 Paul, perhaps citing the Corinthians, writes that 'all of us possess knowledge'. In 8:7, in apparent bold contradiction, he states that 'it is not everyone, however, who has this knowledge [ἡ γνῶσις]'. But Paul's argument has led the Corinthians from an intellectualised 'knowledge' to the 'necessary knowing' (8:2) of relational commitment and love for the one God.[98] It is this type of knowledge, the true relational one, that not all have. Indeed, most translations understand the definite article in 8:7 anaphorically, which would mean that the γνῶσις Paul refers to is that developed in at least 8:6. 8:7a is thus not simply a further contradiction of the Corinthian statement in 8:1a. One must account for how 8:1–6 frames this correction. The meaning of the 'knowledge' has changed, more closely corresponding to Paul's relational knowledge of God in 8:6.

This very brief sketch of a reading of 8:1–7 arguably makes good sense of both syntactical issues and tensions within the text. Although the verses are simply too unclear for absolute certainty in terms of the details of this reading (e.g., whether the Corinthians are actually cited, whether their knowledge was 'cognitive', whether εἴδωλον in 8:4 is to be read as predicative or attributive, whether 8:5–6 is a completed apodosis with protasis, etc.), the important point remains clear: Paul's argument is framed with an emphasis on a relational faith in God, and notably a relational commitment to the *one* God over against idols. *If the interpretive proposal outlined above is correct, then this relational monotheism frames not only 8:1–3 but also 4–7.* Either way, of course,

---

[94] Cf. the theses of Hofius and Woyke as noted above (n. 53).

[95] Note Gäckle, *Starken*, 39, who speaks of a 'differentiated concession' in 8:5 to 8:4b.

[96] Gäckle, *Starken*, 39.

[97] Eriksson, *Traditions*, 150, citing Cicero. That Paul's general strategy is as Eriksson suggests is affirmed, in one way or another, especially with reference to Mitchell, *Paul*, in most recent commentaries (e.g. Schnabel, *Korinther*, 431–33; Schrage, *Korinther*, 213–15; Fotopoulos, *Food*, 195–207; Thiselton, *Corinthians*, 611–12).

[98] Gäckle, *Starken*, 243 n.639, reaches a similar conclusion though through a different line of reasoning.

this corresponds exactly with the definition of monotheism covered in the previous chapter. And, as shall be maintained in the following, this relational faith in the one God over against idolatry runs seamlessly into Paul's continuing argument which speaks mainly of the relation between believers and the *risen Lord* over against idolatry.

3. The believer's relation to Christ in Paul's argument

Given the above argument, that Paul emphasises the relational nature of faith in the one God and that the 'necessary knowing' of the true God involves love for God, Nicholson's observation is significant. It comes as a conclusion to an examination of Paul's one-God language :

Paul's conception of the one God is not perfunctory, static, or deemphasized. Rather it is vital, dynamic and integral to Paul's argumentation. Paul's concept of the one God lies at the core of and profoundly influences the rest of his arguments.[99]

It will be maintained that this assertion is entirely appropriate in terms of 1 Corinthians 8:1–10:22. Having set this frame for his forthcoming and rather typical monotheistic response to pagan idolatry, Paul speaks of the relation between risen Lord and believer over against idolatry, and does so using Pentateuchal language concerning the unique relation between Israel and YHWH. This is evident first in 8:6 and 12, and finds more developed expression in 10:4, 9, and 14–22.

3.1. 1 Corinthians 8:6, the Shema*, and Paul's relational Christology*

The way in which 8:6 redeploys the words of the LXX version of Deuteronomy 6:4 has been noted above (cf. p. 83). This argument seeks to now draw attention to three simple matters. First, it is important to note *how* Paul has started to work with his major subtext, Deuteronomy. He will return to Deuteronomic themes and language as his case develops, and it is important to note how he does this at the outset of this argument. He does so, in 8:6, by emphasising the relational aspect, as argued above. What is more, as others have ably demonstrated, the Deuteronomic κύριος is, for Paul, Christ, the risen Lord. By doing this, Fee argues, Paul includes Jesus in the 'divine identity' without absolutely identifying Christ the Lord with God the Father, because the Father alone is the 'God' of the *Shema*. Christ is as Lord, Fee argues, here the YHWH of the

---

[99] Nicholson, "Oneness," 40.

Shema, included in the monotheistic rhetoric of there being *one* God as the *one* Lord.[100]

However, while Fee thus opines that '1 Cor 8:6 ... could well serve as the starting point for any discussion of Pauline Christology',[101] the significance of Paul's argument is underestimated in Fee's thesis (cf. chapter 3 above). So, and second, it needs to be remembered in which frame Paul starts to speak of the relation between believers and Christ in this passage. In a context which emphasises true faith in God as not merely about cognition but as relationship, Paul writes: καὶ εἷς κύριος Ἰησοῦς Χριστὸς δἰ οὗ τὰ πάντα καὶ ἡμεῖς δἰ αὐτοῦ. The relational import of this language has been noted above. While Fee's conclusions are arguably correct, the real significance of Paul's point is not fully appreciated if the relational monotheistic context is missed. By reworking this important *Shema* subtext from Deuteronomy in terms of Christ, and by doing so in light of the contrast between the Corinthian 'knowledge' and true "love for God' in 8:1–3, the following conclusion can be drawn: *Precisely in a context that contrasts the monotheistic 'knowledge' of the Corinthians with the relational 'necessary' monotheistic knowing of love for God, Paul includes Christ directly in this relational dynamic, and does so by employing a text in Deuteronomy that was central to the daily prayer life of Jews and to the relationship between YHWH and Israel.*[102] This theme will be seen to be of major concern for Paul in his developing argument.

Third, and a matter that will again be of crucial importance to Paul's further argument, this loyalty to Christ is expressed in a context involving rhetoric against idolatry. Paul formulates his relation-to-Christ language in 8:6 in

---

[100] Cf. e.g. Fee, *Christology*, 585. Note that the Greek κύριος could be used 'to replace the Tetragrammaton in first century Judaism (or earlier)' (Waaler, *Shema*, 427). Against this, McGrath argues that in 1 Cor. 8:6 'we have before us an expanded Shema rather than a split Shema. In other words, something [i.e., Christ the Lord] has been added on the outside, alongside the Shema, rather than on the inside, into the definition of the nature of God himself' (James F. McGrath, *God*, 42). However, to make this judgment, McGrath overlooks how Christ as Lord is spoken of in the rest of 1 Cor. 8–10, as will be undertaken here. Further, the various parallels he cites, in an attempt to show Christ is alongside, not inside, God's 'nature', are pertinent for him only a result of this mistake. The rest of his argument regarding Paul involves an unconvincing rehash of various other arguments against a Pauline divine-Christology (such as subordination language, Dunn's 'argument from silence' etc.) without due consideration of opposing literature, such as Hurtado's case (Larry W. Hurtado, "Pre-70 C.E. Jewish Opposition to Christ-Devotion," *JTS* 50 [1999]: 35–58; Waaler, *Shema*) against the argument from silence. Further, neither does he appreciate the scale of problematic Pauline texts for his own case, dealing at any length only with 1 Cor. 8:6 and Phil. 2:6–11.

[101] Fee, *Christology*, 88.

[102] This thesis does not pretend to exhaust the richness of 8:6, of course. One could make more of δἰ οὗ τὰ πάντα καὶ ἡμεῖς δἰ αὐτοῦ, but enough has been said for our ends.

light of this concrete matter,[103] i.e., against the threat of capitulation to idola-try.[104] Over against the 'many lords and gods' mentioned in 8:5, Paul stresses loyalty to and love for the one God *and* one Lord. Christians are to love and be committed to *this* Lord (and God), not the idols of the world (8:4–5). Against idolatry, Paul affirms the exclusive loyalty of believers to the Lord of the *Shema*, the Lord Jesus Christ. So Bauckham correctly notes:

> The issue [in 1 Cor. 8–10] is the highly traditional Jewish monotheistic one of loyalty to the only true God in a context of pagan polytheistic worship. What Paul does is to maintain the Jewish monotheistic concern in a Christian interpretation for which loyalty to the only true God entails loyalty to the Lord Jesus Christ.[105]

These three issues discussed above will find explicit development in Paul's argument up until 10:22.

3.2. 1 Corinthians 8:12 and sin against Christ

If Paul's monotheism is love for this one God and one Lord (cf. also 1 Cor. 16:22 where love for Christ is seen as *the* central commitment), then, when Paul argues that 'sinning against your brethren and wounding their conscience when it is weak, you sin against Christ', this shows that true faith in God, over against the 'knowledge' of the Corinthians, has not been understood. Just as Deuteronomy 6's monotheism was susceptible to the destructive power of sin, by 'following other gods' (6:14), by testing YHWH (6:16), just as loyalty to YHWH was always threatened by rebellion, so, Paul's argument shows, is loyalty to Christ, the one Lord of the *Shema*. By sinning against your brothers, you sin against *Christ*.

Most commentators speak of a 'climax'[106] or 'ultimate wrong'[107] in this verse, specifically in the mention of 'sin against Christ'. Siegert has noted that the evaluation of a thing is often, in Paul, according to its consequences, either those desired or, as here, those to be avoided.[108] Hence Paul can adjudicate the flow of his argument in light of this consequence: Christ is sinned against, and such activity that leads to this is thus to be avoided.[109]

---

[103] Garland approvingly notes the work of Denaux who 'cautions that it is dangerous to separate the verse [1 Cor. 8:6] from its immediate context to understand it in terms of Paul's Christology' (Garland, *1 Corinthians*, 377). However, 8:6 speaks volumes about Paul's Christology precisely in its context!

[104] Cf. Matthias Konradt, *Gericht und Gemeinde: eine Studie zur Bedeutung und Funktion von Gerichtsaussagen im Rahmen der paulinischen Ekklesiologie und Ethik im 1 Thess und 1 Kor* (Berlin: W. de Gruyter, 2003), 361, 369, 394.

[105] Bauckham, *God of Israel*, 210.

[106] Thiselton, *Corinthians*, 655.

[107] Fee, *Corinthians*, 389. Cf. also Schreiner, *Paul*, 106.

[108] Folker Siegert, *Argumentation bei Paulus: gezeigt an Röm 9–11*, (Tübingen: Mohr, 1985), 207.

[109] Not that this is the only consequence Paul is concerned about; his main point also concerns the sin against 'the brothers'. Indeed, the two concerns are associated as part of Paul's argument (cf. Eriksson, *Traditions*, 162–64).

That said, not all are agreed as to how one should properly understand εἰς Χριστὸν ἁμαρτάνετε, and Schrage suggests that Paul does not literally mean sin against Christ himself, but rather against the body of Christ, i.e., the church.[110] However, a number of points speak against this. First, why should his premise 'οὕτως at the beginning of the verse ... reveals the sentence as a conclusion of V 11', legitimately lead to the conclusion that 'one should not understand this in the sense of Mt 25:31ff, as if what was done to those who suffer was therefore done to the Christ who is met in the poor brothers'?[111] Second, as Garland correctly writes, noting 1 Corinthians 12:27 ('Now you are the body of Christ'): 'if Paul had intended ... [to say the 'body of Christ' as opposed to simply 'Christ'], he would have said it'.[112] Third, as detailed above, Paul's argument in 8:6 concerns the believer's relation to the risen Lord; it is an intrinsic part of the context. Indeed, relational faith in God (and the Lord), it was argued, is the key behind 8:1–7. To attempt to collapse 8:12 into the 'body of Christ', i.e., the church, is to neglect this contextual clue. Finally, the obviously associated passages in 1 Corinthians 10 (vv. 9, 22) effectively refute Schrage's argument all by themselves. In the immediate context Paul speaks of testing and provoking the Lord, so understanding 8:12 as sin against Christ himself is entirely natural. Fourth, Paul's language in his treatment of abuses of the Lord's Supper, especially in 11:27, lend support to the notion that Paul can conceive of Christ being sinned against.[113]

So if Christ *himself* is the one sinned against, how is one to understand the logic in Paul, that when 'sinning against your brothers ... you sin against Christ'? Almost all major commentaries at least make mention of Matthew 25:45 ('Truly I tell you, just as you did not do it to one of the least of these, you did not do it to me'), and others point out the close association Christ has with the church, his body in order to understand Paul's reasoning.[114] In association with the last point, some mention the Damascus road experience of Paul, as recorded in Acts (e.g., 26:14, 15 – 'Saul, Saul, why are you persecuting me?').[115] Eriksson puts the line of reasoning down to a hidden premise in a section of enthymematic logic, namely that 'Christ and the Christians are united'.[116]

However, while the association of believers with Christ is no doubt involved in the deliberation of this verse, in order to account better for the relational context of Paul's argument another way of understanding Paul's

---

[110] Schrage, *Korinther*, 267.

[111] In terms of the logical structure of the passage, far more persuasive is Eriksson's analysis (Eriksson, *Traditions*, 159–66).

[112] Garland, *1 Corinthians*, 390 n.18.

[113] Cf. Konradt, *Gericht*, 418.

[114] Thiselton develops this point, and also indicates the work of Robinson, who parallels Gal. 4:14 with 1 Cor. 8:12 (Thiselton, *Corinthians*, 655).

[115] Thiselton, *Corinthians*, 655.

[116] Eriksson, *Traditions*, 164.

logic suggests itself, one that has until now remained ignored. Namely, perhaps one should think of the sin against Christ here in terms of a Jewish
understanding of sin against YHWH. As Tate writes in relation to Psalm 51:6,
certain...

> ... OT passages make it clear that from an early time in Israel sins against persons were
> believed to be sins against God ... see 2 Sam 12:9, 10, 13; Gen 39:9; Prov 14:31; 17:5.
> Violation of the commandments of God is construed as sin against God himself.[117]

Even though the Psalm title states that David had committed adultery and
made arrangements for the death of Uriah the Hittite, Bathsheba's husband
(cf. 2 Sam. 11–12), the prayer in Psalm 51 to God was 'Against you, *you
alone*, have I sinned'. In Corinth, while it was clear to Paul that sin was done
to members of the church, it was also a simple and natural reflex to see this
sin automatically as sin against Christ. Thus, Paul expresses, though negatively this time, the nature of the relation between the risen Lord and
believers, using language in such a context that draws from and is understandable in light of the language Jews used to denote an aspect of their relation to
YHWH. In this context it should also be remembered that Paul knew the
Psalms well (even if we cannot be sure of the exact number or canonical status of the Psalms), citing them more than any other OT text, apart from
Isaiah.[118]

This relation and loyalty accented monotheistic thinking, drawing on the
terms and concepts of OT faith yet rethought around not just Christology generally, but relation to Christ, will continue in 1 Corinthians 10 in the language
of 'testing Christ', faithful κοινωνία with him over against the same with
idols/demons, and in the language of the (risen) Lord's jealousy in 10:22.

3.3. 1 Corinthians 10:9 and the Pentateuchal language in 10:6–10 concerning the relation between YHWH and Israel

Paul continues, in 1 Corinthians 10, with this concern for loyalty to the one
true Lord over against idols, in such a way that not only places the relation
between risen Lord and believer at the centre of his focus, but is also explicitly expressed and explained with the concepts and themes that these Jews, in
their scriptures, used to denote the relation between Israel and YHWH. This
argument shall be substantiated with particular reference to 10:9 and 14–22,
but in order to capture the true significance of Paul's words for this thesis, his
language must be understood in the light of the myriad and crucial scriptural
allusions.

In 10:1–5, Paul is at pains to associate the Corinthian believers with the
Israelites ('our ancestors'), who, Paul hints at with his language, enjoyed the
same spiritual blessings as them. This sets the stage for the argument in 10:6–

---

[117] Marvin E. Tate, *Psalms 51–100* (Waco: Word, 1990), 17.

[118] Cf. e.g. the references in James M. Scott, "Restoration of Israel," in *DPL*, eds G.F.
Hawthorne, R.P. Martin, and D.G. Reid (Leicester: IVP, 1993), 800.

11 as 'the persons with whom the readers were encouraged to identify in 10:1–4 turn out to be those who desired evil ..., were idolaters ..., engaged in sexual immorality ...' etc.[119] Paul's strategy in 10:6–11 is to 'heap up' examples from the Pentateuchal narratives in which the exodus group were unfaithful to God and suffered judgment as a consequence.[120] This is sandwiched with the twice repeated hermeneutical statement in 10:6 and 11: 'Now these things occurred as examples for us'.

In each of these verses, a negative trait is established: 10:6 'desire evil (ἐπιθυμητὰς κακῶν) as they did', 10:7 'become idolaters as some of them did', 10:8 'indulge in sexual immorality as some of them did', 10:9 'sorely test Christ[121] as some of them did'[122] and 10:10 'complain as some of them did'. After each of these statements, a clue is given as to which narrative Paul is referring to in the Pentateuchal narratives, and is usually (as in 10:7–10) associated with some sort of judgment. With the majority of commentaries, the narratives Paul probably alluded to are found in the following passages:

– Exodus 32:1–6. Idolatry and sexual immorality, rejection of God as sole God of Israel, and consequent judgment (32:27–28, 35)
– Numbers 11. Complaining before the Lord (11:1), judgment (11:1, 19–20, 33), 'craving' (ἐπεθύμησαν 11:4, 34 LXX) and rejection of YHWH (11:20)
– Numbers 21. Complaining (21:4–5), judgment (21:6 – the serpents) and sinning against YHWH admitted (21:7) – This is referred to in 1 Corinthians 10:9, but the verb ἐκπειράζωμεν (sorely testing [God]) only appears in a Psalmic summary (Ps. 77:18 LXX).
– Numbers 25. Sexual immorality (25:1), idolatry (25:2–3 – the MT speaks of 'gods', whereas Rahlfs' LXX has εἴδωλον in 25:2. There is also repeated mention of θυσία), the Lord's anger and judgment (25:3–9)
– Deuteronomy 1. Grumbling (1:27) and rebellion against God (1:26, 41)
– Some also point out the parallels of 10:6–10 with Psalm 105 (106 LXX),[123] which include 'craving' (v. 14), 'grumbling' (v. 25), putting 'God to the test'(v. 14), provoking God to anger (v. 29), judgment (vv. 15, 17–18, 26–27, 29), idolatry (vv. 19–20, 28, 36), rejecting and forgetting God (vv. 13, 21).

---

[119] J. Paul Sampley, "The First Letter to the Corinthians. Introduction, Commentary, and Reflections," in The New Interpreter's Bible, ed. L. E. Keck, et al. (Nashville: Abington, 2002), 913.

[120] Hays, First Corinthians, 165.

[121] The reading 'Christ' over 'Lord' is preferred by almost all modern commentators. Cf. especially Garland, 1 Corinthians, 470–71; Thiselton, Corinthians, 740; Schnabel, Korinther, 524, and the literature they cite. 'Christ' is both the best attested and arguably the most difficult reading.

[122] This is Garland's translation (Garland, 1 Corinthians, 463), and one that better brings out the intensive prepositional ἐκ- than simply 'putting ... to the test' (e.g. NRSV).

[123] Garland, 1 Corinthians, 464.

These Pentateuchal texts all tell various stories about the relation between Israel and YHWH, how it went wrong and the consequences of the breakdown of this relation (judgment). Paul is naturally not simply reciting stories but has his eye on the situation at Corinth. So he writes: 'Now these things occurred as examples for us, so that we might not desire evil as they did (10:6) ... Do not become idolaters as some of them did (10:7) ... We must not indulge in sexual immorality (10:8) ... We must not sorely test Christ (10:9) ... And do not complain as some of them did (10:10)', finishing with the words: 'These things happened to them to serve as an example, and they were written down to instruct us, on whom the ends of the ages have come' (10:11). Scholars have been quick to point out how these points could reflect the temptations experienced by Christians in Corinth.[124] However, the simple point to be made here does not necessitate the repetition of the various associated debates. Paul, with these scriptural allusions and his explicit hermeneutical motive, is attempting to associate the themes involved in the experience of Israel's relation to YHWH in the Pentateuchal narratives, with the experience of the Christians in Corinth.

However, he does this in the service of speaking about the Corinthian believers' relation to *Christ*, the Lord of the 8:6 reworked *Shema*. This is seen in two ways. First, Paul associates the experience of the wilderness genera-tion, 'our ancestors' (10:1), with Christ: 'For they drank from the spiritual rock that followed them, *and the rock was Christ*' (10:4), and 'we must not sorely test Christ, *as some of them did* (καθώς τινες αὐτῶν ἐπείρασαν)' (10:9). Second, again in 10:9, Paul directly associates an event from a Pentateuchal narrative, with vocabulary mediated via a Psalmic summary, with the Corin-thians experience of relation to Christ, i.e. '*We* must not sorely test *Christ*'. Paul, thus, associates the relation between Israel and YHWH in the Penta-teuchal narratives with the relation between the risen Lord and believers in Corinth.

Whether, with Meeks, Exodus 32:6 is the midrashic basis upon which verses 1–13 are built,[125] or whether, with Hays, Paul works mainly with narra-tives in Numbers,[126] it is difficult to say. Paul simply conveys a complex of interrelated themes he knows is evidenced in the Pentateuchal narratives and in the Psalmic summaries of them, and sets them in the service of denoting, with the purpose of educating, the relation between risen Lord and believers in Corinth. In 10:1–13, Paul is focusing upon the necessary loyalty of Christians to the risen Lord, over against the evil desires, idolatry, testing of Christ and sin mentioned in 10:6–10.

---

[124] Cf. the references in Garland, *1 Corinthians*, 460.

[125] Cf. both the summary in Richard B. Hays, *Echoes of Scripture in the Letters of Paul* (New Haven: Yale University Press, 1989), 92, and C. Marvin Pate, *The Reverse of the Curse: Paul, Wisdom, and the Law* (Tübingen: Mohr Siebeck, 2000), 303.

[126] Hays, *Echoes*, 92.

3.4. 1 Corinthians 10:14–21 and fellowship with Christ over against idolatry

The temptation to see 10:14–22 as a separate pericope needs to be resisted, as 'it continues to draw out the immediate practical consequences of the wilderness story'.[127] First, 10:14–21 shall be analysed, followed by an examination of 10:22.

Hays provides a lucid summary of the verses up to 10:21: having appealed to the Corinthians as 'sensible' people, Paul 'holds up for comparison meals of three types: the Lord's Supper (vv. 16–17), Jewish meals in conjunction with sacrifice (v. 18), and meals at the table of a pagan god (v. 19–21)'.[128] What, however, is Paul doing by making these comparisons? Such a question is best addressed by first asking what these comparisons have in common. As Hays answers: 'Each meal creates a relation of *koinônia*'.[129] Κοινωνία and the verb μετέχειν, are the key to this passage.[130] But this raises another question which shall have to be addressed first: what does κοινωνία mean?

The basic meaning of κοινωνία is 'the communion with someone by communally partaking in something'.[131] Yet in the Septuagint the term is never used to denote the communion between God and humans.[132] So some deny that the term has any 'vertical' import in Paul's argument and affirm only that a social or horizontal communion is implied between the worshippers.[133] Others emphasise the ecclesial import of 10:17, and read 10:16 in such a light.[134]

However, a number of points speak convincingly in favour of a vertical dimension, even if the horizontal remains,[135] especially given the likely horizontal implication of 10:17. First, Gäckle argues that Paul has adopted the Hellenistic cultic usage of the word, which certainly assumed a fellowship between the god(s) and the worshipper. Paul did this, he maintains, 'to approximate the Corinthian's horizon of understanding'.[136] Indeed, the paral-

---

[127] Hays, *First Corinthians*, 166, contra e.g., Sampley, "1 Corinthians," 917. Thiselton suggests that the 'theme of covenant clearly provides the thematic link between 10:1-13 and 10:14–22' (Thiselton, *Corinthians*, 750). Cf. also the rhetorical study of Eriksson, *Traditions*, 166–72 which understands 10:1–22 as a whole to form the second *refutatio*. Schnabel, *Korinther*, 547, notes that the conjunction διόπερ links the two sections.

[128] Hays, *First Corinthians*, 167.

[129] Ibid.

[130] This is emphasised by almost all modern commentaries and monographs. But cf. especially Thiselton, *Corinthians*, 776, and the sophisticated rhetorical analysis in Eriksson, *Traditions*, 166–72.

[131] My translation of Hainz, cited in Gäckle, *Starken*, 267; Schnabel, *Korinther*, 550.

[132] Cf. Willis, *Meat*, 174.

[133] While not simply relying on lexical studies but an examination of Paul's context, Willis affirms the horizontal interpretation (Willis, *Meat*, e.g. 188, 197–212). Also, with qualification, cf. Fee, *Corinthians*, 466. In his more recent work, Fee stresses his qualifications even more (Fee, *Christology*, 122).

[134] So, with qualification, Woyke, *Götter*, 242.

[135] Witherington, *Conflict*, 225; Thiselton, *Corinthians*, 761- 62.

[136] Gäckle, *Starken*, 267, translation mine.

lelism in Paul's argument between the Christian κοινωνία and that in pagan idolatry is the decisive point, for Gäckle, that affirms a vertical meaning for κοινωνία in 1 Corinthians 10.[137] This reasoning can be disputed, for while it is of course possible that Paul was aware of the possible meanings of κοινωνία in pagan cultic culture, one cannot be sure.[138] Yet Paul was certainly aware of the associations involved with the κοινωνοὶ τοῦ θυσιαστηρίου of Israel according to the flesh (10:18). In this context Paul would have known the important vertical dimension in Israel's sacrifices. The Psalms indicate involvement in the Temple cult as *a communal meeting with God*, not just as membership in a saved community (so Pss. 27:4; 50:9–15; 63:2–5. Cf. also 1 Kgs. 8:12–13 – and the many other Psalms that were used in the Temple).[139] Even Woyke, who emphasises the horizontal aspect of the κοινωνοὶ τοῦ θυσιαστηρίου in his nuanced treatment of 10:16–20,[140] and who tends to flatten the soteriological aspect of the κοινωνία into another way of defining the significance of the ecclesiological aspect, does not ultimately deny the vertical implications.[141] And rightly so. If Paul knew the subtleties involved in pagan temple terminology, it would simply have affirmed what he knew about the Jerusalem Temple sacrifices.

Second, the synonymity of κοινωνία with μετέχειν in this passage also speaks for a vertical participation, especially given the participatory implications of μετέχειν in 10:17 and 21.[142]

Third, a horizontal aspect is perhaps entirely absent from 10:16 and only explicitly surfaces in the following verse. An ecclesiological interpretation of σῶμα in 10:17 should not be read back into 10:16. The close connection, in 10:16, between Christ's body and Christ's *blood* excludes it.[143]

Fourth, in 1 Corinthians 10 there is a complex of associated themes that speak for a vertical dimension. So, associated with the abuse of the Lord's Supper in 1 Corinthians 11:17–34 are two important factors, namely the judgment-bringing presence of Christ (11:27–32) and the covenantal nature of the meal (11:25). Precisely the same themes find expression at the end of this letter, in 16:22, where Paul uses the language of curse in terms of those who 'have no love for the Lord'. In other words, and to adopt the language used in this discussion, vertical relation to Christ is central to faithfulness to the cove-

---

[137] Ibid., 268.

[138] Woyke, *Götter*, e.g. 256.

[139] Cf. for some of the above references, and many more besides, Brueggemann, *Theology*, 650–79.

[140] Woyke, *Götter*, 245–47.

[141] Ibid., 247.

[142] Cf. Gäckle, *Starken*, 267; Schnabel, *Korinther*, 550; Schrage, *Korinther*, 437; Garland, *1 Corinthians*, 477; Hans Conzelmann, *Der erste Brief an die Korinther* (Göttingen: Vandenhoeck & Ruprecht, 1969), 205; Thiselton, *Corinthians*, 776.

[143] Gäckle, *Starken*, 268 n. 743; Schnabel, *Korinther*, 550–51; Schrage, *Korinther*, 439–40.

nant, celebrated in the Lord's Supper. And those who abuse it stand before the judging presence of Christ. Vertical relationship with Christ is likewise naturally a part of the Christian κοινωνία.

These themes also overlap in 10:14–22, drawing as it does from the same overlap of themes in the Pentateuch. As shall be seen, 10:22 echoes language from Deuteronomy 6:

[14] Do not follow other gods, any of the gods of the peoples who are all around you, [15] because the LORD your God, who is present with you, is a jealous God. The anger of the LORD your God would be kindled against you and he would destroy you from the face of the earth. [16] Do not put the LORD your God to the test, as you tested him at Massah (Deut. 6:14–16, NRSV)

The rhetoric against idolatry in this verse is followed by a stern warning about the jealousy (ζηλωτής) of the God who is *present with you* (ἐν σοί). The obvious overlap of themes with 10:19–22 is clear, as is the testing of God (ἐκπειράζω) in Deuteronomy 6:16 with the testing of Christ (ἐκπειράζω) in 10:9, as seen above. It is not going too far, then, to argue with Hurtado that Jesus, in the Lord's Supper, 'is perceived as the living and powerful *Kyrios* who owns the meal and presides at it, and with whom believers have fellowship as with a god'.[144] Therefore, '[w]riters from Seesemann and Thornton to Hainz and Smit' were correct to 'have insisted that the "vertical" or theological dimension of *sharing in Christ* constitutes the foundation for the derivative "horizontal" or socioecclesial dimension of "fellowship" in a group'.[145] This is not to imply that κοινωνία be understood as two 'directions' or dimensions artificially merged. To be in covenant commitment to the risen Lord is to be a part of the community covenanted to this Lord.[146]

With justification, then, Schnabel can summarise Paul's argument in these verses with the words: 'Loyalty to Jesus Christ excludes loyalty to the "gods"',[147] because Paul can argue that when one eats idol meat with pagan friends, '[o]ne is not merely eating with friends at the pagan temples', but, through the κοινωνία created between the members and the idol, 'one is engaged in idolatry'.[148] Comparisons of κοινωνία are thus made in order to draw a contrast, not between types of food and drink, but 'with the different lords at the meal, demonic lords versus the Lord Christ'.[149] Garland can thus correctly argue, in relation to 10:16–17, that the 'Lord's Supper forges a unique *relationship between believer and Christ* that excludes participation in

---

[144] Hurtado, *LJC*, 146. Cf. also recently Fee, *Christology*, 132–33.

[145] Thiselton, *Corinthians*, 750–51, italics his. Cf. also 751 n.2., and pp. 103–5. Cf. also Thomas Söding, "Ekklesia und Koinonia: Grundbegriffe paulinischer Ekklesiologie," *Catholica* 57, no. 2 (2003): 107–23; Konradt, *Gericht*, 419; Hays, *First Corinthians*, 167.

[146] Cf. the discussion in Eriksson, *Traditions*, 168–69 and Thiselton, *Corinthians*, 750–51. Cf. also Wright's analysis of κοινωνία in relation to Philem. 6 in N.T. Wright, *Climax*, 52.

[147] Schnabel, *Korinther*, 545, translation mine.

[148] Fee, *Corinthians*, 473. Cf. also Garland, *1 Corinthians*, 473.

[149] Garland, *1 Corinthians*, 482.

all other sacral meals at which food is consumed in the presence of the deity'.[150] As noted above, given the association between 'blood' and 'covenant' (1 Cor. 11:25. But also cf. Exod. 24:8; Ezek. 44:7; Zech. 9:11; Mt. 26:28; Mk. 14:24; Lk. 22:20; Heb. 9:18, 20; 10:29; 12:24; 13:20), one can appropriately speak of the covenantal nature of this loyalty in 1 Corinthians 10 over against idolatry.[151] Covenant loyalty to this Lord is what stands in contrast to pagan idolatry in 10:14–21.

Naturally, given the implicit premise in this argumentation – that people can be in κοινωνία with respect to idols – these comparisons raise the question again, which Paul must address: 'What do I imply then? That food sacrificed to idols is anything, or that an idol is anything?' It is for this reason that Paul now associates such idols with demons (10:19–20), which leads, to use the words of Thiselton, to the logical, empirical and institutional *cannot* in 10:21.[152] Paul asserts an utter division between the Lord and these idols/demons, and an absolute separation of the believer from associating with this demon idolatry:[153] 'I do not want you to be partners [κοινωνός] with demons. You cannot drink the cup of the Lord and the cup of demons' (10:20b–21a).

In mentioning δαιμόνιον in this context, Paul is 'directly alluding' to a Greek version of Deuteronomy 32:17.[154] The context of this passage indicates that the demons are strange/foreign/other gods (32:8, 16, 17, 12, 37) and idols (32:21). Yet Paul's relational monotheism, as first detailed in 1 Corinthians 8:1–3, 6, is here spoken of in terms of Christ. Indeed, in developing an argument in terms of the Christian sacraments, Paul is specifically anchoring faith to *Christ*.[155] Paul's relational understanding of faith in God, in contradistinction to idolatry and κοινωνοὺς τῶν δαιμονίων, here finds expression in terms of the κοινωνία with Christ in the Lord's Supper. Thiselton has maintained, the theme of covenantal[156] loyalty expressed in 10:1–13 is continued in 10:14–22,[157] and in the latter finds expression in the κοινωνία and μετέχειν language.[158] Κοινωνία with respect to Christ in the κυριακὸν δεῖπνον becomes the expression of covenant loyalty, of monotheistic loyalty without idolatry.

---

[150] Ibid., 477, italics mine.

[151] Following the rhetorical analysis of Eriksson, one can identify 10:14 ('flee from the worship of idols') as the theme of 10:14–22 (Eriksson, *Traditions*, 167).

[152] Thiselton, *Corinthians*, 776.

[153] Concerning the ontology of the δαιμόνιον, cf. the debate between Woyke, *Götter*, 158–257; Woyke, "Bekenntnis", and Gäckle, *Starken*, e.g. 230–39.

[154] Woyke, "Bekenntnis," 238; Watson, *Paul*, 445–46; Fee, *Christology*, 132.

[155] Thiselton, *Corinthians*, 737.

[156] For more on the covenantal language in 1 Cor. 10:1–22, cf. C. Marvin Pate, *Reverse*, 303f.

[157] Thiselton, *Corinthians*, 750.

[158] Cf. also Eriksson, *Traditions*, 168–69, and the literature he cites.

3.5. 1 Corinthians 10:22 and the consequence of idolatry in Pentateuchal language

Just as in the Deuteronomic passages where idolatry was strongly pitted against commitment to and love for the one God, YHWH, Paul also absolutely contrasts idolatry against commitment to Christ. Just as the people of Israel, the covenant people who threatened to provoke God's anger by betraying their commitment to God with idolatry, the Christians in Corinth were also in danger of the same sins as detailed in the Pentateuchal narratives (cf. also 10:1–13 and the analysis of these verses above).[159] This is why, in 10:22, Paul finishes the section with the warning: 'What! do we intend to rouse the Lord's jealousy? Are we stronger than he?'[160]

Above, it has already been implied that the κύριος of 10:22 is Christ. Indeed, while some commentators lapse into speaking of *God's* jealousy coming to expression in 10:22,[161] this is not what the text says. Rather, κύριος in 10:22, as Bell writes, 'almost certainly refers to Christ'.[162] Both Fee and Bell, who take time to justify a christological referent of the κύριος of 10:22, see the christological κύριος in the previous verse as decisive.[163] Certainly, the immediate context of concern with the believers' κοινωνία with Christ would overwhelmingly support this case. It is the Lord they are not faithfully in κοινωνία with who is provoked. The κύριος is Christ.

Once again Paul draws his language here from the Pentateuch. Bell proposes that Paul, in 1 Corinthians 10:22, 'alludes to [Deut.] 32.21a'.[164] Given the repetition of παραζηλόω in 10:22 from Deuteronomy 32:21 (the only place it is used in the Pentateuch, at least according to Rahlfs' Septuagint), and given the direct allusion to Deuteronomy 32:17 just two verses earlier (in 1 Cor. 10:20), this interpretation seems likely.

---

[159] This is a matter that speaks against Nanos' intriguing thesis that the weak were polytheist non-Christ-believers (Nanos, "Polytheist"), as does Paul's consistent use of ἀδελφός in the Corinthian correspondence to denote Christ-believers, a title Paul gives the 'weak' in 8:11–12.

[160] This translation, especially as it follows a series of sharp contrasts in the previous verses, arguably expresses the force of ἢ παραζηλοῦμεν better than is customary among translators who render the Greek in English as a simple question. So James Moffatt, *The First Epistle of Paul to the Corinthians* (London: Hodder & Stoughton, 1938), 134; and Thiselton, *Corinthians*, 777.

[161] E.g. Garland, *1 Corinthians*, 447, 482; Fee, *Corinthians*, 474; Thiselton, *Corinthians*, 779; Fitzmyer, *First Corinthians*, 394. This same phenomenon of automatically reading texts theologically rather than christologically is also seen in commentaries in relation to 10:9. Cf. e.g. Thiselton, *Corinthians*, 741; Hays, *First Corinthians*, 165.

[162] Richard H. Bell, *Provoked to Jealousy: The Origin and Purpose of the Jealousy Motif in Romans 9–11* (Tübingen: Mohr Siebeck, 1994), 254.

[163] Fee, *Corinthians*, 474 n.57; Fee, *Christology*, 133.

[164] Bell, *Jealousy*, 253. His assessment, in relation to 10:22, is followed by many, e.g. Thiselton, *Corinthians*, 778; Bauckham, "Monotheism," 222; Fee, *Corinthians*, 474; Fee, *Christology*, 133.

However, it is important to note that, in using this language, Paul is reflecting a familiar complex of interrelated themes found in the OT. A similar list of themes common in the Pentateuchal narratives was presented above on p. 95, in relation to 10:6–11. Comparable themes are associated with the narratives mentioning God's jealousy. For example, the allusion suggested by Bell contains a number of themes: God's jealousy because of Israel's hankering after idols (Deut. 32:16–17, 19, 21), neglect of YHWH (32:18), the resultant judgment of God on idol worship (32:19–20, 21b–22 etc), and provocation of God by this idol worship (32:21). Further, in Deuteronomy 6, loyalty to the one God (Deut. 6:4), and warnings not to 'follow other gods [... because God], who is present with you, is a jealous God' (6:14–15), is immediately followed by 'Do not put the LORD your God to the test (6:16), as noted above. Garland helpfully reports the words of Rosner, who claims: 'All Pentateuchal references to God's jealousy have to do with idol-worship'.[165] Indeed, Rosner's suggestion accords well with the causes of God's jealousy in the OT, namely when God's special relationship with Israel is shared with other gods.[166]

The themes within these narratives are reflected in Paul's language in 1 Corinthians 10:14–22. In associating with idols, the Corinthian believers are provoking their Lord Jesus, to whom they are covenanted and in fellowship with, to jealousy (10:22). By mixing the κοινωνία of Christ with partnership with demons, Paul claims that Corinthian Christians provoke the risen Christ to jealousy. Paul 'takes very seriously the Jewish understanding of monolatry as required by God's jealous desire for the sole devotion of his covenant people',[167] and rethinks this around the believers' relation to Christ. Henceforth, beyond the specification of this or that OT source verse, it is most significant that the conceptual themes are interrelated in *both* the OT texts and in Paul.

This complex of interrelated themes also explains the point behind Paul's second rhetorical question in 10:22, 'Are we stronger than he?' Just as Paul has understood the interrelated scriptural themes describing the relation between YHWH and Israel in terms of the relation between believers and Christ, so God's judgment-bringing presence and power is the conceptual background for the judgment-bringing presence of Christ in 10:22. The strength of the Lord is, as Garland writes, 'an implicit threat'.[168] It is the risen Lord's judging presence of which they need to beware.[169] As seen above, by associating with idols and provoking YHWH to anger, the Israelites in these Pentateuchal and Psalmic narratives then suffer the threat and execution of divine judgment. So Paul understands the relation between Israel and YHWH as now finding its reflection in the believer's relation to Christ. This line of

---

[165] Garland, *1 Corinthians*, 483.
[166] Cf. the discussion in Schnabel, *Korinther*, 560.
[167] Bauckham, "Monotheism," 222.
[168] Garland, *1 Corinthians*, 483.
[169] Cf. Konradt, *Gericht*, 394; Schnabel, *Korinther*, 560–61, etc.

thinking will, in Paul's next chapter, be made explicit. In 1 Corinthians 11:29–32 Paul writes that, because of abuses associated with the Lord's Supper, 'many of you are weak and ill, and some have died' (11:20).

Suggestively, Bauckham writes, after discussing the possible Deuteronomy 32 allusion in 10:22, that: 'God's jealousy is closely connected with the Shema'',[170] and that 'Paul has already prepared for his christological appropriation of the themes of monolatry and jealousy [in 10:22] by means of his reformulation of the Shema' in 8:6'.[171] Part of the point of this chapter has been to explore this dynamic throughout 1 Corinthians 8–10. So Paul's Lord 'Jesus Christ' of the *Shema*, the Lord the Corinthians can 'sorely test' (10:9) and can sin against (8:12), is also the jealous Lord of 10:22 who can be provoked by unfaithfulness (idol worship) to acts of judgment. As noted above, an almost exact replication of ideas is found in Deuteronomy 6, an allusion to which was present at the start of Paul's argument (in 8:6). Thus entirely justifiably, Hays insists that Paul's monotheism, in 1 Corinthians 10, climaxing in 10:22, is not 'some abstract principle that sets us free from polytheistic superstition. The God with whom we have to do is the God of Israel, a jealous God'.[172] However, as we have seen, where Hays (significantly!) speaks of God, Paul writes of the risen Lord.

All of the above makes it abundantly clear that the allusions Paul makes to the scriptural narratives are not to be understood as isolated appropriations of this or that particle of God-language. Paul's entire argument, in relation to what Eriksson labels the first finite question. (8:1–13; 10:1–22), has involved, in ways sometimes central to the matter, a consistent appropriation of the language and interrelated themes used to denote the relation between Israel and YHWH, in the service of explaining and indicating the relation between Christ and Christians.

4. Conclusion

Arguably, scholarship involved in the Pauline Christology debate has failed to give due consideration to the broader issues and interrelated themes in Paul's discussion on idol food. Indeed, it would seem that the sort of 'knowledge' which Paul sought to correct with the necessary knowing of relational faith in God, if Gäckle is correct, is ironically that which has spellbound scholarship, with its focus on the 8:6 formulation, together with its prepositions and possible hints at the pre-existence of Christ as Wisdom.

In light of 1 Corinthians 8:1–7, it has been maintained that Paul's Christ-language is best understood in the context of an acknowledgement of Paul's

---

[170] Bauckham, "Monotheism," 222.

[171] Bauckham, "Monotheism," 223. Cf. also Conzelmann, *Korinther*, 206.

[172] Hays, *First Corinthians*, 159.

relational and commitment orientated monotheism. Once framed in this way, the significance of Paul's constant recourse to the relation between risen Lord and believers over against idolatry can be grasped. Paul repeatedly refers to the believers' commitment and relation to Christ, and does so using language and categories drawn from the complex of interrelated themes and concepts that describe the relation of Jewish believers with YHWH over against idolatry, sin, and judgment. The God to whom Jews owe covenant allegiance, and the stories told and retold in the scriptural narratives that affirm, express and explain this relation with all of its thematic interrelations, are retold, by Paul, and rethought around the relation between risen Lord and Christians, in such a way that evidences the same sort of thematic interrelations found in those scriptural stories to which Paul so often alludes.[173] The uniqueness of God in Deuteronomy, MacDonald urges, should not be separated from the relationship between God and his covenant people. Likewise the significance of Paul's Christ-language should not be separated from the relation between risen Lord and believers, especially when it is framed in terms of this relationally accented faith in God's uniqueness. As an examination of the relation between risen Lord and believers has shed light on Paul's language in 1 Corinthians 8–10, the complex of interrelated themes and language in Paul's undisputed letters concerning this relation need to be examined more extensively before christological conclusions can be drawn. The following three chapters of this thesis will be devoted to just that task.

---

[173] To be noted is that Paul's hermeneutic here is probably neither christocentric (so Moisés Silva, "Old Testament in Paul," in *DPL*, eds G.F. Hawthorne, R.P. Martin, and D.G. Reid [Leicester: IVP, 1993], 630–42), ecclesiocentric (so Hays, *Echoes*, 84, 86), nor simply soteriological without qualification (so Watson, *Paul*, 19). It involves both Christ and the church, in relationship.

Chapter 6

The Christ-relation in Paul's undisputed letters

1. Introduction

The above exegesis of 1 Corinthians 8:1–10:22 indicates that a focus on the relation between the risen Lord and believers could play an important part in determining whether one should speak of a Pauline divine-Christology. It will now be seen that this relation manifests itself, in Paul's undisputed letters, in various ways. It will be maintained that it is reflected in Paul's Christ-shaped aims, goals and motivations, in a variety of direct devotional language and practices, in the passionate nature of this devotion, in what Paul contrasts with this devotion, in the presence and activity of the risen Lord, yet also in the absence of this Lord, in communication between the risen Christ and believers, and in the nature and character of his risen lordship. These categories, formed on the basis of an inductive study of the letters, will be explored deductively by gathering data under the relevant subheadings from the undisputed letters, in canonical order. There is no space for a detailed examination of all data, yet this chapter does not seek to focus on only a few passages. Indeed, the method of focusing only on 'key' verses has arguably fed a neglect of wider and interrelated themes in Paul's christological rhetoric. We will heed Schlatter, and attempt first to see what is 'right in front of our eyes',[1] and so this chapter rather aims to uncover the *breadth* of relevant material, generating a cumulative case. This is to say, we will not proceed "vertically",[2] breaking the primary text up into small pieces (beyond employing general subheadings), following this with immediate conclusions drawn from heavily annotated exegesis. Instead, we will emphasise the overarching construal of Paul's language. In this way, not only will patterns of data be clarified, but also their relative importance and internal relationships in Paul's theology. This method will thus arguably facilitate a better grasp of the breadth *and* significance of the relevant Pauline material.[3] This chapter will consequently demand much from its readers as it attempts an "horizontal" kind of analysis, one which gathers Pauline data and refuses summary until the conclusion of the chapter.

---

[1] Cited in Schreiner, *Paul*, 16. See chapter 1, p.5 above.

[2] I use Campbell's language here, summarised in chapter 1, n.10.

[3] Of course, where exegetical certainty is impossible within the space restraints, the conclusions will remain tentative. The point is to grasp important patterns in Paul's letters.

2. Paul's Christ-shaped goals and motivations

In Romans 1:5 Paul states that he has received grace and apostleship through Christ 'to bring about the obedience of faith among all the Gentiles'. The reason for this is then stated: it is done 'for the sake of his [i.e., Christ's] name'. To a certain extent this would appear to function as the opposite of that expressed in 2:24, that 'the name of God is blasphemed among the Gentiles because of you'. Later in Romans, in 14:9, Paul writes: 'For to this end Christ died and lived again, so that he might be Lord of both the dead and the living'. In Romans 9:1–4 it could be argued that Paul's ultimate concern was not for Christ but Israel ('I could wish that I myself were accursed and cut off from Christ for the sake of my own people').[4] However, not only is this exceptional language, but the text conceptually echoes Exodus 32:32, where Moses asks God to blot him out of the 'book' if YHWH does not forgive Israel.[5] Paul was thus not necessarily concerned about Israel more than Christ any more than Moses was concerned about Israel more than YHWH. In Romans, then, Paul's goals and motivations are found in his mission 'for the sake' of Christ, and in the claim that the end of Christ's death and resurrection, the goal of it all, is that Christ be Lord of the living and dead.

Turning to 1 Corinthians, in 6:13 Paul states that the purpose of the body is 'for the Lord' as the Lord is 'for the body'. What the latter phrase means need not here detain us, but the former requires some elaboration. As is generally recognised, the σῶμα is more than Bultmann projected, namely 'man is *soma* when he is objectivized in relation to himself by becoming the object of his own thought, attitude, or conduct'.[6] Rather, if Käsemann is correct, with his insistence on a correlation between the 'body of Christ' (the church) and the human body, then the σῶμα 'signifies man in his worldhood and therefore in his ability to communicate [i.e., in his relationality]'.[7] Thus, when Paul writes that the σῶμα is 'for the Lord' he indicates that the believer in his/her entire communal physicality is 'for the Lord'.[8]

The purpose of Paul's advice for the unmarried, in 1 Corinthians 7, is spelt out in a number of ways in 1 Corinthians 7:32–35. Yet in 7:35 Paul sums up the main aim. He advises 'with a view to promoting that which is appropriate

---

[4] Käsemann, *Romans*, 258.

[5] James D.G. Dunn, *Romans* (Waco: Word, 1988), 525; Robert Jewett, *Romans: A Commentary* (Minneapolis: Fortress, 2007), 560; Peter Stuhlmacher, *Paul's Letter to the Romans*, reprint, German original 1989 (Edinburgh: T&T Clark, 1994), 145; Ben Witherington, III and Darlene Hyatt, *Paul's Letter to the Romans: A Socio-Rhetorical Commentary* (Grand Rapids: Eerdmans, 2004), 250; Thomas R. Schreiner, *Romans* (Grand Rapids: Baker, 1998), 480; Moo, *Romans*, 558–59, esp. n.21.

[6] Rudolf Bultmann, *Theology of the New Testament* (London: SCM, 1952), 1.202–3.

[7] Thiselton, *Corinthians*, 464. Cf. E. Käsemann, *Perspectives on Paul* (London: SCM, 1971), 114; and Fee, *Corinthians*, 256 n.32.

[8] Garland, *1 Corinthians*, 238; Thiselton, *Corinthians*, 591, 1276–280.

and facilitates undistracted devotion to the Lord'. This reflects the expressed desirables in 7:32–34, that the unmarried man/woman is 'anxious about the things of the Lord, how to please to the Lord' (7:32, 34).[9] As has been argued by Siegert, in relation to Paul's argumentation, the Apostle often evaluates things based on consequence,[10] and in this way he ends his argument in 7:35: 'This, I say (τοῦτο ... λέγω)', writes Paul, 'with a view to' (πρὸς τό) unhindered devotion to Christ. That is the purpose and goal of his instruction.

In 2 Corinthians 4:5–11 Christ is presented as the reason and motivation for Paul's endurance of much suffering, and for the nature of his mission to the Corinthians. So Paul writes: 'we proclaim Jesus Christ as Lord and ourselves as your slaves for Jesus' sake' (4:5). Though afflicted in every way (4:8), carrying in the body 'the death of Jesus', they do this *so that* 'the life of Jesus may also be made visible in our bodies'. He continues, 'For while we live, we are always being given up to death for Jesus' sake [διὰ Ἰησοῦν[11]], so that the life of Jesus may be made visible in our mortal flesh' (4:10–11).[12]

Paul's missionary motivations are made more explicit later in 2 Corinthians. Paul states, in 5:9, that 'we make it our aim to please him [Christ]'. Further, he aims to please Christ because 'all of us must appear before the judgement seat of Christ' (5:10). This, in turn, generates another missionary motivation: 'knowing the fear of the Lord, we try to persuade others'.[13] That this 'Lord' is Christ is made clear by the οὖν of 5:11, which connects the mentioned 'fear of the Lord' most obviously with the judgment seat of Christ in 5:10 – a point accepted by the vast majority of scholars.[14] In 5:14 still another

---

[9] This translation of material in 7:32–35 will be discussed below. Cf. also Fee, *Corinthians*, 347.

[10] Siegert, *Argumentation*, 206–9, and cf. the summary in Ian W. Scott, *Epistemology*, 6 n.4.

[11] Thrall discusses the textual variant, διὰ Ἰησοῦ, and notes that διὰ Ἰησοῦν is the most likely reading given the repetition of the phrase in 4:11, and the likelihood that the final letter was simply accidentally omitted, creating the genitive variant (Margaret E. Thrall, *The Second Epistle to the Corinthians Vol. 1* [London: T&T Clark, 2004], 314 n.859).

[12] Stegman, in relation to 2 Cor. 4:11, writes:
'The preposition διά + accusative signifies the reason something exists or the reason something results. It is usually translated "for the sake of" or "because of". I propose that both renderings apply here, but in a special way. Paul undergoes being handed over *for the sake of Jesus*, that is, in loyalty and service to the one whose apostle (2 Cor 1:1) and slave (Phil 1:1) he is. In addition, he is handed over *because of* Jesus' (Thomas Stegman, *The Character of Jesus: The Linchpin to Paul's Argument in 2 Corinthians* [Roma: Ed. Pontif. Ist. Biblico, 2005], 150, italics his).

[13] Paul 'attributes ... judgment to Christ, the Lord whom he strives to please *for that very reason*' (Fee, *Christology*, 572, italics mine).

[14] Contra Victor P. Furnish, *II Corinthians*, AB (New York: Doubleday, 1984), 306, as noted in Fatehi, *Relation*, 14 n.37. Cf. also Thrall, *2 Corinthians Vol. 1*, 401; Rudolf Bultmann, *Der zweite Brief an die Korinther* (Göttingen: Vandenhoeck & Ruprecht, 1976), 147; Harris, *Second Epistle*, 412; C.K. Barrett, *The Second Epistle to the Corinthians* (London: Black, 1973), 163; Paul Barnett, *The Second Epistle to the*

Christ-related motivation is evident: the love of Christ, Paul says, 'urges us on' in mission.[15]

In 2 Corinthians 8:19, Paul speaks of administering the 'generous undertaking' of the collection for the poor in the Jerusalem church by supplying the following reasons: 'for the glory of the Lord himself and to show our goodwill'. That the Lord here refers to Christ is made very likely for three contextual reasons. First, within the same argument, Paul speaks a few verses earlier of 'the generous act of our Lord Jesus Christ' (8:9). Second, in 8:16 Paul plainly speaks of God (the Father), without usage of the title 'Lord'. Third, and more importantly, in 8:23 Paul writes of the 'glory of Christ'. Those who think 'Lord' here refers to God do not attend to these contextual matters.[16] Harris understands the preposition πρός in 8:19 as telic in meaning – 'for the purpose of'.[17] Certainly, Paul's motivations and goals sit very closely together in this verse. Even though Harris emphasises the teleological nature of the passage, he appropriately slips back (unconsciously?) to talk of Paul's reasons and motivations, arguing that '[t]he emphatic αὐτοῦ ... occurring between two instances of ἡμῶν, draws attention to the fact that his motivation was not self-centred; it was desire for the Lord's own glory that impelled his action'.[18] The glory of the Lord was probably Paul's more dominant motivation of the two he mentioned,[19] as implied by the emphatic αὐτοῦ.[20]

Dunn argues, referring to the term δοξάζω, that '[f]or Paul, properly speaking, only God [not Christ] is to be glorified'.[21] He notes the references to the 'glory of Christ' in a footnote adding that they 'are to be taken either as anticipations of the final glory of God or in terms of Christ manifesting what of God is perceptible to human sight'.[22] However, it is difficult to understand

---

Corinthians (Grand Rapids: Eerdmans, 1997), 279; Jan Lambrecht, *Second Corinthians* (Collegeville: Liturgical Press, 1998), 91; Franz Zeilinger, *Krieg und Friede in Korinth: Kommentar zum 2. Korintherbrief des Apostels Paulus. Band 2: Die Apologie* (Köln: Böhlau, 1997), 250; Furnish, *II Corinthians*, 306; etc.

[15] Barnett, *Corinthians*, 280. One is reminded of the similar mixture of themes in Ps. 64:11–12: 'Once God has spoken; twice have I heard this: that power belongs to God, and steadfast love belongs to you, O Lord. For you repay to all according to their work' (cf. also Exod. 20:5–6; Deut. 5:9–10).

[16] Byung-mo Kim, *Die paulinische Kollekte* (Tübingen: Francke, 2002); Harris, *Second Epistle*, 604.

[17] Harris, *Second Epistle*, 604.

[18] Ibid., 604–5.

[19] Ibid., 604.

[20] This assumes the αὐτοῦ is original. However, given that there is little reason why the αὐτοῦ should be inserted, it is the preferred reading, and the alternative, αὐτήν, is most likely an assimilation to the previous τήν (cf. Margaret E. Thrall, *The Second Epistle to the Corinthians Vol. 2* [London: T&T Clark, 2004], 549 n.296).

[21] Dunn, *Theology*, 258–59.

[22] Ibid., 259 n.134.

8:19 with either of the meanings Dunn urges. Paul here speaks of the risen Lord's own glory as related to his goals and motivation for the collection.

Paul later explains that the power of Christ dwelling on him was the reason he could boast all the more gladly of his weaknesses (2 Cor 12:7–9). 'Therefore', Paul continues, 'I am content with weaknesses, insults, hardships, persecutions, and calamities *for the sake of Christ* [ὑπὲρ Χριστοῦ]' (cf. 2 Cor 12:7–10). This Christ-related reason for contentedness in suffering is of no small consequence when the kind of sufferings he experienced are kept in mind (cf. 2 Cor. 11:23–33).

It needs to be mentioned that this focus on Paul's Christ-related goals and aims does not attempt to argue that Paul had no other goals or motivations. So in 2 Corinthians 12:19 Paul can write that 'everything we do, beloved, is for the sake of building you up' (cf. also 1 Thess. 2:19–20). The prevalent data relating to Christ is the concern here.

In Galatians, the purpose for which God revealed 'his Son' in Paul was in order that Paul 'might proclaim him among the Gentiles' (Gal. 1:16). The purpose of the revelation is the proclamation of Christ throughout the world. Later, Paul explains that he no longer lives but that the life he now lives, and thus presumably also its purpose and meaning, is found in 'faith in/the faithfulness of the Son of God' (ἐν πίστει ... τῇ τοῦ υἱοῦ τοῦ θεοῦ' – Gal. 2:20). To cite two older commentaries, 'I have no longer a separate existence', Lightfoot read Paul as saying, 'I am merged in Christ'.[23] Or as Calvin put it, Paul is 'animated by the secret power of Christ'.[24] While in prison, Paul states, in Philippians 1:18, that whatever a person's motivation, what matters is that Christ be proclaimed, 'and in that I rejoice'. That this goal be fulfilled was Paul's only real concern. In 1:20 he explains that 'by my speaking with all boldness, Christ will be exalted now as always in my body, whether by life or by death'. If Paul would eventually leave this prison alive, he did not know, but either way his ultimate goal was that 'Christ be exalted'. Importantly, O'Brien notes that the verb, μεγαλύνω 'occurred frequently in the Psalms, and it is quite possible that Paul has drawn from the wells of this source for the language on which to express the content of his earnest expectation and hope'.[25] For example, one is reminded of LXX Psalms 33:3; 34:26–27; 39:15–17; 56:10.[26] This is not a matter of small coincidence as the concerns of both the Psalms in which the word is used, and Paul's letter, overlap considerably. Both are concerned with the δικαι- word group (e.g. LXX Pss. 34:23, 24, 27, 28; 39:9, 10; 69:27 and Phil. 1:11; 3:6, and importantly 3:9), both with suffer-

---

[23] Joseph B. Lightfoot, *St Paul's Epistle to the Galatians* (London: Macmillan, 1869³), 119.

[24] John Calvin, *The Epistles of Paul to the Galatians and Ephesians*, trans. William Pringle (Edinburgh: Calvin Translation Society, 1854), 74.

[25] P.T. O'Brien, *The Epistle to the Philippians* (Grand Rapids: Eerdmans, 1991), 115.

[26] Cf. G.F. Hawthorne, *Philippians* (Waco: Word, 1983), 43; Stephen E. Fowl, *Philippians* (Cambridge: Eerdmans, 2005), 47.

ing at the hands of the enemies of God (e.g. LXX Pss. 34:2; 39:14–15; 68:26 etc. and Phil. 1:7, 13–14, 17), both with vindication over oppressors (LXX Pss. 34:2, 4, 17, 19, 22–27; 39:1–2, 11, 13–15, 17; 68:24, 27–28 etc. and Phil. 1:18–20, 28), both with faithfulness and perseverance through persecution (LXX Pss. 34:9, 13–14; 39:1, 4–10; 68:30 and Phil. 1:21, 27–28) and both with the expressed desire continually to magnify the Lord (LXX Pss. 34:18, 27; 39:16; 68:30 and Phil. 1:20). While aspects of the historicity of the Philippian prison episode in Acts 16 are disputed, it is noteworthy that Paul and Silas are specifically said to be singing Psalms in prison (Acts 16:25. Cf. also Acts 5:41; Rom. 5:3; 2 Cor. 6:10; Phil. 2:17; Col. 1:24; Jas. 1:2; 1 Pet. 1:6–8 which link suffering and persecution with rejoicing in the Lord).[27] Indeed, the practice of singing hymns while under persecution is well attested in Jewish literature (throughout the canonical book of Psalms, but cf. also 4 Macc. 18:15; Esth. [Greek] 13:17; Pr Azar 1:1), and in the Jesus tradition (Mk. 15:34; Mt. 27:46. Cf. also Lk. 6:22–23). This makes the association of Paul's prison based 'magnify' language with Psalmic contexts even more plausible. Paul's ultimate goal here, to see Christ exalted in death or life, likely employed a Psalmic term that spoke, with liturgical overtones, of the exaltation of God.

The very next verse contains an 'intensely personal confession':[28] 'for to me, living is Christ, and dying is gain'. While commentators have understood the precise meaning of the Greek differently,[29] when τὸ ζῆν and τὸ ἀποθανεῖν are accepted as the subjects of their respective clauses it need not be doubted that in this verse 'Paul asserts that living ... has no meaning apart from Christ; he is the object, motive, inspiration, and goal of all that the apostle does'.[30] Hawthorne summarises the significance of the passage thus:

To say "living is Christ" is to say that for him "life *means* Christ" (Goodspeed, Knox, Moffatt, Phillips). Life is summed up in Christ. Life is filled up with, occupied with Christ, in the sense that *everything Paul does*—trusts, loves, hopes, obeys, preaches, follows (Vincent), and so on—*is inspired by Christ and is done for Christ*. Christ and Christ alone gives inspiration, direction, meaning and purpose to existence.[31]

In this verse, Paul expresses that Christ is his reason for living, his motivation in all he is and does. While the verse may well say more than this, it arguably does not say less.

Paul's goal and motivation orientated reasoning continues in the following verses. As he has already stated in 1:21: 'dying is gain'. Yet he elaborates, in 1:23, that 'my desire is to depart and be with Christ, for that is far better'. Far

---

[27] Paul S. Minear, "Singing and Suffering in Philippi," in *The Conversation Continues: Studies in Paul & John*, ed. Beverly Gaventa and Robert Tomson Fortna (Nashville: Abingdon, 1990), 204, notes the link between Acts 16:25, the Philippian 'hymn' (2:6–11), and Paul's suffering.

[28] O'Brien, *Philippians*, 118.

[29] Cf. O'Brien, *Philippians*, 118–23, for a presentation of the various views.

[30] O'Brien, *Philippians*, 120.

[31] Hawthorne, *Philippians*, 45, italics mine.

better than living, a goal and desire greater than life itself, Paul states, is to be with Christ.

The much examined passage 2:6–11 must also be mentioned. The purpose of God's exaltation of Christ, and the giving of the name above every name, was that 'at the name of Jesus *every knee should bend*, in heaven and on earth and under the earth, and *every tongue should confess* that Jesus Christ is Lord, to the glory of God the Father'. The italicised elements above in 2:10–11 echo language from Isaiah 45:23 which involved the universal recognition of YHWH as the only God. This ultimate goal is here fulfilled when Gentile and Jew alike bend the knee to and confess the name of Jesus, to the glory of God. The added phrase sandwiched in the Isaianic language, 'in heaven and on earth and under the earth' also reflects OT language and serves to emphasise the universality of this ultimate goal.[32]

In Philippians 3 Paul exclaims:

> Yet whatever gains I had, these I have come to regard as loss because of Christ. [8] More than that, I regard everything as loss because of the surpassing value of knowing Christ Jesus my Lord. For his sake I have suffered the loss of all things, and I regard them as rubbish, in order that I may gain Christ (Phil. 3:7–8).

His reason for such radical devaluing of everything (as σκύβαλον 'rubbish' or 'excrement') is the knowledge of Christ. Indeed, it is here for *Christ's sake* that Paul suffered the loss of all things. Paul is aware that the goal of knowing Christ and becoming like Christ have not yet been fully obtained. 'But', Paul reasons, 'I press on' to these goals, 'because Christ Jesus has made me his own'. Admittedly, this translation assumes that ἐφ᾽ ᾧ is being used idiomatically, so that 'the clause provides the motive for Paul's intense desire of laying hold on Christ'.[33] But the Greek may also be understood as indicating purpose.[34] Probably one should not draw too thick a line between these two options, but speaking for the reading indicating motive is Paul's usage of ἐφ᾽ ᾧ elsewhere (Rom. 5:12; 2 Cor. 5:4).[35] If the translation adopted above is correct, then it indicates that Paul's reason for pressing on in passionate and energetic Christ-following, as the previous verses describe, is that Christ has made him his own. If the goal is intended, then Paul states that he presses on 'in order to make Christ Jesus his own'. Either way, whether motive or goal or both, Christ is profoundly at the centre.

In 1 Thessalonians Paul expresses a key aim in his missionary endeavours, that the Thessalonian believers may 'stand firm in the Lord' (3:8). Indeed, Paul exclaims that 'we now live', upon this condition. Paul then explains that the coming presence of Christ is the believer's hope. That 'we will be with the Lord forever' (4:17), and that 'whether we are awake or asleep we may live

---

[32] Bauckham, "Philippians"; Fee, *Christology*, 396–401.

[33] O'Brien, *Philippians*, 425.

[34] Cf. the references in O'Brien, *Philippians*, 425 n.38.

[35] Moisés Silva, *Philippians* (Grand Rapids: Baker, 2005), 176.

with him' (5:10),[36] is the ground for the exhortation to 'encourage one another' (4:18; 5:11). Indeed, unlike those who can only expect 'an avenging Lord' (4:6), in 4:13–5:11 Paul sets out the goal of being with Christ as that which characterises and distinguishes Christians from all others.[37] Oddly, Kreitzer's analysis of 4:15–18 completely neglects to examine the christological significance of this language,[38] as does Matera's discussion on Christology in the Thessalonian correspondence.[39]

Schade concludes, in relation to this passage, that '[t]he history-of-religions formative influence of such expressions [i.e., the hope to be 'with him'] comes into question – if from anywhere – truly only from the expressions represented in 1 Enoch concerning the future existence of the righteous and holy with the Elected/Son of Man'.[40] This nevertheless misses the mark by failing to consider the broader picture of Pauline language in regards to the believer's relation to the risen Lord, as shall be detailed in chapters 7 and 9 above. More pertinent are the numerous passages in the worship texts of the OT and intertestamental literature which speak of such desire and hope for the presence of YHWH (e.g. Pss. 16:11; 21:6; 27:4; 42:2; 51:11; 63:1–8; 84:10; 95:2; 100:2; 105:4; Wis. Sol. 3:14; 13:3; 1QH[a] 15:28–31; 28:5–9). Arguably here, and here alone, one can see something of the reason for the breathless radicalism of the Apostle, who could desire Christ's presence over life itself (Phil. 1:23). Christ's presence is perhaps as much Paul's yearning desire and goal as the presence of YHWH was for Second Temple Jewish worshippers.

In Paul's argument in 1 Thessalonians, the expressions in 4:17 and 5:10 likely reveal his deepest goals. As Nicholl writes in his recent monograph on the 'hope' related themes in the Thessalonian correspondence: 'being "with Christ for ever" was the essence of salvation and the primary focus of Christian hope'.[41] Too often this kind of language has been left out of discussions relating to Pauline Christology, yet it is important data. Leon Morris argues: 'Everything leads up to this [4:17], and after this has been said there is nothing to add. Nothing could more adequately indicate the Christian's bliss'.[42]

---

[36] To be noted is that, in 5:10, Paul also makes clear that this hoped for 'living with Christ' is the goal of Christ's death 'for us'.

[37] Cf. the discussion in Börschel, *Konstruktion*, 224–34.

[38] Cf. Kreitzer, *Jesus*, 125.

[39] Frank J. Matera, *New Testament Christology* (Westminster: Louisville, 1999), 88–91.

[40] Hans-Heinrich Schade, *Apokalyptische Christologie bei Paulus: Studien zum Zusammenhang von Christologie und Eschatologie in den Paulusbriefen* (Göttingen: Vandenhoeck & Ruprecht, 1984[2]), 146, translation mine.

[41] Colin R. Nicholl, *From Hope to Despair in Thessalonica: Situating 1 and 2 Thessalonians* (Cambridge: Cambridge University Press, 2004), 46 n.75.

[42] Leon Morris, *The First and Second Epistles to the Thessalonians* (Grand Rapids: Eerdmans, 1991), 146. It is unnatural and arbitrary to drive a wedge between the 'collective experience of the Lord's coming', and a 'deep personal and religious experience', and to claim that 4:13–18 is all about the former. Cf. Plevnik's critique of J. Dupont, *ΣΥΝ ΧΡΙΣΤΩΙ: L'union avec le Christ suivant saint Paul* (Paris: Louvain, 1952) on this point

This is hope with a specific content.[43] Plevnik can thus speak, in light of this passage, of Paul's 'deep yearning to be with the Lord ... [one] fed by the springs of deep love that the apostle has for the Lord'.[44]

In Philemon 4–5 Paul thanks God ἀκούων σου τὴν ἀγάπην καὶ τὴν πίστιν, ἣν ἔχεις πρὸς τὸν κύριον Ἰησοῦν καὶ εἰς πάντας τοὺς ἁγίους. The majority of scholars and Bible translations reasonably understand the εἰς phrase to modify τὴν ἀγάπην alone, and the πρός phrase just τὴν πίστιν, which means that the verse evidences a chiastic structure.[45] Hence the NRSV translation: 'because I hear of your love for all the saints and your faith toward the Lord Jesus'. However, Dunn responds that 'there is no reason why Paul should not have thought of both love and faith as the sum of the Christian lifestyle and therefore of both as related to both "the Lord Jesus" and "all the saints"'.[46] Either way, a simple conclusion can be uncontroversially maintained in tandem with the observations above in relation to 1 Thessalonians 1:1–2: the motivation for Paul's prayers of thanksgiving was here the committed faith and hope of believers in the risen Lord.

Finally, mention must also be made of Philemon 6. It is, however, difficult to ascertain precisely what is meant by the final phrase, εἰς Χριστόν. Did he mean to speak of all the good, which is ἐν ἡμῖν, *for* Christ? Did it mean *to* Christ, or perhaps 'to bring us closer to Christ', or did he mean something equivalent to 'in Christ' or 'in relation to Christ'?[47] All of these translations are possible and coherent with the material analysed in this section.

3. Various expressions of Christ-devotion

Paul's Christ-related goals and aims, as examined above, already display something of Paul's Christ-devotion. In this section it is necessary to examine more direct Christ-devotion language.

Turning first to Romans, Paul explains that whether Christians observe a day, or not, or eat certain foods, or abstain, they are to do it in honour of the Lord (14:6). He then adds: 'If we live, we live to the Lord, and if we die, we die to the Lord; so then, whether we live or whether we die, we are the Lord's' (14:8). While the referent of the κύριος in 14:11 is disputed ('As I live, says the *Lord*, every knee shall bow to me'), Fee has recently maintained that it

---

(Joseph Plevnik, *Paul and the Parousia* [Peabody: Hendrickson, 1997], 265), in which he correctly emphasises the 'intensly personal character of this hope'.

[43] Plevnik, *Parousia*, 201–2.

[44] Ibid., 267.

[45] Cf. the discussion in Murray J. Harris, *Colossians & Philemon* (Grand Rapids: Eerdmans, 1991), 249–50.

[46] James D.G. Dunn, *The Epistles to the Colossians and to Philemon: A Commentary on the Greek Text* (Carlisle: Paternoster, 1996), 317.

[47] Harris, *Colossians & Philemon*, 252–53.

may well refer to Christ and not God.[48] In 16:5, during a list of greetings, Paul writes of Epaenetus who is ἀπαρχὴ τῆς 'Ασίας εἰς Χριστόν.[49] While most modern translations read: 'first convert in Asia for Christ', or some variation thereof (e.g., NRSV, NIV), this flattens the overtones in the Greek. Paul speaks of Epaenetus as the 'first fruit of Asia for Christ'. As Jewett remarks:

In the Jewish tradition, the 'first fruit' was the first part of a harvest to ripen to maturity, so desirable that it should be sacrificed to Yahweh. The word ἀπαρχή is also common in Greek sacrifices. The expression 'for Christ' clearly indicates to whom the choice offering was brought, indicating the kind of cultic veneration that led to the early development of Christology.[50]

Whether Paul's language here is really evidence of a specifically 'cultic veneration' is debatable. But that this short fragment expresses Christ-devotion is scarcely to be denied. In Romans, then, Christians eat/abstain etc. in honour of the Lord, they live and die to the Lord, Epaenetus is described specifically as the 'first fruit of Asia for Christ', and 14:11 may state that every knee will bow to Christ.

In 1 Corinthians Paul reveals that fundamental to the Corinthian believers' posture to the risen Lord, is ἀπεκδέχομαι, a waiting for this Lord's eschatological revelation (1:7. cf. also Phil. 3:20). A few verses later, in 1:9, Paul explains that God has called these believers εἰς κοινωνίαν τοῦ υἱοῦ αὐτοῦ. The word κοινωνία is difficult to translate, but arguably both its vertical and horizontal dimensions should be acknowledged (as discussed in the previous chapter in terms of 1 Cor. 10:16). That is, it speaks of the fellowship of the church, but it is also fellowship with the risen Lord. As Thiselton writes, a 'genitive following the word koinonia expresses … that of which one participates'.[51] The Christ-relation here involves a waiting for and fellowship with the risen Lord.

At the end of this chapter Paul says that the one who boasts should 'boast in the Lord' (1:31; also 2 Cor. 10:17). Significantly, Paul appears to be alluding to Jeremiah 9:23–24:

Thus says the LORD: Do not let the wise boast in their wisdom, do not let the mighty boast in their might, do not let the wealthy boast in their wealth; but let those who boast boast in this, that they understand and know me, that I am the LORD; I act with steadfast love, justice, and righteousness in the earth, for in these things I delight, says the LORD.

Paul's earlier rhetoric in this chapter, in 1:20–27, involved precisely such a stance against 'the wisdom of the wise'. Paul likewise rejects any possible boasting before God on the grounds of wisdom, power or noble birth (1:26).

---

[48] Fee, *Christology*, 259–67.

[49] That the reading εἰς Χριστόν is to be preferred over the minority reading ἐν Χριστῷ, cf. Charles E. B. Cranfield, *Romans 9–16*, reprint, 1979 (Edinburgh: T&T Clark, 2002[8]), 787.

[50] Jewett, *Romans*, 960.

[51] Thiselton, *Corinthians*, 104.

But whereas the text from Jeremiah speaks of boasting in this: 'that they understand and know me, that I am the LORD', Paul makes the only legitimate boast of a Christ-believer, a boast in the risen Lord.[52] As Fee notes, the significance of this language 'is striking indeed, since the context in Jeremiah has to do with Yahweh's absolute claim to loyalty over all other gods'.[53]

The thematic allusions to Jeremiah 9:23–24 continue into 1 Corinthians 2:2. The LXX of 9:24 speaks of boasting in the 'understanding and knowing that I am the Lord' (συνίειν καὶ γινώσκειν ὅτι ἐγώ εἰμι κύριος). Paul, after denying that he speaks in 'lofty words or wisdom', states that 'οὐ γὰρ ἔκρινά τι εἰδέναι ἐν ὑμῖν εἰ μὴ Ἰησοῦν Χριστὸν καὶ τοῦτον ἐσταυρωμένον.' While the correct interpretation of the sentence and its syntax remains disputed,[54] by taking the οὐ with ἔκρινά,[55] and stressing the demonstrative pronoun (τοῦτον),[56] a likely translation is: 'I did not resolve to know anything amongst you *except Christ and Christ crucified*'. Notably, Paul did not write simply ... εἰ μὴ Ἰησοῦν Χριστὸν ἐσταυρωμένον, but adds καὶ τοῦτον, even though major commentaries often tend to read this passage as if καὶ τοῦτον was effectively not present, as if the object of Paul's knowing becomes a cruciformity. But Paul knows not just a cruciform pattern but *Christ* the crucified.[57] In 1 Corinthians 2:2, Jeremiah's boast in the 'understanding and knowing that I am the Lord' becomes the knowledge of Christ, and Christ crucified.

In 1 Corinthians 6:16–17 Paul contrasts the unity between a prostitute and her customer with that of a believer and the risen Lord (ὁ κολλώμενος τῇ πόρνῃ parallels ὁ δὲ κολλώμενος τῷ κυρίῳ). Sampley writes: Paul 'enlists a powerful metaphor to elaborate the relationship of believers, represented as bodies, to Christ'.[58] Thiselton translates κολλώμενος, in 6:17, as 'the person

---

[52] That Paul means the *risen* Lord in 1:31 is most likely, given the context in which the Lord is identified with Jesus Christ (1:2, 3, 7, 9, 10; 2:8, 16 etc.) and distinguished from θεός (1:3, 9). Also, use of this passage from Jeremiah elsewhere in Paul strongly confirms a christological reading (cf. 2 Cor. 10:17–18), as does Paul's Christ-related understanding of 'boasting' in 2 Cor. 12:8–10; Gal. 6:14; Phil. 1:26; 3:3. Cf. also the reasoning offered in Fee, *Christology*, 130 n.113.

[53] Fee, *Christology*, 130.

[54] Cf. the discussion esp. in Thiselton, *Corinthians*, 211–12, and recently that of Wiard Popkes, "1 Kor 2,2 und die Anfänge der Christologie," *ZNW* 95 (2004): 64–83.

[55] As Thiselton urges against the majority. Nevertheless, the 'οὐ–γάρ–verb (or implied verb)' structure in Paul supports the translation accepted, and οὐ usually does not negate an infinitive. Most recently, however, Popkes has objected to assertions of any certainty in this whole matter (Popkes, "1 Kor 2,2," 65–66).

[56] As Thiselton argues, the frequent use of this pronoun [τοῦτον] is hardly captured by an English pronoun [i.e. 'Jesus Christ and *him* crucified], and a demonstrative pronoun ... would be strained in English. Hence we have repeated the name, which conveys Paul's effect' (Thiselton, *Corinthians*, 212–13).

[57] A more satisfactory discussion is provided by Gorman, *Cruciformity*, 1–2.

[58] Sampley, "1 Corinthians," 862.

who is united in intimacy' (to the risen Lord).[59] Likewise, Powers, in his exegesis of 6:14, writes that 'the Christians' unity with Christ forms the basis of Paul's entire argument ... The apostle views fornication as establishing a personal relationship which is incompatible with the personal relationship between the believer and Jesus'.[60] Arguably, by speaking of being united to the Lord and being 'one spirit with him', this indicates that Paul has in mind a relationship, through the Spirit, between risen Lord and believers of deep relational and personal intimacy, involving commitment to purity. Interestingly, the verb κολλάω is used in the LXX to refer to both sexual encounters *and* the believer's relation to YHWH (cf. e.g. relation to YHWH: Deut. 6:13; 10:20;[61] 2 Kgs. 18:6; Sir. 2:3; Jer. 13:11; sexual relations: 1 Kgs. 11:2; 1 Esd. 4:20; Sir. 19:2).[62]

In 1 Corinthians 7:25–38, Paul addresses the subject of marriage and the unmarried in Corinth. The focus here shall be on 7:32–35, a passage which can be divided as follows:

- 7:32a I want you to be free from anxieties.
- 7:32b (A) The unmarried man is anxious about the things of the Lord, how to please the Lord.
- 7:33–34a (B) But the married man is anxious about the affairs of the world, how to please his wife, and he is 'pulled in two directions'[63] (μεμέρισται).
- 7:34b (Å) And the unmarried woman and the virgin are anxious about the things of the Lord, so that they may be entirely holy (ἁγία καὶ τῷ σώματι καὶ τῷ πνεύματι).
- 7:34c (B̊) But the married woman is anxious about the things of the world, how to please her husband.
- 7:35 I say this for your own benefit, not to put any restraint upon you, but with a view to promoting that which is appropriate and facilitates undistracted devotion to the Lord.

Two points about the translation. First, arguably ἁγία καὶ τῷ σώματι καὶ τῷ πνεύματι is best translated as 'entirely holy'. Paul is speaking not about anthropological compartments, but about the quality of devotion to the risen

---

[59] Thiselton, *Corinthians*, 466, contra Porter's emphasis on 'obligation' as discussed by Thiselton on p. 467.

[60] Dan Powers, *Salvation Through Participation: An Examination of the Notion of Believer's Corporate Unity with Christ in Early Christian Soteriology* (Leuven: Peters, 2001), 150–51.

[61] Note the references to this verse in the classic treatment of 'Man's personal relationship with God' in the OT, with special emphasis on the concept of the fear of the Lord, in Walther Eichrodt, *Theology of the Old Testament. Vol. 2*, trans. J. A. Baker (Philadelphia: Westminster John Knox, 1967), Pt 3, XXI.

[62] Cf. also Garland, *1 Corinthians*, 235.

[63] Thiselton, *Corinthians*, 590.

Lord, an interpretation suggested by the parallelism between A and À.[64] Second, the best translation of ἀλλὰ πρὸς τὸ εὔσχημον καὶ εὐπάρεδρον τῷ κυρίῳ ἀπερισπάστως, in 7:35, remains disputed,[65] and 'close translation is scarcely possible'.[66] That admitted, the translation offered above is certainly plausible, and it reflects well the two concerns of marriage and the quality of devotion to Christ. The same cannot be said of Garland's translation: 'but [I am saying this] to promote what is seemly and constant before the Lord [that you might live] undistractedly'.[67] This is based on the addition of the words 'to promote what is' and 'that you might live' to make sense of the Greek, an insistence that the two accusative adjectives (εὔσχημον and εὐπάρεδρον) are linked by the same definite article, and that the adverb ἀπερισπάστως simply 'appears at the end of the clause for emphasis' and hence does not qualify εὐπάρεδρον alone.[68] However, the translation of εὐπάρεδρον as 'constant' is unconvincing, and most major commentaries translate εὐπάρεδρον as 'devotion'.[69] The tight linking of the adjectives with the article τό is an important structural force that guides Garland's translation. Yet the τό may gain its semantic significance, not in its relation to the following two adjectives, but in its relation to the preceding πρός. Thiselton's translation: 'what is appropriate to undistracted devotion to the Lord',[70] is possible, but the adjectives are connected with a καί, and Thiselton's translation ignores this. Rather, the καί reflects the dual themes of devotion and marriage in 7:32b–34c. Εὔσχημον relates to marriage while εὐπάρεδρον τῷ κυρίῳ ἀπερισπάστως concerns Christ-devotion. The context thus clarifies the meaning of the awkward syntax.

On the basis of the translation offered above, a number of points can be made. First, as Garland, following Schrage, writes: 'The combination of body and spirit [in 7:34] describes the whole person and means that she strives to be holy in every way and is totally devoted to the Lord'.[71] It is noteworthy that, because of the thematic parallelism, Paul clearly associates holiness so directly with 'pleasing the (risen) Lord'. Ἅγιος is, of course, common Jewish language used in view of Israel's relation to YHWH, who are to 'be a people holy to the LORD your God' (cf. e.g. Lev. 19:2; 22:32 LXX; Deut. 7:6; 14:2,

---

[64] There is thus no need to think Paul cites a Corinthian position which he does not fully accept (contra C.K. Barrett, *A Commentary in the First Epistle to the Corinthians* (London: Black, 1971²), 181). Cf. also Raymond F Collins, *First Corinthians* (Collegeville: Liturgical Press, 1999), 296.

[65] Cf. the useful discussion in Garland, *1 Corinthians*, 319.

[66] Barrett, *1 Corinthians*, 182.

[67] Garland, *1 Corinthians*, 319. The material in the square brackets is included by Garland.

[68] Garland, *1 Corinthians*, 335.

[69] Πάρεδρος means 'sitting beside' and had frequent religious overtones.

[70] Thiselton, *Corinthians*, 566.

[71] Garland, *1 Corinthians*, 335.

21; 26:19; 28:9 etc.), and of those who are especially close to God, the Levi-
ties and priests (2 Chr. 23:6; 35:3 etc.). Second, Paul strives to facilitate
undistracted devotion to the risen Lord.[72] What matters, what Paul wants to
encourage, is personal devotion to the Lord, to live to please the Lord and to
be anxious about the things of the Lord, and so to be entirely holy.

In 1 Corinthians 11:23–26, Paul repeats a Lord's Supper tradition. As he
relays, Christ said to do this 'in remembrance of me'. Hurtado and Fee have
made much of this data, especially given the former's concern for specifically
cultic devotion to Christ in Paul's letters. And as Fee correctly notes: 'meals
in honor of a deity were a part of the entire ancient Near Eastern world,
including Israel'.[73] In this context, remembering too the reference to 'Christ
our Passover' in 1 Corinthians 5:6–8, it is significant that 'the κυριακὸν
δεῖπνον of 11:20 is the Christian celebration of Passover'.[74] Hence, 'Christ the
Lord has assumed the role of honoree that in Judaism had for centuries
belonged to Yahweh alone and that in surrounding cultures belonged to the
various "gods" and "lords" of the pagan cults'.[75]

In 1 Corinthians 12 Paul turns to address the use, and abuse, of spiritual
gifts. He speaks, at the start of his argument, of the Holy Spirit inspired confession that 'Jesus is Lord' (12:3). Hurtado in particular has pointed to the
cultic context of this particular confession of Christ's lordship.[76] Thiselton
writes that the confession 'Jesus is Lord', here, is 'a spoken act of personal
devotion and commitment which is part and parcel of a Christ-centered worship and lifestyle'.[77] Given this context, Fee may well be correct to understand
the κύριος, in 12:3, as standing for the Tetragrammaton.

Although this connection with the Tetragrammaton is not part of the present context, it is the
crucial matter in the next two occurrences of this confession (Rom 10:9; Phil 2:10–11). The
"Lord" (*Adonai* = κύριος) of the Shema is Jesus ... The devotion that was once the special
province of Yahweh alone is now to be directed toward Christ himself: the Lord is *Jesus*.[78]

An important theme in 1 Corinthians 15 is hope. As a part of Paul's rhetorical
argument, he asks what conclusions follow the denial of Christ's resurrection.
He ends his reasoning by stating that 'ἐν Χριστῷ ἠλπικότες ἐσμέν μόνον, we
are of all people most to be pitied' (15:19). Most modern commentators
understand the μόνον as qualifying the entire clause, both the ἐν τῇ ζωῇ ταύτῃ

---

[72] That Paul here speaks about the *risen* Lord is clear from the wider context, where
κύριος is clearly associated with Jesus (cf. the references to 'Jesus tradition' in 7:10; 7:22;
8:6).

[73] Fee, *Christology*, 122.

[74] Ibid., 123.

[75] Fee, *Christology*, 123. Cf. also chapter 5 above.

[76] Hurtado, *LJC*, 113, 142, 198; Hurtado, *OG²*, 12, 112.

[77] Thiselton, *Corinthians*, 926, italics suppressed.

[78] Fee, *Christology*, 124.

and the perfect periphrastic ἠλπικότες ἐσμέν.[79] Thus, Barrett's translation (recently followed by Garland): 'If in this life we have hoped in Christ – that and nothing more', is to be preferred over the NIV translation ('If only for this life ...').[80] This, along with the intensive[81] meaning of the periphrastic perfect ('we have set our hope and continue to hope'[82]), has the effect of delimiting the thorough nature of this hope. It is a hope that colours all life, invades every pore of the believer's personal and communal orientation in existence. Read in the context of 15:29–34, in which Paul points out the practical consequences and disorientation if Christ were not risen from the dead, one can add that hope in Christ is central to the existence of a Christian, in all of life, death and in all struggles.

In 2 Corinthians 3:15–16 Paul contrasts those who have a veil over their minds with those who have this veil removed. It is removed, says Paul, 'when one turns to the Lord'.[83] Many understand ἐπιστρέψῃ ('turn to'), in 3:16, as a 'quasi-technical term for "conversion"'.[84]

Paul then continues, in 3:18, stating that 'we all, with unveiled faces' are 'seeing the glory of the Lord as though reflected in a mirror'. It is hotly debated whether 'Lord' here refers to Christ, the Spirit or God.[85] Arguably there are good contextual reasons to favour the christological reading. Indeed, Fee, once a proponent against the Christology view, has since, in his recent

---

[79] At least the most recent commentaries assume this reading (e.g. Thiselton, *Corinthians*, 1221, Garland, *1 Corinthians*, 702). Some slightly older commentaries note the presence of a debate on this matter (e.g. Fee, *Corinthians*, 744, Barrett, *1 Corinthians*, 349).

[80] Barrett, *1 Corinthians*, 349 and Garland, *1 Corinthians*, 697.

[81] Cf. Thiselton, *Corinthians*, 1221.

[82] Garland, *1 Corinthians*, 702.

[83] The implied subject of the temporal clause of 3:16 is disputed. While the NRSV translation has been adopted for this thesis, Thrall lists six different interpretive options (Thrall, *2 Corinthians Vol. 1*, 269–71).

[84] E.g. as cited here, Fee, *Christology*, 177; but cf. also Thrall, *2 Corinthians Vol. 1*, 271; Fatehi, *Relation*, 296 and those he footnotes in n.69.

[85] Cf. e.g. James D.G. Dunn, "2 Corinthians 3:17. 'The Lord Is the Spirit'," in *The Christ and the Spirit: Christology*, reprint, originally published in 1970 (Edinburgh: T&T Clark, 1998), 115–25; L. J. Belleville, *Reflections of Glory. Paul's Polemical Use of the Moses-Doxa Tradition in 2 Corinthians 3.1–18* (Sheffield: JSOT Press, 1991); Harris, *Second Epistle*, 306–13; Thrall, *2 Corinthians Vol. 1*, 268–82; Gordon D. Fee, *God's Empowering Presence: The Holy Spirit in the Letters of Paul* (Peabody: Hendrickson, 1994), 310–14; Furnish, *II Corinthians*, 242; Richardson, *Paul's Language About God*, 156; N.T. Wright, *Climax*, 183–84; Witherington, *Conflict*, 382; Max Turner, *The Holy Spirit and Spiritual Gifts: Then and Now* (Carlisle: Paternoster, 1999), 116. Cf. also the further references cited in Fatehi, *Relation*, 290 n.51. One must question Harris' claim, published in 2005, that the christological reading of 3:16–18 is still the 'dominant view' (Harris, *Second Epistle*, 310).

2007 work, changed his mind entirely and now affirms it.[86] The Lord of glory is probably Christ.

Whether the participle, κατοπτριζόμενοι, in 3:18 is to be understood as 'reflecting' or 'beholding' is also disputed. The former translation is maintained by Belleville, Wright and Na.[87] However, the slim philological evidence is in support of the 'beholding' reading.[88] Not only that, but the appearance of the verb ἀτενίζω in 3:7 and 3:13 is contextual evidence that links glory and looking at/gazing/beholding.[89] One can add to this Paul's remark in 4:4 that 'the god of this world has blinded the minds of the unbelievers ... to the light of the gospel of the glory of Christ'. The positive would thus imply some sense of seeing and perceiving the glory of Christ.[90] Additional to this, Volker Rabens notes that 'προσώπῳ as a distributive singular renders an interpretation as believers "coming face to face with one another" unlikely'.[91] The 'beholding' reading is thus to be preferred.

With these exegetical issues noted, one could, as Fee does, simply point out the apparent 'God-language' in this passage as it is applied to Christ.[92] However, the point to draw from this is not only that Paul can speak of beholding the Lord (a matter of course reflected in the Psalmic expressions of beholding the glory of YHWH: e.g., Pss. 17:15; 27:4; 42:2; 63:1–3). Also important are the themes which Paul associates with this exegetical result: the beholding leads to transformation by the Spirit. To understand this complex of themes it will be necessary, albeit briefly, to examine 1) the nature of sin, in Paul, 2) what Paul thought could be transformed, 3) the association between Christ and desire, and 4) how the beholding of the glory of Christ may be understood in this context.

---

[86] Fee, *Christology*, 179. He offers three reasons: '(1) Paul regularly appropriates the Septuagint's κύριος = Yahweh as referring to Christ; (2) Paul *consistently* uses κύριος in all other passages to refer to Christ; and (3) in concluding the present argument, Paul ... explicitly says that he preaches ... "Jesus Christ as Lord"' (italics his).

[87] Belleville, *Reflections of Glory. Paul's Polemical Use of the Moses-Doxa Tradition in 2 Corinthians 3.1–18*, 279–86; N.T. Wright, *Climax*, 185; Ignatius Na, "The Meaning Of KATOPTRIZOMENOI in 2 Cor 3,18," *ED* 55, no. 1 (2002): 33–44.

[88] It is, however, probably going too far to claim that the linguistic evidence is 'clearly against' the 'reflecting' reading, as Furnish does (Furnish, *II Corinthians*, 214). Note Hafemann's qualification of the 'evidence' from the NT-era for the 'reflecting' reading supplied by Belleville (Scott J. Hafemann, *Paul, Moses, and the History of Israel: The Letter / Spirit Contrast and the Argument from Scripture in 2 Corinthians 3* (Tübingen: Mohr Siebeck, 1995), 409 n.231).

[89] 'The link between 3:13 and 18 makes it evident that κατοπτριζόμενοι (v. 18), as the counterpart to μὴ ἀτενίσαι (v. 13), must refer to beholding the glory of God as in a mirror, not reflecting it' (Hafemann, *Paul*, 411).

[90] This also lends support for understanding the infinite of αὐγάζω in 4:4 as 'see' rather than 'shine'.

[91] Rabens, *Spirit*, 8 n.28.

[92] Fee, *Christology*, e.g., 182. Cf. also Hafemann, *Paul*, 416.

1) Sin appears to sometimes be inversely associated with 'glory' in Paul's mind, in that it is the exchange of God's value and glory for idolatry (cf. Rom. 1:21–23; 3:23).[93] One must also add that sin and desire are related in Paul. Based on Romans 7:8, which states that 'sin, seizing an opportunity in the commandment, produced in me all kinds of [negative] desire [ἐπιθυμίαν]',[94] Berger suggests that, for Paul, '[d]esire is the means by which sin rules over human beings'.[95] One could also refer to 1 Corinthians 10:6–11 which links sin and desire (ἐπιθυμέω).[96] While it is doubtful that Paul thought of these matters in any systematic sense, there appears to be a Pauline link between 'sin' and 'desire'. Putting these points together, this means that sin, for Paul, is often understood in terms of the way in which a desire or valuing of God's glory is exchanged for the desire for idols (cf. Rom. 1:23).

2) As a theme in 3:18 is transformation (μεταμορφόω), what did Paul usually think could be transformed, in a believer? Did Paul envisage a transformation of those very desires that, as noted above, are to be associated with sin? Berger, in arguing for the reality of internal change, points to Paul's expression 'obedient from the heart', in Romans 6:17. Paul's argument in 2 Corinthians 3:3 would imply that real change happens in the heart of Christ-believers, especially as Paul's language here likely draws on language from Jeremiah 31:31–34 (LXX 38) and Ezekiel 36:25–27,[97] texts which explicitly speak of internal transformation. Add to this Philippians 2:13, where Paul writes that it is God who is working in believers to cause them to *will* and act according to God's pleasure,[98] and a simple conclusion follows: Paul understood transformation to involve the transformation of human desire, resulting in obedience from the heart (see also Rom. 8:5; 2 Cor. 4:16; Phil. 4:12). *When Paul speaks of 'transformation', it is thus likely to have at least included a transformation of sinful desire to a desire for God's glory.*[99]

3) Now to the question: how does Christ relate to desire in Paul? Paul often contrasted desire for Christ with various negatives. As shall be argued below, starting on p. 133, Paul contrasted Christ-devotion with such matters as the appetites of those who cause dissension and offence (cf. Rom. 16:17), sin,

---

[93] John Piper, "The Demonstration of the Righteousness of God in Romans 3.25, 26," in *The Pauline Writings. A Sheffield Reader*, eds Stanley E. Porter and Craig A. Evans (Sheffield: Sheffield Academic Press, 1995), 199.

[94] Cf. also Jas. 1:14-15.

[95] A point emphasised by Berger (Klaus Berger, *Identity and Experience in the New Testament* [Minneapolis: Fortress, 2003], 133–7).

[96] Cf. Thiselton, *Corinthians*, 733–34.

[97] Cf. Fatehi, *Relation*, 197.

[98] Cf. the comentary on 2:13 in Markus Bockmuehl, *The Epistle to the Philippians* (London: Black, 1997), 154.

[99] On the language of 'transformation' and 'desire', cf. also the reflections in Markus Bockmuehl, "The Conversion of Desire in St. Paul's Hemeneutics," in *The Word Leaps the Gap: Essays on Scripture and Theology in Honor of Richard B. Hays*, eds J. Ross Wagner, C. Kavin Rowe, and A. Katherine Grieb (Cambridge: Eerdmans, 2008), 498–513.

including 'evil desire' (1 Cor. 8:12; 10:6–9, 22), etc. Likewise, as seen above, Paul associates devotion to Christ with being 'entirely holy' (1 Cor. 7:34). Correspondingly, desire for Christ can be understood to have functioned in Paul, at some level, as a counterweight to sinful desire. Berger suggests that, in Paul, 'faith is the positive correlate of desire' and that '[o]nly one who knows what desire is can rightly appreciate what faith is ... Only a faith that is itself "emotional" can be a *counterweight* to desire'.[100] Of course, this faith has, in Paul, a special Christ-focus. Further, at various points in this chapter it will be argued that a *desire* for the presence of the risen Lord was important in Paul's Christ-relation.

By reconstructing these various trajectories in Paul's thought, it can be argued that sin, with its desire for that which is not divine glory, would likely have been understood, at least to an extent, as *counterweighted by the life of faith in and desire for the glory of the risen Lord.*

4) With these issues clarified, how does the theme of 'beholding' sit next to that of 'transformation' in 2 Corinthians 3:18? It needs to be recognised that beholding the glory of God was often associated, in Paul's Jewish tradition, with *desire* for God. Importantly, in the Psalms there is evidence that the delight of the Psalmist was the presence, glory and face of God. There appeared to be an experience of spiritual delight that, importantly, came through *beholding* the Lord (cf. Pss. 17:15; 27:4; 42:2; 63:1–3. Cf. also among others, Wis. of Sol. 7:26–29; *Odes of Sol.* 14:5).[101] Such Psalmic themes would have been well known to the early church, a matter deducible from the fact that '[m]uch of the NT hymnology stands in the OT tradition of confessional statements'.[102] Of course, there is also clear evidence that Psalms were used and sung in the early church (cf. e.g. 1 Cor. 14:26; Col. 3:16; Eph. 5:19), and Paul cited or alluded to the Psalms, apart from Isaiah, more than any other OT text.[103] Desire for God grows through beholding.

One can now draw these lines of reasoning together. If sin, for Paul, involves an exchanging of desire for the glory of God for desire for idols, Paul likewise expected a transformation of these evil desires through the Gospel. Paul, as will be explored below, understood Christ-devotion as the opposite of sinful desire. The Apostle lived life with Christ-shaped desires; Christ, his presence and glory, became the centre of his desires and hopes. By beholding the glory of Christ, desire for Christ develops, counterbalancing sinful desire. In other words, 3:18 is evidence for a Spirit-created relational change between

---

[100] Berger, *Identity*, 137, emphasis mine.

[101] Cf. Deryck Sheriffs, *The Friendship of the Lord: An Old Testament Spirituality* (Carlisle: Paternoster, 1996), 139–46; Rabens, *Spirit*, 170.

[102] R.P. Martin, "Hymns, Hymn Fragments, Songs, Spiritual Songs," in *DPL*, eds G.F. Hawthorne, R.P. Martin, and D.G. Reid (Leicester: IVP, 1993), 420. Cf. also William Oscar Emil Oesterley, *The Jewish Background of the Christian Liturgy* (Oxford: Clarendon Press, 1925).

[103] Cf. the statistics in James M. Scott, "Restoration," 800. Cf. also Hengel, *Studies*, 260.

the risen Lord and believers, one that, as Rabens has argued,[104] relates to the religio-ethical life of believers, or as Paul puts it in 3:18, their transformation (μεταμορφόω) into the same image from glory to glory.[105]

It could, of course, be charged that the above argument is importing concepts into the text that are not there. This need not be denied, but the way it has been done is arguably not inappropriate. The concepts brought together in 3:18 demand some explanation, and the above is offered as a tentative answer to how Paul could do that, in so far as it is relevant to this thesis.

Important material in 2 Corinthians 5:9–15 has already been noted in terms of Paul's goals and motivations. In this context Paul claims that Christ-believers do not live for themselves but for 'him who died and was raised for them' (5:15). Indeed, this was the very reason Christ died (5:14). Christ is the one for whom believers live.

Paul, in 2 Corinthians 8, boasts about the churches of Macedonia to the Corinthians, and in doing so states that 'they gave themselves first to the Lord and, by the will of God, to us' (8:5). This appears similar to Philippians 2:11, where confession of Christ was also 'to the glory of God'. Here their act of financial giving was coupled with the giving of their very selves to the Lord. Not only was their financial giving a model for the Corinthians, so was their Christ-devotion, their 'dedication' to Christ.[106]

In the same chapter, Paul commends Titus for the task of gathering finances for the collection. In this argument he notes, having maintained that the collection is 'for the glory of the Lord himself', that no one 'should blame us about this generous gift', *for* (γάρ) Paul and his team 'consider what is good [προνοοῦμεν ... καλά] not only before the Lord but also before humans' (8:21). It is likely that Paul is here alluding to Proverbs 3:4 in which the father teaches his child not to forget his teachings so that he will find favour (καὶ προνοοῦ καλὰ) ἐνώπιον κυρίου καὶ ἀνθρώπων.[107] The parallel is clear. On the basis of this allusion, some commentators have argued that Paul, in 8:21, means the Lord God, not Christ.[108] But contextual clues indicate that the risen Lord is in view (cf. the christological import of the κύριος of 8:19 – the

---

[104] Rabens' thesis concerning the Spirit and ethical transformation offers a more comprehensive perspective than needs to be developed here. Cf. his exegesis of 2 Cor. 3:18 for more details concerning Pneumatology and ethical transformation in this verse (Rabens, *Spirit*, 158–84).

[105] The stress on the religious-ethical import of this verse has been convincingly maintained by Rabens through an analysis of the significance of 'the same image', and this in critical dialogue with Frances Back, *Verwandlung durch Offenbarung bei Paulus: eine religionsgeschichtlich-exegetische Untersuchung zu 2 Kor 2,14–4,6* (Tübingen: Mohr Siebeck, 2002), which problematically argues that the verse does not involve an ethical dimension. See Rabens, *Spirit*, 176–83.

[106] Harris, *Second Epistle*, 567.

[107] Cf. Harris, *Second Epistle*, 607; Fee, *Christology*, 188–89.

[108] Furnish and Lambrecht, as noted in Fee, *Christology*, 189 n.73. Likewise, Harris argues the κύριος is the Lord God because it was in Prov. 3:4 (Harris, *Second Epistle*, 608).

κυρίου δόξαν of 8:19 compared with the δόξα Χριστοῦ of 8:23). It is before this Lord that Paul lives and seeks to do right.

In 2 Corinthians 10 Paul defends his ministry in a rather direct manner. He states that 'if you are confident that you belong to Christ [Χριστοῦ εἶναι], remind yourself of this, that just as you belong to Christ [Χριστοῦ], so also do we' (10:7). While the exact meaning of Χριστοῦ εἶναι is disputed, what is clear is that a boast is made in terms of this designation. It was apparently the desirable self-designation, to be of Christ, which, in this context, probably means 'to belong to Christ'.[109]

In 2 Corinthians 11:2 Paul writes: 'For I am jealous for you with a jealousy such as God has, because I betrothed you to one husband in order to present you as a pure maiden to Christ himself'.[110] While a good deal of debate revolves around Paul's role in the metaphors of betrothal, marriage, bride and groom, what needs to be recognised here is the fact that Paul uses these images in terms of the relation between the risen Lord and believers. Paul describes this relation with metaphors which, in the OT, 'regularly describe the relation of Yahweh to his people, Israel'.[111]

The mention of the 'YHWH as husband of Israel' metaphor is found in Isaiah 54:5–6, the context of which concerns Israel's re-gathering and restoration after exile. The employment of the metaphor in Isaiah 62:5 concerns, once again, the vindication and salvation of God's people. In fulfilling his promise, God will rejoice over his people 'For as a young man marries a young woman, so shall your builder marry you, and as the bridegroom rejoices over the bride, so shall your God rejoice over you' (62:5). In Jeremiah 3, the metaphor is used in terms of the reunification of the twelve tribes ('the house of Judah shall join the house of Israel', 3:18) and their return from exile to the Land (3:18–19). Exile happened because 'as a faithless wife leaves her husband, so you have been faithless to me, O house of Israel' (3:20). Of course, Hosea is replete with the metaphor. While the nation's sin is like adultery against YHWH, after punishment (2:13) there will be a day when 'I [the Lord] will take you for my wife forever; I will take you for my wife in righteousness and in justice, in steadfast love, and in mercy. I will take you for my wife in faithfulness; and you shall know the LORD' (2:19–20).[112]

With Paul, however, the metaphor finds expression in terms of the relation between Christ and believers. Arguably Paul's scriptural citations in 2 Corinthians 6:16–18 in particular (namely 2 Sam. 7:14; Ezek. 20:34; Isa. 43:6; 52:11) demonstrate that he 'sees the beginning fulfilment of the promised res-

---

[109] As in most translations (e.g. NRSV; NIV). Cf. the discussion in Harris, *Second Epistle*, 688.

[110] Harris, *Second Epistle*, 730.

[111] Ibid., 737.

[112] For a more complete analysis of relevant Jewish texts in this context, cf. Ortlund Jr., *Whoredom*.

toration of God's people already taking place in the establishment of the Corinthian church'.[113] The eschatological event of God's restoration, and the accompanying marriage of God to his people is expressed, by Paul, in terms of the relation between risen Lord and believers, of the marriage between Christ and believers. The eschatological relation between YHWH and Israel is here the pattern for the relation between the risen Lord and Christ-believers.

Further, just as in Hosea where the nation's sin is like adultery against YHWH, so the Corinthians are to be presented to Christ as παρθένον ἁγνήν, as pure or chaste virgins. Their relation to the risen Lord must remain undefiled by anything that, as Paul will go onto say, leads away from a single-mindedness and purity in relation to Christ (11:3).[114] The ἁπλότητος ('single-ness') expressed in 11:3 corresponds with the betrothal to the *one* husband of 11:2.[115] Harris speaks of the word here to mean 'that singleness of mind and purpose that finds expression for Christians in an exclusive preoccupation with pleasing Christ ([2 Cor.] 5:2). The person who is characterized by ἁπλότης has no divided loyalties and is not duplicitous but shows unswerving commitment to a person or cause'.[116] As Paul explicitly states, this 'unswerv-ing commitment' expressed devotion to Christ. Indeed, in Paul's promise, mention of *one* husband further expresses the 'exclusivity of the relationship' between Christ and believers.[117] The ἁγνότητος of 11:3 likewise corresponds to matters stated in 11:2, namely the chastity and purity with which Paul desires the Corinthians to be presented before Christ.[118] The themes of devo-tion to Christ, eschatological relation to YHWH and exclusive commitment to the one Husband overlap in Paul's argument.

Galatians 2:16 is important in the πίστις Χριστοῦ debate. But whether διὰ πίστεως Ἰησοῦ Χριστοῦ and ἐκ πίστεως Χριστοῦ should be rendered as sub-jective genitives, as referring to Christ's own faithfulness, need not detain this discussion. That Paul speaks of the Christian's faith in Christ is not disputed in terms of the phrase ἡμεῖς εἰς Χριστὸν Ἰησοῦν ἐπιστεύσαμεν. At the heart of Paul's gospel is, of course, this faith in Christ, or, as Dunn translates it, '"believing into Christ" (= commitment to Christ)'.[119] The verb πιστεύω is here used as an intransitive, the prepositional phrase (εἰς Χριστὸν Ἰησοῦν) indicating the person in whom this faith, or trust, is invested.[120] Fee writes of

---

[113] Scott J. Hafemann, "The Covenant Relationship," in *Central Themes in Biblical Theology: Mapping Unity in Diversity*, eds Scott J. Hafemann, Paul R. House (Grand Rapids: Baker Academic, 2007), 60.

[114] The longer reading of 11:3, namely ἀπὸ τῆς ἁπλότητος καὶ τῆς ἁγνότητος τῆς εἰς τὸν Χριστόν, is convincingly defended in Harris, *Second Epistle*, 731.

[115] Harris, *Second Epistle*, 731.

[116] Ibid., 740.

[117] Ibid., 737.

[118] Ibid., 731.

[119] Dunn, *Galatians*, 139. Dunn also notes Rom. 10:14 and Phil. 1:29.

[120] Martyn, *Galatians*, 252 n.129.

Paul's 'personal language' in 2:20, and Paul's 'very personal way of speaking', adding that 'it is nearly impossible to explain Paul's Christology without taking seriously his utter devotion to Christ' which, he asserts, is expressed in 2:20.[121]

In these verses Paul speaks of his being crucified with Christ, of himself no longer living but Christ living in him, of the life he lives in the flesh as lived ἐν πίστει ζῶ τῇ τοῦ υἱοῦ τοῦ θεοῦ, 'who loved me by giving himself for me'.[122] By being crucified with Christ, Paul presumably means an ongoing experience of identification with Christ and his cross.[123] It means, as Gorman argues, 'a personal spirituality of being indwelt by Christ'.[124] These verses would thus imply that, for Paul, all of his life revolved around this Son of God who loved him; Christ was the heartbeat of Paul's whole life, the presence which energised, inspired and motivated him.[125]

That Paul did not mean to state these things about himself as exclusive from other Christians in Galatia, and rather meant them as exemplary or indicative of the experience of other Christians, is suggested in the repetition of these themes in Galatians as they are applied to others. So Christ 'gave himself for *our* sins' (Gal. 1:4), 'God has sent the Spirit of his Son into *our* hearts' (4:6), '*those who belong to Christ Jesus* have crucified the flesh' (5:24), '*we* have come to believe in Christ Jesus' (2:16. cf. also 5:5–6).[126]

While the matter of 'belonging to Christ' has been noted above, in Galatians 3:29 Paul explains that 'belonging to Christ' makes one a seed of Abraham, an heir according to the promise. To be a member of the covenant people is here defined not in terms of Torah, confession of the *Shema* or anything other than being Χριστοῦ. Central to the identity of the people of God, for Paul, is that they belong to Christ (cf. also 5:24).

It could be argued that Galatians 4:14 is a difficulty for the present argument concerning Christ-devotion in Paul's letters. Paul writes that 'though my condition put you to the test, you did not scorn or despise me'. Rather, Paul says, the Galatians 'welcomed me as an angel of God, as Christ Jesus'. This would seem to put reception of Paul himself, and the mentioned 'angel of God', on a par with welcoming Christ Jesus. This could thus mean Christ-devotion in Paul is nothing more than Paul would expect toward an angel.

---

[121] Fee, *Christology*, 223.

[122] For this translation of the phrase as a hendiadys, cf. Michael J. Gorman, *Inhabiting the Cruciform God: Kenosis, Justification, and Theosis in Paul's Narrative Soteriology* (Cambridge: Eerdmans, 2009), 58 n.48.

[123] Gorman, *Cruciformity*, 32–33.

[124] Ibid., 40.

[125] Cf. Gorman, *Cruciformity*, 45–47.

[126] Wright argues that Paul's personal language here, as in Romans 7, should be understood corporately, as speaking about what happens to all Jews who believe in the Messiah (Tom Wright, *Justification: God's Plan and Paul's Vision* [London: SPCK, 2009], 99–100).

Indeed, it could be argued that 'Jesus Christ' stands in apposition to, and consequently identifies, the mentioned 'angel of God', marking Christ out as an angel. However, three points speak against drawing such conclusions. First, this example, rather than providing the definitive measure of Christ-devotion in Paul, would be exceptional and unusual. Second, Fee has made a good case that the expression ἄγγελον θεοῦ reflects the LXX phrase denoting *the* angel of the Lord (who 'often turns out to be a representation of Yahweh himself'[127]), not merely *an* angel.[128] Third, Fee also argues that it is unlikely that an appositional relationship exists between ἄγγελον θεοῦ and Χριστὸν Ἰησοῦν as the identification of Christ, even with the theophanic angel of YHWH, would be unusual in Paul. Instead, 'we seem in fact to be dealing with progression here ... which would mean that Christ is a full rung higher than the angelic theopanies of the OT'.[129] While one cannot insist too strongly on these points, Fee, in light of the broader pattern of evidence in Paul, is arguably correct.

The much discussed passage, Philippians 2:6–11, was examined above in terms of Paul's goals, and will be analysed below in relation to the character of Christ's lordship. All that needs to be noted here is that *if* the passage was used as a hymn in the corporate worship of the early church, as has often been argued,[130] then the singing of this 'hymn' about Christ would have constituted a feature of the 'corporate devotional *practice* of early Christians'.[131] Dunn's rejoinder that the 'hymn' is 'not addressed *to* Christ, but gives[s] praise to God *for* Christ'[132] would be pertinent if the biblical Psalms were always addressed *to* God and did not sing *about* God. But there are, of course, plenty of Psalms simply *about* God. Besides, it is far from obvious that Philippians 2:10–11 must be addressed only to God, not Christ, especially as it is at the name of Jesus that every knee bends.

While some understand the imperative χαίρετε in Philippians 3:1 as a farewell formula ('good-bye'),[133] this is unlikely. In all other uses of the imperative form in the letter,[134] namely in 2:18 and 4:4, the meaning is clearly

---

[127] Fee, *Christology*, 230.

[128] Ibid.

[129] Ibid., 231.

[130] Larry W. Hurtado, "Philippians 2:6–11," in *Prayer from Alexander to Constantine: A Critical Anthology*, ed. Mark Kiley (London: Routledge, 1997), 235–39; Hurtado, *LJC*, 146–48; Hurtado, *OG²*, 96–97; Hengel, *Jesus*, 80; Hengel, *Studies*, 155. But against speaking of this passage as a 'hymn', cf. Stephen E. Fowl, *The Story of Christ in the Ethics of Paul* (Sheffield: JSOT Press, 1990), 31–45; Fee, *Christology*, 373–74.

[131] Hurtado, *LJC*, 148, italics his; Hurtado, *Earth*, cf. 84–87.

[132] Dunn, *Theology*, 259.

[133] Cf. the references in O'Brien, *Philippians*, 348 n.11.

[134] The literary integrity of Philippians is doubted (most recently in John Reumann, *Philippians: A New Translation with Introduction and Commentary*, AB [New Haven: Yale University Press, 2008], cf. 3), but note the discussion in O'Brien, *Philippians*, 10–18, which makes a decent case for the unity of the letter.

'rejoice'.[135] Furthermore, the theme of rejoicing is a major theme throughout the letter,[136] making any other meaning of the imperative unlikely. Fee notes that 'this idiom ['rejoice in the Lord'] occurs throughout the Septuagint as a primary expression of Israelite piety'.[137] Oddly, he omits to mention Joel 2:23 in his analysis, which reminds one more forcefully of Paul's language given not only the use of the verb χαίρω (unlike the majority of passages Fee cites) but also that, in Joel 2:23, one finds the imperative form of the verb (χαίρετε) used in conjunction with the dative κυρίῳ. There is thus an echo in Paul's language concerning the relation between the risen Lord and believers with the same language as in Joel 2:23 (χαίρετε καὶ εὐφραίνεσθε ἐπὶ τῷ κυρίῳ θεῷ ὑμῶν) concerning the relation between Israel and YHWH.[138]

Philippians 2:6–11 (and 3:20–21 in Fee's work) is generally considered the major christological passage in Philippians, if not in all Paul's undisputed letters.[139] However, neglected material in Philippians 3:7–10 may be as important, or even more so, in terms of Paul's Christology.[140] It has already been examined above in terms of Paul's goals, aims and motives. Though it will be necessary to return to this passage below in examining the passionate nature of Paul's Christ-devotion, here it suffices to draw attention to a few features. Paul writes of τὸ ὑπερέχον τῆς γνώσεως Χριστοῦ Ἰησοῦ τοῦ κυρίου μου. Not only does Paul regard everything as loss because of this knowledge of Christ (and a few verses later, in 3:10, Paul will further express his desire to 'know Christ'), it is also personal: 'my Lord'. This knowledge of Christ, given its personal nature and its all-surpassing value, arguably means it is to be understood within the horizon of language in Paul's scriptures that spoke of Israel's (or the individual Israelite's) knowledge of God (as is also reflected in Paul's letters elsewhere: Rom. 11:33; 2 Cor. 2:14; 10:5). Fee rightly notes how this knowledge is contextually linked with Paul's boasting in Christ Jesus in Philippians 3:4.[141] As was noted above in relation to 2 Corinthians 1:31–2:2, one is thus reminded of Jeremiah 9:24: 'let those who boast boast in this, that they understand and know me, that I am the LORD'.

In 1 Thessalonians 3:8 Paul writes: 'For we now live, if you continue to stand firm in the Lord'. That Paul can 'live' is probably an idiomatic express-

---

[135] O'Brien, *Philippians*, 312, 348–49, 485–86.
[136] 'The verb "to rejoice" and its cognates turn up sixteen times in Philippians' (O'Brien, *Philippians*, 312).
[137] Fee, *Christology*, 408.
[138] That the κύριος of 3:1 is reference to Christ, not the Lord God, is clear from the conjunction of 'Lord' and 'Christ' at regular points in the previous chapter (2:11, 19, 24, 29–30), and in the following (3:8, 20).
[139] 2:6–11 and 3:20–21 are, for Fee, 'the two major christological passages in the letter' (Fee, *Christology*, 372).
[140] Cf. Koperski, *Knowledge*, 323–4.
[141] Fee, *Christology*, 408–9.

ion for the 'removal of anxiety',[142] and probably also means to convey, given the link with 2:19–20, the addition of that which is positive, i.e. hope and joy. What does στήκετε ἐν κυρίῳ mean? A number of suggestions have been made, particularly with reference to ἐν κυρίῳ. So it is argued that Paul means to speak, here, of 'the Christian existence as determined by the Christ-event',[143] or of that which relates especially to 'human conduct',[144] or Paul means to stress '"the Lord" as the source of the community's strength and fidelity'.[145] However, a number of wider factors in 1 Thessalonians need to be remembered. In 1 Thessalonians 3, Paul's main concern is the continued faith of the community. This faith is expressed in relational terms throughout the letter. So, it is before this Lord that Paul can boast of the Thessalonians (2:19–20); it is this Lord who can intervene and work in believers bringing about increased love and holiness (3:12–13); and this Lord whose presence is the goal of Paul's hopes and desires (4:17, 5:10). This fidelity to Christ is thus not merely concerned with moral behaviour alone, nor is it focused purely on a historical event, though it is grounded in this. To stand firm in the Lord is about the believer's devotion to the risen Lord.

Finally, in 1 Thessalonians 1:2–3 Paul 'always gives thanks to God for all of you', and does so 'remembering your work of faith and labour of love and steadfastness of hope in our Lord Jesus Christ'. Whether 'in our Lord Jesus Christ' should be understood to qualify the work of faith and labour of love as well as the steadfastness of hope is difficult to say, and most modern commentaries simply ignore the question.[146] Speaking for the more extensive qualification is the following: the triad of faith, hope and love occur together regularly in early Christian writings.[147] Given this, the objective genitive may modify all of the preceding in light of their natural association with one another. Furthermore, the ὑμῶν that begins the 'lengthy object'[148] of the sentence is dependent on ἔργου ... κόπου ... ὑπομονης.[149] This extended object culminates in the objective genitive τοῦ κυρίου ἡμῶν Ἰησοῦ Χριστου, and thus suggests it relates to the entire triad. What is more, though Paul does speak of God, not Christ, as the object of faith in 1:8, the entire third chapter implies that faith is expressed in whether or not the Thessalonians are 'stand-

---

[142] E. Richard, *First and Second Thessalonians* (Minnesota: Liturgical Press, 1995), 161.

[143] Cf. C.A. Wanamaker, *The Epistles to the Thessalonians* (Carlisle: Paternoster, 1990), 136 and Richard, *Thessalonians*, 162.

[144] F.F. Bruce, *1 & 2 Thessalonians* (Waco: Word, 1982), 67, following Moule.

[145] Richard, *Thessalonians*, 162.

[146] Morris, *Thessalonians*, 42.

[147] Wanamaker, *Thessalonians*, 75; Green, *Thessalonians*, 89.

[148] To use the language of Richard, *Thessalonians*, 46.

[149] Cf. Bruce, *Thessalonians*, 12.

ing fast' in the *Lord* (3:8).[150] Speaking against this reading is that the focus on just 'hope' in Christ sits very comfortably with the rest of the letter that has the eschatological events centred on Christ very much at the fore. But these eschatological hopes do not exclude a love for Christ but perhaps rather assume it, as Paul explicitly states in 1 Corinthians 16:22. Joseph Plevnik writes: 'For Paul, the centering on Christ is essential for hope, for this centering indicates his love for Christ. It is because of this love that he wants to be with Christ forever'.[151] Nevertheless, the vast majority of scholars and Bible translations read τοῦ κυρίου ἡμῶν Ἰησοῦ Χριστοῦ as the object only of ἐλπίδος.

4. The passionate nature of this Christ-devotion

In discussing Paul's motives and goals above, and other expressions of Christ-devotion, the nature of this devotion has occasionally been addressed. It is now necessary to examine some more explicit expressions of the passionate or fervent nature of the Christ-devotion detailed above.[152]

In Romans 12:9–21 Paul offers a series of instructions. In 12:11 Paul writes: τῇ σπουδῇ μὴ ὀκνηροί, τῷ πνεύματι ζέοντες, τῷ κυρίῳ δουλεύοντες. The Greek lacks a finite verb while the dative corresponds to the list of datives starting in 12:9, continuing to 12:12.[153] This makes a precise translation difficult, but the rather consistent structure in Greek implies that the two

---

[150] Fee has recently suggested that 'their faith and hope are in or toward Christ, while their "love" is most likely toward others' (Gordon D. Fee, *The First and Second Letters to the Thessalonians* [Grand Rapids: Eerdmans, 2009], 23). This is certainly possible, but it is difficult to say any more than this.

[151] Plevnik, *Parousia*, 214.

[152] It is not atypical for 'psychology of religion' studies to distinguish between the degrees of intensity and intimacy of religious experiences. However, this study proceeds inductively on the basis of Paul's own language. It does not seek to import psychology of religion distinctions into this discussion (such as one finds in Theißen, *Erleben*, 115, between confirmative, responsive, ecstatic and revelational experiences).

[153] This is clear in the Greek:
⁹ Ἡ ἀγάπη ἀνυπόκριτος.
  ἀποστυγοῦντες τὸ πονηρόν,
  κολλώμενοι τῷ ἀγαθῷ,
¹⁰ τῇ φιλαδελφίᾳ εἰς ἀλλήλους φιλόστοργοι,
  τῇ τιμῇ ἀλλήλους προηγούμενοι,
¹¹ τῇ σπουδῇ μὴ ὀκνηροί,
  τῷ πνεύματι ζέοντες,
  τῷ κυρίῳ δουλεύοντες,
¹² τῇ ἐλπίδι χαίροντες,
  τῇ θλίψει ὑπομένοντες,
  τῇ προσευχῇ προσκαρτεροῦντες
(Romans 12:9–12. Cf. also Moo, *Romans*, 770–71 n.3)

τῷ sentences belong together. Of note here is that the verb ζέω means 'to bubble, boil, ferment, seethe, and was frequently used in a metaphorical sense to describe high emotion'.[154] These points together suggest that Paul understood the Christian's experience of serving the Lord as one involving a zealous boiling over in the spirit (or perhaps Spirit).

In Romans 15 Paul states that he 'will not venture to speak of anything except what Christ has accomplished through me to win obedience from the Gentiles' (15:18). The conjunction of 'obedience' together with 'Gentiles' naturally reminds one of the opening of the letter, in which Paul explained that he was given grace and apostleship 'to bring about the obedience of faith among all the Gentiles for the sake of his [Christ's] name' (Rom. 1:5). Indeed, this is the only other time in the letter in which (human) obedience is associated with the Gentiles. So it is noteworthy that Paul claims that he makes it his 'ambition (φιλοτιμούμενον) to proclaim the good news, not where Christ has already been named' (15:20). It is Paul's *ambition* (cf. also 2 Cor. 5:9; 1 Thess. 4:11) to proclaim this Gospel for the sake of Christ's name, bringing about the obedience of the Gentiles.

1 Corinthians 1:7 has been analysed above and it was noted that the posture of 'waiting for the revealing of the Lord' was employed (cf. also Phil.3:20). BDAG notes various examples where the verb ἀπεκδέχομαι is best understood as awaiting *eagerly*. Paul, in 1 Corinthians 2:2, states that 'I did not resolve to know anything amongst you *except Christ* and Christ crucified'. Christ alone was the object of Paul's knowing in Corinth. His argument in 1 Corinthians 7:32–35 sheds further light on the passion involved in the Christ-relation, where Paul's advice is given 'with a view to promoting that which is appropriate and facilitates *undistracted* devotion to the Lord'.

1 Corinthians 15:58 ends the long 'resurrection' chapter with a word of exhortation in which Paul instructs the Corinthians to be 'steadfast, immovable, *always excelling in the work of the Lord*' (περισσεύοντες ἐν τῷ ἔργῳ τοῦ κυρίου πάντοτε – 15:58). The verb περισσεύω conveys, as Thiselton argues, 'two interrelated nuances': that of abounding and that of excess.[155] Paul writes with the goal to facilitate 'confidence in the worthwhile and responsive character of the work of the Lord, which is not [to be] grudgingly measured but given *with abundance* and *more and more*'.[156] Most translations choose either one or the other of these nuances, e.g., 'excelling' (NRSV), 'abounding'

---

[154] Jewett, *Romans*, 763.

[155] Thiselton, *Corinthians*, 1305.

[156] Thiselton, *Corinthians*, 1306, italics his. This focus on the present life in relation to the Lord, one set on the basis of Christ's saving work, is also entirely consistent with Paul's view of Christian maturity, as Samra cogently argues (James George Samra, *Being Conformed to Christ in Community: A Study of Maturity, Maturation and the Local Church in the Undisputed Pauline Epistles* [London: T&T Clark, 2006]. Cf. also the analysis of 2 Cor. 3:18 above).

(ESV, KJV, RSV). However, Fee's somewhat looser translation perhaps best renders the meaning with 'give yourself fully' (also the NIV).[157]

In 2 Corinthians 10 Paul claims that 'we destroy arguments and every proud obstacle raised up against the knowledge of God, and we take every thought [or 'scheme' – πᾶν νόημα] captive into obedience to Christ' (10:4–5). Paul probably does not mean that he was psychologically inspecting literally every thought, but whatever it precisely means, every thought or scheme, Paul says, must be taken into the obedience of Christ.

2 Corinthians 11:2–3 was examined above. It was argued that the singleness (ἁπλότητος) and the language of *one* husband indicated the necessary 'unswerving commitment' of the Christian to Christ, or, as Harris put it, of the 'singleness of mind and purpose that finds expression for Christians in an exclusive preoccupation with pleasing Christ'.[158]

The prayer conversation between Paul and the risen Lord, detailed in 2 Corinthians 12:8–9, will be examined below. All that needs to be pointed out here is the superlative nature of Paul's language in 12:9. That the 'power of Christ may tabernacle/dwell in me' is the ground for Paul's 'more gladly' (ἥδιστα ... μᾶλλον) boasting in his weaknesses.

In Philippians 1:20 Paul writes: κατὰ τὴν ἀποκαραδοκίαν καὶ ἐλπίδα μου. The κατά phrase refers back to the previous verse, either to ἀποβήσεται, εἰς σωτηρίαν, or both.[159] Either way, a sensible translation will recognise this connection. So O'Brien adds 'this' in his translation: 'This is in accordance with'.[160] It is in accordance with Paul's τὴν ἀποκαραδοκίαν καὶ ἐλπίδα. It is possible that the 'hope' is epexegetical of the 'eager expectation', and even that the construction is a hendiadys.[161] The translation offered here simply leaves these possibilities open: 'This is in accordance with my eager expectation and hope'.[162] This expectation and hope then appears to be given a purpose in the following ὅτι clause.[163] The two verbs of this clause are αἰσχυνθήσομαι, with Paul as the subject, and μεγαλυνθήσεται with Christ as the subject. This corresponds with the matter that Paul's 'expectation is stated first negatively, then positively'.[164] The ἐν οὐδενί is contrasted, after the conjunction ἀλλά, with the second part of the ὅτι clause, with the ἐν πάσῃ. This

---

[157] Fee, *Corinthians*, 808.

[158] Harris, *Second Epistle*, 740.

[159] O'Brien, *Philippians*, 112; Hawthorne, *Philippians*, 42.

[160] O'Brien, *Philippians*, 107.

[161] Cf. the NEB's 'my hope-filled eager expectation'.

[162] Hawthorne, citing Kennedy, explains: 'ἀποκαραδοκία is "the concentrated hope which ignores other interests and strains forward as with outstretched head"' (Hawthorne, *Philippians*, 41).

[163] As most commentators argue, but cf. Hawthorne, *Philippians*, 42, who argues that the ὅτι phrase relates back not to the 'hope' but to the οἶδα of 1:19. Either way, the relation between the hope and the exaltation of Christ remains, as is clear from his translation on p. 32.

[164] O'Brien, *Philippians*, 113.

second clause is the longest of the two parts of the clause giving 'the proper emphasis to the glorification of Christ, the main point of the clause'.[165] The final phrase, 'whether by life or by death', was perhaps, as Hawthorne has argued, a 'stock expression that means "totally," or "all-encompassingly"'.[166] The expressed eager expectation, the content of the positive Christ-exaltation part of the clause, and the final phrase, 'whether by life or by death', all indicate the zealous nature of Paul's Christ-devotion.

In Philippians 3 Paul's tone is very personal. Here, the passionate nature of Paul's Christ-devotion is further evidenced in the extreme language in Philippians 3:8, where he states that he considers *all things* to be 'loss' (πάντα ζημίαν εἶναι) 'on account of (διά with accusative case) the surpassing-ness (here using a substantivised participle ὑπερέχον) of the knowledge of Christ Jesus my Lord'.[167] Further, Paul regards all things (τὰ πάντα) as rubbish or excrement (σκύβαλον) that he may 'gain Christ'. The passionate nature of Paul's knowledge of Christ could hardly be expressed more forcefully. All things, in light of the surpassing-ness of the knowledge of Christ, are σκύβαλον.

In the next chapter, Paul writes to the Philippians, as noted above, that they 'rejoice in the Lord' (4:4). All that needs to be added here is to note the adverb: πάντοτε. These Christ-believers are to rejoice in the risen Lord *always* (cf. also 4:10 where Paul writes that he rejoices *greatly* [μεγάλως] in the Lord).

As shall be explored below, Paul's prayer-wishes in 1 Thessalonians are directed to the risen Lord (1 Thess. 3:11–13). Given this prayer model provided by Paul here, it is perhaps noteworthy that in the same letter the Apostle requests that these Christians 'pray without ceasing' (5:17). Of course, one cannot and should not try to prove that Paul only meant prayer to Christ, but the letter has shown that such prayer also involved prayer to the risen Lord. Indeed, right next to this command to pray without ceasing is the command to 'rejoice always' (5:16), an imperative used frequently with reference to the risen Lord and not, at least in the extant Pauline letters, in relation to God.

5. What Paul contrasts with Christ-devotion

At numerous points in the undisputed letters, Paul contrasts some aspect of Christ-devotion with various negatives. It will prove illuminating to the general purpose of this thesis to establish exactly what Paul explicitly contrasted with Christ-devotion, and not merely the logical opposite of this devotion

---

[165] Jerry L. Sumney, *Philippians: A Greek Student's Intermediate Reader* (Peabody: Hendrickson, 2007), 27.

[166] Hawthorne, *Philippians*, 43. In support, he cites Rom. 8:38 and 1 Cor. 3:22.

[167] As Sumney notes, 'τῆς γνώσεως ... is dependent on τὸ ὑπερέχον and seems to be epexegetical; that is, the surpassing value is the knowledge' (Sumney, *Philippians*, 78).

(such as claiming that *not* calling on the name of the Lord means one will *not* be saved, cf. Rom. 10:9–13)

The first passage to examine is Romans 16:18. Paul exhorts the Roman Christians to avoid those who 'cause dissensions and offences, in opposition to the teaching that you have learned' (16:17). 'For such people', Paul continues, 'do not serve our Lord Christ, but their own belly [κοιλία]'. As Jewett argues, to 'serve the belly implies that the opponents are slaves to their appetite and to other bodily pleasures'.[168] Serving 'our Lord Jesus Christ' was the opposite, for Paul, of 'belly serving'.[169]

Mention must be made of 1 Corinthians 6:13 where Paul writes: 'The body is meant not for fornication but for the Lord'. The sinful activity of fornication is contrasted directly with the body's purpose to be 'for the Lord'.

In 1 Corinthians 7:32–35, as noted above, Paul develops an enthymematic argument concerning the desirability of remaining unmarried. To facilitate this point Paul draws a distinction between the unmarried and the married. The former are 'anxious about the things of the Lord, how to please the Lord' to be 'entirely holy' (= 'holy in body and spirit') (7:32, 34), while the latter are 'anxious about the things of the world, how to please his/her wife/husband' (7:33, 34). While Paul will state that marrying is no sin (7:36), he makes it clear, in 7:32, that his exhortation involves a contrast of devotion to the Lord with concern for the things of the world. Furthermore, the implication of Paul's statement about unmarried women being entirely holy would suggest that distraction from 'devotion to the Lord' (7:35) means that one cannot be entirely holy (i.e., holy in body and spirit). But this admittedly states more than Paul explicitly says.

As was seen in chapter 5, Paul argues, in 1 Corinthians 8–10, that the opposite of Christ-devotion is sinning against Christ (8:12), testing him (10:9), capitulation to idolatry (10:20–21) and provoking him to jealousy (10:22), a matter which implies the threat of judgment. A similar line of thought concerning judgment is picked up in 1 Corinthians 11, in Paul's discussion concerning the Lord's Supper. 'Whoever', Paul writes, 'eats the bread or drinks the cup of the Lord in an unworthy manner will be answerable for the body and blood of the Lord' (11:27). The phrase 'body and blood' probably makes a christological, rather than an ecclesiological, understanding of 'body' more likely in this sentence as the latter, 'blood', is difficult to explain were the σώματος referring to the gathered community.[170] Furthermore, Konradt adds that '"body" – according to the wide consensus of critical exegesis – is ... not to be understood physically as "Flesh", but describes the Per-

---

[168] Jewett, *Romans*, 991. Cf. also the NIV; NRSV; ESV; NAB; NASB; RSV.

[169] Cf. Karl O. Sandnes, *Belly and Body in the Pauline Epistles* (Cambridge: Cambridge University Press, 2002), 267.

[170] Cf. e.g. Thiselton, *Corinthians*, 889–94; Garland, *1 Corinthians*, 552–53; Schnabel, *Korinther*, 661; Konradt, *Gericht*, 418; Barrett, *1 Corinthians*, 273.

son [of Christ]'.[171] Thiselton's examination of the word ἔνοχος coheres well
with Konradt's thesis: 'in Koine Greek [ἔνοχος with the genitive] came to
denote the *person against whom the crime is committed*'.[172] So Fee writes that
'an abuse of the "body" is an abuse of Christ himself'.[173]

After the exhortation in 11:28 (δοκιμαζέτω δὲ ἄνθρωπος ἑαυτόν), Paul
returns to σῶμα-language in 11:29. Once again, and consistent with the suggested interpretation of σῶμα above in relation to 11:27, it is most plausible
that an ecclesiological rendering of 'body' in 11:29 is to be resisted.[174] Thus
διακρίνων τὸ σῶμα is arguably best understood to mean a mindfulness, to use
the words of Thiselton, 'of the uniqueness of Christ, who is separated from
others in the sense of giving himself for others in sheer grace'.[175] By failing to
remain mindful of the 'uniqueness of Christ' Christians can sin against Christ,
and incur the consequent judgment from the Lord himself (11:30–32).

In speaking of the 'perishing' in 2 Corinthians 4, Paul writes that 'In their
case[176] the god of this world has blinded the minds of the unbelievers, to keep
them from seeing the light of the gospel of the glory of Christ, who is the
image of God' (4:4). As was argued above in relation to 2 Corinthians 3:18, it
is by beholding the glory of the risen Lord that one is transformed. However, ὁ
θεὸς τοῦ αἰῶνος, probably 'the satan',[177] has blinded minds to keep them from
seeing this glory. Paul's apocalyptic worldview involved a dualism between
various spiritual forces set against God.[178] Yet at the centre of Paul's apocalyptic imagination stands the satan's blinding of the minds of unbelievers, to
stop them from seeing 'the light of the gospel of the glory of *Christ*'.

In 2 Corinthians 5:15 Paul writes that Christ 'died for all, so that those who
live might live no longer for themselves, but for him who died and was raised
for them'. The dualism of thought implicit here is that one may live either for
themselves or Christ. Indeed, in the next sentence he reiterates this dualism of
thought in terms of knowing Christ: 'even though we once knew Christ
according to the flesh, we no longer know him in that way' (5:16). Arguably,
Paul intends to distinguish here between two spheres of knowing.[179] On the

---

[171] Konradt, *Gericht*, 418.

[172] Thiselton, *Corinthians*, 889, also following the BDAG.

[173] Fee, *Corinthians*, 533 (cf. 558–59 for a fuller discussion). Cf. also Thiselton,
Corinthians, 890; Konradt, *Gericht*, 438.

[174] Cf. the extended discussion and references in Thiselton, *Corinthians*, 891–94.

[175] Thiselton, *Corinthians*, 893. This is not to negate any social concern in Paul's
argument, but rather to recognise it as secondary and dependent upon necessary
participation in and identification with the Lord and his self-giving grace.

[176] Ἐν οἷς refers back to ἐν τοῖς ἀπολλυμένοις. Cf. the discussion in Harris, *Second
Epistle*, 327.

[177] Cf. Harris, *Second Epistle*, 328.

[178] Cf. Edward Adams, *Constructing the World: A Study in Paul's Cosmological
Language* (Edinburgh: T&T Clark, 2000); and the discussion in Dunn, *Theology*, 104–10.

[179] Of course, κατὰ σάρκα could have a more neutral meaning, but this is unlikely in 2
Cor. 5:16.

one hand there is the world dominated by Sin, by the 'god of this age', by, to import language from Galatians, the 'elemental spirits' (στοιχεῖα – Gal. 4:3, 9), and by the flesh. On the other hand there is the world of new creation in Christ (2 Cor. 5:17), life in the Spirit of Christ (Rom. 8:9, as opposed to the flesh as in 8:4–5, 12–13. Cf. also 2 Cor. 3:3, 6). At the hinge of these worlds is how Christ is 'known'.

Paul's language in 2 Corinthians 11:2–3 is again of importance. His jealousy, 'such as God has', is based upon his eschatological betrothal of the church to one husband, to Christ, and the threat that their single-mindedness and purity in relation to Christ is in danger. In particular, Paul is afraid that this compromise will happen 'as the serpent deceived Eve by its cunning' (11:3). This compromise is related to the ultimate sin of all, to the 'fall'. Elsewhere, Paul speaks of the 'fall' in terms of Adam, as the entrance of universal death into the world (Rom. 5:14; 1 Cor. 15:22). Such a deception, with which the serpent duped Eve, is the root of Paul's fear that the Corinthian Christians will be led away from single-mindedness and purity in devotion to Christ.

In Galatians 1:10, having proclaimed a curse on those who proclaim another gospel, Paul rhetorically states: 'If I were still trying to please men, I would not be the slave of Christ'.[180] Of course, 'slave of Christ' was one of Paul's self-designations, but here he contrasts it with 'pleasing humans'. They are mutually contradictory. This 'slave of Christ' language needs to be remembered when one reads, a few chapters later, that 'formerly, when you did not know God, you were enslaved [ἐδουλεύσατε] to beings that by nature are not gods' (4:8). In Galatians 5:4 Paul writes: 'You who want to be justified by the law have cut yourselves off from Christ; you have fallen away from grace'. To be cut off from Christ is to be severed from grace and to fall prey to the attempt to be justified ἐξ ἔργων νόμου.

In recommending Timothy to the Philippians, Paul exclaims that 'I have no one like him who will be genuinely concerned for your welfare' (Phil. 2:20). 'For all others', Paul continues, 'seek their own interests, not those of Christ' (2:21). There would appear to be some measure of rhetorical exaggeration in Paul's language, in order to best recommend Timothy. But what is noteworthy for the present purpose, is to see how Paul recoursed, in his rhetoric, to a division between those who seek Christ's interests, on the one hand, and those who seek their own, on the other.

In Philippians 3 Paul, with tears, explains how many live as enemies of the cross of Christ (3:18). In the next verse Paul describes these enemies further, through a repetition of relative pronouns, each followed by an assertion: 'whose end is destruction, whose god is the belly, and whose glory is in their shame'. The final substantival participle, while not employing the relative pronoun, speaks of the same people, of the 'many' of the previous verse: 'their minds are set on earthly things'. This change, with the use of the adjective

---

[180] This translation is offered in Dunn, *Galatians*, 48.

ἐπίγειος, sets up the contrast with 'heaven' in the following verse.[181] Unlike these people, 'our citizenship is in heaven, and it is from there that we are expecting a Saviour, the Lord Jesus Christ' (3:20).The dividing line between the 'them' and 'us' revolves around the respective relations to the cross of Christ. The 'us' are expecting their saviour from heaven; the others have their minds set on earthly things.

6. The presence and activity of the risen Lord

In Romans 8:9–10 Paul writes that 'Anyone who does not have the Spirit of Christ does not belong to him. But if Christ is in you ...'. It will be necessary to return to the expression 'Spirit of Christ' below, but for now it suffices to point out Paul's notion of the indwelling Christ. To what extent one should take Paul literally here is an important question,[182] but it would seem clear that a fundamental facet of the Christ-believer is that Christ, however this is precisely understood, dwells in him or her.

In discussing the difficult relations between members in the Roman church, Paul emphasises the need to avoid judging one another. So he reasons: 'Who are you to pass judgment on servants of another? It is before their own lord that they stand or fall. And they will be upheld, for the Lord is able to make them stand' (Rom. 14:4). While important textual variants prefer to read 'God' instead of 'Lord', as the one who is able to make believers stand, κύριος is the reading accepted by most, and this probably means the *risen* Lord.[183] If this reading is accepted, then the passage expresses the idea that Christ's active present power is able to sustain the Christ-believer in their religious-ethical life.

In speaking about his ministry in Romans 15, Paul explains his work: 'For I will not venture to speak of anything except what Christ has accomplished through me to win obedience from the Gentiles, by word and deed, by the power of signs and wonders, by the power of the Spirit of God' (Rom. 15:18–19). Paul states that in his missionary activity, Christ himself is at work. It will be necessary to return to this passage below in determining exactly how Paul understood this activity of Christ, but for now it suffices to note this activity. Indeed, a few verses later Paul promises to visit Rome, and from there to set out to Spain. When he comes, he argues, 'I know that when I come to you, I will come in the fullness of the blessing of Christ' (Rom. 15:29). Christ's active blessing accompanies Paul in his missionary work.

---

[181] Sumney, *Philippians*, 94.

[182] Cf. discussion in Rabens, *Spirit*, 37, 40–49.

[183] So Moo, *Romans*, 840–41; Wilhelm Thüsing, *Per Christum in Deum: Studien zum Verhältnis von Christozentrik und Theozentrik in den paulinischen Hauptbriefen* (Münster: Aschendorff, 1969), 34; Cranfield, *Romans 9–16*, 704.

As Paul began Romans (cf. 1:7), so he ends with the blessing that 'the grace of our Lord Jesus Christ be with you' (16:20). Christ's grace is to be a present and active reality for the Roman Christians. But to examine what this grace means, it will be necessary to turn to the language in the Corinthian correspondence.

Within 1 Corinthians the risen Lord is, for Paul, present and active in a remarkable number of ways: (1) in his outworking, gracious activity and enabling in the Christian community, (2) in appointing leaders (3:5), (3) within Paul, making the apostle trustworthy, (4) over/in the social and communal situatedness of all people (7:17), and (5), over/in the seemingly contingent course of historical events (4:19; 16:17). Each point will now be analysed in turn.

Christ is present and active in the Corinthian Christian community. This is first seen in the grace formulas. At the beginning and end of 1 Corinthians, Paul writes: 'Grace to you and peace from ... the Lord Jesus Christ' (1:3) and 'The grace of the Lord Jesus be with you' (16:23). Grace is *from* the risen Lord, and Paul wishes it to 'be with' (μεθ' ὑμῶν) the Corinthians.[184] Modern commentators, especially since Bultmann's focus on grace as 'event',[185] have emphasised the dynamic and active nature of this grace. Hence Bultmann writes of grace in Paul as 'this now occurring act of grace',[186] as 'the power that determines the life of the individual'.[187] He indeed understands this grace as practically synonymous with 'power', especially in verses like 1 Corinthians 15:10 and 2 Corinthians 12:9.[188] Modern commentators have seized upon this 'event' language, especially as it has been filtered to them through Dunn,[189] and thus write, as, e.g., Fee does, that 'for Paul "grace" does not mean an attitude or disposition of God; it denotes rather the wholly generous *act* of God'. Thiselton too writes that the grace, in 1:3, 'constitutes an event rather than a disposition'.[190]

However, care is needed here. Though some modern commentators draw upon the 1975 formulations of Dunn, his later works, such as his 1988 Romans commentary, and, most recently, his 1998 *Theology of Paul the Apostle*, have formulated the issue more circumspectly, such that 'event' is not entirely played off against 'disposition'. For example, in the latter work he

---

[184] Of course, this grace is also from God, but this chapter seeks simply to examine the data relevant to the Christ-relation.

[185] Bultmann, *Theology*, 1.288–92. At about the same time, cf. also Barth, *CD*, II/1, e.g. pp. 197f, 263 etc.

[186] Bultmann, *Theology*, 1.289.

[187] Ibid., 1.291.

[188] Bultmann, *Theology*, 1.291, followed recently in Dunn, *Theology*, 48.

[189] James D.G. Dunn, *Jesus and the Spirit* (London: SCM, 1975), e.g. 209, 254.

[190] Fee, *Corinthians*, 35 n.29, italics mine; Thiselton, *Corinthians*, 81, italics mine. Cf. also 81–82, n.123. Cf. also Wolfgang Schrage, *Der erste Brief an die Korinther (1)* (Zürich: Benziger, 1991), 106.

writes that grace in Paul 'denoted *not simply* an attitude or a disposition *but also* the act *which expressed the attitude*'.[191] Rather than grace as disposition or event, it is better to speak of the present outworking of the graciousness of Christ. It is an *active, powerful and 'under girding'* grace in the church. This makes sense particularly because the standard form of an ending in the contemporary letters was the injunction 'be strong'.[192] Paul's 'christianised' version demonstrates what makes them strong – the effective grace of Christ in their midst.[193]

Dunn argues, in relation to Romans 1:7, that the grace-wish can be understood in the following way: 'May you know the generous power of *God* undergirding and coming to expression in your daily life',[194] i.e., as a prayer-wish. As with so many of the verses analysed in this chapter, commentators seem to default into reading 'God' into 'Lord [Jesus]' passages, even when the christological referent is clear. In Romans 1:7, as well as 1 Corinthians 1:3, grace is just as much 'from Christ'. But this point aside, Dunn has spotted a feature of this Pauline language that 1 Corinthians scholars have hinted at now and then: Paul's talk of the grace of Christ is perhaps also a prayer-wish.[195] In other words, the experience of Christ's active graciousness is perhaps in some sense related to prayer, as shall be explored below.

While the above passages clearly demonstrate the basic argument that Christ is, for Paul, present in his gracious activity in the church, it is less obvious if the complex and highly debated text in 1 Corinthians 5:3–4 suggests the same. The important phrase for our purpose is 'and my spirit is present with the power of our Lord Jesus' (καὶ τοῦ ἐμοῦ πνεύματος σὺν τῇ δυνάμει τοῦ κυρίου ἡμῶν Ἰησοῦ). Fatehi argues:

Whatever the difficulties of exegeting this verse, there can be no doubt that Paul regarded the risen Lord's presence and power as one of the necessary elements to be present in the gathered community in order to accomplish the task at hand.[196]

However, one of the various interpretive possibilities offered by this verse, actually favoured by Thiselton, *does* admit doubt that Paul was speaking of the present power of the Lord. The 'power of the Lord Jesus' would, on

---

[191] Dunn, *Theology*, 322, italics mine.

[192] A fact Fee mentions but without making this association (Fee, *Corinthians*, 839).

[193] This gracious enabling presence of Christ is something some commentators have ambitiously suggested 'encompassed everything' in the letter (e.g. Thiselton, *Corinthians*, 1352, citing Hays). The implication is thus that Paul's understanding of Christ's active graciousness is something central and foundational to the entire letter. Of course, this claim has support in the obvious fact that both 1:3 and 16:23 appear at key positions at both the start and end of the letter.

[194] Dunn, *Romans*, 20, italics mine.

[195] Cf. Garland, *1 Corinthians*, 30, and the references he cites. But also see R.P. Martin, *2 Corinthians*, 232.

[196] Fatehi, *Relation*, 11.

Thiselton's preferred reading, refer to the institutional authority of the church that the risen Lord legitimises.[197]

It is clear, however, that the risen Lord is active in appointing church leaders and missionaries. In 1 Corinthians 3:5 Paul writes 'What then is Apollos? What is Paul? [They are only] Servants through whom you came to believe, even *as the Lord assigned the role to each*'. Arguably, the context is conclusive that 'Lord' here is to be taken as a reference to Christ, and not God, as can be substantiated by the fact that Paul speaks of Christ as the 'foundation' (θεμέλιος) in 3:11, in a way that parallels the purpose and argument of ὁ κύριος in 3:5.[198] Hence, for Paul, Christ is a present and very active force in the formation and mission of the church, appointing its leaders, assigning them, as Thiselton writes: 'in his sovereign choice'.[199]

The risen Lord is present and active in Paul making the apostle trustworthy, as is evident in 1 Corinthians 7:25. The same verse makes clear that the Lord here is Christ, not the Father (cf. mention of the 'word of the Lord', namely of the pre-Easter Christ in 7:22 and 25).[200] It is therefore inaccurate of Garland to write, in relation to this verse, that '*God's* mercy made him [Paul] "sufficient" as a minister ... and certified him as "trustworthy"'.[201] It is the mercy of the risen Lord, Christ's *active mercy* at work in Paul, that makes him πιστός.

The risen Lord appears also sovereignly to appoint the social and communal situation of the Corinthian believers. In 1 Corinthians 7:17 Paul writes: 'Only, let every one lead the life which the Lord has assigned to him, and in which God has called him' (RSV). Is this κύριος meant to identify the risen Lord? The case has been made that the parallelism (between ἑκάστῳ ὡς ἐμέρισεν ὁ κύριος and ἕκαστον ὡς κέκληκεν ὁ θεός) suggests θεός gives κύριος a theological, rather than a christological meaning.[202] Fee's confidence that this is not so is substantiated by reference to the change in subject and verb (including tense) in the parallelism.[203] In support of Fee, the contextual issues mentioned above in relation to 7:25 tip the balance in favour of reading κύριος here christologically.[204]

---

[197] Cf. Thiselton, *Corinthians*, 394, and his comment that this interpretation 'has most to commend it on the grounds of its status as a speech-act'.

[198] This is a point missed by commentators in reference to 3:11. On Christ as the Lord, here, cf. Fee, *Corinthians*, 131 n.10, who maintains that the definite article before κύριος indicates the reference to be christological 'as it almost always does'. However, κύριος is 'almost always' christological anyway, so the value of Fee's reasoning may be questioned.

[199] Thiselton, *Corinthians*, 300.

[200] Cf. Friedrich Wilhelm Horn, *Das Angeld des Geistes: Studien zur paulinischen Pneumatologie* (Göttingen: Vandenhoeck & Ruprecht, 1992), 227.

[201] Garland, *1 Corinthians*, 321, italics mine.

[202] S. Scott Bartchy, *Mallon Chresai: First Century Slavery and the Interpretation of 1 Corinthians 7:21* (Missoula, Mont.: SBL, 1973).

[203] Fee, *Corinthians*, 310.

[204] Fee is more confident and writes: 'As usual in Paul this ['Lord'] refers to Christ, not God' (Fee, *Corinthians*, 310 n.16).

If this is correct, which seems likely, then first, that which the Lord assigned refers, in the broadest sense, to the domestic matters discussed in the surrounding verses, and of course directly to the matters of marriage and status.[205] This means that in whatever domestic or social situation believers in Corinth found themselves, they have been 'assigned' this by the risen Lord, a fact that will provide the basis for Paul's argument in the next few verses.[206] Second, this last point can be pressed a little further. As Barrett comments, in this verse 'Paul is not thinking primarily of a vocation *to* which man is called, but of the condition *in* which a man is' (hence above the RSV translation is adopted, over the NRSV).[207] Indeed, the following verses (7:18–20) suggest that the call of God is to be associated with conversion. The 'life that the Lord has assigned', if the parallelism of 7:17 is not misunderstood, is thus the pre-conversion state of the addressees, it is the life they lived *in which* God called them. This pre-conversion life, Paul claims, was allotted and determined by the sovereignty of the risen Lord. Third, while not wanting to suggest that Paul was a modern individualist,[208] the repeated use of ἕκαστος in this verse indicates that the sovereign determination of Christ in relation to the pre-conversion social and domestic situation of these believers was such that the risen lordship encompassed each and every individual.[209]

1 Corinthians also gives reason for accepting a Pauline understanding of Christ as active in and sovereign over the seemingly contingent course of historical events. Paul writes:

i) 'But I will come soon (ταχέως), if the Lord wills (θελήσῃ)' (1 Cor 4:19)
ii) '... I hope to spend some time with you, if the Lord permits (ἐπιτρέψῃ)' (1 Cor 16:7)

Commentators have focused on the apparent contradiction between the ταχέως in 4:19 and Paul's comment in 16:8, where he explains his plan to stay in Ephesus until Pentecost.[210] The result is that an appreciative analysis of the implied understanding of the sovereignty of the risen κύριος is often neglected.[211]

---

[205] Cf. how Thiselton arranges and titles the material in Thiselton, *Corinthians*, 484–562.

[206] Cf. e.g., Garland's argument that 7:17 is the 'Statement of the basic principle' which will be explained, restated and expanded on till 7:24 (Garland, *1 Corinthians*, 301).

[207] Barrett, *1 Corinthians*, 168, though note the important qualifications made in Thiselton, *Corinthians*, 548.

[208] Thiselton, *Corinthians*, 301.

[209] Cf. e.g. Fitzmyer, *First Corinthians*, 307. A modern scholarly overreaction to 19th and early 20th century individualism probably needs to be admitted (cf. Gary W. Burnett, *Paul and the Salvation of the Individual* [Köln: Brill, 2001] and the insightful comments in Samra, *Conformed*, 28–32). Of course, such overreactions can be found precisely in the late 19th and early 20th centuries too (cf. the unguarded comments in William Wrede, *Paul*, trans. Edward Lummis, reprint, 1908 [Eugene, OR: Wipf & Stock, 2001], 114)!

[210] Cf. Barrett, *1 Corinthians*, 389–90.

[211] But cf. Fee, *Christology*, 139, 583; Fatehi, *Relation*, 12.

Certain contextual features lend positive support to a christological reading of κύριος in both 4:19 and 16:7.[212] One can refer to the clear christological κύριος in 5:4, 5; 15: 57–58 (and very likely also in 4:17), and the repeated mention of κύριος in 1 Corinthians 16 culminating in the important final verses (16:22–23) where the christological emphasis is certain. Reference to Romans 1:10 ('asking that by *God's will* I may somehow at last succeed in coming to you'. Cf. also Rom 15:32) does not resolve the matter in terms of God as Lord, as in the two verses above Paul is writing about the will and permission of the κύριος, and Paul was quite able to hold θεός and κύριος together without collapsing the meaning of one into the other.[213] Therefore, it is not entirely appropriate, when commenting on 4:19, for Garland to write that 'Paul's travel plans are always conditioned upon the will of *God*'.[214] It is likely that Schrage is correct to note that the concept of sovereignty expressed in these verses encompasses more than simple travel plans, but is reflective of an understanding of 'all of human life as conditioned by the divine will'. However, his mentioning, in light of this verse of 'the will of *God* who is guiding his life' diverts from the specifically christological force of the passage.[215] Fee is more careful in his formulation in writing of the 'divine will' in 4:19, and of Paul's plans being 'subject to Christ' in 16:7.[216] The risen Lord is portrayed, almost as a side-thought, as sovereign over Paul's travel plans, and hence, if Schrage's recourse to the so-called *conditio Jacobaea* is appropriate, over all of the contingencies of the created order, over the 'entirety of human life'.[217] Paul's language can certainly be read to lead to this conclusion, even if it ultimately says more than Paul does in his specific arguments.

In 2 Corinthians once again the 'grace and peace' formula is to be noted (2 Cor. 1:2; 13:13). However, one possible translation that would speak against its inclusion in this argument, suggesting a Pauline understanding of the presence and activity of the risen Lord, can now be addressed more pertinently, given the presence of the following verse (2 Cor. 1:3). It is at least a grammatical possibility to translate 1:2 as if both ἡμῶν and κυρίου Ἰησοῦ Χριστοῦ are dependent on πατρός. However, as Harris argues, such a reading is made unlikely by 1:3 'which speaks unambiguously of God as the "Father of our Lord Jesus Christ"; it would be a tautology uncharacteristic of Paul for v. 2 to make virtually the same affirmation'.[218] While Harris focuses his other arguments against this reading on grammatical and textual issues,[219] another

---

[212] Cf. also the reasoning in Fee, *Corinthians*, 87 n.42.

[213] Cf., e.g., 1 Cor. 8:6 and the thesis of Richardson, *Paul's Language About God*.

[214] Garland, *1 Corinthians*, 148, italics mine.

[215] Schrage, *Korinther*, 362, italics mine.

[216] Fee, *Corinthians*, 191, 820. Cf. now Fee, *Christology*, 139.

[217] Schrage, *Korinther*, 362, esp. n.296.

[218] Harris, *Second Epistle*, 136. He offers four other reasons for rejecting dependence on πατρὸς.

[219] Harris, *Second Epistle*, 136.

important reason for doubting this reading is Paul's regular reference to the 'grace of Christ' (Rom. 16:20; 2 Cor. 13:13; Gal. 6:18; Phil. 4:23; 1 Thess. 5:28; Philem. 25. Cf. also 2 Thess. 3:18 and 1 Tim. 1:14).

The above argument also speaks against those who would understand the reference to 'grace' in relation to Christ, as indicative of a salvation-history event alone.[220] Paul has in mind, in 2 Corinthians 13:13, a grace that he wishes to be '*with* you all' (μετὰ πάντων ὑμῶν). Better is Bultmann's judgment that grace, in 13:13, is 'like in the opening greeting of 1:2 etc., the salvation-grace which bestows not only justification, but all goodness that is grounded in Christ'.[221] This grace is a present and active reality in the life of the Christians, and as Thrall writes: 'When Paul speaks of the grace of Christ ... [in 13:13] he has in mind a personal relationship between Christ and the Corinthians'.[222]

Given that 1:2 ties both the risen Lord and God to the same preposition (ἀπό), and that Lord is linked with God in the benediction of 13:13, some have been quick to claim, on this basis, a divine-Christology.[223] However, such a line of reasoning proceeds too quickly. For example, Harris argues that, in light of the evidence in 1:2, 'the deity of Christ is here implicitly affirmed, for a monotheistic Jew would never juxtapose a mere human being with God as a comparable fount of spiritual blessing'.[224] However, this perhaps underestimates the sort of language used in Second Temple Judaism in relation to various intermediary figures.[225] What is important is not merely this isolated datum, but its place within a pattern of evidence.

In examining the presence and activity of the risen Lord in 2 Corinthians, one must address Paul's phrase ἐν προσώπῳ Χριστοῦ in 2:10. Is it a synecdoche or a Semitic idiom meaning 'the presence of Christ'? And is it to be understood eschatologically, i.e. as referring to Christ's future presence? These questions shall now be addressed in turn.

If ἐν προσώπῳ Χριστοῦ is to be understood as a synecdoche, then 'face' is used to indicate the person of Christ.[226] However, in order to then make sense of the phrase in 2:10, it would be necessary to understand this synecdochic

---

[220] As, e.g., R.P. Martin, *2 Corinthians*, 496, 505; R. H. Strachan, *The Second Epistle of Paul to the Corinthians* (London: Hodder & Stoughton, 1935), 146; Barrett, *2 Corinthians*, 56, 344 (who argues grace is, in 13:13, 'an observable event in history' and, in relation to 1:2, an 'antecedent being and act of God which are the ground of all Christian existence'); Frank J. Matera, *II Corinthians: A Commentary* (Louisville: Westminster John Knox, 2003), 314 ('Believers first experience the graciousness of Jesus Christ who died for all ... On the basis of this gracious act, they come to know the love of God').

[221] Bultmann, *Korinther*, 253, translation mine.

[222] Thrall, *2 Corinthians Vol. 2*, 918.

[223] E.g., Harris, *Second Epistle*, 136, 938.

[224] Harris, *Second Epistle*, 136.

[225] For more on this, cf. chapter 9 below.

[226] Cf. Thrall, *2 Corinthians Vol. 1*, 180; Matera, *II Corinthians*, 61; Harris, *Second Epistle*, 232.

reading as an indication of Paul's understanding of his role as one representing Christ.[227] But if Paul had wanted to indicate his representative role before Christ, evidence within 2 Corinthians suggests that he would have expressed himself differently (cf. 5:20 ὑπὲρ Χριστοῦ).[228]

Indeed, there are numerous reasons to prefer the semitic idiom reading. First, the idiom was well known in the Jewish scriptures (cf. לִפְנֵי as ἐν προσώπῳ in Prov. 4:3; 25:7).[229] Likewise, as Thrall indicates, ἐν προσώπῳ αὐτοῦ likely translates לְפָנָיו in Proverbs 8:30.[230] Scott also points to a number of passages in the LXX that use the phrase in the sense of 'close physical proximity to another person (cf. Jer. 52:25; 2 Macc. 14:24 ...)'.[231] Second, contextual clues suggest this idiomatic reading. Thrall argues: 'Paul seems to be concerned to show his awareness that his acting is witnessed by God or by Christ', and she refers to 2:17; 4:2; 5:11; 8:21.[232] Scott maintains that in the immediate context, namely 2:14–4:6, Paul 'is a Moses-like revelatory mediator who has direct access to the very presence of God'.[233] Finally, within 2 Corinthians, in 10:1, 'face' is understood as the opposite of 'absence', thus implying presence.[234] Together with the majority of commentators, it is thus arguably best to understand ἐν προσώπῳ Χριστοῦ as a semitic idiom, meaning the 'presence of Christ'.[235]

Some scholars have emphasised an eschatological aspect to Paul's words, implying that the presence of Christ indicated is not a present, but a future, presence. Furnish claims that '[i]n both 5:10 ... and 8:21 ... the references are to the final judgment. An eschatological reference is implicit in the present verse [2:10] as well'.[236] Similarly, Barnett sees an eschatological nuance in the phrase ἐν προσώπῳ Χριστοῦ. To cite him, it means '"in the presence of

---

[227] Cf. e.g., Harris, *Second Epistle*, 232.

[228] As noted in Thrall, *2 Corinthians Vol. 1*, 180.

[229] As pointed out in Furnish, *II Corinthians*, 157.

[230] Thrall, *2 Corinthians Vol. 1*, 180.

[231] James M. Scott, *2 Corinthians* (Peabody: Hendrickson, 1998), 49.

[232] Thrall, *2 Corinthians Vol. 1*, 181.

[233] James M. Scott, *2 Corinthians*, 49. Of course, this point has less value if, together with many partition theories, 2:14 is understood as the start of a separate letter or letter fragment.

[234] Cf. Barnett, *Corinthians*, 131, fn. 48.

[235] E.g. Lambrecht, *Second Corinthians*, 32; Thrall, *2 Corinthians Vol. 1*, 180–81; Barrett, *2 Corinthians*, 93; R.P. Martin, *2 Corinthians*, 38–39; Harris, *Second Epistle*, 232–33; Barnett, *Corinthians*, 130; James M. Scott, *2 Corinthians*, 49; Furnish, *II Corinthians*, 157; Craig S. Keener, *1–2 Corinthians* (Cambridge: Cambridge University Press, 2005), 161; Matera, *II Corinthians*, 60; Strachan, *Corinthians*, 71; Werner Kleine, *Zwischen Furcht und Hoffnung: eine textlinguistische Untersuchung des Briefes 2 Kor 1–9 zur wechselseitigen Bedeutsamkeit der Beziehung von Apostel und Gemeinde* (Berlin: Philo, 2002), 147; Bultmann, *Korinther*, 54; ESV; ASV; NAB; NASB; NIV; NJB; NKJV; NRSV; RSV; etc.

[236] Furnish, *II Corinthians*, 157–58.

Christ" (i.e., *eschatologically*, with Christ as a witness – so Furnish, Thrall)'.[237]

However, though the eschatological *consequence* implied in Paul's words is to be accepted, the eschatological element can be over pressed. First, though Paul can speak of accountability before the eschatological judgment seat of Christ (as Furnish notes, in 5:10), Paul can also speak of the present consequences of disobedience to the Lord (as in 1 Cor. 11:28–34), and so the relevance of Paul's forgiveness 'in the presence of Christ' cannot be pushed in a solely eschatological direction if understood in terms of judgment. Second, Furnish's reference above to 8:21 hardly supports an eschatological reading itself, even if Paul may have eschatological consequences in mind. The passage is also about pleasing the Lord in the present, specifically by undertaking the collection for the glory of the Lord. Third, one may question if Barnett's 'i.e.', as cited above, is justifiable. Certainly his reference to Thrall is unwarranted as she does not mention eschatology at all, in this connection, but rather emphasises contextual issues that indicate the current presence and activity of Christ.[238] Fourth, in the following verse Paul adds that he forgives, for the sake of the Corinthians, in Christ's presence 'so that we may not be outwitted by Satan'. In the Pauline corpus, and especially within the Corinthian correspondence, the activity of Satan tends to be associated with present state-of-affairs, even if they imply eschatological significance (cf. 1 Cor. 5:5, 7:5; 2 Cor. 11:14, 12:7; and also 1 Thess. 2:18; Rom. 16:20). The 'schemes' (νόημα) of Satan, of which Paul is aware, are probably potential present problems, which forgiveness in Christ's presence counter.

In 2 Corinthians 2:12 Paul writes θύρας μοι ἀνεῳγμένης ἐν κυρίῳ. The major issue of concern in relation to this thesis is the precise function of ἐν κυρίῳ. Is it meant to indicate the sphere of Paul's activity, i.e., that it is 'in the service of the Lord'?[239] Or, is ἐν κυρίῳ the agent of the passive perfect participle, ἀνεῳγμένης, thus meaning 'by the Lord' or 'in the Lord's sovereignty'?[240] It will be suggested in the following that the latter translation is the most likely, even if the matter remains beyond certainty.[241]

First, Thrall argues: 'whilst some ἐν κυρίῳ phrases in Paul (e.g., Rom 16:12) may have the sense "in the Lord's service", in the present context the sphere of opportunity has been noted already in the preceding εἰς τὸ εὐαγγέλιον τοῦ Χριστοῦ'.[242] Second, many commentators refer to 1 Corinthians 16:9 ('for a wide door for effective work has opened to me') as a relevant parallel. In this very context, in 16:7, Paul speaks of the sovereignty of the

---

[237] Barnett, *Corinthians*, 131 n.48, italics mine.

[238] Thrall, *2 Corinthians Vol. 1*, 181.

[239] Cf. Thrall, *2 Corinthians Vol. 1*, 184 n.388.

[240] Harris, *Second Epistle*, 238.

[241] Contra the unsubstantiated claims in Matera, *II Corinthians*, 64, and Barnett, *Corinthians*, 135, esp. n.10.

[242] Thrall, *2 Corinthians Vol. 1*, 184 n.388.

(risen) Lord in relation to his travel plans (cf. above). Thus, Paul speaks of travel plans directed by Christ in the same breath as doors of work being opened, implying that the door in 2 Corinthians 2:12 was opened *by* the Lord. Third, just two verses previously Paul spoke of 'the presence of Christ', thus suggesting that Paul has in mind an activity of the risen Lord. Fourth, the semantic relation of the passive perfect participle is best complemented by the ἐν κυρίῳ if it is understood as the agent of the 'theological passive' of this participle, again implying that the door is opened *by* this Lord.[243] Fifth, a similar verse in a passage of scripture well known to Paul, that also includes the language of 'doors' and 'opening', has the subject of the activity clearly defined, in the same sentence, as the Lord (cf. Isa. 45:1, where κύριος ὁ θεὸς says that ἀνοίξω ἔμπροσθεν αὐτοῦ θύρας, 'I will open doors before him [Cyrus]).[244]

These five points arguably tip the balance in favour of reading ἐν κυρίῳ in terms of agency. It is appropriate, then, that the majority of scholars understand the ἐν κυρίῳ phrase as indicating that the door is opened by the Lord.[245] So we can conclude with Kleine:

Rather, the passive used in this context, with the addition of ἐν κυρίῳ, indicates that success in mission is a gift of the Lord himself. Jesus Christ himself, as the source and content of Paul's gospel, causes the success of mission.[246]

Whether the 'open door' metaphor is meant to refer to the 'receptivity in the hearts of those who hear the gospel'[247] or just the practically favourable circumstances found by Paul in his mission in Troas,[248] or even both, Paul understands the power of the risen Lord as, to use Thrall's language,[249] the 'divine activity' behind this, and the cause of this 'open door'.

2 Corinthians 3:3 is potentially an important verse in relation to the present argument concerning the activity and presence of the risen Lord. The most important work to date concerning this subject is the WUNT monograph by

---

[243] Cf. Kleine, *Furcht*, 150. To be noted is that Furnish urges that the passive be emphasised in translation (Furnish, *II Corinthians*, 169).

[244] This parallel is suggested in James M. Scott, *2 Corinthians*, 58.

[245] E.g., Harris, *Second Epistle*, 235 (who is however less confident in his actual commentary, but his translation apparently belies his preference); Matera, *II Corinthians*, 64; James M. Scott, *2 Corinthians*, 58; Thrall, *2 Corinthians Vol. 1*, 184; Barrett, *2 Corinthians*, 94; Kleine, *Furcht*, 150; Eckhard J. Schnabel, *Early Christian Mission Vol. 2: Paul and the early church* (Leicester: Apollos, 2004), 1248; Furnish, *II Corinthians*, 169 (though he is more ambiguous); R.P. Martin, *2 Corinthians*, 41–42. Lambrecht does not commit himself (Lambrecht, *Second Corinthians*, 33), while of the major commentators, only Barnett is confident enough definitely to reject an agency reading, though he provides no reasons for his decision (Barnett, *Corinthians*, 135, esp. n.10).

[246] Kleine, *Furcht*, 150, translation mine.

[247] Thrall, *2 Corinthians Vol. 1*, 184.

[248] Cf. the opinion of Windisch cited in R.P. Martin, *2 Corinthians*, 41.

[249] Thrall, *2 Corinthians Vol. 1*, 184.

Mehrdad Fatehi.[250] However, in his discussion, one that aims to establish the presence and activity of the risen Lord through the Spirit, he resolves the debate concerning the genitive ἐπιστολὴ Χριστοῦ rather too offhandedly by simply stating, in a footnote, that he accepts 'a subjective genitive, with the majority of the scholars'.[251] If this genitive, however, relates to the noun in a qualitative sense (i.e., that Christ is the *content* not *author* of the letter) then Fatehi's whole argument in this section fails. Thus, arguably more attention needed to be paid to the growing number of German scholars who read this genitive qualitatively.[252] However, while their concerns need to be heard, a good case can still be made for a *genitivus auctoris* reading, one which understands Christ as the author of the letter, a position consistent with the majority of English speaking scholarship.[253] This is so as the context does not need to stress what is *in* the letter, but rather that it exists and who it is from.[254]

---

[250] Fatehi, *Relation*, 196–201.

[251] Ibid., 196 n.96.

[252] So Mathias Rissi, *Studien zum Zweiten Korintherbrief: der alte Bund, der Prediger, der Tod* (Zürich: Zwingli-Verl., 1969), 21; and more recently Jens Schröter, *Der versöhnte Versöhner: Paulus als unentbehrlicher Mittler im Heilsvorgang zwischen Gott und Gemeinde nach 2 Kor 2,14–7,4* (Tübingen: Francke, 1993), 48–73; Bernd Kuschnerus, *Die Gemeinde als Brief Christi: die kommunikative Funktion der Metapher bei Paulus am Beispiel von 2 Kor 2–5* (Göttingen: Vandenhoeck und Ruprecht, 2002). Others argue that the genitive should be read as concerned with both Christ as author and content of the letter. So Klaus Scholtissek, "'Ihr seid ein Brief Christi' (2 Kor 3,3). Zur einer ekklesiologischen Metapher bei Paulus," *BZ* 44 (2000): 193; Eve-Marie Becker, *Schreiben und Verstehen: paulinische Briefhermeneutik im Zweiten Korintherbrief* (Tübingen: Francke, 2002), 214. This is not to imply that German scholarship is unanimous on this issue (cf. e.g. Christian Wolff, *Der zweite Brief des Paulus an die Korinther* [Berlin: Evangelische Verlagsanstalt, 1989], 59; Bultmann, *Korinther*, 75; Kleine, *Furcht*, 189, who all read Christ as the author of the letter), but simply that modern German works defending this view are the most thorough in their presentation for the qualitative case. For other German works that affirm what can be called a genitive of quality, as opposed to a genitive of authorship, cf. the references in Thrall, *2 Corinthians Vol. 1*, 244 n.248; Back, *Verwandlung*, 131 n.12; and M. Margareta Gruber, *Herrlichkeit in Schwachheit: Eine Auslegung der Apologie des Zweiten Korintherbriefs 2 Kor 2,14–6,13*, FB (Würzburg: Echter, 1998).

[253] Cf. R.P. Martin, *2 Corinthians*, 51; Frederick W. Danker, *II Corinthians* (Minneapolis: Augsburg Publishing House, 1989), 52; Hays, *Echoes*, 127; Barnett, *Corinthians*, 167 n.37; Matera simply considers the subjective genitive reading 'More likely' (Matera, *II Corinthians*, 77). For more English language commentators who prefer the 'Christ as author' reading cf. the material cited in Thrall, *2 Corinthians Vol. 1*, 224 n.249.

[254] So Thrall, *2 Corinthians Vol. 1*, 224. Similarly, Harris recently argued: 'To construe Χριστοῦ as an objective genitive ("a letter about Christ") or a possessive genitive ("a letter belonging to Christ") is inappropriate in a context that places no emphasis on the content of the letter or ambiguity about its possession (cf. ἡμῶν, 3:2). Rather, Paul wishes to avoid giving the impression in v. 2 that either he or the Corinthians actually authored the letter: the letter was "from Christ" (genitive of source also subjective genitive)' (Harris, *Second Epistle*, 263). Cf. also Furnish, *II Corinthians*, 182.

With Fatehi's exegetical decision accepted, the significance of the verse can be clarified. Fatehi himself maintains how the significance of the Christology implied in the verse is best grasped, namely when the analogy of an author of a letter and the means by which he writes, is read in terms of the likely scriptural allusions (cf. Exod. 31:18; 32:15; Ezek. 11:19; 36:26; Jer. 31:33; Prov. 3:3; 7:3).[255] He writes:

[I]t is Christ who is identified as the one who writes on the hearts of the new covenant people by means of the Spirit. In other words, Christ is the new covenant counterpart of the Yahweh of Exodus 31 who wrote the law on the two stone tablets by his finger ... One may conclude that in this passage *the Spirit functions as the Spirit of Christ, mediating his power of recreation and ethical transformation.*[256]

In other words, 3:3 is further evidence, within 2 Corinthians, that Paul understood Christ as present and active. Furthermore, 3:3, if the exegesis above is correct, describes the presence and activity of Christ as working within the hearts of the Christian believers ('written ... on tablets of fleshly hearts [ἐν πλαξὶν καρδίαις σαρκίναις]')[257] through the Spirit ('written ... with the Spirit [ἐγγεγραμμένη ... πνεύματι] of the living God').

In 2 Corinthians 12:7–10 Paul relates a prayer-conversation with the risen Lord. The structure of 12:7–10 is obvious and forms a unit in this section of 2 Corinthians 12.[258] Paul prays to the risen Lord to remove the mentioned 'thorn'.[259] As Keener writes: 'That God is sovereign over Satan and uses him fits OT and mainstream Jewish perspectives (see analogously Job 1:6–2:6)'.[260] Herein lies the significance in light of our present argument. Paul prayed to the Lord *because he must have believed that the risen Lord could do something about the 'thorn'*. Whatever this 'thorn' was, Paul believed Christ was present and active to relieve him of the problem (ἵνα ἀποστῇ ἀπ᾽ ἐμοῦ). Thus, Thrall can write of the 'transcendent divine power' involved in this passage.[261] Perhaps the scholarly search for reasons as to *why* Paul prays to Christ in this situation has led to an under-appreciation of this most obvious point, that Christ is understood as sovereign over the situation described in 12:7. That various authors who nevertheless believe the κύριος of 12:8 is

---

[255] Cf. the notes in all the major commentaries, e.g. R.P. Martin, *2 Corinthians*, 52; Harris, *Second Epistle*, 265; Garland, *1 Corinthians*, 159 etc.

[256] Fatehi, *Relation*, 201, italics mine, and cf. also 197.

[257] As Fatehi notes, the significance of Christ as active within hearts through the Spirit 'holds even if one takes "tablets of fleshly hearts" to refer to Paul's own heart' (Fatehi, *Relation*, 201 n.117).

[258] Harris, *Second Epistle*, 827. The structure of the passage has already been noted above.

[259] That κύριος refers to the risen Lord will be detailed below.

[260] Keener, *1–2 Corinthians*, 240.

[261] Thrall, *2 Corinthians Vol. 2*, 823.

christological have used θεός-language to refer to this sovereignty is understandable but it is not what the text says.[262]

The Lord's answer is also significant: 'but he said to me, "My grace is sufficient for you, for power is made perfect in weakness"' (12:9a). Harris has helpfully diagrammed the chiastic structure of the verse as follows:[263]

A ἀρκεῖ   C´ ἡ δύναμις
B σοι   B´ ἐν ἀσθενείᾳ
C ἡ χάρις μου A´ τελεῖται

Not only is there obvious parallelism between 'grace' and 'power' (C C´), but the γάρ functions as an explanatory connective, linking the two,[264] such that they function almost as synonyms. Thus for Paul, 'the "graciousness" of Christ is much more than a benign attitude towards himself: it is an exercise of divine power'.[265]

Paul's response to Christ is also significant for the present argument: 'So, I will boast all the more gladly of my weaknesses, so that the power of Christ may dwell in me' (12:9b). Of particular significance is Paul's use of the verb ἐπισκηνόω to describe the power of Christ in relation to himself. Most scholars understand Paul to be echoing the Hebrew notion of the presence of God in the Tabernacle and first Temple, the *Shekinah*.[266]

In 2 Corinthians 13:3–5 Paul speaks of Christ as 'powerful in you', and 'living in you'. Three points can be made in relation to this passage concerning the Pauline understanding of the presence and activity of the risen Lord. First, Paul immediately goes on to claim, with a chiasmus,[267] that Christ 'is

---

[262] Cf. Franz Zeilinger, *Krieg und Friede in Korinth: Kommentar zum 2. Korintherbrief des Apostels Paulus. Band 1: Der Kampfbrief, Der Versöhnungsbrief, Der Bettelbrief* (Köln: Böhlau, 1992), 108–9; Josef Zmijewski, *Der Stil der paulinischen "Narrenrede": Analyse der Sprachgestaltung in 2 Kor 11,1–12,10 als Beitrag zur Methodik von Stiluntersuchungen neutestamentlicher Texte* (Köln: Hanstein, 1978), 369; and the many examples in R.P. Martin, *2 Corinthians*: E.g., 'God's power upon him' (p. 393, italics mine, as in these following citations), 'he had ceased to petition *God*' (418), 'Instead of asking *God* yet again to remove the thorn' (420). Cf. also p. 412 and 422; Note also Bruce J. Malina and John J. Pilch, *Social-Science Commentary on the Letters of Paul* (Minneapolis: Fortress, 2006), 159.

[263] Harris, *Second Epistle*, 862.

[264] Barnett, *Corinthians*, 573.

[265] David Michael Stanley, *Boasting in the Lord: The Phenomenon of Prayer in Saint Paul* (New York: Paulist, 1973), 57. This is noted by almost all the major commentaries, but cf. especially Bultmann, *Korinther*, 229; R.P. Martin, *2 Corinthians*, 419 and Harris, *Second Epistle*, 863. Zmijewski's claim that ἡ δύναμις in 12:9 refers to *God's* power (Zmijewski, *Narrenrede*, 383–84) is refuted by Furnish, *II Corinthians*, 530, and Harris, *Second Epistle*, 863 n.187.

[266] Cf. the list of proponents in R.P. Martin, *2 Corinthians*, 421, and Fatehi, *Relation*, 15 n.40. A couple of important voices have nevertheless objected (cf. Thrall, *2 Corinthians Vol. 2*, 828; Furnish, *II Corinthians*, 531).

[267] Scholars that notice the chiasmus are listed by Thrall, *2 Corinthians Vol. 2*, 881 n.80. Cf. also Harris, *Second Epistle*, 912.

not weak in dealing with you, but is powerful in you' (13:3b). In light of the following verse, what Paul exactly meant with these words is disputed. For the purpose of this argument, all that needs to be maintained is that Paul understood the risen Christ as powerful in his relation to the Corinthians, the chiastic structure highlighting the 'personal relationship of Christ to the Corinthians' in this context.[268] It could be argued that Paul was merely being ironic in this claim.[269] However, even if he was, Paul was clearly not attempting to refute the proposition, and the most that can be said is that he was redefining it.

Second, 13:4 yields relevant evidence. It can be divided as follows:[270]

4a καὶ γὰρ ἐσταυρώθη ἐξ ἀσθενείας,
4b ἀλλὰ ζῇ ἐκ δυνάμεως θεοῦ.
4c καὶ γὰρ ἡμεῖς ἀσθενοῦμεν ἐν αὐτῷ,
4d ἀλλὰ ζήσομεν σὺν αὐτῷ ἐκ δυνάμεως θεοῦ εἰς ὑμᾶς.

Following Aejmelaeus, it is probably best that the καὶ γὰρ ... καὶ γάρ is interpreted the same way both times.[271] Furthermore, the repeated ἐκ (ἐξ) is also best not treated too flexibly, giving it one translation one moment, and another the next.[272] In light of the arguments proposed by Harris, it arguably makes most sense to translate each as 'because of'.[273] These observations lead to the following translation:

4a For indeed he was crucified because of weakness,
4b but he lives because of the power of God.
4c For indeed we are weak in him,
4d but in dealing with you we will live with him because of the power of God

In 4d Paul is clear that in dealing with the Corinthians (εἰς ὑμᾶς) 'we will live with him', i.e., with Christ. The above structural plan shows that 4b is paralleled with 4d, such that Paul's apostolic team living with Christ is paralleled with the present (ζῇ – an indicative present active verb form) life of Christ. The living Christ will thus be with (σὺν αὐτῷ) the apostolic team in their future visit to Corinth. As Harris argues, 'in the expression ζήσομεν σὺν αὐτῷ

---

[268] Harris writes: 'εἰς ὑμᾶς (A) οὐκ ἀσθενεῖ (B) ἀλλὰ δυνατεῖ (B') ἐν ὑμῖν (A') forms a chiasmus that has the effect of highlighting items A and A''(Harris, *Second Epistle*, 912. Cf. also Thrall, *2 Corinthians Vol. 2*, 881).

[269] E.g. Lars Aejmelaeus, *Schwachheit als Waffe: die Argumentation des Paulus im Tränenbrief (2. Kor. 10–13)* (Göttingen: Vandenhoeck & Ruprecht, 2000), 357.

[270] Following the pattern suggested in Lambrecht, *Second Corinthians*, 224. Cf. also Harris, *Second Epistle*, 914; Barnett, *Corinthians*, 603.

[271] Contra e.g. Harris, *Second Epistle*, 914; Lambrecht, *Second Corinthians*, 224. Cf. Aejmelaeus, *Schwachheit*, 360–63, a work missed by Harris in his recent NIGTC commentary.

[272] Some translate the first as 'in', i.e. 'in weakness', and the second as 'by', i.e. 'by the power of God' (Furnish, *II Corinthians*, 571; Lambrecht, *Second Corinthians*, 221, 224).

[273] Harris, *Second Epistle*, 914, following and developing Barrett, *2 Corinthians*, 335–36. Cf. also BDAG (which refers to 2 Cor. 13:4 as an example).

ἐκ δυνάμεως θεοῦ εἰς ὑμᾶς Paul is speaking of his imminent visit to Corinth when, in unison with Christ and with God's power, he would act decisively ... against unrepentant evildoers within the congregation'.[274] Thus, as 'a result of his fellowship with Christ (σὺν αὐτῷ)' Paul 'shared in the power of his risen Lord (vv. 3b, 4a)'.[275]

It could be argued that the 'living' in 4d refers not to Paul's visit to Corinth, but rather to the resurrection life.[276] This is suggested on the basis of the future tense of ζάω used together with σὺν αὐτῷ (cf. the eschatological overtones of this pairing in 1 Thess. 4:14), and the parallel between the ζῇ ἐκ δυνάμεως θεοῦ in 4b (and the resurrection of Christ) with 4d. In light of this, some have attempted to bring the eschatological resurrection theme into their interpretation of Paul's planned visit to Corinth. For example, Barrett claims Paul thinks 'God will grant him such a measure of resurrection life' that 'will suffice to deal with the situation in Corinth'.[277] Likewise, Murphy-O'Connor thinks Paul is portraying his coming visit to Corinth in terms of resurrection.[278] To be clear, even if the eschatological overtones are accepted, this need not negate reference to the upcoming visit to Corinth, as the entire context[279] and the use of the words εἰς ὑμᾶς make clear.[280] Gräbe is thus correct to write, in relation to 13:4, of Christ as '[r]esurrected in power' becoming 'actively present through his apostle' even though '[l]ife with Christ certainly belongs primarily to the future'.[281]

Third, in 13:5 the presence and activity of the risen Lord is expressed in terms of Christ being ἐν ὑμῖν. Thrall rightly contends that it would be a mistake to drive a wedge between 'among you' and 'in you' in translating ἐν ὑμῖν.[282] While the force of the ἐν is certainly metaphorical, over against any

---

[274] Harris, Second Epistle, 916.

[275] Ibid., 917.

[276] Cf. Ulrich Heckel, Kraft in Schwachheit: Untersuchungen zu 2. Kor 10–13 (Tübingen: Mohr Siebeck, 1993), 133, who writes: 'Because of the parallelisation with the Christ-event in V. 4a, the future form ζήσομεν has to have an eschatological meaning and – at least – relate to eternal life' (italics his, translation mine).

[277] Barrett, 2 Corinthians, 337. Cf. also Aejmelaeus, Schwachheit, 371.

[278] Cf. J. Murphy-O'Connor, The Theology of the Second Letter to the Corinthians (Cambridge: Cambridge University Press, 1991), 133. For another suggestion as to how eschatological language could be used in a very concrete historical sense in Paul, cf. Andrew Perriman, The Coming of the Son of Man (Milton Keynes: Paternoster, 2005).

[279] Harris, Second Epistle, 916. Cf. also Petrus J. Gräbe, The Power of God in Paul's Letters (Tübingen: Mohr Siebeck, 2000), 152: 'The argumentation in this entire pericope is specifically related to the Corinthians (cf πρὸς ὑμᾶς [13,1], ἐν ὑμῖν [13,3], εἰς ὑμᾶς [13,4])' (italics his).

[280] Thrall, 2 Corinthians Vol. 2, 886–87; Aejmelaeus, Schwachheit, 368–71.

[281] Gräbe, Power, 157, italics mine.

[282] Thrall, 2 Corinthians Vol. 2, 891 esp. n.159. Also Harris, Second Epistle, 921. Harris cites Martin (R.P. Martin, 2 Corinthians, 478, 480) as also recognising what he calls the dual sense of ἐν. But Martin, contra Harris, appears to prefer simply to translate the texts as 'among you'.

sense of the indwelling as *forma substantialis*,[283] it is not arguably best understood as *only* metaphorical *as opposed* to a literal sense. Christ's presence 'in'
the believer and the community, to adopt the language employed by Rabens in
his dialogue with Horn, is perhaps best understood, in light of Aaron's gradi-
ent model of meaning as a continuum between literal and metaphorical, as an
intimate union with the Christ who is really present.[284]

Some, desiring to avoid collapsing 'in the faith' into 'the life of Christ in
the believer', do not emphasise the parallelism of the passage.[285] Harris argues
that 'the faith' in 13:5 likely does not denote 'personal trust in Christ' given
that the context emphasises 'the need for proper Christian conduct'. Barnett
likewise argues that 'in the faith' is propositional and thus 'in contrast' to the
experiential 'Christ Jesus is in you'.[286] But it remains clear that the presence
of Christ is paralleled with being 'in the faith',[287] so one can conclude that the
whole life of faith is associated, in Paul, with the presence of Christ.

Turning to Galatians, Fee has argued that Paul's use of ἐν in 1:6, 16; 2:20;
3:11–12, 26, is best understood as locative.[288] This would mean that Paul's
claim concerning the divine revelation of the Son, in Galatians 1:16, was 'in
me' (ἐν ἐμοί), that Christ was revealed in Paul. This same sense of the
indwelling of Christ in Paul is expressed in Galatians 2:20, where Paul writes
that he no longer lives but that 'Christ lives in me'. Later in his argument Paul
speaks of the sending of 'the Spirit of his Son' into the hearts of believers
(4:6). This indwelling of Christ also finds expression in terms of the believer's
maturation. So Paul is 'in the pain of childbirth until Christ is formed in you
[Galatians]' (4:19). Once again, and as discussed above, Paul finishes his letter thus: 'May the grace of our Lord Jesus Christ be with your spirit' (6:18).

In Philippians, once again Paul starts his letter with the words: 'Grace to
you and peace from God our Father and the Lord Jesus Christ' (1:2). A few
verses later Paul speaks of his longing for the Philippian Christians 'with the
compassion of Christ' (1:8). If ἐν σπλάγχνοις Χριστοῦ means to indicate the

---

[283] As Horn suggests in terms of the Spirit's indwelling in 1 Cor. 3:16; 6:19; Rom. 8:9 and
1 Thess. 4:8. See now Volker Rabens, *The Holy Spirit and Ethics in Paul: Transformation
and Empowering for Religious-Ethical Life*, WUNT II/283 (Tübingen: Mohr Siebeck,
2013²), 75.

[284] Rabens, *Spirit*, 48 n.107.

[285] Thrall, *2 Corinthians Vol. 2*, 888.

[286] Barnett, *Corinthians*, 608.

[287] This is noted by, e.g., Heinz-Dietrich Wendland, *Die Briefe an die Korinther*, reprint,
1932 (Göttingen: Vandenhoeck & Ruprecht, 1972¹³), 257; Barrett, *2 Corinthians*, 338;
Zeilinger, *Krieg 1*, 138–39; R.P. Martin, *2 Corinthians*, 478.

[288] Gordon D. Fee, "Paul's Use of Locative ἐν in Galatians: On Text and Meaning in
Galatians 1.6; 1.16; 2.20; 3.11–12 and 3.26," in *The Impartial God: Essays in Biblical
Studies in Honour of Jouette M. Bassler*, ed. Calvin J. Roetzel and Robert L. Foster
(Sheffield: Sheffield Phoenix Press, 2007), 170–85.

'compassion' (lit. 'bowels') of Christ himself, as is most likely (cf. p. 171 below), then Paul implies that Christ is emotionally present in Paul.[289]

In 1:19 Paul writes of his deliverance 'through your prayers and the help of the Spirit of Jesus Christ'. Christ's own Spirit, through prayer, will secure Paul's deliverance.

In speaking of obtaining his goal in Philippians 3:12–21, as discussed above, Paul writes that he presses on 'because Christ Jesus has made me his own' (3:12). Paul's conversion is spoken of, here, not as God's act, though Paul would not deny this, but rather as Christ's act in making Paul his own. This is, in some ways, a smaller expression of that power of Christ stated at the end of this section, where Paul speaks of the transformation of 'the body of our humiliation' by 'the power that also enables him to make all things subject to himself' (3:21). Christ's own power was active in converting Paul, and will be expressed finally and universally in the eschatological future.

As noted above in relation to Paul's appeal to the risen Lord in 2 Corinthians 12, prayer to Christ directly implies a Pauline belief that this Lord can do something about his request. The same can be said of the prayer in 1 Thessalonians 3:11–13; the prayer-wish only makes sense if the Lord can indeed 'direct our way to you' (3:11). Whatever problems were stopping Paul in returning (2:18) to the Thessalonians could be changed by Christ's intervention.[290] To start his prayer 'May the Lord', as in 3:12, only makes sense if this Lord can indeed make the Thessalonians 'increase and abound in love for one another and for all' (3:12), and indeed 'strengthen' their 'hearts in holiness' (3:13). Whether the infinitival purpose clause of verse 13 ('to establish your hearts as blameless') is an additional prayer-wish (even though it is not related to the optative verb of verse 11),[291] or whether it is a 'statement concerning the outcome of the Lord's increased gift of love'[292] is not important. Either way it is the hearts (καρδίας, i.e., 'the thinking, willing, and feeling dimension of human existence, in modern terms the human personality'[293]) of the Thessalonian Christians that will be strengthened in holiness by the risen Lord.[294] Of course, this is all simple evidence against Horn who wrongly

---

[289] 'Paul's deeply emotional expression of Christian affection in this verse is not primarily the sign of a gushing temperament, but of a gushing christology' (Bockmuehl, *Philippians*, 65). Cf. the discussion in O'Brien, *Philippians*, 71–72; Joachim Gnilka, *Der Philipperbrief / Der Philemonbrief* (Freiburg: Herder, 1968), 50.

[290] Here τὴν ὁδὸν ἡμῶν apparently refers to the physical path Paul needed to make back to Thessalonica.

[291] As Wanamaker, *Thessalonians*, 143–44.

[292] E.g. Richard, *Thessalonians*, 175.

[293] Wanamaker, *Thessalonians*, 144.

[294] Fee has recently argued that this passage is another example of the 'extraordinary dividing up of the *Shema*', much like that evidenced in 1 Cor. 8:6 (see Fee, *Thessalonians*, 130). This verse, among many others, is rather conspicious for its absence in McGrath's misleading treatment of monotheism in Paul's letters (James F. McGrath, *God*, 38–54).

argues that Paul had no notion of a present and active risen Lord at the time he wrote 1 Thessalonians.[295]

As in the other letters, Paul finishes with the words: 'May the grace of our Lord Jesus Christ be with you' (5:28), as discussed above. It is this grace (and peace) theme that one, finally, also finds in Philemon. So Paul writes again: 'grace to you and peace from ... the Lord Jesus Christ' (Philem. 3),[296] and 'the grace of the Lord Jesus Christ be with your spirit' (Philem. 25).

7. The absence of the risen Lord

Having examined the nature of the risen Lord's presence and activity in Paul's undisputed letters, it is important to now inspect how Paul also understands Christ to be in some sense *absent*. This conjunction of Christ's presence *and* absence in the Pauline epistles has not been given the attention it deserves, and even less so in terms of Paul's Christology.

7.1. Until he comes

Stretched across the canvas of 'the ages', between the 'now' and the 'not-yet', Paul's experience of the presence and absence of the risen Lord finds expression.[297] In terms of this argument it means that the risen Lord is present, yet at the same time also absent, and the Pauline communities await a fuller, eschatological presence.

For example, in 1 Corinthians 11:26 Paul notes that the Corinthians 'proclaim the Lord's death' *until* he comes (ἄχρι οὗ ἔλθῃ). In other words, the Lord has not yet come in the sense meant here, but he will do. Likewise in 1 Corinthians 13:12 Paul confesses that 'now (ἄρτι) we see in a mirror, dimly,

---

[295] Horn, *Angeld*, 147.

[296] Once again, the ellipses is justified given the focus of this chapter. The relation between God and Christ language will be explored later.

[297] Kreitzer notes: 'Most scholars now accept that Paul's Jewish heritage and background, including its twofold division of temporal history into two aeons, the "now" and the "not-yet", is determinative for his eschatological worldview' (L.J. Kreitzer, "Eschatology," in *DPL*, eds G.F. Hawthorne, R.P. Martin, and D.G. Reid [Leicester: IVP, 1993], 255, and 256-57. Cf. also A.T. Lincoln, *Paradise Now and Not Yet: Studies in the Role of the Heavenly Dimension in Paul's Thought with Special Reference to His Eschatology* [Cambridge: Cambridge University Press, 1981], e.g. 8). The German scholarly scene tends to posit more development in Paul's eschatological thinking than the Anglo-American works (cf. e.g. the references given in Schnelle, *Paulus*, 672 n.15 and Konradt, *Gericht*, 476 n.15) but they still accept this basic dualism of thought: 'believers are already living in the end times, but the end is not there, yet!' (Schnelle, *Paulus*, 670, translation mine). The appropriateness of a mystical understanding of the language 'now-and-not-yet' has recently been challenged in Andrew Perriman, *Re:Mission. Biblical Mission for a Post-Biblical Church* (Milton Keynes: Paternoster, 2007), 39–40, who argues that the 'now' is simply prophetic, not an actual inauguration of a future in the present.

but then (τότε used 'in the temporal sense rather than the logical'[298]) we will see face to face'. The expression 'face to face' is most likely of Semitic origin (פָּנִים אֶל־פָּנִים), and is used to denote, among other things, the presence of YHWH in a sense that is not true all the time, a special presence of God.[299] Interestingly, Paul's use of πρόσωπον elsewhere tends to indicate presence, as in 2 Corinthians 10:1 (cf. also, e.g., 1 Thess. 2:17). That Paul speaks of *Christ's* face here – not God's – is not certain, but Paul, also in the Corinthian correspondence, can speak of the glory of God ἐν προσώπῳ Ἰησοῦ Χριστοῦ (2 Cor. 4:6). Indeed, Paul's eschatological language usually entails christologically accented themes indicating, for example, the unveiling of Christ (cf. 1 Cor. 1:7–8), the day of the Lord Christ (1 Cor. 1:8; 5:5; 2 Cor. 1:14),[300] and the hope of being with Christ forever (cf. 1 Thess. 4:17–18; 5:10; 2 Cor. 5:8; Phil. 1:23). It is thus likely that Paul here speaks of the face of Christ. Either way, Paul assumes a future time when the Lord comes, obviously implying that the Lord has not yet come (cf. Gal. 3:19). The risen Christ, for Paul, is in some sense not yet present, has not yet come, cannot yet be seen face to face, language that connotes presence. These things await the eschaton.

7.2. The παρουσία of Christ

Christ's absence is further reflected in Paul's παρουσία-language. In 1 Corinthians 15 Paul's treatment of things eschatological finds more detailed expression, and once again Paul emphasises the coming of the Lord as something yet to happen. So he writes: 'But each in his own order: Christ the first fruits, *then at his coming* (ἐν τῇ παρουσίᾳ αὐτοῦ) those who belong to Christ' (1 Cor. 15:23. Cf. also 1 Thess. 2:19; 3:13; 5:23). The order concerns who is resurrected and when, and Paul adds that the resurrection of those who belong to Christ will happen at his παρουσία.

But what does παρουσία mean? Paul uses the word a few times in the undisputed letters mostly in reference to the 'coming' or arriving of one of his co-workers (1 Cor. 16:17; 2 Cor. 7:6–7), but also of the 'bodily presence' or simply 'presence' of Paul himself in contrast with his absence (2 Cor. 10:10; Phil. 2:12).[301] A couple of these occurrences are significant for the simple reason that they are used in such a way that the παρουσία of this or that person is contrasted with the *absence* of that person. For example, Paul rejoices 'at the παρουσία of Stephanas and Fortunatus and Achaicus' because these co-workers 'have made up for your absence' (1 Cor 16:17). The word translated

---

[298] Thiselton, *Corinthians*, 1067.

[299] Cf. Thiselton, *Corinthians*, 1070, for references. Also cf. Joel S. Burnett, "The Question of Divine Absence in Israelite and West Semitic Religion," *CBQ* 67, no. 2 (2005): 215–35 and Hendrik Bosman, "The Absence and Presence of God in the Book of Exodus a Theological Synthesis," *Scriptura* 85, no. 1 (2004): esp. 3.

[300] Cf. Plevnik, *Parousia*, 3.

[301] Cf. the statistics and analysis in Plevnik, *Parousia*, 4.

as 'absence', ὑστέρημα, means a deficiency, and here seems to indicate a deficiency of the presence of the Corinthians. Paul expresses this very sentiment in his repeated desire to come to the Corinthians, to be present with them and not separated from them. In Philippians 2:12 Paul urges the believers to 'work out' their salvation 'not only in my presence (παρουσία), but much more now in my absence (ἀπουσία)'. Silva indicates that the structure of the verse clearly parallels ἐν τῇ παρουσίᾳ μου with ἐν τῇ ἀπουσίᾳ μου as elements in a chiasm.[302] In a similar manner, Paul quotes his opponents in 2 Corinthians 10:10 as claiming 'his bodily presence is weak'. The phrase 'bodily presence' translates παρουσία τοῦ σώματος, literally the presence of Paul's body. Probably σῶμα here functions to signify Paul himself.[303] Paul's opponents thus contrast Paul's letters, his communication when he himself, his body, is physically absent, with Paul's 'actual or personal' presence,[304] his παρουσία. In all these cases, the παρουσία of the named individuals is contrasted with a notable lack of presence, with an absence of those people. Perriman uncontroversially states:

The meaning of the word *parousia* apart from its use in the New Testament with reference to Christ is not difficult to determine. It signifies, in effect, the *coming as to be present of a person or group*. In other words, if it means "presence", it generally carries with it the thought that the one who is present has only recently arrived or might otherwise have been absent.[305]

All of this has a clear implication for the present argument, especially as there is no reason to suppose that the word παρουσία, in Paul, when used in relation to Christ, has developed a different technical sense indicating a developed eschatological scheme.[306] When Paul speaks specifically of the future παρουσία of Christ, he thus also implies that Christ is at the present time *absent*.

This argument is confirmed in 1 Thessalonians. The most relevant section to analyse is the much discussed passage, 4:13–5:11. Though it remains disputed exactly which problems Paul sought to address in these verses, and which background text (Exod. 19:10–18 and/or the Hellenistic παρουσία) best illuminates Paul's thinking, the argument to be maintained here is simple. The

---

[302] Silva, *Philippians*, 118.

[303] Cf. the discussion in L.J. Kreitzer, "Body," in *DPL*, eds G.F. Hawthorne, R.P. Martin, and D.G. Reid (Leicester: IVP, 1993), 72–73. Dunn puts it clearly: 'Every time σῶμα appears in Paul modern readers need to be reminded that it does not denote the physical body as such, rather a fuller reality which includes the physical but is not reducible to it' (Dunn, *Romans*, 319). Thrall argues that 'body' here means Paul's 'whole outward character and personality' (Thrall, *2 Corinthians Vol. 2*, 631) and cf. also Harris, *Second Epistle*, 699.

[304] To adopt the language used in Harris, *Second Epistle*, 699.

[305] Perriman, *Coming*, 52. Cf. also N.T. Wright, *Jesus and the Victory of God* (London: SPCK, 1996), 341; Geerhardus Vos, *The Pauline Eschatology* (Grand Rapids: Eerdmans, 1953), 75; Ben Witherington, III, *Jesus, Paul, and the End of the World: A Comparative Study in New Testament Eschatology* (Downers Grove: IVP, 1992), 152.

[306] Plevnik, *Parousia*, 4.

climax of both of the sections of eschatological teaching (4:13–18 and 5:1–11) ends with the crucial promise: 'so we will be with the Lord forever' (4:17) and 'whether we are awake or asleep we may live with him' (5:10). The flip side of this is, of course, that the Thessalonians were *not yet* 'with the Lord'. The hope of his presence was related to the eschatological παρουσία.

The implication of this is straightforward and should not be the source of dispute. Paul tends to use the word παρουσία in such a way that is explicitly contrasted with 'absence'. The occasional reference to the παρουσία of Christ (1 Cor. 15:23; 1 Thess. 2:19; 3:13; 5:23) implies Christ's absence at the time of Paul's letter writing.

Before we proceed, it is necessary to engage with the recent proposals of Perriman whose thesis could be understood to undermine the reasoning adopted thus far. Based on an analysis of a variety of intertextual echoes, especially from the book of Daniel, Perriman argues that Paul's 'παρουσία of Christ' language is first and foremost 'a *story* about the rescue and vindication of the church',[307] and is to be situated in concrete response to and in the context of 'a conflict with Roman imperialism'.[308] Hence, Paul's language is not simply about the absence and future presence of Christ in and of themselves. The language alludes to a wider story of suffering and vindication. Thus, he argues, when Paul speaks of his preference to be with the Lord rather than absent from him (in passages to be examined below), the modern exegete should not think this a matter of 'personal piety'. Rather, this desire comes 'out of the experience of intense suffering'.[309] Perriman thus suggests that Paul's language, which denotes the absence and future hoped for presence of Christ, are essentially pointing primarily to *something else*, to the experience of present suffering, and the hope for future vindication over the enemies of the people of God. Indeed, it should be emphasised that Paul was not simply sketching the foundations of an academic theism, as if he were coldly ascribing to the risen Christ descriptions of immanence and transcendence for the sake of theological exactitude or novelty alone.

Perriman's argument, that universalising tendencies have separated the modern exegete from 'the pain and fearfulness ... that gave meaning and urgency to these [eschatological] visions', is to be heeded.[310] However, he arguably sets up, or at least overplays, a false either/or (i.e., either personal piety or suffering) and overlooks the piety and personal longing for the presence of God that was also a part of the Jewish religious language and hope as evidenced throughout the OT and intertestamental literature – and this often precisely at points of suffering (e.g. Pss. 16:11, 21:6, 27:4, 42:2, 51:11, 63:1–8, 84:10, 95:2, 100:2, 105:4; Wis. Sol. 3:14, 13:3; 1QHᵃ 15:28–31, 28:5–9

---

[307] Perriman, *Coming*, 176, italics his.
[308] Ibid., 162.
[309] Ibid., 104.
[310] Ibid., 5.

etc).³¹¹ Hence, in discussing the related expression, 'to be with Christ', O'Brien argues that the most appropriate general background is the Psalter (citing LXX Pss. 16; 139:14; 20:7; 138:18; *1 En.* 62:13–14; 105:2).³¹² Notably, as argued above, these expressions of the presence and absence of Christ were very real existential longings and experiences, not of secondary importance which really spoke about something else. Arguably this can be claimed without neglecting Perriman's valid complaint against overly universalising and abstract readings. The παρουσία language in Paul is thus further evidence of the implied understanding of the present absence of Christ.

7.3. Away from the Lord

2 Corinthians 5:6–8 is relevant for the argument developed here concerning the Pauline understanding of the absence of Christ. While it would arguably be a mistake to think Paul was expressing himself with clearly defined theological categories in these verses,³¹³ they still reveal something of Paul's understanding of Christ's absence. On the surface of things, Paul appears to simply claim that 'while we are at home in the body' (i.e., Paul's state-of-affairs while writing the letter, as the previous verses make clear) '*we are away from the Lord*' (ἐκδημοῦμεν ἀπὸ τοῦ κυρίου). Then, after emphasising that his present situation is marked out by faith, not by outward appearance,³¹⁴ he expresses his original proposition positively: 'we would rather³¹⁵ be away from the body and at home with the Lord'. If this reading is correct then these verses function as confirmation of the argument pursued here, namely that Paul understood the risen Lord as, in a very important sense, absent. Indeed, tᴗe metaphor of exile/being at home involved, in the verbs Paul employs in 5:6 and 8 (ἐνδημέω and ἐκδημέω), emphasis on a specifically spatial aspect of this absence from the Lord.³¹⁶

However, a number of arguments have been raised against this reading that need to be addressed. The first is offered by Murphy-O'Connor who argues that 2 Corinthians 5:6b 'is a Corinthian slogan stemming from the

---

³¹¹ Noteworthy is that though the word, παρουσία, is seldom found in the LXX, it is employed by Josephus to denote 'the benevolent presence of Yahweh' (*Ant.* 3.80; 9.55; 18.284–86 – cf. Plevnik, *Parousia*, 5 n.10; and Perriman, *Coming*, 54).

³¹² O'Brien, *Philippians*, 133–34.

³¹³ Cf. Andrew Perriman, "Paul and the Parousia: 1 Corinthians 15.50–7 and 2 Corinthians 5.1–5," *NTS* 35, no. 4 (1989): 519.

³¹⁴ This translation of οὐ διὰ εἴδους is at least an option discussed in most commentaries, and has arguably the most going for it, especially in light of the suffering motif analysed in Perriman, "Paul".

³¹⁵ Cf. the discussion on this disputed translation of εὐδοκοῦμεν μᾶλλον below.

³¹⁶ Cf. esp. Thrall, *2 Corinthians Vol. 1*, 386; Fowl, *Philippians*, 51.

pneumatikoi.[317] 'Being at home in the body we are in exile from the Lord', as he translates the relevant section, is 'one of the most problematic statements in the Pauline letters ... [and] contradicts one of the most basic tenets of Pauline theology, namely, that the whole being of believers is infused with the grace of Christ'.[318] Murphy-O'Connor thinks these words so problematic because, referring to Furnish, they imply 'life in the body is incompatible with life in Christ',[319] they 'could be read as a major concession to those at Corinth who denied any importance to the body'. This makes it all the more difficult to account for, given the stress on the body in 2 Corinthians 5:10, for which 'only a polemical concern' can adequately account.[320] Paul is thus combating a false Corinthian view in 5:6b.

His arguments of greatest substance for this position are as follows: First, 'the verbs *endêmein* and *ekdêmein* are foreign to the language of both the LXX and the NT', a fact he thinks is best explained by the hypothesis that the language originates from the Corinthian *pneumatikoi*.[321] Second, the 'introductory formula *eidotes hoti* is exactly parallel to *oidamen hoti*, which introduces the [generally accepted] Corinthian slogans in *1 Cor* 8:1a and 4'.[322] Third, the 'two slogans in *1 Cor* 8:4 are modified by the following verse, which begins with *kai gar*, whose clarificatory function mirrors that of *gar* in *2 Cor* 5:7'. Fourth, '*2 Cor* 5:8 rejects the implication of 5:6b'.[323] This Paul does 'by simply substituting [in 5:8] *ek* for *en* and *pros* for *apo*, thereby introducing the idea of motion, which links the two states'.[324] He thus does not statically separate 'away from the body' and 'at home with the Lord', as appears to be the case in 5:6.

This reasoning, however, arguably fails to convince. In terms of the grounds which Murphy-O'Connor specifies as reasons for supposing 5:6b involves unbearable theological tension in Paul, the following can be said. 5:6b, far from implying that 'life in the body is incompatible with Christ', simply indicates what the verses analysed above show: that only at the παρουσία will believers truly be 'with the Lord' in the full eschatological sense.[325] As Dunn writes: 'those who share "in Christ" and "with Christ" are

---

[317] J. Murphy-O'Connor, "'Being at Home in the Body We Are in Exile from the Lord': (2 Cor. 5:6b)," *RB* 93 (1986): 214 (in all of the following citations from his article, italics are his). It is irrelevant to the following to establish exactly who the *pneumatikoi* are, so this part of his argument will not be summarised.

[318] Murphy-O'Connor, "Being," 214. Here he cites 2 Cor. 12:9.

[319] Murphy-O'Connor, "Being," 215.

[320] Ibid., 216.

[321] Ibid.

[322] Ibid., 216–17.

[323] Ibid., 217.

[324] Ibid., 218.

[325] The eschatological sense is here emphasised because Paul could speak of being 'with the Lord' in the present (cf. e.g. 2 Cor. 13:4), and the past (cf. Dunn, *Theology*, 403, 467 – contra Harris, *Second Epistle*, 402).

caught, as it were, between the two comings'.[326] It is this same eschatological frame that needs to be remembered. Dunn has stressed the many tensions in Paul's letters based on this 'now' and 'not-yet',[327] and thus Murphy-O'Connor's claim that 5:6b 'contradicts' the truth that the whole life of believers 'is infused with the grace of Christ' is to over-realise the eschatological tension in Paul. 5:6b is hence probably not a straightforward devaluation of the body but rather a statement concerning the 'not yet' of Christian life, a recognition in line with the suffering of Apostolic life (cf. 1 Cor. 15:19). The suggested polemical addition of 'body' in 5:10 is indeed likely,[328] but even if this is right it is improbable that 5:10 is correcting any-thing in 5:6b. In order to claim this, one must surely insist that 5:6b implies that living in the body is in some way unimportant in terms of the coming judgment, but it does not.

Turning to the reasons Murphy-O'Connor supplies for reading 5:6b as a citation, the first point concerning the presence of the *hapax legomena* would only carry weight if accompanied by other supporting evidence. There is no reason why Paul would not have felt able to use these words himself. As we shall see, there is arguably no complementary support for Murphy-O'Connor's thesis. The second point has been rightly challenged by Harris who argues that 'the presence of an introductory εἰδότες ὅτι ... is an insufficient pointer to a slogan, when εἰδότες is linked to θαρροῦντες οὖν πάντοτε by καί (contrast 1 Cor. 8:1, 4)'.[329] The third point assumes a parallel use of language with the first few verses of 1 Corinthians 8, but this association has already been undermined in response to the previous. Rather, and contra Murphy-O'Connor, the γάρ of 5:7 likely functions in relation to 5:6b by way of expla-nation.[330] The fourth and final point of any potential weight assumes too great a distinction between 5:6 and 8, a strict distinction that carries more than can be put on the shoulders of the different prepositions (and the supposed 'ingressive aorist' ἐνδημῆσαι).[331] It is therefore little surprise to learn that Murphy-O'Connor's argument has not won the support of the major commen-tators.

A second, and more subtle, argument has been proposed, most prominently by Furnish, that could undermine the present thesis concerning Christ's absence as in these verses, namely that Paul speaks, in 5:6–8, of the Christian

---

[326] Dunn, *Theology*, 468.

[327] Dunn, *Theology*, 466–98. Cf. also Thrall, *2 Corinthians Vol. 1*, 386.

[328] But cf. Konradt, *Gericht*, 486.

[329] Harris, *Second Epistle*, 395 n.170. Cf. also Thrall, *2 Corinthians Vol. 1*, 386 n.1376: 'the εἰδότες which introduces v.6b is strictly parallel to the θαρροῦντες, which expresses Paul's own view'.

[330] So Harris, *Second Epistle*, 396; Lambrecht, *Second Corinthians*, 85. Barnett thinks the γάρ 'introduces a clarification of the previous statement' (Barnett, *Corinthians*, 270 n.16).

[331] Cf. the discussion in Harris, *Second Epistle*, 401.

experience of growing nearer to Christ *in this life*. It is concerned with 'processes and attitudes within the present world'.[332] In other words, Paul always considers the Lord as present, and believers are absent from him only in terms of recognition, i.e., to the extent that believers are not properly orientated toward Christ. So Furnish argues: '[O]rientation (commitment) is involved here, not location'.[333] It would appear that Paul's use of the verb εὐδοκέω would confirm this reading, a verb which means more exactly 'decide' than 'prefer'. It is rightly noted that to prefer the eschatological presence of the Lord is easy to understand, but how can one decide for the presence of the Lord without thinking of suicide? Furthermore, this reading would make better sense of the ethical injunctions in 5:9. In other words, Paul is expressing a conscious choice to live nearer the Lord, and is thus not making a statement about the risen Lord's 'spatial' absence or location vis-à-vis the believer.

However, and first, it is debatable that one can correctly exclude something of the sense of 'prefer' in translating εὐδοκέω here, especially as it is used together with μᾶλλον.[334] Thrall notes that the text can be translated as 'to be willing to a greater degree' and so comes 'very close to the meaning of "prefer"'.[335] In other words, it can still appropriately be translated as 'prefer' in this context. Second, even if one accepts the sort of reading suggested by Furnish, it is not necessary that one should exclude the notion of the risen Lord's real absence by setting 'orientation' against 'location' as Furnish does. While he disputes, in light of his reading, the pertinence of mention of Philippians 1:23 in terms of his reading of 2 Corinthians 5:6–8, by claiming it is 'misleading to cite Phil 1:23' here,[336] why should this obvious thematic parallel be dismissed? Third, other counter arguments have been proposed against the entire perspective promoted by Furnish, criticisms that have been accepted and adopted in the most recent commentaries on 2 Corinthians.[337] Not least of these is the importance of the context of the passage that, especially in 5:1, implies Paul is thinking about Christian death, and so 'departing from the body' is to be more naturally understood as death, rather than simply orientation in life.[338]

One last interpretive possibility could be maintained in potential contradiction to the argument being pursued here concerning Paul's understanding of the real and 'spatial' absence of the risen Lord. Perriman, in a manner reminiscent of his arguments concerning the παρουσία detailed above on page 157,

---

[332] As summarised in Thrall, *2 Corinthians Vol. 1*, 389, and cf. the references in the footnotes for more representatives for this view.

[333] Furnish, *II Corinthians*, 303.

[334] Cf. the extensive discussion in Thrall, *2 Corinthians Vol. 1*, 389–91; and Harris, *Second Epistle*, 399–400.

[335] Thrall, *2 Corinthians Vol. 1*, 390.

[336] Furnish, *II Corinthians*, 303.

[337] E.g. Thrall, *2 Corinthians Vol. 1*, 388–90, and Harris, *Second Epistle*, 394–403.

[338] Cf. the additional arguments proposed in Thrall, *2 Corinthians Vol. 1*, 390.

seems to suggest that being 'with the Lord' is actually to be understood not simply as presence with the Lord, but as language which more directly refers, again, to *something else*. 'Being "with the Lord"', he writes, 'refers neither to death nor to the parousia but to the wished-for pre-possession of the heavenly body'.[339] Remembering Perriman's concern to avoid overly abstract readings of Paul's eschatology,[340] one could therefore argue that it would be a mistake to over press Paul's language of absence (as well as 'presence') in terms of abstract theologising in theistic categories. However, even if the general thrust of Perriman's exegesis is accepted,[341] it is not clear that being 'with the Lord' can so easily be taken really to mean something else. Being 'with the Lord' was not an irrelevant hope in Second Temple Judaism, as detailed above, nor is this an anachronistic reading of Paul, as the exegesis in this thesis of 1 Thessalonians 4:17–18; 5:9–10 and Philippians 1:23 shows. To speak of Paul's very deep travail in light of the painful reality of the 'spatial' absence of the risen Lord is not to dislocate interpretation into a dubious eisegesis of dry theistic theologising, but is rather to look into the passions and pains of the Apostle himself.

The initial reading of this passage presented above is thus to be preferred. Indeed, it makes sense of the context well. If one takes seriously the wider narrative thrown up in Paul's thought world by the exile motif of the spatial metaphor language in 5:6 and 8, one can also comfortably explain, without needing to accept Furnish's proposals, why the faith in 5:7 is sandwiched in between these two verses, and why 5:9 and 10 involve urges to live life so as to please the Lord in light of the coming judgment. It is precisely because the people of God remain in 'exile' from the presence of the Lord that life now can be seen as a time of testing, as is so prominent in Israel's wilderness wandering narratives. Paul was naturally perfectly aware of these stories, but he also saw in them clues to Christian identity, as 1 Corinthians 10:1–13 shows.[342] Besides, no good reason has been found to neglect an emphasis on Paul's real sense and experience of the absence of the risen Lord. As Thrall writes: 'life in this world means life in exile, life apart from the Lord'.[343] Harris adds: 'to be living on earth in a physical body inevitably means distance – indeed exile – from the risen Lord'.[344]

---

[339] Perriman, "Paul," 520.

[340] Cf. the discussion on page 157 above.

[341] To be noted is that his argument, in terms of 2 Cor. 5, helps to explain the meaning of the εἶδος in 5:7.

[342] To develop these arguments further would be outside the scope of the present argument. For more on this complex of themes cf., e.g., Sylvia C. Keesmaat, *Paul and His Story. (Re)Interpreting the Exodus Tradition* (Sheffield: Sheffield Academic Press, 1999), esp. 34–48.

[343] Thrall, *2 Corinthians Vol. 1*, 386.

[344] Harris, *Second Epistle*, 395.

Of course, a similar cluster of ideas, as that in 2 Corinthians 5:6–8, is found in Philippians 1:20–24, specifically 1:23–24. Paul writes from prison (Phil. 1:7, 13–14, 17), as one experiencing the weight of suffering for the sake of the gospel (e.g., 1:17, 29 etc.). In 1:23 he argues that he is 'torn between two' options.[345] On the one hand, he could continue living ἐν σαρκί (1:22), which would mean fruitful labour for Paul (1:22), and this would clearly be the better thing for the Philippians (1:24). On the other hand, Paul's desire is actually 'to depart' (ἀναλύω - a Greek euphemistic metaphor for death[346]) and 'be with Christ' (σὺν Χριστῷ εἶναι), which would be by far the better of the two options for Paul himself. It would be a mistake to suggest that this desire is to be understood as Paul's longing to be free simply from persecution and suffering for the gospel.[347] Rather, he wants to depart *and be with Christ*. Indeed, as O'Brien argues: 'The prepositional phrase εἰς τὸ ... ἀναλῦσαι καὶ σὺν Χριστῷ εἶναι indicates grammatically the direction of the apostle's strong desire, and this is tantamount to describing its content'.[348] The emphasis is upon the experience of the presence of Christ, and is thus to be understood together with 2 Corinthians 5:8, 1 Thessalonians 4:17–18 and 5:10–11 (where Paul writes 'and so we will be with the Lord forever. *Therefore* encourage one another with these words').

All of this implies a very obvious conclusion. Paul's desire to be with Christ means that Paul is in some sense not yet with Christ. In the same way, within the Philippian correspondence, Paul can write that 'the Lord is near' (4:5). However, 'near', whether this is meant spatially or temporally,[349] is not 'here'. Paul does not yet live with the Lord in the eschatological sense indicated in these verses. He is not yet 'with the Lord', in the presence of the Lord, in the eschatological sense for which Paul hopes. Christ is absent from the apostle while he lives in the body.

7.4. Christ is in heaven

It has been argued that Christ is, for Paul, in some very real sense *absent*. The risen Lord is not yet seen face to face, has not yet 'come', his presence (παρουσία) is future, Paul does not yet live 'with the Lord' and is 'away from the Lord'. This naturally raises the question as to where, then, Christ actually is. For Paul, where is Christ now? Happily, even a cursory reading of the Pauline material yields an answer to this question, one that is hardly disputed. For example: '"Do not say in your heart, 'Who will ascend into heaven?'"' (that is,

---

[345] For translations involving the word 'torn', cf. Fowl, *Philippians*, 50–51; NET; NIV; NLT.

[346] Cf. O'Brien, *Philippians*, 130.

[347] Thus contra, e.g., Palmer (cited in O'Brien, *Philippians*, 122–23), and Arthur J. Droge and James D. Tabor, *A Noble Death: Suicide and Martyrdom Among Christians and Jews in Antiquity* (San Francisco: Harper, 1992), as cited in Fowl, *Philippians*, esp. 55.

[348] O'Brien, *Philippians*, 129.

[349] Cf. the discussion in O'Brien, *Philippians*, 488–90.

to bring Christ down)' (Rom. 10:6); 'Christ Jesus, who died, yes, who was raised, who is at the right hand of God' (Rom. 8:34); 'But our citizenship is in heaven, and it is from there that we are expecting a Saviour, the Lord Jesus Christ' (Phil. 3:20); 'you turned to God from idols, to serve a living and true God, and to wait for his Son from heaven' (1 Thess. 1:9–10); 'For the Lord himself, with a cry of command ... will descend from heaven' (1Thess. 4:16) etc. (cf. also 1Cor. 15:47–49; 2 Cor. 12:2; Eph. 6:9; Col. 4:1; 2 Thess. 1:7). The Lord is not simply 'here' for Paul, he is in some sense absent and in heaven at the right hand of God.

8. An absent Lord whose presence is mediated by the Spirit

If the above argumentation is correct then Christ is in some sense present and active in the church and the world in various ways, *yet at the same time* also absent. How is this to be understood? Numerous passages were examined above that suggest an answer. In Romans 8:9–10 Paul writes:

> But you are not in the flesh; you are in the Spirit, since the Spirit of God dwells in you. Anyone who does not have the Spirit of Christ does not belong to him. But if Christ is in you, though the body is dead because of sin, the Spirit is life because of righteousness.

Because the Spirit of God, the Spirit of Christ, dwells in believers, so does Christ. The major study of the Spirit's relation to the risen Lord in Paul maintains that to speak of the 'Spirit of Christ' refers 'to the Spirit in its capacity to mediate the risen Lord's own presence and activity'.[350] Indeed, the author of this work, Fatehi, draws the same conclusions from analysis of both Galatians 4:6 ('God has sent the Spirit of his Son into our hearts'),[351] and Philippians 1:19 ('the help of the Spirit of Jesus Christ').[352] In Romans 12:11 Paul writes of being 'ardent in spirit, serving the Lord', which most commentators understand to refer to the Holy Spirit. So Jewett writes that for 'Paul the Spirit was the Lord's presence in believers'.[353] In Romans 15:18–19 Paul describes his missionary activity:

> For I will not venture to speak of anything except what Christ has accomplished through me to win obedience from the Gentiles, by word and deed, by the power of signs and wonders, by the power of the Spirit of God.

Paul can speak of what Christ has accomplished through him as it happened 'by the power of the Spirit of God'. So Fatehi writes in analysis of these verses that 'what Christ has done through him [Paul], he has done *by the power of the Spirit*'.[354]

---

[350] Fatehi, *Relation*, 229.
[351] Ibid., 215–20.
[352] Ibid., 221–29.
[353] Jewett, *Romans*, 763.
[354] Fatehi, *Relation*, 172, italics his.

All of this is good evidence, especially in the hands of Fatehi, that Christ is experienced and described as present in the Pauline communities *through the Spirit*.[355] It needs only be noted, at this point, that all Spirit-language in Second Temple Judaism (and in Paul) is exclusively God-language and speaks of 'God's activity as he *relates* himself to his world, his creation, his people'.[356]

9. Communications between the risen Lord and believers

There are a few valuable studies of prayer in Paul, and they at least touch upon prayer to the risen Lord. However, less recognised in terms of Paul's Christology is the communication *from* Christ *to* believers (including Paul). Communication between the risen Lord and believers is two-way. Ostmeyer's recent study of the language and theology of prayer in the NT thus correctly asserts that 'communication' functions as a better terminology than 'prayer', as the former is wide enough to encompass both verbal and non-verbal types of encounters between God, Christ and believers in the NT, in a way that 'prayer' struggles to do.[357] Indeed, Ostmeyer also recognises that it is precisely this communication between risen Lord and believers that reflects the nature of the relation between them. So he argues, 'The ... individual [NT] author's comprehension of Christ corresponds with their idea of how believers connect with God or Christ, or in which way they should commune with them'.[358] However, the conclusions Ostmeyer draws arguably miss the mark, so it will be necessary to engage with his study at certain points

9.1. Communication from Paul and believers to Christ

Material in Romans 10:9–13 is relevant. 10:9–10 expresses the content and nature of the Christian confession: it is made with the mouth, and states that 'Jesus is Lord'. 10:11–13 makes the addressee of the confession likely to be Christ. This is arguably no confession that 'Jesus is Lord' to the Father, but it is rather spoken to the risen Lord. So the 'him' in 10:11 is likely the one who is believed in and, in 10:12–13, the one who is called upon. This calling upon the Lord ensures 'you will be saved' (σωθήσῃ), and that these believers will receive the generosity of the risen Lord. Paul uses the verb ἐπικαλέω three times in Romans 10:12–14 (cf. also 1 Cor. 1:2). Jewett argues that the

---

[355] 'The same Spirit that exclusively mediated and still mediates the active presence of God, comes to be experienced as mediating also the active presence of the risen and exalted Christ' (Fatehi, *Relation*, 311).

[356] Fatehi, *Relation*, 303, italics mine, himself citing Lloyd Neve, *The Spirit of God in the Old Testament* (Tokyo: Seibunsha, 1972).

[357] Karl-Heinrich Ostmeyer, *Kommunikation mit Gott und Christus: Sprache und Theologie des Gebetes im Neuen Testament* (Tübingen: Mohr Siebeck, 2006), 29–30.

[358] Ibid., 37, translation mine.

'expression ἐπικαλεῖν αὐτόν ... is a technical expression for praying',[359] a judgment certainly reflected by its common employment in Rahlfs' LXX.[360]

It is at least possible that the κύριος, in Paul's citation of Psalm 117 in Romans 15:11 ('Praise [αἰνεῖτε] the Lord, all you Gentiles, and let all the peoples praise [ἐπαινέω] him'), is to be understood christologically, a case made more likely given Fee's recent christological reading of a similar passage in Romans 14:11.[361] If 15:11 is christological, and it remains debatable, then the communication of believers to the risen Lord involves the explicit vocabulary of praise.

In 1 Corinthians 16:22 Paul writes μαράνα θά, which most understand as 'Our Lord, come' (imperative), not as the also possible indicative, 'Our Lord has come'. Indeed, given Paul's hope for the speedy return of Christ (1 Cor. 11:26), plus the imperative formulation of the parallel expression in Revelation 22:20, the imperative is to be preferred.[362] While Ostmeyer accepts the imperative reading he also seeks to distinguish the 16:22 exclamation from prayer proper. While this passage is, in his opinion, 'the only direct invocation to Christ within the Pauline epistles', he opines that it is to be understood 'not so much as actual prayer, but primarily as a formulaic invocation'.[363] One wonders, however, whether this is splitting semantic hairs. Why does μαράνα θά cease to be prayer if it is 'a formulaic invocation'? It is communication, from a human, with a heavenly being (here Christ), hence the label 'prayer' seems appropriate. Indeed, why, having maintained that 'communication' is better terminology than 'prayer', is Ostmeyer all of a sudden concerned to distinguish 'a formulaic invocation' from 'prayer'?

Obviously 2 Corinthians 12:8, and Paul's triple appeal to the Lord, deserves examination. The structure of 12:7–10 is clear, and forms a unit in this section of 2 Corinthians 12.[364] In 12:7 Paul details the matter that was bothering him and which provoked the appeal in 12:8. 12:9a recounts the risen Lord's answer and 12:9b–10 presents Paul's response to this answer.[365]

---

[359] Jewett, *Romans*, 633.

[360] E.g. Gen. 4:26; 12:8; 13:4; 21:33; 26:25; 33:20; Exod. 29:45f; Deut. 4:7; 12:5, 11, 21, 26; 14:23f; 16:2, 6, 11; 26:2; 28:10; 1 Sam. 12:17f; 2 Sam. 22:4, 7; 1 Kgs. 17:21; 18:24–28; 2 Kgs. 5:11; 1 Chr. 4:10; 13:6; 16:8; 2 Chr. 6:20, 33; Est. 4:8; Job 5:8; 27:10; Pss. 4:1; 14:4; 18:3, 6; 20:9; 31:17; 50:15; 53:4; 56:9; 75:1; 79:6; 80:18; 81:7; 86:5; 89:26; 91:15; 99:6; 102:2; 105:1; 116:2, 4, 13; 118:5; 138:3; 145:18; 147:9; Isa. 55:5f; 64:7; Jer. 10:25; 11:14; Lam. 3:55, 57; Hos. 7:7; Joel 2:32; Amos 4:12; Jonah 1:6; Zeph. 3:9; Zech. 13:9; Jdt. 6:21; 8:17; 9:4; 16:1; Wis. Sol. 7:7; Sir. 2:10; 46:5, 16; 47:5; 48:20; 51:10; Bar. 3:7; 2 Macc. 3:15, 22, 31; 7:37; 8:2; 12:6, 28, 36; 13:10; 14:34, 46; 15:21f; 1 Esd. 6:33; 3 Macc. 1:27; 5:7; 6:1; 4 Macc. 12:17.

[361] Fee, *Christology*, 259–67.

[362] Ostmeyer, *Kommunikation*, 68.

[363] Ibid., 68, translation mine.

[364] Harris, *Second Epistle*, 827.

[365] Cf. Zmijewski, *Narrenrede*, 375, for a good summary of the structure of the passage.

Concerning the identity of the κύριος, all the major commentaries are agreed that it should be understood christologically. First and foremost this is clear from the dialogue in the following verses. Paul prays to the Lord and the one who answers with talk of 'my grace' and 'power'[366] is indirectly named in 12:9b in relation to this power, i.e. it is the 'power of Christ'.[367] Viewing the larger context, it should also be noticed that the 'visions and revelations of the *Lord*' (12:1) to be detailed in 12:2–7 are mentioned immediately after a verse in which Paul distinguished between God and the Lord Christ (cf. 11:31 'The God and Father of the Lord Jesus').[368]

It has nevertheless been argued that Paul does not pray to the risen Lord here in the same sense in that he would pray to God. This is indicated, so argues Ostmeyer, by Paul's terminological choices.[369] He writes:

For Paul's invocation, circumscribed as it is with παρακαλέω, God would not be the right addressee. Moreover, the Apostle would likely choose different prayer vocabulary to address God, for παρακαλέω contains - even if considerably less strongly - the aspect of sending for someone. This, however, would not strike the appropriate tone with God.[370]

However, as BDAG notes, there are numerous examples where the verb *is* used in terms of prayer to a god, not least in Josephus where it speaks of Samuel's 'appealing to God [παρακαλεῖ τὸν θεὸν] to extend his right hand over [... the Israelites] in their battle with the Palestinoi'. It continues: 'God was receptive to his *prayers* [εὐχῶν] ... he indicated victory and conquest for them' (*Ant*. 6:25).[371] Apparently this prayer did meet God in the right tone.

Finally, important material is found in 1 Thessalonians 3:11–13. This passage is called a 'prayer-wish' because Paul uses the optative mood rather than the imperative, and begins with the reflective pronoun αὐτός. The first issue of relevance that has caused debate concerns the use of the singular verb, κατευθύναι, with the doubled subject, both ὁ θεὸς καὶ πατὴρ ἡμῶν *and* ὁ κύριος ἡμῶν Ἰησοῦς. Morris maintains that this grammatical oddity is simply

---

[366] While the reading 'my power' is arguably later (cf. e.g. Harris, *Second Epistle*, 830), the major commentators agree that this accurately captures the meaning of the passage (e.g. R.P. Martin, *2 Corinthians*, 419; Barnett, *Corinthians*, 573 n.30). Harris goes as far as to contend that the definite article is possessive (Harris, *Second Epistle*, 830, a thesis affirmed with more certainty on p. 863).

[367] Cf. Thrall, *2 Corinthians Vol. 2*, 819.

[368] Harris, referring to Zerwick, also reasons that a christological reading is affirmed by the fact that the 'Lord' in 12:8 is definite (τὸν κύριον), something he considers typical of passages meant to be understood christologically (Harris, *Second Epistle*, 860).

[369] Ostmeyer, *Kommunikation*, e.g. 81, 98.

[370] Ibid., 85, translation mine.

[371] This translation is from Flavius Josephus, *Flavius Josephus: Judean Antiquities Books 5–7*, trans. Christopher Begg, Steve Mason and Louis H. Feldman (Leiden: Brill, 2005), 102. The LXX version of this story in 1 Sam. 7:9, which Josephus appears to work with (Josephus, *Flavius Josephus: Judean Antiquities Books 5–7*, 102 n.95, uses the verb βοάω.

a manifestation of Paul's belief in the divinity of Christ.[372] Likewise, Richard presumes the theological significance of the construction. However, as has already been noted, Richard asserts that Paul's Christology was 'low',[373] and thus he attempts to explain the double subject as a 'clumsily modified' gloss that changed an original genitive to a nominative case.[374] While this suggestion is creative, his theological and linguistic reasons are unconvincing.[375] Besides, there is simply no MS evidence to support his claim. It is better to follow Wanamaker and not to attempt to squeeze too much christological significance out of the grammatical anomaly of a single verse with double subject.[376] The second issue concerns the debate about whether the 'Lord', in 3:12, refers to God or to Christ. The vast majority maintain that Christ is the intended reference because of the usage of 'God' and 'Lord' in verses 11 and 13, and the explicit identification of the latter with Jesus in both verses.[377] A simple argument can now be asserted: Paul expresses a prayer-wish to the risen Lord.[378]

Of course, Paul's usual custom was to pray to the Father through Christ (cf. 1.20; Rom. 1:8; 7:25; Phil. 1:3; 4:6 etc.). Some deny Paul actually prayed to Christ,[379] yet 1 Corinthians 1:2; 16:22; 2 Corinthians 12:8 and 1 Thessalonians 3:12–13 are fairly clear evidence that he did communicate with the risen Christ and expect that his Lord could hear and answer his petitions. Is this prayer? As has been detailed above, Christ was, for Paul, present yet also absent, active yet also in heaven. So when Paul speaks to this risen Lord the practical dynamics, whatever the specific vocabulary used, will have looked very much like prayer to God, who was likewise present yet also absent; active yet also in heaven.

9.2. Communication from Christ to believers and Paul

In 2 Corinthians 10:18 Paul writes that 'it is not those who commend themselves that are approved, but those whom the Lord commends'. This language of commending (συνίστημι) is important in 2 Corinthians (e.g. 3:1; 4:2; 5:12;

---

[372] Morris, *Thessalonians*, 107.

[373] Cf. Richard, *One and Many*, 328.

[374] Richard, *Thessalonians*, 167–68.

[375] There is no reason to divide verse 11 from 12 on the grounds that one is eschatological and the other salvific. Furthermore, even if verse 11 is to be understood as 'eschatological', this does not exclude any connection of this verse with Christ (Richard refers to 1 Thess. 5:9, but what about 4:13–5:11?).

[376] Wanamaker, *Thessalonians*, 142.

[377] Cf. Abraham J. Malherbe, *The Letters to the Thessalonians*, AB (London: Doubleday, 2000), 212; and the literature cited in Fatehi, *Relation*, 9 n.23, both for and against this identification.

[378] Oddly, Ostmeyer does not examine the theological or christological significance of this prayer-wish.

[379] Hans Windisch, *Der zweite Korintherbrief* (Göttingen: Vandenhoeck & Ruprecht, 1924), 388; Stanley, *Boasting*, 53; and Matera, *II Corinthians*, 284.

6:4; 7:11; 10:12, 18; 12:11). Though it is not precisely clear what Paul meant by being commended by the Lord, it is nevertheless the basis of his being approved (δόκιμος). Paul believed that Christ himself, in some way, approved Christian ministers. If Paul can claim that 'the Lord commends', it is not an unreasonable assumption that the risen Lord somehow directly communicated this commendation, especially if a scenario similar to that described in Acts 13:1–2 is to be assumed.

In 2 Corinthians 12:1 Paul speaks of 'visions and revelations of the Lord'. Whether the genitive κυρίου is subjective, with Christ as the source of the revelations, or objective, with Christ as the content of the visions, is difficult to say. Perhaps the choice is a false one. Indeed, Fee argues that Ezekiel's 'visions of God' (ὁράσεις θεοῦ) function as the best template for understanding Paul's visions here. While God was certainly the content of Ezekiel's visions (Ezek. 1:1–28), it was also God who gave them. The majority position favours the subjective genitive reading, though Fee notes a problem with this view, namely that what mattered in these experiences was not merely the reception of a revelation, but that Christ was seen.[380]

In 2 Corinthians 12:9 Paul writes that Christ 'said to me, "My grace is sufficient ..."'. The catalogue of difficulties listed in 2 Corinthians 11:23–29 is likely echoed in 12:10, and in all of these difficulties Paul is reassured because Christ has spoken. Ostmeyer has rightly argued that prayer can involve nonverbal communication, as evidenced in the desperate prayer of the Tax-collector mentioned in Luke 18:9–14. Indeed, in 'this way of praying his relationship with God comes to expression'.[381] Much the same could be said of the nature of Paul's response to Christ's communications in 2 Corinthians 12. Paul's embrace of the risen Lord's words alter Paul's perception of reality.

In 2 Corinthians 13:3 Paul mentions the Corinthians' demand[382] for proof that 'Christ is speaking in me' (13:3a). Whatever one understands this proof to consist of,[383] it is apparent that the Corinthians wanted evidence that Christ speaks through Paul.[384] In other words, the Corinthians were concerned, in their own way, to be addressed by Christ, not merely Paul. They believed, therefore, that the risen Lord would speak through certain chosen people. Their demand consisted in proof of this.

Common Jewish rhetoric against idolatry involved the claim that the idols were dumb, and incapable of speaking. This is especially so in Deutero-Isaiah.

---

[380] Fee, *Christology*, 194.

[381] Ostmeyer, *Kommunikation*, 37.

[382] Furnish, *II Corinthians*, 570.

[383] Cf. the discussion in Thrall, *2 Corinthians Vol. 2*, 879–81. Her argument that the Corinthians probably expected some display of authoritarian power and judgment is very possible.

[384] This interpretation, of course, assumes an instrumental reading of ἐν ἐμοί, an interpretation made likely by the context (for this cf. Thrall, *2 Corinthians Vol. 2*, 879; Harris, *Second Epistle*, 912).

Unlike dumb idols, however, in Paul's letters the risen Lord was believed to communicate with his people.

10. The nature and character of Christ's risen lordship

10.1. Paul's understanding of Christ's character

As has been noted already, Bauckham's christological project employs the notion of 'identity'. He writes:

> Reference to God's identity is by analogy with human personal identity, understood not as a mere ontological subject without characteristics, but as including both character and personal story (the latter entailing relationships). These are the ways in which we commonly specify "who someone is".[385]

Bauckham, however, has not yet examined specifically Christ's *character* in the Pauline letters. But examination of Christ's characteristics will further this study of the Christ-relation in Paul's letters.

As has already been observed in relation to the presence and activity of Christ, Paul regularly speaks of Christ's grace (cf. the grace formulas at the beginning and end of the letters: Rom. 1:7; 16:20; 1 Cor. 1:3; 16:23; 2 Cor. 1:2; 8:9; 13:13; Gal. 1:3; 6:18; Phil. 1:2; 4:23; 1 Thess. 5:28; Philem. 3, 25). As argued above, this grace is not to be understood as an 'event rather than a disposition',[386] but as an event *and* disposition, as is especially clear in 2 Corinthians 8:9. Stegman argues that in '2 Cor 8:9 χάρις denotes "gracious care or help", in the sense of beneficent *disposition* toward others'.[387] This disposition is also evident in 12:9 where the risen Lord addresses Paul, in personal conversation, saying 'my grace is sufficient for you'. Christ's grace is truly power, but it remains a defining characteristic of his lordship. Christ *is* gracious.

Paul can also characterise the risen Lord in terms of his love. So he asks, 'Who will separate us from the love of Christ?' (Rom. 8:35). As Jewett has argued, the phrase τῆς ἀγάπης τοῦ Χριστοῦ 'is clearly a subjective genitive, referring to the love Christ shows to the undeserving'. One can thus argue that the use of the verb χωρίζω ('divide, separate') is used, in this context, to describe the 'severance of personal relationships'; to be separated from Christ's love implies a 'breach of relationship'.[388] This *characteristic* of the risen Lord entails relationship.

Paul writes of 'the love of Christ' also in 2 Corinthians 5:14, as discussed above. Speaking for a subjective genitive translation of the ἀγάπη τοῦ Χριστοῦ in this verse, Harris notes that '[n]o one doubts that believers' love

---

[385] Bauckham, *God*, 7 n.5.
[386] Thiselton, *Corinthians*, 81, italics mine. Cf. also 81–82, esp. n.123.
[387] Stegman, *Character*, 191.
[388] Jewett, *Romans*, 543.

for Christ motivates their actions, but here Paul is concentrating on an earlier stage of motivation, namely the love shown by Christ'.[389] In this context one must remember the very personal confession (using personal pronouns in the singular) in Galatians 2:20, that the Son of God 'loved me by giving himself for me' (ἀγαπήσαντός με).[390]

In Philippians 1:8 Paul writes about how he longs 'for all of you with the compassion (lit. bowels – σπλάγχνα) of Christ Jesus'. While this can be translated as 'compassion of Christ', other interpreters understand the term as essentially synonymous with love or affection.[391] So O'Brien writes that Philippians 1:8 shows that 'Christ loves the Philippians in and through Paul'.[392] This all of course presupposes, but uncontroversially, an instrumental reading of the ἐν in the phrase ἐν σπλάγχνοις Χριστοῦ Ἰησοῦ and a subjective genitive understanding of Χριστοῦ.[393]

In Romans 10:12 Paul writes that 'the same Lord is Lord of all and is generous to all who call on him'. The verb translated 'generous' is πλουτέω which means 'to be rich'.

Paul can also characterise the risen Lord as faithful. In Romans 14:4 Paul writes that 'servants of another' will be upheld for the Lord is able to make them stand'. While this passage was examined above in relation to Christ's presence and activity, the point to make here is Paul's confidence that these servants *will* stand (cf. Paul's employment of the indicative future passive of the verb ἵστημι). The implication of this reasoning, and that which makes sense of Paul's confidence that they will stand, is that the risen Lord is faithful to make them stand (cf. the connected ideas in 2 Thess. 3:3 'But the Lord is faithful [πιστὸς δέ ἐστιν ὁ κύριος]; he will strengthen you and guard you from the evil one').

Of course, at this point one is forced to at least glance at the πίστις Χριστοῦ debates, for if the genitive is subjective then it refers not to (human) faith in Christ, but to Christ's faithfulness. Fee has recently addressed the issue in terms of Paul's Christology, concluding that though the construction 'might possibly refer to "the faithfulness of Christ" (e.g., Rom 3:22, on the pattern of "God's faithfulness" in 3:3 and Abraham's in 4:12, 16)', it is unlikely to do so in Galatians. At present, scholarship is probably about evenly balanced between those who adopt the subjective, on the one hand, and those who prefer the objective reading, on the other, though possibly slightly more opt for

---

[389] Harris, *Second Epistle*, 419. Cf. also Stegman, *Character*, 168–70.

[390] For this translation, cf. n.122.

[391] Sumney, *Philippians*, 13; O'Brien, *Philippians*, 71–72.

[392] O'Brien, *Philippians*, 72.

[393] Cf. Bonnie Bowman Thurston and Judith Ryan, *Philippians and Philemon* (Collegeville: Liturgical Press, 2005), 51; Hawthorne, *Philippians*, 25.

the objective.[394] Rather than enter this complicated and lengthy debate, it simply suffices to argue that were a subjective genitive reading accepted in any of the disputed cases (Rom. 3:22, 26; Gal. 2:16, 20; 3:22; Phil. 3:9), then there is further ground for asserting Paul's understanding of his Lord as faithful. Indeed, arguably a decent case can be made for a subjective genitive reading of at least Romans 3:22 and Galatians 3:22.[395]

Stegman maintains that 2 Corinthians 4:13 is evidence for Paul's understanding of the faithfulness of Christ.[396] He argues that Paul appropriates LXX Psalms 114–115 in 2 Corinthians 4:13, and 'draws upon a christological reading of these texts, a reading that unfolds a rich portrait of Jesus and his πίστις'.[397] He also argues that Christ's faithfulness is in view in 2 Corinthians 13:5 ('examine yourselves to see whether you are living in the faith'), but the following rhetorical question 'Do you not realise that Jesus Christ is in you?' is hardly unambiguous for this case,[398] and at the most makes his proposal a slight possibility.

When Paul speaks of Christ, the last Adam, as πνεῦμα ζῳοποιοῦν in 1 Corinthians 15:45, much discussion revolves around whether or what type of resurrection body Paul believes Christ has.[399] However, a point that needs to be stressed, that is often overlooked, is the importance of the present active participle. It is likely that this participle looks back to 15:22 ('so all will be made alive in Christ'),[400] which means that '"[g]iving life" is synonymous with raising the dead (Rom. 4:17; 8:11; 2 Cor. 3:6)'.[401] However, this life-giving function is one Paul would have recognised in his scriptures, with reference to the verb ζῳοποιέω. In 2 Kings 5:7, upon reading a letter, the king exclaimed: 'Am I God, to give death or life (ζῳοποιέω)'. Ezra prays:

---

[394] For recent discussion, cf. e.g. R. Barry Matlock, "The Rhetoric of πίστις in Paul: Galatians 2.16, 3.22, Romans 3.22, and Philippians 3.9," *JSNT* 30, no. 2 (2007): 173–203; Roy A. Harrisville, "Before πίστις Χριστοῦ: The Objective Genitive as Good Greek," *NovT* 48, no. 4 (2006): 233–41; Fee, *Christology*, 223–26; Karl Friedrich Ulrichs, *Christusglaube: Studien zum Syntagma pistis Christou und zum paulinischen Verständnis von Glaube und Rechtfertigung* (Tübingen: Mohr Siebeck, 2007); Dunn, *Theology*, 379–85; Douglas A. Campbell, *The Quest for Paul's Gospel: A Suggested Strategy* (London: T&T Clark, 2005), 208–32.

[395] Campbell, *Gospel*, 208–32. Bird, while reserved in his judgments about the genitive in Rom. 3:22, asserts that 'there is no question as to whether it [the faithfulness of Jesus] is conceptually present in [Rom.] 5.18–21' (Michael F. Bird, *The Saving Righteousness of God: Studies on Paul, Justification and the New Perspective* [Milton Keynes: Paternoster, 2007], 147).

[396] Stegman, *Character*, 146–68.

[397] Ibid., 146.

[398] *Pace* Stegman, *Character*, 360.

[399] Cf. Thiselton, *Corinthians*, 1276–84.

[400] Schnabel, *Korinther*, 971; Fee, *Corinthians*, 788.

[401] Garland, *1 Corinthians*, 735.

You are the LORD, you alone; you have made heaven, the heaven of heavens, with all their host, the earth and all that is on it, the seas and all that is in them. To all of them you give life (ζωοποιεῖς), and the host of heaven worships you (Neh. 9:6).

The Psalmist states his confidence that God 'will revive (ἐζωοποίησάς) me again' (Ps. 71:20 [70:20 LXX]). Likewise in Paul, God is the one 'who gives life (ζῳοποιοῦντος) to the dead' (Rom. 4:17), and in 2 Corinthians 3:6 the divine Spirit is the one who 'gives life' (ζῳοποιεῖ). Paul begins 1 Corinthians 15:45 by citing the LXX of Genesis 2:7, where 'the man became a living being' (ὁ ἄνθρωπος εἰς ψυχὴν ζῶσαν). Paul's contrast is clear: the last Adam, became a *life-giving* spirit (πνεῦμα ζῳοποιοῦν).[402] In the Genesis text, of course, it is God who 'formed the man of dust of the earth, and breathed upon his face the breath of life', so that the man became a living soul. Perhaps there is more significance, then, in characterising Christ as a life-*giving* spirit in 1 Corinthians 15:45 than is often recognised. Either way, Christ is, for Paul, life-giving.

In 2 Corinthians 10:1 Paul speaks of the 'gentleness and forbearance of Christ' (πραΰτητος καὶ ἐπιεικείας τοῦ Χριστοῦ).[403] In a study of the character of Jesus in 2 Corinthians, Stegman argues that:

The allusion to Christ in 2 Cor 10:1 ... evokes two interconnected aspects of the character of Jesus. First, πραΰτης refers to his quality of gentleness exhibited especially in his role as teacher and master (cf. John 13:13–14), a gentleness marked by love and dissociated from the use of coercion. Second, ἐπιείκεια refers to Jesus' forbearance, manifested in particular by patience, slowness to anger, non-retaliation, and his willingness to forgive.[404]

For Paul, Christ is thus 'slow to anger', and one could note certain texts (e.g., 2 Macc. 2:22; 10:4; Bar. 2:27; Pr Azar 1:19), where the mentioned ἐπιείκεια belongs to God.

Until now Paul's understanding of the character of Christ has been shown to involve love, compassion, faithfulness, grace etc. Yet Paul could also speak of Christ as an avenging Lord (1 Thess. 4:6 ἔκδικος κύριος). There is some debate as to whether κύριος here refers to God or the risen Christ. Those maintaining God is in view, with κύριος, tend to do so by noting how God is usually associated with 'avenging' language.[405] Richard thus argues, with reference to Romans 2:16, that for Paul, '[s]trictly speaking, judgment is the role of God and Jesus is God's agent in this activity'.[406] Hence Paul, in using the OT language of judging, must be referring to God with κύριος. However, that

---

[402] Fee, *Corinthians*, 788.

[403] This translation is defended in Stegman, *Character*, 121–29. Writing about the phrase πραΰτητος καὶ ἐπιεικείας τοῦ Χριστοῦ, Stegman also argues that 'the genitive Χριστοῦ can*not* be anything but subjective' (122, italics his).

[404] Stegman, *Character*, 128–29.

[405] Morris, *Thessalonians*, 124. Tentatively Malherbe, *Thessalonians*, 233. However, by the time Malherbe reaches 1 Thess. 4:9, he appears to have decided absolutely for the referent as God, not Christ (212).

[406] Richard, *Thessalonians*, 204.

he understands Romans 2:16 to be Paul's 'strictly speaking' is an arbitrary move. One could equally state that 'strictly speaking' *Christ* was Paul's judge, based upon 1 Corinthians 4:4 and 2 Corinthians 5:10. And that Paul is using OT language here proves nothing. Paul *regularly* employed OT language in terms of Christ.[407] Furthermore, in the immediate context κύριος is frequently referred to explicitly as Jesus (4:1, 2), and God is likewise spoken of not as κύριος but as θεός (4:1, 3, 5, 7, 8). One should therefore conclude, with the majority of commentators, that the 'Lord' in this passage refers to Christ.[408] Against the vices named in 1 Thessalonians 4:3–6, Christ is an avenging Lord. In this respect, one is also reminded of Christ's response to those who abuse the Lord's Supper in 1 Corinthians 11. Those who eat and drink in an unworthy manner (11:27) 'eat and drink judgment against themselves' (11:29). Paul adds: 'For this reason many of you are weak and ill, and some have died' (11:30).

10.2. The scope and nature of Christ's risen lordship

In detailing the risen Lord as present and active by the Spirit, yet in a sense also absent, present in heaven at God's right hand, the nature of Christ's lordship has already been addressed. However, there is further material in the undisputed Pauline epistles directly relevant to the question of the nature and scope of Christ's lordship that must now be examined.

The proper punctuation of Romans 9:5 remains hotly disputed. To cite the primary translational options:

1) ... Christ as to his earthly life, who is God over all, blessed forever;
2) ... Christ as to his earthly life, who is over all things. May God be blessed forever.
3) ... Christ as to his earthly life. May God who is over all things be blessed forever.[409]

Fee opts for the third translation possibility,[410] yet the matter is far from settled.[411] However, what concerns this thesis is not whether Christ is called 'God' but whether Christ is described as 'over all'. Rather than enter the long and complex debates surrounding the minutiae of syntax, it suffices to point out that two of the three main possibilities for this passage (options 1 and 2 above) read Christ as 'over all'.

Evidence for reading 1 or 2 above is found in Romans 10:12, where Paul claims, as discussed above, that there is 'no difference between Jew and Greek, for the same Lord of all is rich to all those calling upon him'. This

---

[407] Cf. many places in Fee, *Christology*.

[408] Reference here can be made to Bruce, *Thessalonians*, 85; Green, *Thessalonians*, 197; Wanamaker, *Thessalonians*, 156; Ben Witherington, III, *1 and 2 Thessalonians: A Socio-Rhetorical Commentary* (Grand Rapids: Eerdmans, 2006), 117.

[409] Adapted from the analysis in Fee, *Christology*, 273.

[410] Fee, *Christology*, 272–77.

[411] Cf. the critical remarks in Matthew Montonini, Review of Fee's *Pauline Christology*, on the *Review of Biblical Literature* web site.

Lord is Lord *of all* (κύριος πάντων). In Romans 14:9 Paul expresses the scope of Christ's lordship in terms of the goal behind Christ's dying and resurrection (ἔζησεν): 'so that he might be Lord of both the dead and the living'. This Lord is thus, according to Romans, Lord of all, Lord of both the dead and living, and perhaps also 'over all' (ἐπὶ πάντων).

In 1 Corinthians 10:26 Paul, to support the Corinthians in buying anything from the μάκελλον, cites Psalm 24:1 (LXX 23:1): 'the earth and its fullness are the Lord's'. Capes, on the basis of:

(1) ethical considerations, (2) other occurrences of κύριος in the context, and (3) the structure of Paul's entire discussion - particularly with reference to creation - indicate[s] that Paul applied Ps 24:1, an Old Testament Yahweh text, to the Lord Jesus.[412]

Capes is likely correct, and the exegetical analysis of 1 Corinthians 8:1–10:22 proposed above speaks in favour of his reading. However, given that Paul's argument changed direction in 10:23, and given that this argument ends, in 10:31, with reference to doing 'everything for the glory of God',[413] it is perhaps best to remain undogmatic regarding the precise referent of this κύριος.[414] Nevertheless, it is a real possibility that Paul refers to the earth and its fullness, via citation of the Psalm, as belonging to Christ.

In Philippians 3:21 Paul speaks of the 'the body of our humiliation' (σῶμα τῆς ταπεινώσεως ἡμῶν) that Christ himself will transform 'according to the power that also enables him to make all things subject to himself'. As the αὐτόν refers to Christ,[415] 'Christ is able not only to transform the body, but "also to subject" (καὶ ὑποτάξαι) the entire universe (τὰ πάντα) to himself'.[416]

A point regarding the *nature* of Christ's risen lordship needs to be mentioned. In Galatians 1:1, 11–12 Paul places Christ's lordship in a duality. On the one hand, Paul was not sent 'by human commission nor from human authorities' (ἀπ' ἀνθρώπων ... δι' ἀνθρώπου), but rather, and on the other hand, through Jesus Christ ...' (Gal. 1:1). Likewise, the gospel Paul proclaims 'is not of human origin' (1:11 – κατὰ ἄνθρωπον), nor was it received 'from a human source' (1:12 – παρὰ ἀνθρώπου). It was, rather, received 'through a revelation of Jesus Christ' (1:12). In this dualism, Paul places the human on one side and Christ on the other. While obviously not implying a kind of proto-docetism,

---

[412] Capes, *Yahweh Texts*, 145, and cf. his discussion in 140–45. Also confident of the christological nature of this κύριος is Hurtado, *LJC*, 112.

[413] Fee offers a third reason for doubting that 'Lord' here refers to Christ, namely that Paul makes no christological point in 10:26 (Fee, *Christology*, 134). But does Paul really need to make a christological point for this Lord to refer to Christ?

[414] Cf. the balanced judgment in Fee, *Christology*, 133–34.

[415] O'Brien, *Philippians*, 465.

[416] O'Brien, *Philippians*, 466. Most commentators treat the αὐτῷ as reflexive (so Bockmuehl, *Philippians*, 236; Fowl, *Philippians*, 159, 175; Thurston and Ryan, *Philippians and Philemon*, 135; Silva, *Philippians*, 185; Fee, *Christology*, 405), and arguably only a desire to harmonise this passage with 1 Cor. 15:27 would lead to the suggestion that αὐτῷ should refer to God.

this duality between Christ, and that which is ἄνθρωπος, is noteworthy. Also in Galatians, Paul could speak of the pre-Christian lives of the Galatians as a time when they were 'enslaved to beings that by nature are not gods' (4:8 – ἐδουλεύσατε τοῖς φύσει μὴ οὖσιν θεοῖς). Nevertheless, he can use the verb δουλεύω with reference to Christ (cf. Rom. 12:11; 14:18; 16:18), and one is therefore tempted to emphasise the implication that the Galatians are now enslaved to Christ, who is thus by nature divine. This would correspond rather neatly at least with the duality expressed in Galatians 1:1, 11–12.

11. An overview and summary of the Pauline Christ-relation

In terms of Paul's Christ-shaped aims, goals and motivations, though the aims of Jesus have been discussed in at least one important monograph,[417] nothing similar, to the knowledge of this author, has been published on Paul. Hence the comments in this chapter concerning Paul's Christ-shaped goals and motivations must remain preliminary. Nevertheless, certain results emerged. In Romans the goal of Paul's mission to bring about the obedience of faith among the Gentiles was for the sake of Christ's name (Rom. 1:5. Cf. also Gal. 1:16). The end of Christ's death and resurrection was that he be Lord of the living and the dead (14:9). In 1 Corinthians Paul states that the purpose of the body is for the Lord (6:13), and Paul's goal in his ethical instruction concerning marriage was ultimately to promote undistracted devotion to the Lord, to promote lives that please the Lord and are entirely holy in this devotion (7:32–35). In 2 Corinthians, Christ is presented as the motivation for enduring such suffering and persecution – even to the point of death. Yet Paul's overriding concern was that, through suffering and weakness, the life of Christ would be made visible (4:5–11. Cf. also 2 Cor. 12:7–10). Paul's mission is further described as motivated by the desire to please Christ, as well as by Paul's fear of the Lord and Christ's own love (5:9–14). Further, the collection there described was undertaken 'for the glory of the Lord himself' (8:19). In Philippians, Paul's goal was that Christ be exalted (1:20), whether by life or by death. Indeed, for Paul, life itself is summed up in Christ – everything he does is done for Christ (1:21). Even more poignantly, the presence of Christ, for Paul, is his ultimate desire and yearning, more than life itself (1:23). Indeed, Paul's grasp of these goals and motivations encompasses a cosmic sweep, such that every tongue is destined to confess to Christ that he is Lord (2:9–11). Perhaps more important still are Paul's claims in Philippians 3. Everything, the entirety of all he could boast of in his pre-Christophany life, is regarded as rubbish or excrement *because of* the knowledge of Christ. Indeed, the goal of knowing Christ causes him to 'press on', and Christ himself motivates this because he made Paul 'his own'. Likewise in 1 Thessalonians Paul

---

[417] Ben F. Meyer, *The Aims of Jesus* (London: SCM, 1979).

reveals his deepest yearning: to be with Christ forever (4:17; 5:10). More could be added to this summary, but enough has been detailed to give a sense of the depth and importance of Christ as goal and motivation in Paul's life. Surely, here we encounter Christ-devotion.

In terms of the various other expressions of Christ-devotion, still more can be added. Christians, Paul argues, live and die to the Lord, eat or abstain from certain foods etc. in honour of the Lord (cf. Rom. 14:6–8). Every knee, so continues Paul, will bow to this same Lord (14:11? But cf. Phil. 2:9–11). Some Christians are described as the first-fruits *for Christ* (Rom. 16:5), and are specified as those who eagerly await their Lord (1 Cor. 1:17; Phil. 3:20). Christ-believers are called into communion and fellowship not only with each other but also with their Lord (1 Cor. 1:9), and they boast in the Lord Jesus (1:31). Paul, in his mission to the Corinthians, determined to know Christ and nothing but Christ crucified (2:2), and in 6:17 Paul employs memorable language to detail the intimate unity between Christ and believers, one contrasted with unity with prostitutes. Holiness is described in terms of devotion to the Lord, and Paul in the same context speaks of living to please the Lord with undistracted devotion (7:32–35). The cultic meal (performed in honour of a deity) was done in 'remembrance' of Christ (11:23–26) and the confession 'Jesus is Lord' is perceived as the work of the Holy Spirit (12:3). Paul's life is based on an exclusive hope in Christ, a hope which, it becomes clear in his argument in 1 Corinthians 15, invades every pore of the Christian's existence, whether in life or death. In 2 Corinthians 3 believers 'turn to' (ἐπιστρέψῃ) the Lord and behold the glory of the Lord, which leads to their transformation. This implies a Spirit inspired growth of desire for the risen Lord, through beholding Christ's glory, such that this desire functions to counterbalance sinful passions (3:16–18). A little later Paul speaks of believers as those who do not live for themselves but for the risen Lord (5:15), and as those who give themselves *first* to the Lord (8:5). Paul and his team, when considering what to do, think of what would be good before the Lord (8:21). To be a believer in Christ, and central to their identity, is to 'belong to Christ' (10:7. Cf. also Gal. 3:29; 5:24). They are betrothed to Christ, their one husband, and are to be presented as a pure maiden to this Lord, single-minded in their Christ-devotion (ἁπλότης – 11:2–3). Of course, Christians are those who believe into Christ (Gal. 2:16), and Paul, in this context, can speak of Christ as the heartbeat of his whole life, the presence which inspired and filled him (2:20). Possibly Philippians 2:6–11 is evidence that believers sang songs about Christ in their corporate gatherings. They also rejoiced in the Lord (Phil. 3:1), and Paul speaks in exalted language of his personal knowledge of the risen Christ (3:7–10), and of his boasting in this knowledge (cf. 3:4 and 2 Cor. 1:31–2:2). Finally, turning to 1 Thessalonians, believers 'stand firm' and hope in the Lord, expressions all reflecting their love for the Lord (Plevnik).

In terms of the passionate nature of this Christ-devotion, while some of the above already discloses the passion involved, the fervency of this Christ-devotion is revealed in further ways. Serving the Lord is spoken of in terms of a *boiling over in the spirit* (Rom. 12:11). Paul's *ambition* is to proclaim Christ (15:20. Cf. also 2 Cor. 5:9; 1 Thess. 4:11). Believers *eagerly* wait for the Lord (1 Cor. 1:7), Paul knows *only* Christ and him crucified in his mission to Corinth (2:2). Ethical instruction about marriage is given to facilitate *undistracted* devotion to the Lord (7:32–35). Believers are to *always excel and abound* in the work of the Lord (15:58). Every thought is taken captive into the obedience of Christ (2 Cor. 10:4–5) and believers are to be *unswervingly and single-mindedly committed* in their devotion to Christ (11:2–3). That Christ be exalted is Paul's *eager expectation and hope*, one that he wishes will find expression in the *totality* of his existence (Phil. 1:20). Perhaps most forcefully, Paul considers *all things* as rubbish or excrement compared to the *surpassingness* of the knowledge of Christ (3:8). Paul encourages believers to rejoice in this Lord and to do so *always* and *greatly* (4:4, 10).

In terms of what Paul contrasts with Christ-devotion, the opposite of serving the Lord is to serve the belly (Rom. 16:18). Fornication with the body is contrasted with the body being for the Lord (1 Cor. 6:13), while being anxious about the things of the world is matched against undistracted devotion to Christ (7:32–35). Rather than the sort of relation to the risen Lord which Paul desired, some in Corinth sin against Christ, test him and provoke him to jealousy through their capitulation to idolatry and loveless behaviour (8:12; 10:9, 20–22; 11:28–32). It is also none other than the god of this world who blinds unbelievers to the glory of Christ (2 Cor. 4:4). To not live for the Lord is, by implication, to live for oneself, and 'to know' according to the flesh (5:15–16). To give up on pure devotion to Christ is to be deceived as the serpent deceived Eve (11:3). To live so as to please humans would mean one is not a servant of Christ (Gal. 1:10), and Paul laments that many seek only their own interests and not, in contrast, those of Christ (Phil. 2:21). Further, as in many of Paul's arguments, there exists a dividing line between 'us', who expect Christ from heaven, and 'them', who set their minds on earthly things (3:18–20).

The presence and activity of Christ is described in a variety of ways. Christ indwells believers (Rom. 8:9–19). The Lord is able to make believers stand (14:4). Christ is active in Paul's mission (15:18–19, 29). The grace of the Lord is active in the Pauline churches (e.g. Rom. 1:17; 16:20 etc.). 1 Corinthians portrays the risen Lord as present and active in, among other ways, appointing leaders (3:5), within Paul himself, making him trustworthy, in the social and communal situatedness of all people (7:17), and even over/in the seemingly contingent course of historical events (4:19; 16:17). A wide spread of evidence across the rest of the letters paints a similar picture (cf. as discussed above, e.g. 2 Cor. 1:2–3; 2:10, 12; 3:3; 13:2–5, 13; Gal. 1:16; 2:20;

4:19; 6:18; Phil. 1:2, 8; 1 Thess. 5:28; Philem. 3, 25 etc.). In 2 Corinthians 12:7–10 Paul's prayer-conversation with the risen Lord further shows his expectation of the presence and activity of Christ in his life to answer his prayers. This is also evident in the prayer-wish in 1 Thessalonians 3:11–13 and the expectation that the Spirit of Jesus Christ will respond to the prayers of the Philippians (Phil. 1:19). What is more, a couple of chapters later Paul speaks of the power of Christ active in his conversion, and even of the power which enables Christ 'to make all things subject to himself' (3:21). Christ is, for Paul, tangibly present and active in the ancient Mediterranean world in a variety of ways.

What makes the previous conclusions so remarkable is that Christ is at the same time, for Paul, *absent*. He speaks of the Lord as not yet present, as not yet come (1 Cor. 11:26). Christ cannot yet be seen face to face (1 Cor. 13:12). The παρουσία language (e.g. 1 Cor. 15:23; 1 Thess. 2:19; 3:13), which speaks of the future coming of the Lord, implies that, for Paul at the time of his letter writing, Christ was absent (ἀπουσία) – hence Paul's longing for Christ's presence as detailed above. In 2 Corinthians 5:6–8 Paul writes that 'while we are at home in the body we are away from the Lord', Christians are not yet 'at home with the Lord' but away from him (cf. also Phil. 1:20–24; 1 Thess. 4:17–18; 5:10–11).

Though, for Paul, Christ is present and active, this Christ is also absent. He is in heaven at the right hand of God (Rom. 8:34; 10:6; Phil. 3:20; 1 Thess. 1:9–10 etc.). So how is Christ present and absent at the same time? Various clues in Paul's letters lead to the conclusion that Christ's presence was understood to have been mediated by the Spirit (Rom. 8:9–10; 12:11; 15:18–19; Gal. 4:6; Phil. 1:19).

Paul's letters also evidence that this present yet absent Lord engages in various communications with Christians. They communicated to Christ in a number of ways. The confession 'Jesus is Lord' was likely made to Christ himself, and believers 'call upon' him (Rom. 10:9–13. Cf. also 1 Cor. 1:2). If the Romans 15:11 'Lord' is Christ, then this communication involved praise of Christ. The μαράνα θά of 1 Corinthians 16:22, likely an early communal prayer, was addressed to the risen Lord. Paul's thrice repeated appeal to the risen Lord in 2 Corinthians 12 must also be mentioned, as should the prayer-wish of 1 Thessalonians 3:11–13. However, it is also clear that the risen Lord himself communicated to believers; the conversation was two-way. Though evident in a few verses (e.g., 2 Cor. 10:18?; 12:1; 13:3), it is clearest in 2 Corinthians 12:9 where Christ verbally responds to Paul's prayer-appeal for the removal of the 'thorn'.

Christ is characterised in Paul's letters in numerous ways. Though not always explicitly with the following adjectives, Christ is, in substance, portrayed as gracious (e.g., 2 Cor. 12:9), loving (Rom. 8:5; 2 Cor. 5:14), compassionate (Phil. 1:8), rich (or generous – Rom. 10:12), faithful (14:4; Rom. 3:22;

Gal. 3:22; 2 Cor. 4:13), life-giving (1 Cor. 15:45), gentle and forbearing (2 Cor. 10:1) yet also avenging (1 Thess. 4:6. Cf. 1 Cor. 10:22; 11:27–30).

Finally, though Christ's risen lordship is possibly spoken of as 'over all' (Rom. 9:5), it is clear that in 10:12 he is called Lord *of all*, and in 14:9 as Lord of both the dead and the living. Though 1 Corinthians 10:26 possibly speaks of the earth and its fullness as belonging to Christ, it is clearer that Philippians 3:21 speaks of the power of Christ in terms of the ability to subject all things to himself. Though this evidence details the scope of Christ's lordship for Paul, something of its nature is apparent from the contrasts in Galatians 1:1, 11–12, where Christ is contrasted with the merely human.

At various points the apparently deliberate overlap of this sort of Christ-relation language with Second Temple Jewish God-relation language was noted. In terms of devotion to Christ, Hurtado concentrates on its *cultic* expression. Yet without wanting to negate his legitimate focus, most of the matters included in Hurtado's pattern of data, such as prayer, the Lord's Supper, hymns, invocation and confession of Christ and prophecy, have naturally found expression in the above as part of a different and larger pattern of data.[418]

---

[418] Cf. the material analysed in, e.g., Hurtado, *LJC*, 138–51.

Chapter 7

The Christ-relation: a pattern of data Paul would recognise?

1. Introduction

The previous chapter outlined the general contours of the Christ-relation in the undisputed Pauline letters. It is now necessary to explore an important question, namely to what extent the data in the previous chapter is a pattern Paul would recognise. Is this language merely thrown together from the four corners of Paul's letters, or would Paul have recognised those data as appropriately discussed under one heading (the Christ-relation), as a pattern? This chapter suggests that Paul would recognise the previous chapter's Christ-relation data as a pattern, and it thus functions as the best perspective from which to assess christological significance. Indeed, because Paul would recognise this material as a pattern, one can gain insight into his own christological convictions, as will be detailed in chapter 10.

2. Paul's extensive employment of elements of the proposed pattern

It will first be noted that the evidence analysed above in terms of the relational pattern is found extensively throughout the undisputed Pauline Epistles. Only in the following chapters has no material of direct relevance for the study of the relation between risen Lord and believers been found: Romans 3–6; 11; 13; 1 Corinthians 9; 14; 2 Corinthians 7; 9; 1 Thessalonians 2. In even these cases, some reference could sometimes be made. In other words, the majority of Romans, the large majority of 1 Corinthians, 2 Corinthians and 1 Thessalonians, and material in all chapters of Galatians, Philippians and Philemon was considered directly relevant. Of course, this is not the case with almost all other arguments relating to Pauline Christology in modern scholarship. So, a point of this thesis is to highlight the large amount of relevant data for the construction of its argument.

The initial significance of this for the present argument, that the relational pattern is one Paul would himself recognise, is that this relational data are not peripheral to Paul but central to his concerns, theology and life. But before this point is developed, there is even more concerning the relation between the risen Lord and believers that has not yet been mentioned and needs to be at least noted, especially given its relevance to the present concern about patterns. This 'even more' refers to the 'in Christ' and 'in the Lord' language that permeates Paul's letters, omitted from the above discussion for reasons of space. Had it been included, the only chapters without directly relevant material would have been Romans 11; 13; 1 Cor. 9; 14; 2 Cor. 7; 9

It is to be noted that Dunn argues the 'in Christ, in the Lord' language gives 'immediate access to a characteristic and distinctive trait within Paul's theology'.[1] He continues: 'Paul's perception of his whole life as a Christian, its source, its identity, and its responsibilities, could be summed up in these phrases ["in Christ/in the Lord"] ... the language and the perspective' this language 'embodied had become an integral part of the warp and woof both of his theology and, not least for Paul himself, of his living and relationships'.[2] This is one reason why Schweitzer famously wrote that the 'doctrine of righteousness by faith is therefore a subsidiary crater, which has formed within the rim of the main crater – the mystical doctrine of redemption through the being-in-Christ'.[3] While much of Schweitzer's precise understanding has been rightly challenged, especially the importation of overly subjective and mystical categories into Paul's 'in Christ' language, its centrality is acknowledged by most.[4]

In reaction to the overly subjective interpretations of those associated with the *Religionsgeschichtliche Schule*,[5] the objective aspect of being 'in Christ' came to be emphasised (i.e., that it refers to the concrete salvific event of redemption in Christ).[6] But this probably led to an overemphasis of the other extreme and, while not dismissing the objective nature of much of the language it is now recognised that the 'in Christ' language is used in more than one way in Paul.[7] As there is no space in this thesis to engage this debate it

---

[1] Dunn, *Theology*, 397.

[2] Ibid., 399.

[3] Albert Schweitzer, *The Mysticism of Paul the Apostle*, trans. B. D. Montgomery, William, reprint, 1931 (New York: Seabury Press, 1968), 225.

[4] E.P. Sanders, *Paul and Palestinian Judaism: A Comparison of Patterns of Religion* (London: SCM, 1977), 502–08; Dunn, *Theology*, 395. Cf. also Schreiner, *Paul*, 156–57; Mark A. Seifrid, "In Christ," in *DPL*, eds G.F. Hawthorne, R.P. Martin, and D.G. Reid (Leicester: IVP, 1993), 433.

[5] Cf. references to Deissmann, Bousset and others in chapter 2 above.

[6] Käsemann, *Romans*, 96. Cf. also the discussion in Fatehi, *Relation*, 263–65. While not directly related to the 'in Christ' debate, for the nature of this reaction, cf. Rudolf Bultmann, *Glauben und Verstehen I* (Tübingen: Mohr Siebeck, 1933), 'Die Christologie des Neuen Testaments' 245–67 (now in Rudolf Bultmann, "The Christology of the New Testament," in *Faith and Understanding I* [New York: Harper & Row, 1969], 262–85).

[7] So Moule, *Origin*, 55, discussing ἐν. Cf. also A.J.M. Wedderburn, "Some Observations on Paul's Use of the Phrases 'in Christ' and 'with Christ'," *JSNT* 25 (1985): 83–97; Schreiner, *Paul*, 158; Seifrid, "In Christ," 433–34; N.T. Wright, *Climax*, 46.

can at least be noted that some have rightly argued that the language can often be understood relationally,[8] subjectively, existentially, experientially,[9] and perhaps even mystically in some sense,[10] in both an individual and social dimension (cf., as discussed by Dunn, Rom. 6:11; 8:1; 16:3; 1 Cor. 1:2, 30; 15:8; 2 Cor. 5:17; Gal. 1:22; 2:4; 3:28 etc.).[11] Fatehi, while discussing Paul's 'in Christ' language, notes:

[I]n many cases the idea of living under the authority and power of Christ as Lord seems to be present. Christians are in Christ in the sense that they live in the sphere of his lordship ... according to Paul Christians are "in Christ" also in the sense that they are in union with him through the Spirit.[12]

The main point of the above is the following proposition: the 'in Christ' language, which is at some level to be associated with the relation between risen Lord and believers, is further evidence of the centrality and scope of this relation throughout Paul's letters. Indeed, all of the different categories mentioned above, and according to which the exegetical study was divided, are found in *every* individual undisputed letter (apart from the 'absence of Christ' in Galatians and a few other themes from Philemon which may surely be excused given its size. Nevertheless, it still evidences two, namely the presence and activity of Christ, and Paul's Christ-shaped goals). This means that all of the major subdivisions of themes above are found together in all of the letters.

3. A unified existential reality

Furthermore, as made clear in the previous chapter, as well as in the short comments above concerning the 'in Christ' language, this Christ-relation was an *existential reality* in Paul's life. It was not merely a collection of loose ideas. The absence and desired presence of Christ was for Paul the force behind his most deeply expressed yearnings. The presence of Christ was also, as far as the Apostle was concerned, an experienced reality. His Christ-shaped goals and motivations were a deep part of his daily life and most profound desires, driving him through all manner of persecution and suffering; they were not a collection of theological abstractions. Furthermore, the various expressions of Christ-devotion were the basis of one specific argument after another, as if the Apostle defaulted in his concerns to the necessity of pure

---

[8] Schnelle, *Paulus*, 549; Dunn, *Theology*, 395 n.27; Andrie du Toit, "'In Christ', 'in the Spirit' and Related Prepositional Phrases: Their Relevance for a Discussion on Pauline Mysticism," *Neot* 34, no. 2 (2000): 287–98.

[9] Dunn, *Theology*, 400–401; du Toit, "'In Christ'."

[10] Dunn, *Theology*, 395, 401, 408.

[11] Ibid., 398, 401 n.55.

[12] Fatehi, *Relation*, 274. Cf. also Eduard Lohse, *Paulus: eine Biographie* (München: Beck, 1996), 230; J.A. Ziesler, *Pauline Christianity* (Oxford: OUP, 1990[2]), 50–51.

devotion to Christ (e.g. 1 Cor. 7:32–35; 2 Cor. 11:2–3). Likewise, Paul was not making a theological point in praying to the risen Lord, as detailed in 2 Corinthians 12:7–10. It expressed and came from the urgency of real need, and Christ's communications to him were likewise treated with zealous embrace. These various disparate elements concerning the relation between the risen Lord and believers were, thus, part of Paul's existential reality, and found their unity in his life as a whole, not in a projected system of detached theological propositions. His own life passions and experiences testify to the essential interconnectedness of the above material as a pattern.

4. Elements of the proposed pattern are regularly brought together by Paul

Finally, and perhaps most importantly, the appropriateness of speaking of the above material as a pattern that Paul would recognise, under the head 'the relation between the risen Lord and believers', is that at various points in the undisputed letters Paul brings the various elements together in *single* arguments. It is not an artificial pattern imposed upon the letters.

So, in Romans 10:6–13 Paul argues in such a way that brings expression to communication with Christ (10:9 'confess with your lips that Jesus is Lord' with the 10:12 Lord who is 'generous to all who call upon *him*'), Christ's absence (10:6 'who will ascend into heaven? [that is, to bring Christ down]), Christ-devotion (10:9 'confess with your lips that Jesus is Lord'; 10:11 'believes in him'; 10:12 'generous to all *who call on* him'; 10:13 'calls on the name of the Lord'), and depiction of his lordship's scope (10:12 – 'Lord of all') and the character (10:12 – 'generous to all') of the risen Lord.

Likewise, in Romans 14:4–11 Paul brings together various elements concerning the broad pattern of the relation between the risen Lord and believers that were categorised separately above. So in the same breath he speaks of the presence and activity of the Lord (14:4 'the Lord is able to make them stand'), of Christ-devotion (14:6 'those who observe the day / eat, observe / eat it in honour of the Lord'; 14:8 'whether we live or whether we die, we are the Lord's'; 10:11 'As I live, says the Lord, every knee shall bow to me'), and of his understanding of Christ in terms of ultimate goals (14:9 'For to this end Christ died and lived again, so that he might be Lord of both the dead and the living').

Similarly, in 1 Corinthians 1:2–3 Paul speaks of communication with the risen Lord (1:2 'call on'), of the character (1:3 'grace') and scope (1:2 'their Lord and ours') of the risen lordship, of devotion to the risen Lord (1:2 'call on the name'), and the presence and activity of the risen Lord (1:3 'grace ... from ... the Lord'). In 1 Corinthians 6:13–17 Paul speaks of how Christ relates to his understanding of important goals (6:13 'the body is meant ... for the

Lord'), of Christ-devotion (6:17 'united to the Lord'), and of the presence of his Lord (6:17 'one spirit with him [the Lord]'). Paul, having stated that he is trustworthy by the Lord's mercy (7:25), expresses his understanding of the presence and activity of the risen Lord, and then turns to detail his expectation for Christ-devotion (7:32, 34 'anxious about the things of the Lord, how to please the Lord', 10:34 'holy in body and spirit' – note also with what Paul contrasts this devotion in this passage), and his Christ-related highest goals (7:35 'I say this with a view to promoting ...[that which] facilitates undistracted devotion to the Lord'). In the last verses of the letter, Paul, within two verses, speaks of Christ-devotion (16:22 'love for the Lord'; 'Our Lord, come!'), about that with which it is negatively contrasted (16:22 'let anyone be accursed who has no love for the Lord'), about the presence, character and activity of Christ (16:23 'the *grace* of the Lord Jesus *be with you*'), and of communication with the risen Lord (16:22 'Our Lord, come!').[13]

In 2 Corinthians, one could point to the cloud of themes in 3:16–4:11 where Paul expresses Christ-devotion both in positive terms (3:16 'turns to the Lord'; 3:18 'beholding the glory of the Lord') and with the negative with which he contrasts it (4:4 'the god of this world has blinded the minds of the unbelievers, to keep them from seeing the light of the gospel of the glory of Christ'). He expresses understanding of the presence and activity of the risen Lord (3:17 'now the Lord is the Spirit'; 3:18 'this [transformation] comes from the Lord, the Spirit') and his Christ-shaped goals (4:5 'for Jesus' sake'; 4:10 'carrying in the body the death of Jesus, so that the life of Jesus may be made visible in our bodies'; 4:11 'given up to death for Jesus' sake, so that the life of Jesus may be made visible in our mortal flesh'). 5:6–16 speaks, in the same breath, of the absence of the risen Lord (5:6 'we are away from the Lord'; 5:8 'we would rather be away from the body and at home with the Lord'), about the Lord's 'seeing' of Paul and his team's work and his future judgement (5:9–10 'we make it our aim to please him. For all of us must appear before the judgment seat of Christ, so that each may receive recompense for what has been done in the body, whether good or evil'), of Christ-devotion, both in negative contrast (5:16 'even though we once knew Christ from a human point of view') and positive expression (5:11 'knowing the fear of the Lord'; 5:15 'might live no longer for themselves, but for him who died'; 5:16 'we know him [Christ] no longer in that way'), of Paul's Christ-shaped goals and motivations (5:8 'we would rather be away from the body and at home with the Lord'; 5:9 ' we make it our aim to please him'; 5:11 'knowing the fear of the Lord, we try to persuade others'; 5:14 'the love of Christ urges us on'; 5:15 'And he died for all, so that those who live might live no longer for themselves, but for him who died'), and of the character of the risen Lord (5:14 'the love of Christ').

---

[13] These verses will be discussed in the next chapter.

For a similar conglomeration of themes within single arguments one could point to 2 Corinthians 8:9, 19–21 (Christ-devotion, the character of the risen Lord, and Christ-shaped goals); 10:1, 5, 7–8, 17–18 together with 11:2–3 (the character of the risen Lord, Christ-devotion both negatively and positively expressed, the presence and activity of the risen Lord, Christ's communications). Very important also is 12:8–10, where Paul speaks of communications from the risen Lord (12:9) and to the Lord (12:8), the Lord's presence and activity (implied in 12:8, and explicit in 12:9), the character of the risen Lord (12:9), Paul's Christ-shaped goals (12:9–10), and Christ-devotion (the nature of Paul's response to Christ expressed in 12:9–10, but it is implied in most of the material in these verses). All this within the space of three verses. The end of 2 Corinthians speaks of communications from the Lord (13:3), the Lord's presence (13:3–5), and his character (13:3 judgment in power?; implied in 13:10), while 13:13 speaks of the presence and character of the risen Lord ('the grace of the Lord Jesus Christ ... be with you all').

This same convergence of Christ-relation elements in specific arguments finds further expression in Galatians, Philippians and 1 Thessalonians, but because the point has already been made forcefully enough it will suffice to note the relevant verses and the themes brought together. So in Galatians 1, Paul speaks of communications from Christ, the nature of Christ's risen lordship, Christ-devotion, the presence and activity of the Lord, and Paul's Christ-shaped goals (cf. Gal. 1:1, 10–12, 15–16). In the next chapter Paul expresses Christ-devotion, the presence of this Lord and Paul's own Christ-shaped goals (cf. Gal. 2:16, 19–20). Philippians is brimming with various interlocked themes. In Philippians 1 alone, Paul expresses understanding of Christ's character (1:2, 8), the risen Lord's presence and activity (1:2, 14, 19), Christ's absence (1:23), his Christ-related ultimate goals and motivations (1:13, 18, 20, 23, 29), and his Christ-devotion (1:21, 26). Philippians 3, after Philippians 1, is one of the most significant chapters in the undisputed letters for this thesis. It mentions Christ-devotion (3:3, 8, 10, 20), Christ-related ultimate goals and motivations (3:7–9), the scope of Christ's risen lordship (3:21), and the presence and activity of the risen Lord (3:12). 1 Thessalonians 3:8–13 speaks of Christ-devotion, Christ-related goals, communication with the risen Lord, and the presence and activity of the Lord – all within a few verses, interweaving the themes. 1 Thessalonians 4 continues this mixing of the themes analysed above, speaking of the character of the risen Lord (4:6), his implied absence (4:17), and Paul's Christ related ultimate goals (4:17–18, also reflected in 5:10–11).

What has been analysed above in various categories in the previous chapter is a pattern of themes that Paul himself regularly brought together in individual arguments and sections.

5. Conclusion

In order to deny that the 'Christ-relation' is an appropriate heading for the cluster of Pauline data examined above, one would have to mount a case that would arguably run against Paul's understanding of his experiences and numerous individual arguments in his letters. The importance and scope of the Christ-relation material for Paul, as well as its existential reality and unity in his life, suggests it was a pattern Paul recognised, whether in his individual arguments, across whole letters, or in his own passionately expressed existential grasp of the risen Christ and his relation to this Lord. It is this larger pattern, and not lists of abstractions about the title κύριος and Christ's 'divine prerogatives' (Fee), that is the appropriate pattern in light of which christological conclusions should be drawn.

Chapter 8

1 Corinthians 16:22. Approaching Paul in light of the Christ-relation

1. Introduction

It will prove appropriate, given that the exegetical proposals of the last chapters were introduced via an examination of Paul's argument in 1 Corinthians 8–10, to conclude this section via meditation upon another 1 Corinthians passage, namely 16:22. By approaching the verse in terms of the Christ-relation, matters otherwise overlooked or downplayed will become visible.

2. Present scholarly concerns in relation to Paul's Christology in 16:22

Scholars concerned with the question of Paul's Christology in relation to 16:22 almost always only analyse the significance of the μαράνα θά,[1] and this in terms of two subjects. First, it is usual practice to focus on the expressed Aramaic christological title, *marêh*. As noted above, the history of christological analysis of the NT has expended a tremendous amount of energy on the so called 'christological titles', so it is no surprise that considerable weight has been placed on the slim shoulders of this *marêh*. Indeed, if one studies the exact data analysed by scholars in relation to 16:22, it so often boils down to the precise referent of the word *marêh*. For example, Davis, in commenting upon 16:22, writes: 'The [christologically significant] question ... is, what does the title "Lord" מר mean when applied to Christ?'.[2] Arguably, his analysis then focuses too exclusively on etymological matters, and so it is no surprise that his results remain inconclusive concerning christological sig-

---

[1] The lack of spaces between letters in the original unical manuscripts, textual disagreements, and the questions surrounding the original Aramaic, which the Greek transliterates, creates a wide number of opinions concerning how one reads μαράνα θά. However, most translate the text as 'Our Lord, come!', and it shall be so understood in the following. Cf. the discussion in Thiselton, *Corinthians*, 1349–352, who largely follows Eriksson, *Traditions*, 290–98. Note also the comments by Casey, "Worship," 223–24, for analysis missed by commentaries and works related to Pauline Christology.

[2] Davis, *Name*, 138.

nificance.[3] Davis is by no means alone in this restricted focus, it is one that has dominated scholarship throughout the middle of the twentieth century, and continues to do so in many publications.[4] Not only does a solely etymological study crash against the rocks of modern linguistics,[5] it also tends to fail to consider the significance of the wider context in which the title is used.

A focus on the christological significance of devotion to the risen Lord, especially in Hurtado's publications, is thus to be welcomed. This is the second major concern of Pauline Christology scholars in relation to 16:22, and one that has increased focus upon the recognition of μαράνα θά as a *prayer* to the risen Lord. So Hurtado, following Cullmann,[6] points out the meaning of *marêh* is best understood not just diachronically, but rather in the context in which it was used, i.e., the cultic communal gatherings. Thus, so the argument goes, the meaning of *marêh* is best understood with divine overtones.[7] Hence Hurtado argues that this prayer 'indicates an incorporation of Jesus into the corporate, public devotional life of the early Christians in a way otherwise reserved for God'.[8]

However, Hurtado's critics, while also focusing upon the question of potential 'Christ-devotion',[9] challenge Hurtado's confidence that 16:22 constitutes such positive evidence. Hence, Casey complains that such a 'Christ-devotion' thesis can hardly carry the weight put upon it if this is one of the only and major pieces of evidence in the Pauline corpus available.[10] Casey's argument against Hurtado, is, in relation to this verse, that the evidence is simply 'not enough'; it is too 'sparse'.[11] Indeed, one feels sympathetic with Casey's complaint if the evidence really is so 'sparse'. But is it? Has a scholarly 'stalemate' been reached? Or has an inappropriate scope of evidence been consulted, one which has sidelined important material?

---

[3] Ibid., 139.

[4] Cf. Capes, *Yahweh Texts*, 44; Paula Fredriksen, *From Jesus to Christ: The Origins of the New Testament, Images of Jesus* (New Haven: Yale University Press, 1988), 139; I.H. Marshall, *The Origins of New Testament Christology* (Leicester: IVP, 1976), 99; Douglas J. Moo, "The Christology of the Early Pauline Letters," in *Contours of Christology in the New Testament*, ed. Richard N. Longenecker, (Grand Rapids: Eerdmans, 2005), 189; etc. There is small recognition of broader themes in Fee, *Christology*, 120–22, but it is still left underdeveloped.

[5] For a basic overview of many of the issues, cf. P. Cotterell and M. Turner, *Linguistics and Biblical Interpretation* (London: SPCK, 1989).

[6] Cullmann, *Christology*, 213.

[7] Hurtado, *OG²*, 107.

[8] Hurtado, *LJC*, 141–42.

[9] 'Does this prayer mean that Christ was worshipped?' (Casey, "Worship," 224).

[10] Casey, "Worship."

[11] Ibid., 222.

3. Reengaging 16:22 in terms of the relation between the risen Lord and believers

Besides the importance of the much discussed μαράνα θά,[12] there are another two strands of evidence in this verse of considerable significance as comes to light when the question is framed in terms of the relation between risen Lord and believers: 1) the meaning of the mentioned 'love' and 2) the curse. New light can be shed on the significance of the μαράνα θά in light of these additional two points.

Klaus Berger recently asked, 'What does Paul love?'. In answer to this, Berger asserts that 'in contrast to many modern believers, Paul cannot say, "I love Jesus" ... the relationship to this lord and king could not be any closer, but it is not called love. Paul loves heaven.'[13] However, as was seen in relation to 1 Thessalonians 4:17–18 and 5:10–11, Paul's great hope in relation to the 'day of the Lord' appears not to be an abstract idea of heaven, but that he may always be 'with the *Lord*'. Not only that, the entire tenor of passage after passage throughout the Pauline corpus is concerned with the quality of the believer's devotion to the risen Lord. Furthermore, and to anticipate a counter argument, that Christ is 'Lord' does not exclude the idea of love, as recent studies in master/slave relations and 'friendship' confirm.[14] Although all of this is enough to dismiss Berger's peculiar assertion, Paul's comment in 16:22, of course, fully refutes it. The positive corollary of his statement is clearly that believers love (φιλέω) the Lord.

But to explore the significance of 16:22 for this wider thesis, it must be a᠎ked: what does this 'love' mean? Some scholars have attempted to highlight the aspect of 'feeling' connoted by the word: 'φιλεῖ ... stresses the emotional aspect of love', writes Bachmann.[15] Indeed, this would be in accord with the examples cited in at least Thayer's Greek lexicon which carefully notes the wider Graeco-Roman usages. However, more scholars have wanted to affirm

---

[12] That the κύριος refers to Christ, not God is arguably clear from the context. This is most obvious in the christological use of κύριος in the preceding and following verses. However, it is also explicit in the use of the μαράνα θά of 16:22, which is almost universally taken as reference to Christ – and not God. Bultmann once attempted to argue it referred to God, but he was motivated more by the need to explain away the, at least for his scheme, problematic christological implications of prayer to the risen Lord (Rudolf Bultmann, *Theology of the New Testament*, trans. Kendrick Grobel [New York: Scribner's, 1951], 52. Cf. the recent comments in Schrage, *Unterwegs*, 164 n.378).

[13] Berger, *Paulus*, 35.

[14] Master/slave: e.g., Dale B. Martin, *Slavery as Salvation: The Metaphor of Slavery in Pauline Christianity* (New Haven: Yale University Press, 1990); Harris, *Slave*. On 'friendship', cf. John T. Fitzgerald, "Paul and Friendship," in *Paul in the Greco-Roman World: A Handbook*, ed. J. Paul Sampley (Harrisburg: Trinity Press International, 2003), 328, 'two parties to a friendship would rarely have looked like equals'.

[15] Philipp Bachmann, *Der erste Brief des Paulus an die Korinther* (Leipzig: Deichert, 1936⁴), 478.

the aspect of loyalty in Paul's usage. Thus, Barrett writes that the verb indicates 'personal loyalty to the Lord Jesus', and means 'the adoration and religious consecration of the believer to his God'.[16] Moffatt brings both aspects, feeling and loyalty, together in his explanation of the φιλέω. It refers to 'loyalty, whole-hearted devotion to him'. He adds: 'Paul insists, as usual, that absolute devotion to him [i.e. the Lord]... is the characteristic of all saints'.[17]

Taking a rather different tack, Sampley translates the phrase as: 'if anyone does not have friendship with / love the Lord'.[18] He may well be correct, especially, as Fitzgerald has recently argued, φιλέω is naturally associated with themes of friendship, and also with κοινωνία, a subject very important in Paul's language in 1 Corinthians regarding the believer's relation to the risen Lord.[19] The initial impression, then, is that the 'love' Paul speaks of involves deeply felt and sincere devotion to Christ, perhaps with overtones of friendship.[20]

But before the argument can proceed along an analysis of the various options for understanding what is meant by 'love' here, it is necessary to turn to another aspect of 16:22, namely the curse formula. Besides, it would be a linguistic mistake to import all possible meanings of love into this verse. And however φιλέω is understood, Paul's statement is made in the negative, and involves a curse on all those who do *not* love the Lord. Thus 16:22 contains another element, alongside 'love', that of cursing.

Now it is tempting to argue that such language suggests association with the *covenantal* blessings and curses of Deuteronomy 27–30,[21] as potentially employed by Paul in differentiated ways (Gal. 3:10, 13; Rom. 9–11; 1 Cor. 10:22; 14:21; Phil. 2:15).[22] A number of recent scholars have rightly argued

---

[16] Barrett, *1 Corinthians*, 397.

[17] Moffatt, *Corinthians*, 281–82. Eriksson does something similar by noting that the verb can 'be interpreted in two ways'. However, he doesn't attempt to understand the two concepts together, and simply states what he considers those two concepts are, i.e. first, as moral obligation, and second, as 'personal devotion' to the Lord (Eriksson, *Traditions*, 295).

[18] Sampley, "1 Corinthians," 1002.

[19] Fitzgerald, "Paul and Friendship."

[20] For more on the theme of friendship in Paul, cf. Fitzgerald, "Paul and Friendship", and Ben Witherington, III, *Friendship and Finances in Philippi: The Letter of Paul to the Philippians* (Valley Forge, Pa: Trinity Press International, 1994).

[21] This association is also maintained by Eriksson, *Traditions*, e.g. 292, and he is followed by Thiselton, *Corinthians*, 1350–352. Cf. also John P. Heil, *The Rhetorical Role of Scripture in 1 Corinthians* (Leiden: Brill, 2005), 8; Fee, *Christology*, 120.

[22] Cf. esp. Guy Prentiss Waters, *The End of Deuteronomy in the Epistles of Paul* (Tübingen: Mohr Siebeck, 2006).

for an appreciation of Paul's use of this OT narrative.[23] Indeed, not insignificant is the similar mixture of themes in 1 Corinthians 11 and Paul's discussion concerning the Lord's Supper. There too, in a context involving 'the new covenant' (11:25), Paul speaks of the coming of the Lord (11:26) and judgment for sin (11:27, 28, 31–32) involving illness and even death (11:30). Likewise, in 16:22, mention of the judgment of curse, love for Christ, and the coming of the Lord are arguably connected by implicit reference to the covenant.[24]

With this in mind, some scholars have understandably gone on to speak of the covenantal nature of the love in 16:22. Certainly, this would cohere well with 1 Corinthians 8:3 (arguably implicit too in 8:6) where love for God is the distinguishing mark of the 'necessary knowing', as indeed the command to love God functions as the centre of the covenant in Deuteronomy 6:4–5.[25] Eriksson comments: 'both the concept of "loving God" and the curse belong to covenantal terminology'.[26] This would be to argue that the covenant is the implied conceptual premise making sense of the connections in this verse. The argument would thus run as follows: in 16:22 we have something similar to Paul's argument developed in 1 Corinthians 8–11, and especially 8:6, where Paul reworked the *Shema* both theologically and christologically, dividing the 'God' and the 'Lord' between God the Father, and the Lord Jesus Christ respectively. This implies that Paul is speaking of covenantal love for the Lord Christ in 16:22, the exclusive love demanded by the risen Christ over all other loyalties. For Paul, the point and focus of covenant faithfulness, then, appears to be this love for Christ, the absence of which leads to the curse.

However, care must be taken as the LXX term in Deuteronomy, when speaking of the covenant 'blessings and curses' is not ἀνάθεμα-language at all. Instead, it uses the word κατάρα (cf., e.g., Deut. 30:1, 19).[27] In Deuteronomy, ἀνάθεμα-language is used to speak of that which is given over to utter destruction; it is not the covenant curse at all. So it would seem that Eriksson, Thiselton and others are wrong to import covenant themes into this verse via the 16:22 language of 'curse'. This does not mean that they would thereby be

---

[23] E.g. N.T. Wright, *Climax*, chap. 7; N.T. Wright, *Paul: Fresh Perspectives* (London: SPCK, 2005), 108–29, 138–40; Eriksson, *Traditions*, for specific references, see below. For more extensive research on this point, see C. Marvin Pate, *Reverse*, and the shorter treatment in C. Marvin Pate, *Communities of the Last Days* (Leicester: Apollos, 2000), esp. chap. 6; Waters, *End*; Steve Moyise and Maarten J. J. Menken, eds, *Deuteronomy in the New Testament: The New Testament and the Scriptures of Israel* (London: T&T Clark, 2007).

[24] The Pauline curse formula, repeated in Gal. 1:8–9, has likewise been associated with the Deuteronomic tradition in a number of works. Cf. Karl O. Sandnes, *Paul – One of the Prophets?* (Tübingen: Mohr, 1991); C. Marvin Pate, *Reverse*, 175–76.

[25] Cf. also Waaler, *Shema*, 314, who writes that 'the redirection of love from God (1Cor 8:4–6, cf. 8:3) to the Lord in 1Cor 16:22 is comparable to the redirection of the "one Lord" statement from the Father to the Lord Jesus Christ in 1Cor 8:4–6'.

[26] Eriksson, *Traditions*, 292.

[27] This was pointed out to me by Larry Hurtado.

necessarily wrong to speak of the love here in terms of 'covenant loyalty', given the thematic resonance with other covenantally permeated Pauline passages, as noted above.[28] But one must not overpress the evidence, especially as Paul used the word φιλέω[29] instead of the expected ἀγαπάω.[30]

But what is clear is that there seems to be a very real and existential aspect to this love, as the μαράνα θά prayer suggests. Hence Moffatt calls the prayer a 'passionate ejaculation',[31] Hays calls it a 'fervent prayer',[32] Eriksson writes of Paul's longing for the parousia, and points to the '*pathos* function of the conditional curse and the added maranatha'.[33] 16:22 is in this way 'quivering with passion'.[34] Certainly the proximity of curse language on those who do not love Christ, is at least evidence for such claims. Paul, in speaking of φιλέω love in relation to the risen Lord, albeit negatively, implies the necessity of a deeply felt and consuming personal loyalty to the risen Lord.[35]

This already teases out potential significance from the μαράνα θά usually overlooked. However, there is more. As noted above in the response to Berger's claim that Paul loved heaven, but not Christ as such, 1 Thessalonians 4:17–18 and 5:10–11 were mentioned. There, Paul expressed his hope and desire: to be with the Lord forever. Arguably, something of this very hope and passion comes to expression in this prayer, as noted a couple of paragraphs above. Having spoken a curse on all who do not love the Lord, his passion for the risen Lord expresses itself in this prayer, a prayer for the coming of the risen Lord himself.

---

[28] Thiselton, *Corinthians*, 1351.

[29] For the relationship between these two verbs, and whether they are synonyms, cf. the recent discussion in Stephen Voorwinde, "Ἀγαπάω and Φιλέω – Is There a Difference?" *RTR* 64, no. 2 (2005): 76–90. Notice that the verb φιλέω is never found in the imperative form in the NT (and is only used twice as an imperative in the LXX, and then only when it is used to indicate kissing. Cf. Song 1:2 and Gen. 27:26), while ἀγαπάω is regularly commanded (e.g. Matt. 5:44; Luke 6:27, 35; Eph. 5:25; Col. 3:19; 1 Pet. 1:8; 2:17; 1 John 2:15).

[30] Schrage opines that the use of this verb φιλέω (it being the only occasion in the extant Pauline corpus) indicates that it is a traditional formula, and so belongs together with the μαράνα θά as part of a tradition (Wolfgang Schrage, *Der erste Brief an die Korinther [4]* [Zürich: Benziger, 2001], 464, 472). This is speculative.

[31] Moffatt, *Corinthians*, 282.

[32] Hays, *First Corinthians*, 292.

[33] Eriksson, *Traditions*, 296–97.

[34] Cf. Moffatt, *Corinthians*, 280.

[35] In this respect it is arguably not without significance that more than just a few commentators and scholarly monographs gloss 'God' into their comments on this verse, especially in relation to the love and curse themes examined above (e.g. Barrett, *1 Corinthians*, 397 [noted above. Cf. n.16]; Eriksson, *Traditions*, 296, followed by Thiselton, *Corinthians*, 1350; Garland, *1 Corinthians*, 774, etc). It is also possible, but speculative, that Paul chose the word φιλεῖ in deliberate parody of the Cynic 'friend of the gods' language (cf. examples of this language in F.G. Downing, *Cynics, Paul and the Pauline Churches. Cynics and Christian Origins II* [London: Routledge, 1998], 216–20).

Furthermore, as was noted above, scholars understand this passage also as evidence of an early (because Paul is repeating a presumably well-known Aramaic tradition[36]) prayer formula to the risen Lord. Thus, a comparison with the prayer to the risen Lord in 2 Cor 12:8 is not out of place. There has been some fuss regarding whether Paul's praying to Christ was here corporate or personal in nature,[37] but either way, the risen Lord was one whom Paul believed would hear prayer. Even though he was well aware that the man Christ Jesus lived and died in Palestine, he nevertheless believed Christ could hear (and respond to) the prayers of believers in Corinth. So in the very context in which Paul mentions the importance of loving devotion to Christ, the evidence is clear that he also indicates longing for the presence of this risen Lord, and likewise consequently expected this same risen Lord to hear and answer the prayer. Of course, that 16:22 contains prayer for the coming of the Lord implies the absence of this Lord, as well as the implied ability of this Lord to hear the prayer. The significance of this prayer is not simply that it reflects a cultic devotional pattern, but that it also implies wider factors relating to the relation between risen Lord and believers, such as presence and absence, desires and loves. Casey can respond to Hurtado with the objection 'not enough' simply because the most appropriate set of issues has been underappreciated.

But the oversight is not just Casey's. All bar two scholars (known to the author) engaged in the Pauline Christology debates,[38] fail to analyse more than simply the μαράνα θά of 16:22. The argument undertaken in this section has shown that this is an underestimation of even 16:22. What we have in 16:22 is an example of the importance Paul placed on love for Christ and his risen lordship, which expressed itself in prayer, itself implying a network of other related issues, such as spiritual desires and Christ's absence yet ability to answer prayer etc.

It can also be noted that there is a possibility that 16:22 functions as the *peroratio* of the content and purpose of the entire letter of 1 Corinthians.[39] While such suggestions are difficult to assess or prove, the relation of believers to the risen Christ is so often the main burden and concern of the Apostle in 1 Corinthians, as demonstrated in one concrete Pauline argument after another, as the exegesis in chapters 5 and 6 above has maintained. So, in

---

[36] Cullmann, *Christology*, 208–09, followed also by Hurtado in his numerous publications.

[37] Bultmann, *Theology*, 1:128, and cf. the discussion in Hurtado, *OG²*, 105.

[38] The exceptions to prove the rule are Fee, *Christology*, 120–22, and Waaler, *Shema*, e.g. 314. However, Waaler's reflections on christological significance are underdeveloped, and even Fee's two-page analysis omits much of significance from his discussion.

[39] As argued in Eriksson, *Traditions*, 275, chap. 8. Thiselton follows Eriksson's conclusion that 16:22–24 makes 'sense only as part of the *peroratio* of the whole letter' (Thiselton, *Corinthians*, 1348, citing Eriksson).

light of the material overviewed above, Eriksson's suggestion that 16:22 serves as the letter's *peroratio* is at least a plausible inference. Thus Fee may, with more justification than he perhaps realised, suggest that the 'if anyone does not love the Lord' clause 'covers the whole letter'.[40] Central to the whole letter has been the believer's relation to the risen Lord, and this often understood with the language, relational overtones, practices and passions associated with second Temple Jewish relation to YHWH.

4. Conclusions

It has been argued that 16:22 is another example which shows the importance Paul placed on the relation between the risen Lord and believers. Within a single verse, a variety of the elements of this relation find expression, whether it be Paul's Christ-devotion, what Paul contrasts with this devotion, the passionate nature of devotion, communications with the risen Lord, or, because of appeal for this Lord to 'come', Christ's absence. And once again, with these themes on the table, the complex of interrelated motifs in Judaism that denoted the relation of Israel to YHWH are not far away, and are to an extent used to express, as a pattern, the believer's relation to Christ.

---

[40] Fee, *Corinthians*, 838.

Chapter 9

Jewish relation to figures other than God, and the Pauline Christ-relation

1. Introduction

The pattern of data in Paul's undisputed letters concerning the Christ-relation has now been analysed. The christological significance of this data could be demonstrated through an examination of those texts Paul drew upon as Scripture, to demonstrate how Paul's Christ-relation, as a pattern, corresponds with the pattern of God-relation data found therein. Indeed, at various points in chapters 5, 6 and 8 above it was seen that Paul often explicitly, and thus deliberately, drew upon the scriptural pattern of God-relation themes to elucidate the Christ-relation (cf. e.g., 1 Cor. 8:1–10:22 in terms of various Pentateuchal narratives). This shows that the interrelated scriptural God-relation themes are rethought, by Paul, in terms of the relation between risen Lord and believers.

Here it is necessary to engage with a few potentially significant texts which some have argued pose a problem to the theses developed especially by Bauckham and Hurtado. In these texts, it has been maintained, evidence comes to light which refutes Bauckham's neat categories of divine identity as well as Hurtado's focus on the offering of worship as the identifying factor of who God is. Fletcher-Louis, for example, points to (among other cases) the worship of Adam as the image of God in the *Life of Adam and Eve*, and argues that this shows early Pauline communities had resources to understand devotion to the risen Lord in a way that did not mean they must break with Jewish monotheism.[1] Barker argues that the reverence accorded the High Priest helps explain Christ-devotion in Paul.[2] Horbury can associate the worship of Christ with Jewish messianism and the praise of Jewish kings.[3] To a greater or lesser extent, and while sometimes admitting Christian development of such traditions, Christ-devotion can be explained, they argue, with the literary resources of devotion to figures other than God.[4] Hence, it is argued that, despite Paul's reliance on OT texts, a straight line should not be drawn from

---

[1] Fletcher-Louis, "Worship"; Fletcher-Louis, "Alexander."

[2] Barker, "Priest."

[3] Horbury, *Messianism*, esp. 109–52.

[4] Cf. also Chester, *Messiah*, 394–95, though he is admittedly more circumspect and nuanced about how he formulates his arguments.

the worship of Christ to a divine-Christology, at least not in the way especially Hurtado has urged, with emphasis at the same time on a strict monotheism.[5] Indeed, precisely these apocryphal and pseudepigraphal examples, so many arguments go, best explain the later development of the Christian worship of Christ, not least in Paul.

As Paul's Christ-relation has already been examined in terms of various OT texts in chapters 5–8, it is now time to examine what are arguably the most important of these apocryphal and pseudepigraphal texts for the present thesis, namely Sirach 44–50, the *Life of Adam and Eve* and the Similitudes of Enoch.[6] Having examined those pseudepigraphal and apocryphal texts it will be possible to critically engage with the methods and argumentation of a representative work of those criticising Hurtado *et al.*, namely Horbury's *Jewish Messianism and the Cult of Christ*.

2. A background to Paul's Christ-devotion in the worship of figures other than God?

2.1. Pauline Christ-devotion and Sirach 44–50

A number of scholars make the claim that the sort of devotion and praise offered to Simon son of Onias in Sirach 50 helps to explain the Jewish origin of devotion to Christ in early Christianity. Horbury will be engaged below, but mention should be made of the various skilful arguments proffered by Fletcher-Louis. In agreeing with Loren Stuckenbruck, that the Jewish precedent for the worship of Jesus in earliest Christianity is not to be found in the worship offered to angels, Fletcher-Louis argues for another precedent, namely the worship given to 'a particular righteous humanity which in one way or another had become divine or angelmorphic'.[7] He feels driven to offer some kind of explanation as 'there are insurmountable barriers to Jewish

---

[5] Hurtado, *LJC*, e.g. 36–37.

[6] Of course, a more complete argument would include analysis of at least various passages in Ezek. Trag. and Josephus, not to mention Philo. But in the first two there is very little that is of significance, and Paul's relational understanding of Christ does not compare well with Philo's λόγος, about which Paul was apparently uninterested. Indeed, while Philo's questions often revolved around the difficulty of reconciling the transcendence and immanence of God, Paul does not attempt to solve any such problem and indeed perpetuates it in the Christ-relation language: Christ is likewise both present and absent. Besides, it is noteworthy that Philo continues the trend of firmly distinguishing God's uniqueness in his various texts, even if it does not follow Bauckham's strict rules (as pointed out in Chester, *Messiah*, e.g. 20–21). In Philo, too, one finds much of the pattern of God-relation language. Though there is no space to justify this claim, at least elements of the case that would be constructed can be found in Jutta Leonhardt-Balzer, *Jewish Worship in Philo of Alexandria* [Tübingen: Mohr Siebeck, 2001], summarised in e.g. 274–75).

[7] Fletcher-Louis, "Worship," 112.

Christians remaining monotheists and worshipping Jesus if, as it is assumed, such worship is utterly foreign to Jewish theology and devotional behaviour'.[8] One of the five texts Fletcher-Louis cites as evidence of the worship of 'a particular righteous humanity' is Sirach 44–50.[9] He argues that these 'closing chapters of Sirach are, as a whole, a serious challenge to the view that the worship offered to the One Jewish God was hermeneutically sealed off from any veneration of a created reality'.[10] While there is no space here to engage the arguments of Fletcher-Louis in any depth, it should be pointed out that he argues the material in Sirach means the 'historical problem of the worship of Jesus is at once greatly eased'. And while he admits that the worship of Jesus in early Christianity is to an extent discontinuous with the tradition exemplified in Sirach, this discontinuity consists, he argues, in the fact that the worship of Jesus is the worship of a particular *person*, not just an *office*.[11] In sum of his whole argument he asserts that the worship of certain righteous individuals is the ...:

... key to the history-of-religions context for the worship of Jesus. It is no coincidence that two of the clearest instances of New Testament hymns to Christ rely heavily on Image of God theology (Phil 2 and Col 1:15–20).[12]

It is argued here, however, that to understand the sort of material found in Sirach 44–50 as an explanation of Christ-devotion in Paul – which is part of the broader relational pattern in the same – is entirely misleading. To show this it will be helpful to summarise the relevant evidence in these chapters concerning the relation to figures other than God:

– Devotion to the figures: The Greek section title added to the start of chapter 44 ('Hymn in honour of our ancestors'); 44:1 (Let us now sing the praises of famous men').
– Communication to the figures: To Solomon in 47:14 ('How wise you were') and to Elijah in 48:4 ('How glorious you were, Elijah').
– Specifically in terms of Simon son of Onias: In 50:4 he is the implied saviour ('he considered how to save his people'); and 50:5–12 goes into great detail explaining his glorious appearance.

This last point requires elaboration. Barker examines the procession of the high priest, in this text, from out of the inner sanctuary and notes that elsewhere 'in the Hebrew Scriptures, the one who emerges from the holy place is unambiguously the LORD' (she cites Isa. 26:21; Mic. 1:3; Hab. 2:20).[13] The high priest is thus, Barker argues, YHWH himself.[14] However, this crude mash-

---

[8] Ibid.
[9] It will be necessary to return to his arguments in relation to *L.A.E.* below.
[10] Fletcher-Louis, "Worship," 116.
[11] Ibid., 119.
[12] Ibid., 128.
[13] Barker, "Priest," 102–03.
[14] Ibid., 107.

ing together of texts related by common theme does not answer why devotion to the high priest does not match the general pattern of devotion to YHWH in the literature of Second Temple Judaism generally.[15] Further, if one is pressed to reassess the weight of her argument in light of the following engagement with the primary texts, her thesis will arguably fair even worse. Fletcher-Louis has noted, together with C.T.R Hayward, the parallels between Sirach 24 and 50, which they take to imply that 'the high priest is an incarnation of Wisdom'.[16] Apart from also embodying the glory of God,[17] Fletcher-Louis continues: 'Simon is worshipped at the climax of the crescendo of praise offered to Israel's righteous heroes from the beginning of chapter 44:1'.[18] While some of this can be disputed,[19] let it be assumed for now that he is correct on these points. It will prove illuminating to return to assess the significance of these issues having compared the devotion to figures other than God, as listed above, with the God-relation language in Sirach 44–50. The God-relation texts can now be noted:[20]

– God's presence, activity and sovereignty: At the very beginning of these chapters we are told that it was 'the Lord [who] apportioned to them [the ancestors] great glory' (44:2). In addition, multiple other references to God's dynamic presence and activity in these chapters can be listed (e.g. 44:21–23; 45:3, 5–8, 19, 26; 46:5, 9; 47:6, 13, 22; 48:10, 20). This is understood together with assuming God's presence is in heaven (48:20).

---

[15] Cf. chapter 2 above for noted critical responses to Barker's theses.

[16] Crispin H.T. Fletcher-Louis, *All the Glory of Adam: Liturgical Anthropology in the Dead Sea Scrolls* (Leiden: Brill, 2002), 73–74; Fletcher-Louis, "Worship," 116.

[17] Fletcher-Louis, *Adam*, 72–73. Mulder also claims: 'Simon is the personification par excellence of the priesthood, of wisdom and of glory' (Otto Mulder, *Simon the High Priest in Sirach 50: An Exegetical Study of the Significance of Simon the High Priest as Climax to the Praise of the Fathers in Ben Sira's Concept of the History of Israel* [Leiden: Brill, 2003], 353).

[18] Fletcher-Louis, "Worship," 117. His thesis that 'the whole of Sirach 44–50 must be related theologically to a remarkable reworking of the *Shema* in 7:27–31' (118) is speculative and will be profoundly qualified by appreciation of the material difference between relation to God and devotion to the ancestors in these chapters, as will be demonstrated below.

[19] Rightly, Goshen-Gottstein writes in comment of Sir. 44–50 that '[p]raise is traditionally reserved for God. Ben Sira himself obviously uses praise in a wider sense' (Alon Goshen-Gottstein, "Ben Sira's Praise of the Fathers," in *Ben Sira's God: Proceedings of the International Ben Sira Conference*, ed. Renate Egger-Wenzel [Berlin: W. de Gruyter, 2002], 238–39). Cf. also Jan Liesen, "'With All Your Heart': Praise in the Book of Ben Sira," in *Ben Sira's God: Proceedings of the International Ben Sira Conference*, ed. Renate Egger-Wenzel (Berlin: W. de Gruyter, 2002), 199–220.

[20] Mulder argues that the way relationship with God is portrayed in the Hebrew text is changed in the later Greek translation (Mulder, *Simon*, 321–25). However, while this is a matter that deserves more attention, the differences are not of the kind that this present argument must attend to them.

– Devotion to God: Enoch pleased God (44:16); Abraham kept the law of the Most High (44:20); Aaron ministered to God (45:15), offered sacrifices to him (45:16, 21), and the Lord himself is Aaron's portion (45:22); Phinehas was 'zealous in the fear of the Lord' (45:23), and entered a covenant of friendship with God (45:24); Joshua was a 'devoted follower' of 'the Mighty One', 'so that all the Israelites might see how good it is to follow the Lord' (46:10). Of David it says that 'in all that he did he gave thanks to the Holy One, the Most High, proclaiming his glory; he sang praise with all his heart, and he loved his Maker' (47:8).[21] More could be added here, but cf. also 47:10, 22; 48:22; 49:3–4, 12.

– Notably, the text contrasts 'sin', 'wicked grumbling', 'idolatry' and 'turning away from the lord' (46:7, 11) with this devoted following of God.[22] Note also how Josiah 'kept his heart fixed on the Lord' (49:3), and how Josiah, David and Hezekiah are then immediately contrasted with the 'great sinners', who 'abandoned the law of the Most High' (49:4).

– The text describes God's communications to humans (44:21; 45:3, 5; 46:17; 49:8), and communication (prayer) directed to God (45:26; 46:5, 16; 47:5, 8; 48:20).

– God is characterised in the text in various typical ways. Mention is made of his wrath (48:10); love (45:1; 46:13) and mercy (e.g. 47:22).[23]

If one remembers the pattern of Christ-relation data in Paul, it is surely surprising that so much has been made of the very limited material in Sirach 50, because the general pattern of evidence in chapters 44–50 concerning the God-relation is *far* closer to the Christ-relation in Paul. Indeed, the interrelated themes in Sirach 44–50 are uncannily close to the various ways the Christ-relation is expressed in Paul.

It will be noticed that mention of chapter 50 was left out of the above bullet points in terms of the God relation. The reason for this is that chapter 50 (the one which speaks of Simon son of Onias) is particularly abundant with statements concerning the God-relation, and will be treated separately now:

– Devotion to God: Simon is remembered because he repaired the temple (50:1); the text speaks of the Lord's offerings, of service at the altar which is a 'pleasing odour to the Most High' (50:13–15); 'All the people', we are told, 'fell to the ground on their faces to worship their Lord, the Almighty,

---

[21] Cf. Liesen, "Praise," 208.

[22] For a more extensive discussion of these contrasts as a literary device, cf. Teresa R Brown, "God and Men in Israel's History: God and Idol Worship in *Praise of the Fathers* (Sir 44–50)," in *Ben Sira's God: Proceedings of the International Ben Sira Conference*, ed. Renate Egger-Wenzel (Berlin: W. de Gruyter, 2002), 214–20.

[23] Jeremy Corley, "God as Merciful Father in Ben Sira and the New Testament," in *Ben Sira's God: Proceedings of the International Ben Sira Conference*, ed. Renate Egger-Wenzel (Berlin: W. de Gruyter, 2002), 33–38. Corley, however, does not analyse how the evidence in Sirach overlaps with Paul's understanding of the character of *Christ*.

God Most High' (50:17); the 'God of all' is to be blessed (50:22); and the 'fear of the Lord' encouraged (50:29); 'the people of the Lord Most High' offer prayers and worship (50:19); Simon himself glories in God's name (50:20). Of course, such texts as this show why the praise of Simon, and as shall be seen that of Adam too, hardly raise 'very serious problems for Jewish monotheism', as Chester claims in comment on Adam. These figures themselves worship God!

– The presence and activity of God: He smells the odour at the altar (50:15); he hears the fanfare (50:16); the people receive a blessing from the Most High (50:21); God 'everywhere works great wonders' (50:22 – precisely as the 'Most High' [50:21], a name presumably expressing transcendence); God fosters the people's growth from birth and deals with them according to his mercy (50:22).

– There is human communication to God (50:19, 23–24)

– God is characterised as the Merciful One (50:19),[24] and the text repeats mention of his mercy (50:22, 24).

All of this is just in Sirach 50. The very first verses of the next chapter (51) go on to speak of the God-relation further, of prayer and praise of God, his absence (in heaven distinguished from earth – 51:9), yet also of his presence and activity, mercy and kindness, etc.

Remembering the pattern of language in Paul concerning the Christ-relation, i.e., the broader context into which his Christ-devotion is to be put, a pattern that Paul arguably would himself have recognised as such, the following proposition appears obvious: if one is searching for the best parallels for understanding the appropriate pattern of Christ-devotion language in Paul, one will indeed find it in the relational language in Sirach 44–50, *but as it concerns God, not the ancestors or Simon*. It will now be obvious that the relational analysis developed in terms of Paul has also facilitated a more satisfactory handling of these chapters in Sirach, and thus the ability to compare this text with Paul.

2.2. Pauline Christ-devotion and the Life of Adam and Eve

In discussing evidence from the Latin *Life of Adam and Eve*, Fletcher-Louis claims that a certain scene in the text 'provides a corrective to Hurtado's claim that there is no Jewish precedent for the worship of Christ'.[25] D. Steenburg argues that the worship of Christ in earliest Christianity was partially legiti-

---

[24] 'In the Hebrew portions of the Book of Ben Sira, the verb *racham* and its derivations are exclusively used for God' (Pancratius Beentjes, "God's Mercy: 'Racham' [Pi.], 'Rachum', and 'Rachamim' in the Book of Ben Sira," in *Ben Sira's God: Proceedings of the International Ben Sira Conference*, ed. Renate Egger-Wenzel [Berlin: W. de Gruyter, 2002], 113).

[25] Crispin H.T. Fletcher-Louis, *Luke–Acts: Angels, Christology and Soteriology* (Tübingen: Mohr/Siebeck, 1997), 142.

mated by texts such as the *Life of Adam and Eve* in which God commands angels to worship Adam, the image of God.[26] In the Latin version, Satan explains to Adam why he was expelled from heaven:

When God blew into you the *breath of life* and your countenance and likeness were made *in the image of God*, Michael brought you and made (us) worship you in the sight of God. And Michael went out and called all the angels, saying, 'Worship the image of the LORD God, as the LORD God has instructed'. And Michael himself worshiped first, and called me and said, 'Worship the image of God, Yahweh'. And I answered, 'I do not worship Adam'. And when Michael kept forcing me to worship, I said to him, 'Why do you compel me? I will not worship one inferior and subsequent to me. I am prior to him in creation; before he was made, I was already made. He ought to worship me' (*L.A.E.* 13:3–14:3).[27]

As the text goes on to explain, Satan and his minions were then summarily dismissed from heaven. Once again, a list of all of the relevant data in the entire document concerning the relation to a figure other than God will now be presented:

– Devotion: God commands all the angels to worship Adam, the image of God (cf. 13:3–14:3, cited above).
– Prayer to a figure other than God: Not generally noticed in the debates surrounding Pauline Christology is the scene, in the 19th chapter of the Latin version, in which Eve begs the 'lights of heaven' to tell Adam about her pains (19:3), because God has not heard her (19:2). It appears that the 'lights' (angels) hear Eve, and in 20:1 the text simply states that 'Adam said, "Eve's complaint has come to me"'.

And that is all there is of any serious relevance in the Latin. Still, there is precisely nothing of relevance in the Greek versions of the *Life of Adam and Eve*. Indeed, both of these listed items must be strongly qualified. First, the question of whether this worship is that usually reserved for God remains open. It should be added that this worship is done 'in the sight of God' (13:3), and is undertaken precisely because Adam is God's image (13:3). Perhaps Fletcher-Louis and others are correct that worshiping Adam, here, is much the same as the relation between the idol and the god it represents in pagan worship. However, the text immediately details that the worship is done because God has 'instructed' it (14:1), and not to do so incurs the wrath of *God* (15:2). It is 'worship' of Adam under the command and authority of God. Furthermore, Satan responds by claiming Adam 'ought to worship me' (14:3) – again implying that the worship mentioned is not strictly that which God receives, as Satan's complaint is not about the worship of God, but that Adam is prior to him in creation (and thus he still recognises that God made him and is thus not subsequent to God).

---

[26] D Steenburg, "The Worship of Adam and Christ as the Image of God," *JSNT* 39 (1990): 95–109.

[27] James H. Charlesworth, ed., *The Old Testament Pseudepigrapha, 2 Vols.* (New York: Doubleday, 1983), 2.262. The Latin *adorare* is behind the English translation 'worship'.

Concerning the second listed item, as the text makes clear, God will not listen to Eve (cf. 19:2), and it seems that these intermediary angels act as a kind of mobile-telephone service in the absence of God's listening ear – a matter which it will be necessary to revisit below. And the scene continues with Adam's prayers to God (20:3). Certainly, this is a special instance: God will not listen to Eve because of the trouble she has brought on the whole human race (the text is rather merciless in ascribing to Eve, not Adam, the main weight of the fault for the 'fall').

The pattern of data in the various versions concerning the God-relation can now be listed, although, given the vast amount of material, comments will be kept to a minimum. The God-relation data in the *Life of Adam and Eve* consists in:[28]

- Expressions of devotion to God: fear (26:1), falling down in worship and speaking about the character of God (27:1), 'cast me not from your presence' (27:2 – echoing Ps. 51:11). There are many different further expressions in, e.g. 26:1; 28:1–2; 30:2; 33:2; 36:1; 47:1; 50:3.
- The opposite of devotion is negatively formulated as disregarding 'the command of God' in 26:2; disregarding 'my [God's] words' (26:2) etc. Cf. also e.g. 34:1; 49:2.
- God's presence, activity and sovereignty implied or stated: 2:1; 3:1–2; 4:2–3; 9:4; 17:2; 22:2; 27:1–2; 28:2; 32:2; 33:1; 34:3; 39:1; 40:3; 41:1; 46:3.
- God is in heaven, separated from earth (i.e. absent from earth): 12:1 and 13:2 – see notes above in relation to the second listed item of the bullet list. Cf. also 16:1–2; 25:3–26:1; 29:1–3; 36:1–2; 45:2.
- Communication to God implied or explicit: 5:1; 6:2; 9:3; 17:1; 19:1; 20:2–3; 31:3; 35:2; 40:3; 41:1; 50:3.
- Communication from God: 26:2; 27:3; 48:1.
- God's character: Wrath (15:2–3), mercy (19:2; 27:1; 46:3), holy (27:1), upright (27:1), grace (27:2), great excellence (28:2).

Perhaps simply referencing the verses like this disguises the vast amount of data in the text concerning the God-relation. As noted above, by adding to this list material from the Greek versions, not just the Latin, its size would be multiplied two or three times over. But enough has now been listed to make the point, one that will be elucidated and amplified by conducting a short thought-experiment.

---

[28] For space reasons the analysis will be limited to the Latin version and not include the appendix, even though examination of other versions would only strengthen this argument.

3. A thought-experiment on Paul's Christ-relation, Sirach and the *Life of Adam and Eve*

The following thought-experiment, deliberately tipping the scales against the argument of this thesis, ought to prove illuminating. Even though a growing number of scholars today would deny that the *Life of Adam and Eve* was written by Jews, but by Christians (and the text cited by Fletcher-Louis and others is only found in the Latin),[29] let it be assumed that Paul had a Greek or Hebrew copy of all the chapters of the Latin *Life of Adam and Eve*, which also contained a version of the Adam-worship scene detailed above (none exist, but this is a thought-experiment). Further, let it be assumed that Paul had a copy of Sirach, and that he particularly liked re-reading the chapters analysed above (44–50). Indeed, in this thought-experiment Paul reads only chapters 44–50. On top of this, let it be assumed that he was reading these texts precisely as he was thinking through his convictions about the identity of Christ. To go even further, let us assume that he was reading *only* these texts as he developed his understanding of the identity of Christ.

Against those who have mined Sirach and the *Life of Adam and Eve* for the few scraps of evidence that could explain Christ-devotion on the basis of the praise or worship offered to figures other than God, a very different yet obvious proposition presents itself. The whole pattern of language in Paul regarding the relation between the risen Lord and believers, data, it was argued, Paul himself would have recognised as a pattern, was analysed in the previous 4 chapters of this thesis. It included descriptions of Christ's presence and activity, yet absence. Verse after verse of text detailing various expressions of Christ-devotion (including love for Christ, fear, total committed devotion etc.) were uncovered, and this Christ-devotion was contrasted with matters such as sin, blinded minds, the flesh etc. It was a devotion expressed in the language of passionate zeal, and found form also in Paul's Christ-shaped goals, aims and motivations, etc.

Now given this Pauline pattern, as well as that found in both the *Life of Adam and Eve* and Sirach, it would only be one bound by prior assumptions that would be capable of denying the obvious conclusion.[30] If Paul had only these two texts as he was developing his understanding of the identity of Christ, it would have been the broad pattern of *God*-relation themes in these texts that shaped his thoughts regarding the relation between the risen Lord and believers. Even if Paul had found the worship of Adam to be another way

---

[29] Cf. the references in J.R. Davila, *The Provenance of the Pseudepigrapha: Jewish, Christian, or Other?* (Leiden: Brill, 2005), 232–33.

[30] This mention of 'assumptions' is, of course, a comeback to Fletcher-Louis's claim that those who disagree with his analysis, based in part on analysis of both Sir. and *L.A.E*, are bound by unreasonable assumptions (Fletcher-Louis, "Worship," 119–20). Cf. also Hurtado, *LJC*, 42, for a similar critique of Fletcher-Louis.

to express his devotion to Christ, two points should be made: i) the Adam language was taken up into a completely different level of discourse that consistently put Christ in the God-relation role of these texts. ii) If Paul did employ the texts cited by Fletcher-Louis etc., then it was far from a central feature of his understanding of the identity of Christ, as potential echoes appear only a few times in his letters. This is in stark contrast with the God-relation themes adopted by Paul repeatedly in his letters in detailing the Christ-relation. It would be like trying to compare the amount of words the undisputed Pauline letters devote to, say, Hagar, as contrasted with, say, the cumulative space devoted to the themes of justification, spiritual gifts and resurrection! The material Fletcher-Louis cites is thus of limited value in understanding Paul's Christ-devotion, especially when understood in terms of the broader relational pattern. It is disputable that Paul would have worked at all within the conceptual space offered by Fletcher-Louis and others, as Adam and Wisdom themes in Paul's Christology have recently been challenged in Fee's major work, as noted above in chapters 2 and 3.[31]

The proposition that Paul understood the identity of Christ, and thus the Christ-relation, in light not of the occasional references to Simon or Adam in these texts, but rather in light of the frequent descriptions of the God-relation, is a one made all the more likely for a further reason. Important for Horbury, Fletcher-Louis etc. is that Adam and Simon are worshipped or praised. That is why these scraps of evidence are considered important. However, if this is a background for understanding devotion to Christ in Paul's letters, why did Paul not speak of the praise of Christ more centrally? Indeed, why did he neglect to speak of the worship of Christ at all (at least with the common worship vocabulary relating to the verb προσκυνέω)?[32] In this respect, one is reminded of Casey's (albeit wrongheaded) argument which maintained that the evidence in Paul for the worship of Christ is 'extremely sparse and not really convincing'.[33]

Furthermore, if the limited number of studies concerning Pauline epistemology are anywhere near the target, as shall be noted in the following chapter, then Paul's epistemological leanings in regard to divine knowledge were decidedly *relational*. Knowledge of God, it was also maintained in chapters 4 and 5 above, is about relationship with God, and is likewise formulated relationally. In other words, in thinking through the identity of Christ, and in conceiving how it was to be formulated, he would have likely spent much time pondering the relation between both Christ and believers on the one hand, and God and others in the two texts the thought-experiment gave him.

---

[31] Cf. also Aquila H. I. Lee, *From Messiah to Preexistent Son: Jesus' Self-Consciousness and Early Christian Exegesis of Messianic Psalms* (Tübingen: Mohr Siebeck, 2005), 285–96.

[32] Cf. Dunn, *Theology*, 259.

[33] Casey, "Worship," 222.

Paul, with only the *Life of Adam and Eve* and Sirach in his hands, according to our thought-experiment, would have likely paid much attention to the God-relation in these texts, which would make the extensive overlap with the Christ-relation language in his letters all the more noteworthy.

Finally, the proposal in our thought-experiment means that Fletcher-Louis, in his desire to explain early Christian Christ-devotion within a Jewish background as detailed above, was indeed half right. He was correct that the background was Jewish, but he looked for it in the wrong place when he sought conceptual links in the worship of Adam or Simon. Ironically the most appropriate evidence was staring Fletcher-Louis right in the face every time he opened Sirach 44–50, or the *Life of Adam and Eve*, on almost every page. The *God*-relation language in these texts is almost exactly the same complex of interrelated themes that one finds in Paul's Christ-relation language. Paul's Christ-devotion language is indeed Jewish in its shape and origin, but it is so as a reworking of Jewish God-relation themes. Still more reasons in support of the above proposal will be explored in dialogue with the Similitudes of Enoch, to which it is now necessary to turn.

4. The Pauline Christ-relation and the Similitudes of Enoch

The Similitudes of Enoch are, as Bauckham himself explains, the exception to his rule that one worshipped while seated on the divine throne was necessarily included in the divine identity.[34] Here is a figure, variously called the 'Son of Man', 'the Chosen One', the 'Elect One', 'Messiah' and 'Righteous One',[35] sitting on God's throne and offered worship. Yet this figure also arguably remains distinguished from the deity,[36] the 'Lord of Spirits'. Given that Paul's conversion involved a revelation of Christ as a heavenly being, in some sense distinguished from God, perhaps the Similitudes offer a parallel to the relation between believers and Christ in Paul's letters? Indeed, in contrast to the *Life of Adam and Eve* and Sirach 44–50, data in the Similitudes concerning the Son of Man do indeed parallel the language in Paul describing the Christ-relation. This admittedly exceptional evidence will first be outlined, followed by a section in which the importance of these parallels for Paul's Christ-

---

[34] Bauckham, *God*, 19. Below it will be necessary to reassess whether he is right about this.

[35] The vast majority of Enochic literature scholars understand these names to refer to the same figure. Cf. the discussions in Andrei A. Orlov, *The Enoch-Metatron Tradition* (Tübingen: Mohr Siebeck, 2005), 82; Klaus Koch, "Questions Regarding the So-Called Son of Man in the Parables of Enoch: A Response to Sabino Chialà and Helge Kvanvig," in *EMSM*, ed. Gabriele Boccaccini (Cambridge: Eerdmans, 2007), 228–34; Lester L. Grabbe, "The Parables of Enoch in Second Temple Jewish Society," in *EMSM*, ed. Gabriele Boccaccini (Cambridge: Eerdmans, 2007), 389.

[36] Cf. p. 232 below.

relation will be challenged. This will pave the way to argue that the Lord-of-Spirits-relation in the Similitudes, not the Son of Man data, is a *clearly* closer parallel to the Christ-relation in Paul's letters.

4.1. Relational language and the Enochic 'Son of Man'[37]

While there is not too much of significance in terms of the present discussion in the first parable (*1 En.* 38–44), it does speak of the dwelling of the Chosen One in heaven with 'the righteous and chosen' who 'will be without number before him forever and ever' (39:6). Indeed, this dwelling is described as the desire of Enoch (39:8), so could it be that the author wishes to express a delight in the presence of the Chosen One in a way that parallels Paul's statements in, for example, 1 Thessalonians 4:17–18;[38] 5:10–11; 2 Corinthians 5:8; Philippians 1:23?

Also in the first parable, some may find significance in that, in 40:5, a heavenly figure is portrayed as blessing the Chosen One. However, the chosen ones are also blessed by the same figure in the same verse.

Turning to the second parable (*1 En.* 45–57), the Chosen One is first depicted as sitting on a throne of glory. The wicked see this 'and their spirits will grow strong within them, when they see my chosen ones' (45:3). Some translations read 'Chosen One' instead of 'chosen ones' here,[39] which would imply that the act of beholding the Chosen One on the throne of glory makes their souls grow strong. Is this a weak parallel to, for example, 2 Corinthians 3:18, where beholding the glory of the Lord transforms the believer from one degree of glory to another?

After this, the Chosen One is described as 'another' who was with the Head of Days. His 'face was full of graciousness', which is a significant characterisation of the Son of Man. Does this parallel, in a very small way, the characterisation of the risen Lord in Paul, as detailed above? Additionally, in this scene, when Enoch asks the 'angel of peace' about the Son of Man, he is answered that 'all the treasuries of what is hidden he [the Son of Man] will reveal' (46:3). This certainly parallels language in 1 Corinthians 4:5 which speaks of the coming of the Lord 'who will bring to light the things now hidden in darkness and will disclose the purposes of the heart'.

46:4–5 continues to express the role of the Son of Man as agent of the Lord of Spirit's wrath. In the eschatologically projected vision, the Son of Man is portrayed as on earth, and as such will crush evil kings (46:4–5). Significantly,

---

[37] All the *1 En.* citations, unless marked, are from the new and most authoritative translation: George W.E. Nickelsburg and James C. VanderKam, *1 Enoch: A New Translation* (Minneapolis: Fortress, 2004).

[38] Nickelsburg draws attention to this verse in Paul though fails to mention the matter of the desire involved (George W. E. Nickelsburg, Klaus Baltzer, ed., *1 Enoch: A Commentary on the Book of 1 Enoch* [Minneapolis: Fortress, 2001], 85).

[39] E.g. Daniel C. Olson, *Enoch: A New Translation* (North Richland Hills, Tex.: BIBAL Press, 2004), 87; James H. Charlesworth, *OTP*, 1.34.

he does this 'because they do not exalt him or praise him, or humbly acknowledge whence the kingdom was given to them' (46:5). Does the text imply that the wicked are crushed because they do not exalt or praise the Son of Man?

A couple of chapters later the author describes a scene involving the naming of Son of Man (48–49). In the process, in 48:1–3, the Son of Man seems to be described as pre-existent. While the text speaks of the eternity of the Lord of Spirits (cf. 58:4), the Son of Man was given a name even 'before the sun and the constellations were created, before the stars of heaven were made' (48:2–3), and he was 'chosen and hidden' in the presence of the Lord of Spirits, 'before the world was created and forever' (48:6). Of course, it has been debated precisely what is meant by this 'pre-existence' in terms of the Son of Man. Does it merely express the pre-existence of wisdom?[40] Was Enoch simply pre-existent as a 'project in the mind of God'?[41] The text does not answer these questions, but 'it is difficult to see why his identity would need to be hidden if he did not yet exist' in a real sense.[42] Given this, one wonders why Fee, whose problematic focus on pre-existence in Pauline Christology has already been addressed above, did not consider these texts even worthy of mention. Here is a figure, distinguished at some level from the Lord of Spirits,[43] who is probably described as pre-existent, especially in 48:6. Fee's 'pre-existent thus divine' equation should be questioned.

After this, the author describes the relation between the righteous and the Son of Man at his appearing:

He will be a staff for the righteous,
    that they may lean on him and not fall;
And he will be the light of the nations,
    and he will be a hope for those who grieve in their hearts.
All who dwell on the earth will fall down and worship before him,
    and they will glorify and bless and sing hymns to the name of the Lord of Spirits. For
    this reason he was chosen' (48:4–6)

This eschatological relation of the righteous to the Son of Man involves dependence (leaning), hope and possibly also worship, depending upon the recipient of the worship of those who fall down.

---

[40] Cf. Helge S. Kvanvig, "The Son of Man in the Parables of Enoch," in *EMSM*, ed. Gabriele Boccaccini (Cambridge: Eerdmans, 2007), 202–6.

[41] Collins citing T.W. Manson (John J. Collins, "Enoch and the Son of Man: A Response to Sabino Chialà and Helge Kvanvig," in *EMSM*, ed. Gabriele Boccaccini [Cambridge: Eerdmans, 2007], 225). Cf. also Lee, *Messiah*, 109. In private correspondence, Nelson Moore has drawn my attention to Rev. 13:8, and notes that even though the names of the redeemed were written in the book of life 'from the foundation of the world', this in no way implies their pre-existence. 48:6, however, seems to express the Son of Man's pre-existence less ambiguously.

[42] John J. Collins, "Enoch," 225.

[43] Cf. p. 232 below for a justification of the assertion that the Son of Man is not to be understood as included in the identity of the Lord of Spirits.

A few verses later, the distress of those who 'deny the Lord of Spirits and his Anointed One' (48:10) is described. That which is contrasted with true and acceptable devotion is here spoken of in terms of denying not just the Lord of Spirits, but also his Anointed.

Throughout these chapters, apart from the last when the Son of Man is arguably identified as Enoch,[44] the Son of Man is portrayed as existing in heaven.[45] He comes to earth only in the eschatological future. However, one text would appear to speak of the presence of the Chosen One which exceeds the merely individual, perhaps in a way that parallels Paul's 'in Christ' language. We are told that 'in him' dwells 'the spirit of those who have fallen asleep in righteousness' (49:3). Is the Son of Man a kind of corporate entity, much as Moule argued in relation to Christ?[46] Is this idea also found in Colossians 3:3–4 ('your life is hidden with Christ in God'), or 1 Thessalonians 4:16 ('the dead in Christ')? Of course, immediately one must note that the singular 'spirit' shows that the spirit in question is *God's* spirit, as is indeed the case in Isaiah 11:2, the passage from which 49:3 draws almost verbatim.[47] So Black, who erroneously speaks of 'the *spirits* of the faithful dead', cannot believe this translation stood in the original and wonders whether the text is a corruption.[48]

In the next verse the Son of Man is described as one who will 'judge the things that are secret' (49:4). This conceptually parallels some of Paul's eschatological expressions relating to Christ (Rom. 2:16; 1 Cor. 4:5. Cf. also *1 En.* 51:3).

Chapter 52 begins with various descriptions of Enoch's journeys and visions. Similar to the majority of translations, VanderKam and Nickelsburg translate 52:4 as: 'All these things that you have seen will serve the authority

---

[44] The debate surrounding this issue continues, but most assume that Enoch is indeed identified with the Son of Man at least in chapter 71. But cf. the discussion in Kvanvig, "Parables," 197–210; John J. Collins, "Enoch," 223–26.

[45] 'In the body of the Parables there is no suggestion at all that the Son of Man ever had an earthly career' (John J. Collins, "Enoch," 226).

[46] Moule, *Origin*. But cf. Porter's critique of the notion of corporate personality (S.E. Porter, "Two Myths: Corporate Personality and Language/Mentality Determinism," *SJT* 43 [1990]: 289–307).

[47] The singular is accurately translated in most, e.g. in Olson, *Enoch*, 95; James H. Charlesworth, *OTP*, 1.36; and Nickelsburg and VanderKam, *1 Enoch*, 63. The Ethiopic word translated as 'spirit' in this verse (*manfas / manfasa*) is unambiguously singular. The plural would be either *manfasāta* or *manāfesta* (Wolf Leslau, *Comparative Dictionary of Ge'Ez: [Classical Ethiopic]; Ge'Ez-Engl./Engl.-Ge'Ez ; with an Index of the Semitic Roots* [Wiesbaden: Harrassowitz, 1987], 389). My thanks to Professor Robert Holmstedt for pointing this reference out to me.

[48] Matthew Black, *The Book of Enoch or 1 Enoch: A New English Edition with Commentary and Textual Notes* (Leiden: Brill, 1985), 212–13, italics mine.

of his Anointed One, so that he may be powerful and mighty on the earth'.[49] However, Isaac translates the last part of the text as follows: 'so that he may give orders and be *praised* upon the earth'.[50] Even if the majority translation, represented by VanderKam and Nickelsburg, is accepted, the text still states that the Son of Man will be mighty and powerful on earth. Some may see here a faint reflection of the presence and activity of the risen Lord in Paul.

In 52:6, the mountains listed in 52:2 are described as being 'like wax before the fire' before 'the Chosen One'. Noteworthy is that here the Chosen One, as the agent of God's judgment, 'is depicted [in the Similitudes] with imagery that the early chapter of 1 Enoch ascribe to God'.[51] In this respect it is apropos to mention that the author(s) of the Similitides could also apply OT God and YHWH texts to this figure, as in 52:6,[52] but also, for example, in 62:6.[53] The former passage involves the application of a YHWH text (cf. Mic. 1:3) cited 'virtually verbatim' from Mic. 1.4',[54] to the Son of Man figure. While the Son of Man is not called 'Lord' or 'God', there is ground here, if it is accepted that the text does not merge the divine-identity of the Son of Man with the Lord of Spirits, to challenge the bold christological conclusions of Capes based upon the Pauline employment of YHWH texts in relation to Christ, at least when this is taken as a stand-alone argument for Paul's supposed divine-Christology.[55]

Lest one think that the judgment of the Son of Man is just about a human political scenario, in 55:4 he also sits on the throne of glory judging the angels 'Azazel and all his associates and all his hosts' (note also 61:8 where the Chosen One judges 'all the works of the holy ones in the heights of heaven').

The third parable (58–69) contains the most significant material. In chapter 62 there is yet another description of the role of the Chosen One in the coming judgment. He is enthroned, the spirit of righteousness is poured out upon him, and 'the word of his mouth will slay all the sinners' (62:2). As with the Lord of Spirits (e.g., 67:9), 'no lying word is spoken in his [the Son of Man's] presence' (62:3). The judgment scene is expanded upon in the following verses, describing the pain and terror experienced by the 'kings and mighty'.

---

[49] Cf. also Olson's translation: 'that he may be in command and hold power on earth' (Olson, *Enoch*, 99), VanderKam's earlier suggestion: 'that he may be strong and powerful on the earth (James C. VanderKam, *Enoch: A Man for All Generations* [Columbia: University of South Carolina Press, 1995], 137), and M.A. Knibb's translation in Hedley F. D. Sparks, ed., *The Apocryphal Old Testament* (Oxford: Clarendon Press, 1984), 232. Cf. also Black, *Enoch*, 52.

[50] James H. Charlesworth, ed., *The Old Testament Pseudepigrapha, 2 Vols.* (New York: Doubleday, 1983), 1.37, italics mine.

[51] Nickelsburg and VanderKam, *1 Enoch*, 4. Cf. 1:6 and 52:6, and the comments in VanderKam, *Enoch*, 137; Olson, *Enoch*, 98.

[52] Cf. Black, *Enoch*, 236.

[53] Black, *Enoch*, 218; Davis, *Name*, 76.

[54] Black, *Enoch*, 216. Cf. also VanderKam, *Enoch*, 137.

[55] Capes, *Yahweh Texts*.

In the middle of this scene, the most striking material of all surfaces. In the midst of the judgment, where the mighty recognise the Son of Man 'sitting on the throne of glory', it states that:

[A]ll the kings and the mighty and all who possess the earth
will bless and glorify and exalt him who rules over all, who was hidden.
For from the beginning the son of man was hidden (62:6–7)

This time it is explicit that the object of glorification, exaltation and blessing is the Son of Man, not the Lord of Spirits. Bauckham writes: 'This worship cannot be understood as merely an expression of submission to a political superiority, since the Son of Man is seated on the throne of God'. According to Bauckham's scheme, such a *throne* context means this worship *must* be a 'recognition of the unique divine sovereignty over the world',[56] and hence this passage constitutes the single exception that proves Bauckham's rule that no intermediary figures participate in God's rule or are worshipped.[57]

To come back to 1 Enoch 62, the text continues with:

And all the kings and the mighty and the exalted and those who rule the earth will fall on their faces in his presence;
and they will worship and set their hope on that son of man,
and they will supplicate and petition for mercy from him (62:9).[58]

While the scene then explains how the Lord of Spirits executes the judgment (62:10–12), a number of relevant features need to be noted. The kings worship this Son of Man, and set their hope on him (cf. also 48:4 as discussed above). In this context the kings also supplicate the Son of Man for mercy.

After these scenes, the salvation of the righteous is described. 62:14 states: 'And the Lord of Spirits will abide over them, and with that son of man they will eat, and they will lie down and rise up forever and ever'. Is this meant to convey that the destiny of the righteous is glorious in that they live with the Son of Man (cf. also the discussion relating to 39:6–8 above)?

65:1–69:25 probably constitutes an interpolation,[59] in which some Noachic fragments are inserted. 65:3 reports a scene in which Noah repeats a 'prayer' to Enoch (who is now presumably meant to be in heaven) three times. Natu-

---

[56] Bauckham, *God*, 20 n.33.

[57] Cf. Bauckham, *God*, 19; Bauckham, "Throne.".

[58] One also wonders, in this light, if 63:4 is also partly meant to refer to the Son of Man. The kings and mighty exclaim: 'Now we know that we should glorify and bless the Lord of the kings, and him who rules over all kings'

[59] Most scholars understand this to be an interpolation. Just how much later it was added to the text remains disputed. Hannah argues that it was added very shortly afterwards (cf. Darrell D. Hannah, "The Book of Noah, the Death of Herod the Great, and of the Date of the Parables of Enoch," in *EMSM*, ed. Gabriele Boccaccini [Cambridge: Eerdmans, 2007], 476), and less plausibly Sacchi maintains it was added by the author of the Parables (Paolo Sacchi, "The 2005 Camaldoli Seminar on the Parables of Enoch: Summary and Prospects for Future Research," in *EMSM*, ed. Gabriele Boccaccini [Cambridge: Eerdmans, 2007], 502).

rally, one is reminded of 2 Corinthians 12:8, and Paul's thrice repeated prayer to the risen Lord in heaven. When Noah spots trouble on earth, he sets off 'to the ends of the earth and cries to his great-grandfather, Enoch' (cf. Ps. 61:1–2 'Hear my cry, O God; listen to my prayer. From the end of the earth I call to you, when my heart is faint'). It continues: 'And Noah said three times with a bitter voice, "Hear me, hear me, hear me"'. This appears to be evidence of prayer to Enoch.

Finally, after the extended interpolation of 65:1–69:25, there is a concluding summary to the judgment scenarios of the third parable. It speaks of blessing and glorification and joy 'because the name of that son of man had been revealed to them [presumably the righteous]' (69:26). Gieschen has argued that the 'name' of the Son of Man in the Similitudes indicates 'that he shares the Divine Name of the Ancient of Days, the Tetragrammaton'.[60] 'If the Son of Man shares the Name of the Lord of the Spirits', Gieschen continues:

[H]e can be identified within the mystery of the one God even though he has distinct personhood ... Without the clear identification of the Son of Man within the mystery of YHWH by means of his possession of the Divine Name, his enthronement and worship depicted in 1 En 69 could have been considered idolatry.[61]

Surely this is an impressive list of Son of Man related features which sounds like material found in Paul concerning the Christ-relation. This is especially so in relation to judgment themes (e.g. *1 En.* 41:2, 9; 45:6; 49:4 [where the Son of Man even judges the 'secret things'] 53:2, 7; 54:6–7; 55:3; 60:24–25; 61:9; 62:8–9, 10–12; 68:4), employment of God and YHWH texts in terms of the Son of Man, the use of 'the name' in relation to both Christ and the Enochic Son of Man (cf. e.g. *1 En.* 41:6; 48:7; 50:3–5), the employment of the throne imagery (cf. e.g. *1 En.* 45:3; 51:3; 61:8; 62:2–5; 69:27–29),[62] as well as the language of hope, 'prayer' to and dependence (leaning). If the Son of Man, against Gieschen, is to be understood as non-divine, as, to employ Bauckham's language, distinct from the unique divine identity, then one should perhaps not conclude from Paul's Christ-relation a divine-Christology (again, in Bauckham's sense). As shall be demonstrated now, however, such a conclusion would be a most misleading handling of the actual Enochic and Pauline material.

4.2. Paul's Christ-relation, the Lord of Spirits and the Son of Man

The following 16 points seek to show that Paul's Christ-relation far more closely corresponds with the pattern of data, in the Similitudes, concerning the Lord of Spirits than it does the scattered material relating to the Son of Man.

---

[60] Charles A. Gieschen, "The Name of the Son of Man in the Parables of Enoch," in *EMSM*, ed. Gabriele Boccaccini (Cambridge: Eerdmans, 2007), 238.

[61] Ibid., 249.

[62] As noticed in Bauckham, *God*, 19–20, which caused him to judge this text as so exceptional.

1) It needs to be noted that these data concerning the Son-of-Man-relation in the Similitudes are not an experienced reality, unlike Paul's Christ-relation. The Similitudes text is a series of eschatological visions and there is thus no real existential reality to the Son-of-Man-relation. In a similar way, Hurtado justifiably contrasts the worship of real Jewish groups with that which is merely a literary phenomenon.[63] So the language of 'hope', 'leaning' and worship in 48:4–6 is about what *will* happen. That is, it is not a relational reality for anyone; it is a vision about an as yet unrealised eschatological future.

2) The analysis above of the Son-of-Man-relation in the Similitudes was generally not undertaken thematically because the evidence arguably does not constitute a pattern of data, or one that was supposed to be perceived as a pattern. It needs to be remembered that statements about the Son of Man in the Similitudes are not free-floating ideas that inform the reader about an abstract idea or conception of the 'Son of Man'.[64] Rather, as Leslie W. Walck's research shows,[65] there is not too much material that overlaps in the various chunks of 'Son of Man' related passages Walck has isolated.[66] No element in his list concerning the Son of Man occurs in all five of the chunks of material. Appearing in four of the important passages is only the Son of Man's heavenly status and righteousness.[67] The majority of the Son of Man 'concepts' only have one reference. In other words we are not dealing with a pattern of interrelated data about this 'intermediary'. It was simply a literary vision, not an explanation about a unified experience, and this important point must be remembered.

Indeed, it can also be asked whether the single English translation 'Son of Man' does justice to the various Ethiopic phrases. Does the text wish to portray a monolithic entity, the 'Son of Man'? 'Perhaps it would be wiser', suggests Pierluigi Piovanelli, 'to avoid translating all of them as "Son of Man" in order to make the readers aware of the variety and the complexity of these terminological and exegetical issues'.[68] And is the 'Chosen One' the same as the 'Son of Man'? 'Morna Hooker's research', as Orlov has noted, 'demonstrates that, while Chapters 38–45 use the title "chosen one", Chapters 46 to 48 operate with "son of man"'.[69] Of course, Grabbe is surely correct that the 'present

---

[63] Hurtado, *Origins*, 73.

[64] Cf. chapter 1 ('From Free-Floating "Problems" to Hermeneutical Questions from Life') in Anthony C. Thiselton, *The Hermeneutics of Doctrine* (Cambridge: Eerdmans, 2007), 3–18.

[65] Leslie W. Walck, "The Son of Man in the Parables of Enoch and the Gospels," in *EMSM*, ed. Gabriele Boccaccini (Cambridge: Eerdmans, 2007), 309.

[66] First: *1 En.* 46; Second: 48:2–8; Third: 62–63; Fourth: 69:26–29; Fifth: 70–71.

[67] Walck, "Parables," 309.

[68] Pierluigi Piovanelli, "'A Testimony for the Kings and the Mighty Who Possess the Earth': The Thirst for Justice and Peace in the Parables of Enoch," in *EMSM*, ed. Gabriele Boccaccini (Cambridge: Eerdmans, 2007), 368.

[69] Orlov, *Enoch-Metatron*, 82.

form of the book appears to be thinking of a single figure'.[70] Yet if all this implies the Similitudes were created 'on an ad hoc basis over a period of time',[71] can we be sure what existed as a single literary unit in the first century? It is impossible to be dogmatic about the nature and timing of the postulated later interpolations given the absence of alternative versions of the Similitudes.[72]

3) This leads to another crucial question in relation to the present study, one concerning the dating of the Similitudes. A majority of Enoch scholars argue that Matthew's Gospel evidences knowledge of, and even directly cites from, the Similitudes.[73] Adela Yarbro Collins argues that Mark's messianic secrecy motif may be explainable in light of the hiddenness of the 'Son of Man' in the Similitudes and his 'revelation' to be elected.[74] At least a form of the Book of Watchers was known to the Jerusalem church, if Jude's letter is taken as evidence of such.[75] Yet while most scholars now agree in speculating a date of origin around the turn of the millennium, can we assume that the Similitudes were known to Paul, as Nickelsburg maintains?[76] It must be admitted that it is difficult to know, and many scholars continue to date the Similitudes later than Paul's letters. There are no *clear* citations from the Similitudes in antiquity,[77] and as is well known, no fragments from these chapters of 1 Enoch have been recovered from Qumran, although parts from the Book of the Watchers (1–36), the Astronomical Book (72–82), the Book of Dreams (83–90), and the Epistle of Enoch (91–107) were. Perhaps there were theological reasons it was not found at Qumran, or maybe it was lost. But it is also possible that it was only composed later, too late for Paul to have known it, post AD 70 as some still maintain.[78] If a consensus is emerging, few

---

[70] Grabbe, "Parables," 389.

[71] Michael A. Knibb, "The Structure and Composition of the Parables of Enoch," in *EMSM*, ed. Gabriele Boccaccini (Cambridge: Eerdmans, 2007), 64.

[72] So, Knibb, "Structure," 64.

[73] Cf. e.g. Sabino Chialà, "The Son of Man: The Evolution of an Expression," in *EMSM*, ed. Gabriele Boccaccini (Cambridge: Eerdmans, 2007), 167; John J. Collins, "Enoch," 216; Walck, "Parables," 336–37; Davila, *Provenance*, 133.

[74] Adela Yarbro Collins, "The Secret Son of Man in the Parables of Enoch and the Gospel of Mark: A Response to Leslie Walck," in *EMSM*, ed. Gabriele Boccaccini (Cambridge: Eerdmans, 2007), 338–42.

[75] As maintained in, e.g., Richard J. Bauckham, "James and the Jerusalem Community," in *Jewish Believers in Jesus*, eds Oskar Skarsaune and Reidar Hvalvik (Peabody: Hendrickson, 2007), 86, 94–95.

[76] Cf. e.g. George W. E. Nickelsburg and Klaus Baltzer, *1 Enoch*, 85.

[77] Davila, *Provenance*, 133.

[78] Cf. David W. Suter, "Enoch in Sheol: Updating the Dating of the Book of Parables," in *EMSM*, ed. Gabriele Boccaccini (Cambridge: Eerdmans, 2007), 415–43. Stone writes: 'Overall, I am in agreement with his [Suter's] summary that the Book of Parables was written either toward the turn of the millennium or in the late first century C. E.' (Michael E. Stone, "Enoch's Date in Limbo; or, Some Considerations on David Suter's Analysis of the Book of Parables," in *EMSM*, ed. Gabriele Boccaccini [Cambridge: Eerdmans, 2007], 444).

would date it before the Roman period, and equally few after the first century AD. Beyond that, it is to a large degree speculation. Though this thesis does not hereby support a later date of composition than Paul, it simply needs to be admitted that these possibilities cannot be ruled out, and Paolo Sacchi's rhetoric, that implies the arguments for an early and Jewish origin has effectively closed the discussion,[79] underestimates the amount of sheer speculation involved in the supposed modern consensus.

4) A related question is whether this document is even (non-Christian) Jewish. Milik famously argued the document was Christian, though nobody has followed him on this point.[80] As noted above, Fröhlich has suggested that it cannot be ruled out that the document is of Jewish-Christian origin.[81] Indeed, it is noteworthy that the document 'shows no interest in Torah observance, makes no mention of the temple cult or priesthood, and gives no indication of any sense of Jewish national or ethnic identity'.[82] Additionally, there is no mention of Abraham, Israel or Moses![83] Hence, major distinguishing features of Jewish identity are missing. Davila, together with the vast majority of scholars, argues that a good case can be made for the Jewish composition of the text,[84] but the matter is not entirely clear cut, especially as Davila himself has argued that 'Christians may have written pseudepigrapha without any obvious Christian features'.[85] Most maintain that it is likely that the Similitudes are Jewish and earlier than Paul, but these points must be raised in comparing Paul with these chapters of Enochic literature.

5) The worship of the Son of Man, possibly present in 46:4–5; 48:6 and definitely expressed in 62:6–7, 9, need not imply the significance Bauckham

---

Ida Fröhlich writes: 'I think we should not even rule out the possibility that the authors of the Parables might have been Jewish Christians. This fact would explain the presence of Christian elements in the text. It also would explain the fact that the Enochic collection, finalised with the material of 1 En 37–71, found its way into the Christian tradition' (Ida Fröhlich, "The Parables of Enoch and Qumran Literature," in *EMSM*, ed. Gabriele Boccaccini [Cambridge: Eerdmans, 2007], 351). Jonathan Ben-Dov argues that an examination of the cosmology of the Similitudes, which shows similarities with *Serekh* and later rabbinic materials, 'is an important clue for the study of the provenance of the Parables of Enoch' (Jonathan Ben-Dov, "Exegetical Notes on Cosmology in the Parables of Enoch," in *EMSM*, ed. Gabriele Boccaccini [Cambridge: Eerdmans, 2007], 150), the implications of which could push the date of the Similitudes later.

[79] Sacchi, "Camaldoli," 511.

[80] Cf. the summary in James H. Charlesworth, "Can We Discern the Composition Date of the Parables of Enoch," in *EMSM*, ed. Gabriele Boccaccini (Cambridge: Eerdmans, 2007), 451.

[81] Cf. n.78.

[82] Davila, *Provenance*, 133.

[83] Cf. Koch, "Questions," 228.

[84] Davila, *Provenance*, 134.

[85] J.R. Davila, "The Old Testament Pseudepigrapha as Background to the New Testament," *ExpTim* 117, no. 2 (2005): 55, but cf. his important qualifications to this statement.

has ascribed it. It is so significant for Bauckham because of the divine throne in his divine identity scheme, and because this Son of Man sits on it. But the language in these passages, especially the first and last, sound very much like an earthly or military rout, the political submission of one king to another more mighty (cf., e.g., the images and text on the 'amous Black Obelisk of Shalmaneser III, which depicts Jehu kneeling prostrate 'before "the mighty king, king of the universe, king without a rival ..."' etc.,[86] language used to describe Shalmaneser.[87] Cf. also, for example, Jdt. 2:28–3:2; Pss. 2:10–11; 72:9–11; 2 Sam. 14:22, 33; 18:28; 24:20; Mt. 18:23–35). It must be remembered, Solomon too could sit on the throne of YHWH (1 Chr. 29:23; 2 Chr. 9:8). These Enochic passages likely do not portray the worship of the Son of Man in the way only God should be worshipped (cf., e.g., Ex. 23:24–25), a conclusion that will be confirmed via meditation on the precise nature of the presence and activity of the Son of Man below. Furthermore, it should be noted that the most impressive language in the Similitudes concerning the Son of Man, namely the explicit worship of the enthroned intermediary, is *not* significantly employed by Paul in terms of Christ in the undisputed letters.

6) There is *much* more information in the Similitudes of Enoch concerning the Lord-of-Spirits-relation, than there is concerning the Son-of-Man-relation. As such, the Son of Man language in the Similitudes contrasts strongly with the general picture of the centrality of Christ one finds in Paul's letters (apart from some of the first chapters in Romans), which, in terms of simple preponderance of mention, parallels the Lord of Spirits in these chapters of 1 Enoch.

There is debate concerning the literary relationship between the Similitudes and of the Book of Watchers. Most scholars maintain that the Similitudes were consciously written to continue the first vision (cf. *1 En.* 1:2) in the Book of Watchers, or at least were penned under the strong influence of these opening 36 chapters of 1 Enoch.[88] So, were the Similitudes ever circulated

---

[86] Bernhard W. Anderson, *The Living World of the Old Testament* (Harlow, Essex: Longman, 1993⁴), 284.

[87] David Winton Thomas, ed., *Documents from Old Testament Times: Translated with Introductions and Notes by Members of the Society for Old Testament Study* (London: Nelson, 1958), 46–55.

[88] George W.E. Nickelsburg, "Discerning the Structure(s) of the Enochic Book of Parables," in *EMSM*, ed. Gabriele Boccaccini (Cambridge: Eerdmans, 2007), 23–47; Knibb, "Structure," e.g. 48; Loren T. Stuckenbruck, "The Parables of Enoch According to George Nickelsburg and Michael Knibb: A Summary and Discussion of Some Remaining Questions," in *EMSM*, ed. Gabriele Boccaccini (Cambridge: Eerdmans, 2007), 65–71; Benjamin G. Wright, "The Structure of the Parables of Enoch: A Response to George Nickelsburg and Michael Knibb," in *EMSM*, ed. Gabriele Boccaccini (Cambridge: Eerdmans, 2007), 77; James C. VanderKam, "The Book of Parables Within the Enoch Tradition," in *EMSM*, ed. Gabriele Boccaccini (Cambridge: Eerdmans, 2007), 84, 91; Kvanvig, "Parables," 184. This connection between chapters 1–36 and 37–71 of *1 En.* is disputed by Eibert J.C. Tigchelaar, "Remarks on Transmission and Traditions in the Parables of Enoch: A Response to James VanderKam," in *EMSM*, ed. Gabriele Boccaccini

separately, as a stand-alone text? VanderKam appears to think it did indeed exist as a 'booklet',[89] and Grabbe maintains the Similitudes were meant to be read without necessary reference to the Book of the Watchers.[90] Knibb, on the other hand, thinks that an independent existence of the Similitudes is unlikely.[91] Because Grabbe's position remains a minority view, it is fair to assume that the Similitudes were penned to continue the Book of Watchers. Given this, one could legitimately use the Book of the Watchers, i.e., chapters 1–36, in this comparison. It would confirm that the Pauline Christ-relation far more closely corresponds with the Lord-of-Spirits-relation than the Son-of-Man-relation. Indeed, it is time to turn to specific examples of this correspondence, and thereby to dispel potentially problematic readings of the evidence for the 'Son of Man'-relation detailed above. However, the evidence in the Similitudes alone, not including 1 Enoch 1–36, is sufficient to make the case, and so despite the above comments it will be assumed that the Similitudes text was circulated separately.

7) The Lord of Spirits, like the risen Lord, was understood in terms of a 'theistic' framework, i.e., one that could speak of both the immanence and transcendence of the deity, of the divinity's presence and activity in the world despite, at the same time, speaking of the deity's absence from earth. So the Lord of Spirits is understood as absent from earth, above it, in heaven. The prayers of the righteous ascend 'from the earth' into his presence (47:1–3). There are regular mentions of his throne in heaven, where it is surrounded by heavenly beings (e.g. 60:2). This heavenly zone is explicitly separated from the earth in the cosmology of the Similitudes.[92] The whirlwind snatched Enoch 'up from the face of the earth and set me down within the confines of the heavens' (39:3. Cf. also 40:6; 45:2). 'Heaven is above the earth' (55:2. Cf. also 37:5; 61:6), and the Most High is in heaven (60:22 – sometimes also envisaged as above heaven), while others 'possess the earth' (63:12. Cf. also 67:8). In the presence of the Lord of Spirits there can be no lying word spoken (67:9), a fact which implies that this eschatological presence is different, something more direct than usual (cf. also 67:8).

Yet this Lord is also present and active in the world, despite the, in some sense, very real absence associated with his being in heaven. So there is praise of the Lord of Spirits for 'all his deeds and all his mighty acts' (e.g., 61:13). Things happen in accordance with the will of the Lord of Spirits, including Enoch's own praise of this Lord (39:9). Enoch has wisdom only in so far as it

---

(Cambridge: Eerdmans, 2007), e.g. 105–6. Likewise, Grabbe argues that the Book of Similitudes was meant to be read on its own (Grabbe, "Parables," 393).

[89] VanderKam, "Parables," 81.

[90] Grabbe, "Parables," 393.

[91] Knibb, "Structure."

[92] Suter has argued that the comparison between the heavenly and earthly realities is one of three main comparisons central to the Similitudes (cf. the summary in Kvanvig, "Parables," 180 n.2).

is 'according to the good pleasure of the Lord of Spirits' (37:4). The 'light-nings and the luminaries ... flash for a blessing or for a curse, as the Lord of Spirits wills', and the thunder too 'according to the word of the Lord of Spir-its' (59:1–2). The sun 'emerges and completes its path according to the com-mand of the Lord of Spirits' (41:6), and the flood and the 'sign in heaven' were likewise his activity (54:5, 7; 55:2). Even the angels who are in charge of 'the power of the waters' are under the command of the Lord of Spirits (66:2). The Lord of Spirits also 'strengthened the spirits of the righteous' and 'made a separation between light and darkness' (41:8). The righteous are able to 'con-quer in the name of the Lord of Spirits', and he 'will show this [victory] to the others' (50:2). This Lord confirms the seed of Noah, and scatters those who dwell with him (67:3). Even the Righteous One's 'chosen works depend on the Lord of Spirits' (38:2. Cf. also 40:5; 46:8). The Lord makes his Chosen One to dwell among those who deny the Lord (45:4), and will himself 'trans-form the earth and make it a blessing' (45:5).

This is not so with regard to the Son of Man in the Similitudes at all. It appears that the Son of Man is either in heaven (e.g. 70:1), or, in the eschatological future, on earth (e.g., 45:3–4 'On that day, I shall make my Chosen One dwell among them'; 52:4 as discussed above; 60:5–6).[93] In 1 Enoch 61, for example, the Lord of Spirits summons all in heaven, on the one hand, and those on the land, on the other, to praise him (cf. 61:10, 12). The 'Chosen One' is then specifically associated with those on the land (61:10). In another vision the dwelling of the Chosen One is 'beneath the wings of the Lord of Spirits' (39:7),[94] which draws on Psalmic language and the notion of God's protection and deliverance from (earthly) danger (cf. Pss. 17:8; 36:7; 61:4; 91:4 etc.).[95] Because the 'Chosen One' is explicitly identified as having been made to dwell on earth (45:4–5), the '[m]ighty kings who dwell on the earth' are able to 'witness my Chosen One' (55:4). The throne he sits on is hence probably an earthly one, much as Solomon's when he was described as sitting on the throne of YHWH in 1 Chronicles 29:23; 2 Chronicles 9:8.[96] So this Son of Man is not present and absent. On earth he will 'cause the house of

---

[93] The notion that the Son of Man is Enoch's heavenly double (cf. Olson, *Enoch*, 11–12) is a creative solution to the identification of Enoch with the Son of Man in chapter 71. However, as noted above, the majority of scholars consider this chapter a later interpolation, inconsistent with the portrayal of the Son of Man and Enoch in the rest of the Similitudes. Further, even if this 'heavenly double' notion is accepted, it is quite different from the presence and activity of the (absent) risen Lord through the Spirit one finds in Paul.

[94] Some MSS read 'the chosen' and 'their dwellings'. The text is the translation preferred in Nickelsburg and VanderKam, *1 Enoch*, 52–53. Black, Isaac and Olson allow for both meanings (Black, *Enoch*, 44; Olson, *Enoch*, 79; James H. Charlesworth, *OTP*, 1.31).

[95] Black, *Enoch*, 198; Olson, *Enoch*, 79.

[96] For these references, cf. Olson, *Enoch*, 97. Knibb notes that the 'throne on which God will sit' in the Book of the Watchers (cf. *1 En.* 18:6–9a; 24:1–3; 25:1–3), and which forms the background to the Son of Man's appearance in *1 En.* 52, is precisely the one upon which God will sit 'when he comes to visit *the earth*' (Knibb, "Structure," 56, italics mine).

his congregation to appear' (53:6); he does not do this while in heaven. Indeed, a few verses previously the point of the authority of the 'Anointed One' is that he be 'powerful and mighty *on the earth*' (52:4). Likewise, when it states that the one who was hidden (i.e., the Son of Man) 'rules over all' (62:6), the context of the affirmation appears to be stated in contrast to the earth being possessed by the kings and the mighty. Their judgment, at the hands of the earthly Son of Man, is the sign that his reign is 'over all' (cf. also 46:4–6).[97]

In sum, the Enochic Son of Man is not portrayed as active on earth while in heaven. Hence, Paul's present and active, yet absent, Lord is to be *contrasted* with the decidedly non-'theistic' expressions regarding the Son of Man. On the other hand, Paul's Lord is to be *compared* with the *repeated* Enochic picture of the presence and absence of the Lord of Spirits.

The fact that the Lord of Spirits is both absent yet present and active, while the Son of Man is either one or the other, is an important distinction that helps clarify further the nature of the worship of this intermediary. The Lord of Spirits, to whom people pray, intercede (38:6) and to whom worship is offered, is in heaven. Yet the 'worship' of the Chosen One tends to take place on the horizontal level, on earth. This would cohere with the above argument that the 'worship' of the Son of Man is of the sort offered by serfs or defeated enemies; it corresponds most directly to the acknowledgement or extolling of a victorious earthly king.

8) That Paul's language concerning the relation between the risen Lord and believers better corresponds with the pattern of language concerning the Lord of Spirits, rather than the Chosen One, is seen in the goal-orientated formulations in the Similitudes that speak of the desire for the presence of God and the ultimate eschatological aim and destiny. The eschatological destiny involves, as one would expect, praise of the Lord of Spirits, and so the climax of the second parable (chapters 45–57) crescendos with the event: 'they all fell down and worshiped the Lord of Spirits' (57:3). In speaking of the enthronement of the Chosen One, the text ends with the ultimate goal of praise to the Lord of Spirits. Indeed, it is described as an everlasting worship as 'every spirit' and 'all flesh ... glorifies and blesses your name *forever and ever*' (61:12, italics mine). The ultimate destiny implied, the goal to which the text points: the Lord is praised forever and ever. This is comparable with 69:22 where 'the spirits of the water, of the winds' etc. (69:22) find their food 'in all thanksgiving, and they give thanks and glorify and exalt the name of the Lord of Spirits forever and ever' (69:24). Further, when the wicked kings and the mighty beseech the Lord for respite from the 'angels of his punishment' (63:1), they confess what the text likely assumes is the ultimate ethical injunction and the highest moral activity: 'Now we know that we should glorify and bless the Lord of the kings' (63:4). Importantly, the portion (39:8) of Enoch,

---

[97] Cf. Black, *Enoch*, 236.

'beneath the wings of the Lord of Spirits' (39:7), is that desirable place where 'their mouths were full of blessing, and their lips praised the name of the Lord of Spirits' (39:7). The salvation of the righteous and the chosen is, finally, neatly expressed in that 'the Lord of Spirits will abide over them' (62:14).

Though the Son of Man, in 1 Enoch 39, is where Enoch desires to be, it appears that the source of delight is not directly the presence of the Chosen One. Importantly, the dwelling of the Chosen One is described as 'beneath the wings of the Lord of Spirits' (39:7). So Grabbe can state that the 'central focus of the Parables is on the eternal life of the righteous under the "wings of the Lord of Spirits" ..., praising him, with the Son of Man/Chosen One ruling among them'.[98] The response of those righteous and chosen ones under these wings is as follows: 'their mouths were full of blessing, and their lips praised the name of the Lord of Spirits' (39:7). So Enoch states that '[t]here I wished to dwell', i.e., under the Lord's wings, where they were praising the Lord's name, 'and my spirit longed for that dwelling'. He continues: 'There my portion has been from the first, for thus it has been established concerning me *in the presence of the Lord of Spirits*' (39:8, italics mine). Enoch thus proceeds in 39:9 to praise and exalt the name of the Lord of Spirits, '[a]nd for a long time, my eyes looked at that place'. So while this is the dwelling of the Chosen One, the emphasis is upon the delight of being under the Lord's wings, and the praise that is there offered to the Lord of Spirits.

The same qualification can be added to the Son of Man related eschatological destiny in 62:14. The salvation of the righteous is expressed in that 'the Lord of Spirits will abide over them' (62:14). While they also eat there 'with that son of man' (62:14), the garment of life they receive comes from the Lord of Spirits, and their 'glory will not fade in the presence of the Lord of the Spirits' (62:16). So while the Son of Man is associated with the ultimate eschatological destiny of the righteous in the Similitudes, the emphasis appears to lie with the presence of the Lord of Spirits. Of course, 62:14 could be translated so as to state that the lying down and rising up is that it is with 'that son of man'.[99] While this detail would not change the substance of the preceding argument, the VanderKam and Nickelsburg translation adopted here is to be preferred as it appears to maintain the rhythm of the text better.

In 71:16–17, after Enoch is finally identified as the Son of Man (at least in the extant copies of the Similitudes[100]), the same angel that brings him this

---

[98] Grabbe, "Parables," 391.

[99] So Olson, *Enoch*, 117; Black, *Enoch*, 60; James H. Charlesworth, *OTP*, 1.44.

[100] Nickelsburg maintains that only 70:1–2 is original to the Similitudes, with the rest added later (George W.E. Nickelsburg, "Structure," 43. Also John J. Collins, "Enoch," 221). Knibb postulates that both chapters 70 and 71 'belong to a later stage in the formation of the Book of Parables' (Knibb, "Structure," 62). Chialà has argued that only *1 En.* 70 is original, with 71 being a later addition (cf. Chialà, "Evolution," 162 n.13). Cf. also Benjamin G. Wright, "Structure," 77; Sacchi, "Camaldoli," 505. On the other hand, Kvanvig, for example, maintains that both *1 En.* 70–71 are original (Kvanvig, "Parables").

news also reassures the Son of Man that the righteous will never be separated from him (71:16). Again, the text makes clear that this 'length of days with that son of man' is 'in the name of the Lord of Spirits forever and ever' (71:17). So, though the destiny of the righteous with the Son of Man is part of the eschatological 'package deal', the text makes it clear that the reward and necessary reassurance needs to be given to the *Son of Man*, that the righteous will be with *him*, not the other way around.

As noted above, though the Son of Man is associated with the ultimate eschatological destiny of the righteous, the emphasis lies upon the presence of the Lord of Spirits. This Lord of Spirits language coheres more closely with Paul's eschatological destiny language in, for example, 1 Thessalonians 4:17–18; 5:10–11; 2 Corinthians 5:8; and Philippians 1:23, where it is Christ and his presence that is the direct hope, the destiny, the implied goal and the deepest longing.

9) Apart from those few passages that speak of the eschatological presence of the righteous with 'that son of man', there is next to nothing about the relation between the righteous and the Son of Man. Rather, the emphasis of the text is upon the relation between the wicked and the Son of Man, specifically the catalogue of future troubles promised the unrighteous through this intermediary figure's activities. However, there is the usual relational accent in the language concerning the Lord of Spirits and the righteous. For example, the Lord of Spirits is regularly portrayed as a personal being, and the centrality of relationship with this deity either implied or made explicit. So, Enoch comforts Noah that 'the Lord of Spirits knows that you are pure' (65:11). The Noahic covenant is described as '(a pledge of) faithfulness between me and them forever' (55:2). Enoch speaks his parables 'in the presence of the Lord of Spirits' (37:2). It is implied that mercy is usually sought from the Lord of Spirits (38:6). The text regularly speaks of the centrality of the 'good pleasure' of the Lord of Spirits. He also personally shows Enoch a parable (43:4), etc. Associated with this, and as shall be examined below, the way both the righteous and wicked are characterised is almost exclusively expressed in terms of their relation to the Lord of Spirits. For example, the chosen ones depend on the Lord of Spirits (40:5) etc. Obviously, in all of this it is, again, the Lord of Spirits language, not that concerning the Son of Man, which far more closely corresponds with Paul's Christ-relation language.

10) This link between the Enochic Lord of Spirits language, and Paul's Christ-relation language, is evident in the way the text links beholding the Lord and transformation. As noted above, upon beholding the place under the wings of the Lord of Spirits, Enoch blessed and praised the Lord (39:10). A few verses later, having beheld the worship of those standing in the presence of the Lord's glory (39:12), Enoch says: 'my face was changed' (39:14). Having describes the sun and moon as opposite one another 'in the presence of the Lord of Spirits', he immediately continues to state that 'they give praise and

glory' (41:7). Indeed, even Enoch, shortly to be identified as the Son of Man, upon seeing the 'Head of Days' (71:10) says 'I fell on my face, and all my flesh melted, and my spirit was transformed. And I cried out with a loud voice ... and blessed and praised and exalted ... [and they were] acceptable in the sight of that Head of Days' (71:11–12).

In contrast, such a complex of themes does not find expression in terms of the Son of Man, even in relation to 45:3. There it is the *wicked*, not the righteous, who are doing the beholding, and thus their spirits growing 'strong' implies something very different from 2 Corinthians 3:18. Further, Black, VanderKam and Nickelsburg opt to translate the text not as 'Chosen One', but rather 'chosen ones'.[101] As Olson admits, 45:3 'is corrupt' and difficult to translate.[102] So whether the Son of Man is the object of beholding is disputed. It could be a beholding of the chosen ones. The transformation described in 45:4 is executed by the Lord of Spirits and is not connected with the seeing of the 'Chosen One' (or 'chosen ones').

The witnessing of how the Chosen One 'will sit on the throne of glory' (55:4) is likewise not associated with praise or transformation, but rather with the coming judgment 'in the name of the Lord of Spirits' (cf. also 62:1). One passage does contain at least one element of the mix of themes analysed here, namely the scene when there is rejoicing, blessing and glorification upon having had the name of 'that son of man' revealed to them (69:26).[103] The worship in question, however, appears to be directed to the Lord of Spirits. In other words, the conglomeration of beholding and transformation is unique to the Lord of Spirits, a matter also shared with the risen Lord in 2 Corinthians 3·16–18.

11) Though the relation between the Lord of Spirits and the Son of Man is similar to the relation between Father and Son in Paul's letters, in important ways it is also quite different. The similarities include the Lord of Spirits naming the Son of Man (48:2), that this Son of Man was chosen and pre-destined by the Lord of Spirits (46:3), that he stands before the Lord of Spirits according to His good pleasure (49:4. Cf. also 69:29), and will be glorified by the Lord of Spirits (51:3). With all of these, parallels or at least similarities with Paul's understanding of the relation between Father and Son can be found. But the differences are multiple. The Son of Man is said to stand *before* the Lord of Spirits (e.g., 49:2 – whereas the risen Lord is portrayed usually at *God's right hand*. Cf. Rom. 8:34. He is 'seated' in Eph. 1:20; Col. 3:1). The Son of Man can judge only in so far as God reveals truth to him (60:10 but cf. Charles's translation). The Chosen One is only one among many summoned

---

[101] Black, *Enoch*, 47; Nickelsburg and VanderKam, *1 Enoch*, 59.

[102] Olson, *Enoch*, 86.

[103] This is perhaps the best evidence for Gieschen's case that the Son of Man, in the Similitudes, 'shares the Divine Name of the Ancient of Days' (cf. Gieschen, "Name," 238), but his thesis remains less than persuasive.

by God in 61:10–11. Enoch, in the Noah fragment, has to ask the Lord of Spirits to learn things – a very different picture from 2 Corinthians 12:9. Enoch, later identified as the Son of Man, worships the Lord of Spirits like the rest of God's creation, and is transformed in beholding the Lord (71:2, 10–12). An angel has to affirm to Enoch, the just identified Son of Man, that he will dwell with the righteous forever, saying that the Lord will not forsake him, that the Lord will proclaim peace to him (71:14–15). Of course, the Son-Father picture is quite different in Paul.

12) The nature of communication between the Lord of Spirits and creation is notably distinct from the way the text speaks of the Son of Man. This Lord of Spirits language corresponds with communication with Christ in Paul. To be noted are the visions of the Lord of Spirits, the 'words of the holy one', the wisdom the Lord of Spirits gives, all the things he 'reveals' and his speaking voice (cf. e.g. 37:2, 4; 43:4; 48:7; 52:5; 59:2; 61:6, 13; 67:1). The word that goes forth from 'that son of man' does so precisely 'in the presence of the Lord of Spirits' (69:29), and is part of the 'one voice', together with the Cherubin, Seraphin, all the holy ones etc. that 'bless and glorify and exalt' the 'name of the Lord of Spirits forever and ever' (cf. 61:10–11). Just as Christ is prayed to and speaks from heaven to Paul and Christ-believers, so the Lord of Spirits, in contrast to the Son of Man, is prayed to and speaks from heaven.

Of course, in 1 Enoch 65 there is the evidence of Noah's thrice repeated 'prayer' to Enoch. This passage comes at the beginning of the probable interpolation of 65:1–69:25.[104] This raises a bigger question, formulated incisively by Loren Stuckenbruck: 'When we refer to the Book of Parables, what are we ultimately talking about? ... in what sense can we reasonably speak of the whole of chps. 37–71 as the Parables?'[105] Not only is it universally agreed that there are a number of interpolations into the text,[106] it is difficult to know when they were added and by whom. The relation of the so-called 'Noahic fragments' (including Noah's prayer) to the rest of the Similitudes is 'difficult to ascertain'.[107] Because there are no extant Greek or Aramaic copies of the Similitudes, only the Ethiopic translation, one cannot adjudicate on these matters with too much certainty. But as Stuckenbruck notes:

The failure of the material to make any direct or even indirect allusions to early Christian tradition suggests at least that the original composition *as well as* the editorial insertions and relocations may be ascribed to *non-Christian Jews*. Moreover, the lack of any allusion in the book to Christian tradition, despite the frequency of its references to an eschatological, enthroned "Son of Man" who could be worshipped alongside the Lord of the Spirits ...

---

[104] Cf. n.59 above.

[105] Stuckenbruck, "Parables," 71.

[106] For example, 39:1–2a; 54:7–55:4; 64:1–69:25; some or all of chapters 70–71, etc.

[107] Nickelsburg and VanderKam, *1 Enoch*, 84 n.*a*.

suggests that the editorial activity was carried out during a relatively short time after the original composition.[108]

It is thus a sensible step to treat the text as essentially a unity, albeit remaining aware that this text is likely a (much?) later interpolation.

To return to the Noahic fragment, it should be noted that unlike 2 Corinthians 12:8–10, where Christ spoke to Paul and Paul responds with reverential and devoted embrace of his Lord's words, in 1 Enoch 65:9 Enoch responds to Noah, despite Enoch's impressive stage entrance in 65:4 as follows: '*Go, for I have asked the Lord of Spirits* about the quaking on the earth'. Furthermore, within this fragment the relation between Noah and Enoch is presupposed, based upon the blood link. He cries to his 'great-grandfather' (repeated in 65:2, 5, 9). Further, it is before the Lord of Spirits, not Enoch, that Noah is found pure, and Enoch assures him that 'the Lord of Spirits knows that you are pure and blameless' (65:11). Links to 2 Corinthians 12:8–9 should thus not be exaggerated. The general pattern emerging shows a much closer correspondence between Christ and the Lord of Spirits in this respect.

13) To be noted is the way devotion to the Lord of Spirits is characterised. The faithful *cling* or depend on the name of the Lord of Spirits (46:8), the holy ones are those who '*believe* in the name of the Lord of Spirits forever and ever' (43:4. Cf. also 61:11), they *appeal* to his glorious name (45:3). He receives *prayers* from the dwellers in heaven as well as the holy ones and righteous on earth (47:1–2), and when the Son of Man is revealed, all 'who dwell on the earth ... will glorify and bless and sing hymns to the name of the Lord of Spirits' (48:5). The righteous '*rely* on the name of the Lord of Spirits forever and ever' (61:3), and the response of heavenly beings to his voice is exaltation and glorification (61:6–7. Cf. 2 Cor. 12:9–10). In their[109] blessing, glorifying, exalting, and sanctifying of the name of the Lord of Spirits, 'they will all speak with one voice' (61:9, 11). The wicked, the mighty and kings seek to 'confess their sins in his presence' (63:1), and want to 'make confession', or 'believe',[110] in the presence of his glory (63:5). The spirits of the water, of the winds etc. all 'confess and give thanks before the Lord of Spirits, and they glorify (him) with all their might ... forever and ever' (69:24). Those who are saved are saved in the name of the Lord of Spirits, and all the deeds of this 'age of unrighteousness' 'they have hated in the name of the Lord of Spirits' (48:7). The righteous will 'seek the light and find righteousness with the Lord of Spirits', and there will be 'peace for the righteous in the name of the Eternal Lord' (58:4). Enoch's vision of the 'Head of Days' and his angelic hosts also inspired a 'great trembling' and 'fear' in him (60:2–3). The material concerning devotion to the Son of Man, on the other hand, is slim by compari-

---

[108] Stuckenbruck, "Parables," 71. Cf. also Hannah, "Date", in which he maintains that the Noahic fragements (cf. 64:1–69:25) were interpolated early in the history of the Similitudes.

[109] 'Their' apparently refers to 'the hosts of heaven'.

[110] Olson, *Enoch*, 119; James H. Charlesworth, *OTP*, 1.44.

son. Of course, the worship offered the Lord of Spirits is described as universal (61:9, 11–13; 39:9–14), as offered by angels (40:1) *and* by the Son of Man himself (71:10–12.[111] Cf. also 61:10–11). Given the material concerning Christ-devotion in Paul, as detailed above in chapters 5–8, the overlap in this Lord of Spirits language with Paul's Christ-devotion language is most noteworthy. The devotion to the Son of Man has some parallels with Paul (cf. the 'hope' and 'dependence' noted above), but it does not compete with the overlap of themes in relation to the Lord of Spirits.

14) Noteworthy are the ways used to express the opposite of true godly devotion, and thus also how the wicked are identified. The bad people are called sinners and are defined most often as those who 'deny the name of the Lord of Spirits' (41:2). In 45:1 it is those who deny the Lord of Spirits *and* the name of the dwelling of the holy ones (in 48:10, as noted above, the 'Anointed' is also mentioned as denied, in reflection of Ps. 2. And the text immediately adds: 'Blessed be the name of the Lord of Spirits'), but again in 45:2 it is only the denial of the Lord of Spirits that is mentioned. Indeed, in the next chapter, the denial specifically of the name of the Lord of Spirits is coupled with their 'faith ... in the gods they have made with their hands' (46:7). The wicked, further, are said to not glorify, extol or obey the Lord of Spirits (46:5–6). In 60:6 the wicked are characterised as those 'who do not[112] worship the righteous <judge>', who 'deny the righteous judgment' and 'take his name in vain'. A little later they are characterised as those who 'did not make confession,[113] nor ... glorify the name of the Lord of kings'. Rather, with misplaced hope in 'the scepter of our kingdom and <throne of> our glory' (63:7), they will perish. 67:8 explains that their 'spirits are full of lust, so that their flesh will be judged, because they denied the Lord of Spirits ... and do not believe in his name' (67:8). This broad spectrum of language characterising the wicked is familiar in terms of the material outlined in chapters 5 and 6 above, which detailed the way sin against Christ and sinners were characterised in Paul.

15) It is illuminating to note how the Lord of Spirits is characterised in the Similitudes. He knows all things (63:3. Cf. also 65:11), he is the active creator (61:13; 60:8), his power is desribed as 'splendid' (63:3), and he is called the 'Lord of glory' (63:2. Cf. 1 Cor. 2:8 'crucified the Lord of glory'). He has an 'indescribable' apparel (71:10) and the text says much about the peace and mercy from the Lord of Spirits (38:6; 45:6; 50:5; 58:4; 60:5–6; 60:25; 61:13).

---

[111] With the scholarly majority, when the angel says to Enoch that 'you are that son of man', it is understood to mean the Son of Man detailed in the Similitudes. Of course, the chapter may be a later addition, but it has been argued above that it was likely added, if at all, only a short time after the composition of the 'original' (cf. p. 223 above).

[112] Though note that 'all but one ms omit the negative, which seems necessary, however' (Nickelsburg and VanderKam, *1 Enoch*, 76).

[113] Or 'believe', (Isaac in James H. Charlesworth, *OTP*, 1.44); 'give thanks' (Black, *Enoch*, 238); or 'professed belief' (Olson, *Enoch*, 119).

He is faithful (63:8), has great compassion (50:3–4), is long suffering (60:5–6, 25. Cf. also 61:13), etc. The only way the text speaks of the Son of Man, in this respect, is in two verses, one where it says his face was full of graciousness, like one of holy angels (46:1), and another where it states that the Son of Man 'has righteousness' (46:3. Cf. also 71:16). Once again the Pauline material concerning Christ is, as a pattern, the *much* closer parallel to the Lord of Spirits language.

16) Thus far it has been argued that the Christ-relation, in Paul, much more closely corresponds in numerous ways not with the Enochic 'Son of Man'-relation but with the Lord-of-Spirits-relation. Furthermore, many aspects of the data presented above concerning the Son of Man have been crucially qualified. This leads to the final point to be made in this section: *if* Paul had known the sort of Enochic traditions represented in the Similitudes – and of course we cannot be certain about this – he would appear to have associated the Enochic Son of Man not with Christ Jesus but with believers. Corresponding to the above points, he associates Christ Jesus with data relating to the Lord of Spirits. These points will now be elucidated.

Indeed, as noted above, the Son of Man material speaking of the judging of angels is reflected in Paul in terms of *Christians*, not Christ. Believers, says Paul, will judge angels (1 Cor. 6:3) – this being the only other text known to this author which speaks of the judgment of angels by a figure other than God (contrast Isa. 24:21–23; Mt. 25:41; 2 Pet. 2:4; Jude 6; *1 En.* 10:12–14; 19:1; 21:1–10).[114] In the Similitudes it is the Chosen One who judges angels, but in Paul it is believers. And as this is the only other passage like it, perhaps Paul had indeed read the Similitudes, or at least heard of the Enochic tradition. If this is so, instead of linking Christ Jesus with the Son of Man, Paul associated this intermediary figure with believers. Further, it is striking that Paul never speaks of Christ as 'Son of Man', 'Righteous One', 'Chosen One' or 'Elect One', all the names predominantly used to speak of the text's intermediary figure. Again, similar language was used by Paul in terms of *Christians*, not Christ (cf. Rom. 1:17;[115] 5:19; 8:33; 11:7; 16:13; Gal. 3:11; 1 Thess. 1:4. Cf. also Col. 3:12).

Boccaccini opines:

Paul never uses the *term* " Son of Man", yet his view of the Messiah Jesus as the *kyrios* so closely resembles the *concept* of the Messiah Son of Man of the Parables that one could look

---

[114] For these references, cf. Schnabel, *Korinther*, 308 n.31.

[115] Heliso makes a case that a christological reading of Rom. 1:17 'should be afforded more weight within Pauline scholarship than has been the case thus far' (Desta Heliso, *Pistis and the Righteous One: A Study of Romans 1:17 Against the Background of Scripture and Second Temple Jewish Literature* [Tübingen: Mohr Siebeck, 2007], 254), but his claims remain necessarily modest and cautious. Cf. also Mark A. Seifrid, *Christ, Our Righteousness: Paul's Theology of Justification* (Leicester: Apollos, 2000), 37 n.6.

at the term *kyrios* as a convenient translation and development in Hellenistic terms of the Enochic concept.[116]

Referring to 1 Thessalonians 4:16 he continues: 'At least in one passage ..., *kyrios* replaces "Son of Man" almost as if they were interchangeable terms'.[117] However, apart from Boccaccini's problematic focus on Wisdom categories, and his misrepresentation of Paul's Christology as one which, he argues, depicts a stage lower than that found in the Johannine *logos*,[118] he fails to grasp the vast differences between Paul's Christ and the Enochic Son of Man. Paul's Christ-relation language, it has been argued here, has more in common with the Lord of Spirits language in the Similitudes. It is thus arguably significant that Paul does *not* speak of the Son of Man in 1 Thessalonians 4:16.

It should consequently come as no surprise that Paul could speak of Christ crucified as the 'Lord of glory' (1 Cor. 2:8), just as the author of the Similitudes spoke of the Lord of Spirits (40:3. Cf. also 40:4–7, 10; 41:7). The title is also found in the Book of the Watchers (*1 En.* 22:14; 25:3; 27:3, 5). The Book of Watchers was perhaps known in the Jerusalem community (cf. Jude 14–15), at least this is so if, as Bauckham argues, Jude is not understood as a pseudepigraphal text but was penned by Jude, the brother of Jesus, who was a member of the Jerusalem community.[119] If James was likewise not pseudepigraphal and was penned by James the leader of this community,[120] it is perhaps significant that he spoke of faith in τοῦ κυρίου ἡμῶν Ἰησοῦ Χριστοῦ τῆς δόξης (Jas. 2:1). Is this evidence of a reading of the Enochic traditions in the Jerusalem church such that their own Christology was protected from the Enochic Son of Man "Christology" because the latter was too 'low', because it did not express the full extent of their developing understanding of the Christ-relation? Acts 7:56 portrays the important last words of the first Christian martyr:[121] he sees the 'the heavens opened and the Son of Man standing at the right hand of God'. Though not wanting to change this testimony so as to protect readers from potential misunderstandings, i.e., a reading of the significance of Christ in terms of the christologically inadequate

---

[116] Gabriele Boccaccini, "Finding a Place for the Parables of Enoch Within Second Temple Jewish Literature," in *EMSM*, ed. Gabriele Boccaccini (Cambridge: Eerdmans, 2007), 278.

[117] Ibid., 279.

[118] Cf. Boccaccini, "Finding," 278–83. Note the powerful critique of Boccaccini's proposals in Matthias Henze, "The Parables of Enoch in Second Temple Literature: A Response to Gabriele Boccaccini," in *EMSM*, ed. Gabriele Boccaccini (Cambridge: Eerdmans, 2007), 290–98.

[119] Richard J. Bauckham, *Jude, 2 Peter* (Waco: Word, 1983), 14–17; Bauckham, "Jerusalem," 86; Richard J. Bauckham, *Jude and the Relatives of Jesus in the Early Church* (Edinburgh: T&T Clark, 1990), 171–78.

[120] Cf. Richard J. Bauckham, *James: Wisdom of James, Disciple of Jesus the Sage* (London: Routledge, 1999), 11–25.

[121] On the christological importance of the last words of a martyr, cf. Richard J. Bauckham, "The Worship of Jesus," in *ABD Vol 3.* (London: Doubleday, 1992), 817.

Enochic traditions, Luke, with this danger in mind, perhaps deliberately speaks of *Stephen*, not of Christ, with the language with which the Similitudes spoke of the Son of Man (cf. Stephen's face 'like the face of an angel' in Acts 6:15 and the Chosen One's face 'like one of the holy angels' in *1 En.* 46:1). Indeed, perhaps here is at least one reason why the title 'Son of Man' was abandoned by early Christianity by the end of the first century, even though it was arguably Jesus' preferred self-designation.[122] The Enochic Son of Man implied an understanding of Christ that was too 'low'.

To return to the significance of the Similitudes' title for the deity as 'Lord of glory', perhaps Paul, speaking of Christ in a way not found anywhere as extensively as in 1 Enoch,[123] is developing a subversive reading of the Enochic literature that places Christ on a par with the Lord of Spirits, not the Son of Man. Given that the language of judging angels as well as the 'Lord of glory' is found most clearly only in Paul *and* the Similitudes, or at least in 1 Enoch 1–71, it is suggestive that Paul may have known the Similitudes and read the text such that the Lord of Spirits material was related to Christ and the Son of Man material was related to Christ-believers.[124]

This would thus speak against Gieschen's claim that the Son of Man, in the Similitudes, is presented as divine (in Bauckham's sense – Gieschen footnotes Bauckham[125]) because he is worshipped, sits on the divine throne and because of 'the name' of the Son of Man (cf. *1 En.* 69:26). Further, there are reasons to doubt Bauckham's proposals here, as noted above. To speak of the Son of Man as being identified with the Lord of Spirits in this text is arguably to apply a logical wringer to the text that forces it out of its natural shape. The text does not identify the Lord of Spirits and the Son of Man at all, and the text keeps them quite distinct in a number of ways as the points above show. The divine throne the Son of Man sits on is probably to be related to Solomon's divine throne, and the worship is likewise that offered the victorious military king by the defeated. Further, Gieschen's thesis that the name of the Son of Man is indeed the divine name remains to be proved. Sacchi also feels a discrepancy between assertion and solid proof in Gieschen's thesis when he writes, in response to the Gieschen paper noted above: 'I am not yet certain that Gieschen has truly demonstrated his hypothesis'.[126]

In light of the above 16 points, the following can be maintained. The Christ-relation in Paul *compares* with the Lord-of-Spirits relation, and, at the

---

[122] Cf. the short but salient discussion in Chialà, "Evolution," 178.

[123] Cf. Thiselton, *Corinthians*, 246.

[124] Smith argues that the Similitudes were part of a Jewish mystical tradition which Paul sought to correct in Colossians. Interestingly, Smith's study maintains that Paul corrected the Colossian heresy/philosophy with an emphasis specifically on *Christology* (Ian K. Smith, *Heavenly Perspective: A Study of the Apostle Paul's Response to a Jewish Mystical Movement at Colossae* [London: T&T Clark, 2006]).

[125] Gieschen, "Name," 249 n.38.

[126] Sacchi, "Camaldoli," 508.

same time, *contrasts* on most occasions with data concerning the Son of Man, in terms of all the following themes:

– the amount of the language (and this is true even if *1 En.* 1–36 is not added to the equation)
– presence and activity, yet absence
– goal and motivation language
– beholding and transformation
– communication language
– devotion
– the identification of the wicked in contrast to devotion
– the characterisation of both the Lord of Spirits and Christ.

Furthermore, it must be noted that unlike the relation between the Lord of Spirits and the righteous, there is very little, in the Similitudes, about the relation between the Son of Man and the righteous. Again, Paul's Christ-relation compares with the Lord-of-Spirits-relation, while it contrasts with the Son of Man data. A number of additional points amplify this argument:

– The supposed Son-of-Man-relation in the Similitudes is not an experienced reality, unlike Paul's Christ-relation. It is an eschatological vision about what will happen.
– The Son-of-Man-relation does not constitute a pattern of data.
– Taken together, these two points suggest that one should not really speak of a Son-of-Man-relation at all.
– The dating of the Similitudes, and thus its relevance for Paul, is disputed and the various proposals involve a good deal more sheer speculation than some scholarly rhetoric would imply.
– One cannot even be dogmatic that the text is (non-Christian) Jewish.
– The Son of Man is worshipped in the Similitudes, yet arguably these scenes do not portray the worship of the Son of Man in the way only God should be worshipped. Furthermore, overlap here with Paul's Christ is in any case minimal, for the simple reason that Paul does not employ such explicit worship language of Christ.
– Despite some similarities, the relation between the Lord of Spirits and the Son of Man is, in important ways, quite different from the relation between Father and Son in Paul's letters.
– Because Paul calls Christ the Lord of glory (not Son of Man), there is a direct link between Christ and the Lord of Spirits. However, when using language similar to that concerning the Son of Man in the Similitudes, Paul tended to relate it not to Christ but to believers in Christ, to Christians. If Paul did know of Enochic traditions, perhaps, in this way, he deliberately distanced Christ from the Son of Man, aligning him rather with the Lord of Spirits.

So much for this talk of an 'exception which proves the rule'. Even here, in the heart of the most problematic of all texts for not just Bauckham's divine-Christology, Paul's Christ-relation corresponds far more closely with the Lord-of-Spirits-relation than the 'Son of Man'-relation, despite the occasional overlap between Paul's Christ and the Enochic Son of Man. The case cannot, however, be made with quite the same force as in the thought experiment concerning Sirach and the *Life of Adam and Eve*, simply because the title 'Anointed One' (messiah) is given the Son of Man in 48:10, and there is also undeniable overlap with some Christ-relation themes. But it can still be assumed with confidence that, had Paul read the Similitudes closely, he would have located his understanding of the Christ-relation in the Enochic Lord of Spirits language, in both its general shape as well as in many details.

5. The view from here

The above conclusions are of significance and arguably shed a good deal of light on the many claims concerning the worship of intermediary figures, and the supposed relationship of this sort of evidence with early Christian devotion to Christ. As an example of a work that attempts just such a comparison, it will prove illuminating to examine Horbury's learned argument as detailed in *Jewish Messianism and the Cult of Christ*.[127]

He first argues for the prevalence of messianism in the Second Temple period.[128] Then, citing evidence from, for example, Psalms 8:3; 45; 72; 1 Chronicles 29:20; Daniel 2:46; Sirach 50, 1 Maccabees 3:3–9; 14:4–15; 1 Enoch 48:5; 62:9; etc. he maintains that the ruler-cult, associated with messianism, involved praise of the king. This leads to his claim that '[t]he praise and *proskynesis* envisaged in the Septuagint recall a Hellenistic royal court, and offer antecedents to the Christian praises and worship of Christ'.[129] Of course, the only time *proskynesis* is used in Paul is in 1 Corinthians 14:25, where it is directed to God – never to Christ, but let us press ahead with his argument. New Testament depictions of Christ, he maintains, 'belong within a continuum of messianic praise stretching from the LXX to the rabbinic literature'.[130] So, he argues, for example in relation to Ps. 72:17, that 'here the "blessing" of the king's name is of note as a partial antecedent to the Christian practice of "calling on the name" of Christ', citing 1 Corinthians 1:2 as just such a case.[131] Again, he thinks the 'universal obeisance and praise imagined in Phil. 2. 10–11, with concluding emphasis on the venerated royal name of Jesus and the titles of sovereignty "Christ" (messiah) and "Lord"' recalls

---

[127] Horbury, *Messianism*. Horbury's case has already been engaged above.
[128] This has not convinced everyone, but that is beside the point for this argument.
[129] Horbury, *Messianism*, 132.
[130] Ibid., 140.
[131] Ibid., 132.

'Jewish royal public appearances of this era', citing especially 1 Enoch 46:1 in this context.[132]

This argument is then strengthened with reference to the christological titles in the New Testament. Given that the titles evidence, Horbury argues, strong messianic overtones, it is all the more plausible to understand the devotion offered to Christ in Paul as reflecting devotion found in the ruler-cult (associated with Jewish messianism). This further explains how Christ-devotion could develop within Jewish soil. So in terms of Paul he notes Romans 15:7–12 'where the messiah specifically is envisaged as receiving homage'.[133] He concludes, citing 2 Corinthians 4:4–5 and Philippians 2:5–11, that 'it is envisaged that Christ rules and receives homage and acclamation precisely as messiah'.[134] He summarises:

> The principal New Testament titles of Christ, therefore, themselves suggest that messianism was an important factor in the rise of the cult of Christ. Those reviewed are all likely to have been connected with messianism as well as the cults of the gentile rulers. *They indicate that Christ was accorded obedience, worship and acclamation precisely in his capacity as messianic king.*[135]

In light of the present study, and the material presented above, this reasoning is arguably quite misleading. While messianism may have constituted an impulse towards the worship of Christ,[136] that is the most that can be said. As seen above, the pattern of Christ-relation language in Paul's letters, into which Christ-devotion fits, much better corresponds with the relation between Israel/individual Israelites on the one hand, and YHWH on the other – even in those texts often considered problematic for the likes of Fee, Bauckham, Hurtado etc., and which Horbury regularly cites in favour of his thesis.

Arguably, Horbury has misconceived the actual nature and pattern of Christ-devotion in Paul, and so seeks the explanatory light of the flickering candle offered by the praise of Jewish royalty. The irony is that his candle flame, to loosely continue the analogy, actually casts a shadow against the background of the large blazing fire of the God-relation, which is the real source of light which illuminates Paul's Christ-devotion. While the christological titles, in Paul, may well have strong messianic overtones, and this author is inclined to agree, they are used within a discourse which conceives of the Christ-relation as Jews conceived of the God-relation, a wider discourse that can only be neglected at the cost of misunderstanding Paul. It is because Horbury has not attended to the depth and interconnectedness of the material within Paul himself that he has failed to see how inadequate his own

---

[132] Ibid., 134.
[133] Ibid., 143.
[134] Ibid., 144.
[135] Ibid., 150, italics mine.
[136] Cf. Horbury, *Messianism*, 150.

evidence is to explain devotion to Christ in Paul.[137] In attempting to justify his own argument by analysing what happens 'if the early Christian material itself were made the starting-point', he merely examines christological-titles and does not locate them in the wider contexts Paul's letters offer (as discussed in the previous four chapters).[138] The relation between the risen Lord and believers, in Paul, is, as a pattern, one that can only be compared to the relation between Israel/individual Israelites and YHWH. And it is precisely this Jewish evidence that Horbury has missed in his attempt to understand the Jewish background of Christ-devotion in Paul.

6. The unique divine identity

The above discussion also leads the argument to return to a final matter, initially raised in chapter 4. It was there suggested, in discussing 'monotheism', that God is indeed understood as transcendently unique in Second Temple Judaism, but that the way the texts maintain this uniqueness is through a God-relation pattern of data, one which includes cultic worship but cannot be reduced to that. This chapter has arguably verified this proposal. In the texts analysed above, Bauckham's understanding of what he calls 'YHWH's transcendent uniqueness' is one found in the texts – YHWH is indeed put consistently in 'a class of his own', something seen precisely through an analysis of the God-relation pattern.[139] Aspects of this language may well be (very) occasionally shared with other figures (like the few verses which speak of the 'worship' of Adam), but that is all. Hence the way in which the texts maintain the 'unique divine identity' are not as systematically predictable as Bauckham imagines, as noted above in relation to Chester's critique of Bauckham. Of course, Chester makes this same mistake by claiming that 'it is precisely right to insist on the point that this command to worship Adam [in the *Life of Adam and Eve*] should, unless some convincing explanation can be found, potentially raise very serious problems for Jewish monotheism'.[140] But to claim this raises '*very* serious problems for Jewish monotheism' is to be spell-bound by an external set of categories rather than an inductive study of the text itself, which, in its own way arguably portrays its God as transcendently unique through a unique *pattern* of God-relation data.

Of course, it could be argued that the Son of Man in the Similitudes *is* divine,[141] and that is why there is the thematic overlap that there is with Paul's

---

[137] This is arguably an error perpetuated by Chester, despite his helpful analysis, in his expressed methodological desire to *not* 'set Pauline Christology as the central point' (Chester, *Messiah*, 329).

[138] Cf. Horbury, *Messianism*, 140.

[139] Bauckham, "Monotheism," 210–11.

[140] Chester, *Messiah*, 115.

[141] Cf. esp. Gieschen, "Name".

Christ. So the Son of Man is worshipped, has YHWH texts applied to him, is probably to be understood as pre-existent etc. However, this proposal is problematic in light of the various arguments above. The Son of Man data does not constitute a pattern, nor does it reflect an existential reality, a 'theistic' experience. Further, the one deity in the Similitudes, in the context of the unique God-relation language, is identified via the employment of certain distinguishing titles not shared with the Son of Man (only God is called 'Lord of Spirits', 'Most High', 'Lord of glory' etc.). Taking both together (the unique pattern of relational language in terms of the Lord of Spirits, and the non-sharing of titles), it can be asserted that the text has itself preserved the transcendent uniqueness of YHWH even if it violated Bauckham's rules. Hence the Chosen One is only one of many summoned by the Lord of Spirits to bless, glorify, exalt and praise the Lord of Spirits (61:10–11). In Paul, on the other hand, there is not only a sharing of an important title with the YHWH of the *Shema* (κύριος), but also the pattern of relational data concerning the Lord of Spirits is largely shared by the risen Lord. Indeed, the text maintains the transcendent uniqueness of the Lord of Spirits in a remarkably similar manner to the way Paul speaks of the relation between the risen Lord and believers. The same could be said about the *Life of Adam and Eve* and Sirach 44–50. This data leads inexorably to an obvious christological conclusion, to be detailed in the next chapter.

7. Conclusion

Remembering Paul's pattern of language concerning the Christ-relation, one finds an astonishingly similar pattern of data in the *Life of Adam and Eve*, Sirach 44–50 and in the Similitudes of Enoch. It is not the relation concerning the intermediary or 'historical' figures detailed in these texts that are of much significance. Rather, and repeatedly, the texts portray the unique divine identity through a pattern of God-relation data, and it is this pattern that most closely corresponds with Paul's Christ-relation language. Indeed, especially in the *Life of Adam and Eve* and Sirach 44–50, it is scholarship, lit only by the inappropriate flame of Horbury's candle, that has diverted attention, in terms of Paul's Christ-relation, to those scraps of largely irrelevant texts that detail the 'worship' of figures other than God.

Chapter 10

Paul's Christ-relation and the divine-Christology debate

1. Introduction

The argument of this thesis is ultimately concerned with the Pauline divine-Christology debate. In other words, it does not claim to develop proposals about Paul's Christology generally,[1] nor does it seek to analyse the development of Christology across New Testament witnesses or the early church. Indeed, rather than understand a focused analysis on Paul's Christology as a weakness,[2] it is maintained here that Paul's letters should remain the focus because his evidence has arguably not been recognised for what it is. As noted earlier, Adolf Schlatter has contended that 'the hardest thing to observe is often right in front of our eyes',[3] and so this study has attempted to attend to Paul's own complex of language with more earnestness before seizing upon, for example, the supposed significance of the worship of Adam in the *Life of Adam and Eve*. Seeking comparisons in Second Temple literature with only an impoverished grasp of the actual nature of Paul's Christ-relation, has led many an argument down the wrong track. In the following it will be necessary to seek to assess how this thesis concerning the Christ-relation speaks to the Pauline divine-Christology debate. Then, from this perspective, it will be possible to re-engage the common arguments used against a Pauline divine-Christology.

2. The Pauline Christ-relation is a divine-Christology

Four points will lead to the conclusion that Paul's Christ-relation should mean the affirmation of a Pauline divine-Christology.

First, there is, despite differences, a unique and significant overlap, in content and in shape, between Jewish God-relation language, and Paul's Christ-relation language. As one would expect, this theocentric relational pattern is also represented in *Paul's* God-language. This is not, of course, to say that the Christ and God relations in Paul are exactly the same. Some differences between specific elements of the Christ-relation and the God-relation in Paul

---

[1] As has recently been attempted in Fee, *Christology*.
[2] Contra Chester, *Messiah*, 329.
[3] Cited in Schreiner, *Paul*, 16.

can be isolated. However, basically the same pattern of language is used, and certainly the God- and Christ- relations evidence the same shape and cover the same themes (i.e. both concern and similarly express Paul's goals and motivations, a wide variety of devotion language, the devotion's passionate nature, that which Paul contrasted with this devotion, belief in the presence and activity of God/Christ, communications between God/Christ and believers, the characterisation of God/Christ etc.).

The differences between the Christ- and God- relations in Paul's language are evident:

– In the way God is characterised: there is more emphasis on God's righteousness/justice (Rom. 1:17 [assuming a subjective or possessive genitive reading]; 3:5, 21 etc.). The most that could be said of Christ is that he is God's righteousness (1 Cor. 1:30. But cf. Rom. 8:10). Also, Paul speaks only of God's, not Christ's, immortality (Rom. 1:22), severity (Rom. 11:22) and kindness (χρηστότης – e.g. Rom. 2:4; 11:22. However, Paul also speaks of believers with this language, not just God). Of course, only God is called 'Father', with believers therefore only being God's children (e.g. Rom. 8:14–15; 2 Cor. 6:18). Paul speaks only of God with the rhetorical question 'who has been his counsellor' (e.g. Rom. 11:34), and only God is called 'wise' (Rom. 16:27) and Almighty (2 Cor. 6:18). When Paul speaks of divine knowledge, it is only God who is the subject of the verb 'to know' (e.g. 2 Cor. 11:11; 12:2–3).[4] Only God is called 'living and true' (1 Thess. 1:9) and Paul speaks only of God's ὀργή (e.g. Rom. 1:18; 1 Thess. 2:16).
– In the communications: Paul thanks God a lot, but never Christ (cf. the beginning of almost all of his letters, e.g. Rom. 1:8; 1 Cor. 1:4; Phil. 1:3 but also Rom. 6:17; 14:6; 1 Cor. 1:14; 15:57; 2 Cor. 8:16; 1 Thess. 3:9; Philem. 4 etc.). The text can mention the 'oracles of God' (Rom. 3:2), but never oracles of Christ. Scripture citations (e.g. Rom. 9:25–26) are recognised as the word of *God*, and reflect the speech of God more directly than that of Christ. Only God reveals (ἀποκαλύπτω) (cf. Rom. 1:17f; 8:18; 1 Cor. 2:10; 3:13; 14:30; Gal. 1:16; 3:23; Phil. 3:15).
– In the God-devotion complex of language there is more stress on accountability before God, and only God is 'sought' (Rom. 3:11). Also unique to the God-relation: believers bear fruit to God (Rom. 7:4), and of God Paul can say that 'from him and through him and to him are all things' (followed by a statement of praise – Rom. 11:36). There is more about glorifying God in Paul (e.g. 1 Cor. 6:20) and those who speak in a tongue speak to God, not Christ (1 Cor. 14:2, 28). The adjective εὐλογητός is only used in relation to God (e.g. Rom. 9:5; 2 Cor. 1:3; 11:31), and people are reconciled to God (καταλλάσσω – e.g. 2 Cor. 5:18–20), not Christ. As seen above, Paul can

---

[4] Of course, this may be disputed in light of 1 Cor. 3:20, but arguably the 'Lord' there is God the Father.

speak of the glory of Christ, and of doing the collection for 'the glory of the Lord himself'. However, there is more of an emphasis on glorifying God in his letters (cf. Rom. 1:21; 4:20: 15:6, 9; 16:27; 1 Cor. 6:20; 10:31; 2 Cor. 4:15: 10:13; Gal. 1:5, 24; Phil. 4:20).

– There is some language, also unique to the God-relation, which is used to express that which is opposite to true devotion to God: blasphemy (Rom 2:24. But note that this verb can also be used about negative attitudes toward Paul and his team); only God is rejected (ἀθετέω) by unbelievers (1 Thess. 4:8); and it is only mentioned that one's mind can be hostile against God (e.g. Rom. 8.7).

– When the text describes God's presence and activity there is also some language unique to the God-relation: God 'gave them up' (Rom. 1:26 etc.); he imprisons all in disobedience (Rom. 11:32) and God predestines (e.g. Rom. 8:30; 9:23; Gal. 1:15). Christians are the temple of God, not Christ (1 Cor. 3:16–17; 2 Cor. 6:16). God alone 'calls', though believers can be called 'in Christ' (1 Cor. 7:22) and in 'the grace of Christ' (Gal. 1:6). But the one 'calling' is more directly God, and the divine passive is often used to express this (cf. 1 Cor. 7:15, 17, 20). Likewise, only God is said to have chosen or elected (Rom. 9:11; 11:5, 7, 28; 1 Thess. 1:4).

– The divine goals are also expressed in a unique way in relation to God, especially in Romans. The unity of Jew and Gentile as the people of God has the goal that all may 'glorify God' (Rom. 15:6, 7, 9 – but note a potential reading of Rom. 15:9–12 also puts Christ into this dynamic). In 1 Corinthians the goal is uniquely God's that he may be 'all in all' (1 Cor. 15:28). Thanksgiving is to the glory of God (2 Cor. 4:15), and on another occasion, thanksgiving to God is itself the desired goal (2 Cor. 9:11). In Philippians, while at the eschatological climax of all things it is Christ who will be confessed as Lord, this is still to the glory of God (Phil. 2:11. Cf. also 1:11)

– Finally, one must mention the well-documented subordination language, detailed in chapter 2 above. Associated with this, one can point to numerous other logical conclusions: Only God shines into our hearts the knowledge of the glory of God in the face of Christ (2 Cor. 4:6), only God raises Jesus from the dead, etc.[5]

But that said, the similarities are more considerable, both in detail and shape. Rather than list all relevant references, reference will be made to key discussions in earlier chapters.

– God is characterised in these ways: faithfulness (Rom. 3:3; 1 Cor. 1:9; 10:13; 2 Cor. 1:18), love (Rom. 1:7; 5:5, 8; 8:37–39; 2 Cor. 9:7; 13:11, 13), grace (Rom. 1:7; 5:2, 15; 2 Cor. 6:1; Gal. 2:21 – cf. below for more references in relation to the way 'grace' language indicates God's presence and

---

[5] For an analysis of the differences in God and Christ language, specifically as it relates to the question of worship, cf. the masterful contribution of Dunn, *Worship?*.

activity), (Rom. 1:9; 8:27; 2 Cor. 4:2; 1 Thess. 2:5, 10), judgment of sin (Rom. 1:18; 2:2, 5; 5:9; 9:22, 28; 1 Cor. 5:13; 10:5), forbearance and patience (Rom. 2:4), glory (Rom. 1:22; 3:23; 9:23), peace (Rom. 1:7. Cf. below for more references that relate this peace to God's presence in the church), mercy (Rom. 9:16, 23; 11:32; 2 Cor. 1:3; 4:1; Phil. 2:27), welcoming of sinners (Rom. 14:3. Christ), truth (Rom. 3:4, 7), oneness (Rom. 3:39; 1 Cor. 8:6; Gal. 3:20), and impartiality (Rom. 2:11; Gal. 2:6).

– Christ is likewise characterised in exactly the same ways: faithfulness, love, grace, as witnessing Paul's mission (2 Cor. 8:21), Christ's forbearance and patience (2 Cor. 10:1), glory, peace, mercy, welcoming of sinners (Rom. 15:7), truth (2 Cor. 11:10), oneness (1 Cor. 8:6), and impartiality (Rom. 10:12). For more, cf. the section starting on p. 170 above.

– God-devotion is expressed as follows: it is expected (or expressed as desirable) that people serve, are slaves of and belong to God (Rom. 1:9; 6:22; 1 Cor. 3:9). They boast in God (Rom. 2:17; 5:11; 1 Thess. 1:9), know God (Rom. 1:19, 28; 1 Cor. 15:34; 2 Cor. 2:14; 10:6; Gal. 4:8; 1 Thess. 4:5), love God (8:28; 1 Cor. 8:2), fear God (Rom. 3:18; 2 Cor. 7:1), hope in God (Rom. 4:18; 8:20), pray to God (Rom. 1:9–10; 10:1; 15:30; 2 Cor. 13:7; Phil 1:3–4; 1 Thess. 3:10–13; Philem. 4–6), believe in God (Rom. 4:17, 20–22, 24; Gal. 3:6; 1 Thess. 1:8), believers have turned to God (1 Thess. 1:9); 'live' or are 'alive to' God (Rom. 6:11; Gal. 2:19), they please God (Rom. 8:8; Phil 4:18; 1 Thess. 2:4, 15; 4:1), present themselves to God (Rom. 6:13, 16; 12:1), praise God (Rom. 14:11), and are eschatologically accountable before God (Rom. 14:12) etc.

– Christ-devotion is likewise expressed with exactly the same language: service and slavery (Rom. 1:1; 7:4), boasting, knowing Christ, loving Christ, fearing Christ, hoping in Christ, prayer to the risen Lord, believing in Christ, turning to the Lord, living or being alive to Christ (Rom. 14:8), and pleasing Christ. Believers present themselves to Christ (2 Cor. 11:2), praise him (Rom. 15:11), and are eschatologically accountable before him. For more, cf. the section starting on p. 113 above.

– This God-devotion language is often contrasted with negatives, as a way of identifying the wicked: they do not know God (Rom. 1:21, 28), do not please God (Rom. 8:8), nor fear God (Rom. 3:18). They practise idolatry instead of turning to God (Rom. 1:25) etc.

– In terms of the considerable overlap of Christ-relation language with this, cf. the both section starting on p. 133 above, and that concerning Paul's varied Christ-devotion language (where it is expressed in terms of 'fearing', 'pleasing' and 'knowing' Christ, and by turning from idols). But coming to know Christ is the key turning point in Paul's life, before which, in retrospect, all things seem rubbish.[6] This new life orientation is a new kind of 'knowing' of Christ (cf. 2 Cor. 5:16). Likewise, Paul laments that many seek only their own interests and not, in contrast, those of Christ (Phil. 2:21).

– God-devotion language is expressed in a way that shows it was energetic and passionate devotion. So Paul speaks of serving God in his spirit (Rom. 1:9), that tongues, which is a language spoken to God (1 Cor. 14:2, 28), is something Paul practises 'more than all of' the Corinthians (1 Cor. 14:18). Likewise, Paul regularly speaks of his constant, day and night praying to God (Phil. 1:4; 1 Thess. 1:2–3; 2:13; 3:10–13).

– For the considerable overlap of related Christ-relation language, cf. the section starting on p. 130 above. Interestingly, serving the Lord is spoken of in terms of a 'boiling over' in the spirit (Rom. 12:11).

– Paul speaks of the presence and activity of God: God is active (Rom. 4:17; 8:9; 9:16; 11:23; 13:1–2; 1 Cor. 1:29; 2:12) in Paul's mission (Rom. 14:20; 1 Cor. 2:4; 3:6; 2 Cor. 2:17; 3:4–6; 4:7; 6:7; 12:19; 13:4; 1 Thess. 3:11–13), in the church (1 Cor. 3:16; 7:24; 12:18, 24, 28; 14:25; 2 Cor. 6:16; 9:8, 14; Gal. 3:5; Phil. 1:6; 2:13; 4:19), in the church's worldly situations (1 Cor. 10:13), in individuals (Rom. 9:16–18; 2 Cor. 8:16), in God's grace and peace (Rom: 12:3; 15:13, 15, 33; 16:20; 1 Cor. 1:3, 4; 14:33; 15:10; 2 Cor. 1:2, 12; 8:1–2; 2 Cor. 13:11; Gal. 1:3; Phil. 1:2, 7; 4:7, 9; 1 Thess. 5:23; Philem. 3) etc.

– In terms of the Christ-relation, there is noteworthy and extensive overlap once again. Paul describes the experience of the presence and activity of the risen Lord with similar language: in his mission, in the church, in the church's worldly situations, in individuals, in Christ's grace and peace etc. Cf. the section starting on p. 137 above.

– Paul speaks of communication between God and creatures: (Rom. 1:19; 11:2–5; Gal. 1:15–16; Phil. 3:15).

– For the overlap of the Christ-relation language, cf. the section starting on p. 165 above. To be noted is that the conversational description of the prayer to God in Romans 11:2–5, with its emphasis on God's grace, is interestingly paralleled in 2 Corinthians 12:8–9. There the prayer conversation is with Christ, and once again we find an emphasis on grace, though Christ's.

– God is strongly associated with Paul's ultimate goals, motivations and aims: (Rom. 11:36; 2 Cor. 1:20; 5:13; Phil. 1:11; 2:11; 4:20 etc.)

– For the overlap of related Christ-relation language, cf. the section starting on p. 106 above.

– Importantly, both the God- and Christ-relation language in Paul overlaps extensively in his arguments such that he can speak of various elements of

---

[6] Cf., e.g., Phil. 3:7–10, especially as expounded in Campbell, *Deliverance*, 897–911. In many ways, this passage is the crown-jewel in Campbell's apocalyptic, retrospective and christological engagement with Paul's justification language generally, but his analysis serves our argument here, too.

the above at the same time, and mix them together as part of one existential reality. In both cases the data would seem to constitute a pattern of relational data that Paul himself would have recognised as a pattern.

Hence, and as is evident in light of chapters 5–8 above, Paul speaks of the Christ-relation with the same pattern of language as the God-relation. While there are differences, as noted above, the God- and Christ- relations have the same shape, major themes and basic content. Indeed, at times the overlap is striking.

It is to be observed that even though language in the God-relation was not echoed in the Christ-relation, and vice versa, roughly the same idea was indeed often expressed, albeit with different vocabulary. For example, while Paul speaks only of God's (not Christ's) ὀργή, he does speak of Christ as ἔκδικος, as avenger (1 Thess. 4:6). While only God is the object of the verb 'to glorify' (δοξάζω), Paul still undertakes the collection 'for the glory of the Lord himself' (2 Cor. 8:19). Although only God is the subject of the verb 'to know', it is at least *implied* that Christ knows secrets when he reveals the intentions of hearts etc. at his eschatological return (e.g. 1 Cor. 4:5). Additionally, the amount of God-relation data roughly corresponds to the Christ-relation data. Romans, especially the first few chapters,[7] and 1 Thessalonians are focused more on the God-relation, while Philippians and Galatians more on the Christ-relation (the rest of the letters use about the same space to express the God- and Christ-relations).

In sum, while there are differences in the language describing Paul's God- and Christ- relation, they are strikingly similar on matters of details and, more importantly, in general shape. More generally it would be very difficult to dispute considerable and extensive overlap between Jewish God-relation language and Paul's Christ-relation.

Second, it has been argued that the pattern of God-relation data constitutes the way God was conceived as unique. Not only was a relational monotheism evident in the monotheism of the OT texts Paul alluded to at key points, it was also seen, through examination of the various specialist works, to be an accurate description of OT monotheism more generally. Not only was this relational monotheism posited in Paul, it was just such an understanding of the unique oneness of God, over against idolatry, which characterised Paul's argument in 1 Corinthians 8:1–7. It should not, therefore, be a surprise that God's transcendent uniqueness is likewise expressed relationally. Indeed, in the examination of the Similitudes of Enoch, Sirach 44–50 and the *Life of Adam and Eve*, it was seen that God's unique identity was displayed through a pat-

---

[7] Campbell offers a thesis which could explain why Romans 1–4 seems a little at odds, in this respect, with the majority of the rest of Paul's extant writings. He argues that Paul, via speech-in-character, presents the 'gospel' of the (false) Teacher in Rom. 1:18–32, and subverts it in Romans 1–4 largely in terms of its own underlying commitments. Cf. Campbell, *Deliverance*, esp. chapter 14.

tern of relational data. Only the God of these texts was related to in terms of an interrelated mixture of all of the following:

– the ultimate goals and most significant motivations
– varied descriptions of ardent devotion (which could include specific mention of the cultus), which also, when negatively contrasted, characterised the wicked
– experiences of the active and present power of God who was at the same time also in some sense absent, in heaven
– communications between creation and God
– the characterisation and nature of God and his lordship.

The way Second Temple texts conceived of the uniqueness of God, or, to use Bauckham's words, of God 'in a class of his own', was through this pattern of God-relational data which (as a pattern) only ever concerned God and never any other figure, however highly exalted. While some figures may share one or two of these identifying features (e.g., some are worshipped, some are exaltedly described as pre-existent to creation, others are described as sitting on God's throne, Melchizedek was called 'god', Metatron was called the 'little YHWH',[8] the 'heavenly' Enoch was called upon by Noah, the Son of Man was associated with ultimate goals, etc.), the complete *pattern* remains descriptive of the God-relation alone. This is why the short scene in the *Life of Adam and Eve* involving the 'worship' of Adam does not in any sense pose 'very serious problems for Jewish monotheism', as Chester argued. Even the cultic worship of God, which Hurtado has rightly drawn attention to, was only a part of this pattern (cf. p.60 above).

Third, and with point one and two in mind, the correspondence between Paul's Christ-relation and the Jewish God-relation must be expounded in 5 sub-points.

1) At various moments in the exegesis it was seen that Paul drew upon scriptural God-language to describe elements of the Christ-relation.

2) This relation between the risen Lord and believers was also seen, in 1 Corinthians 8–10, to find expression over against idolatry precisely in a context which contrasted true Jewish relational monotheism over against idolatry. In other words, Paul would appear, at points, to construct his understanding of the Christ-relation in terms of the Jewish God-relation.

3) Significantly, it was argued that Paul himself grasped the various elements of the Christ-relation as a *pattern* of data; they are elements of his letters that belong together for Paul. Hence it is from this that christological significance should be deduced, not (cultic) devotion alone. With this more appropriate Pauline pattern established, one can speak more accurately of a *Pauline* Christology.

---

[8] For Melchizedek as god, cf. 11QMelch 2:10. For Metatron, cf. *3 En.* 12:5.

4) This Pauline Christ-relation pattern reflects, in terms of its general shape, the God-relation pattern. This Christ-relation found expression in Paul's Christ-shaped goals and motivations, in the wide variety of Christ-devotion language, in the passionate nature of this devotion, in what Paul contrasted with this devotion, in the belief in the presence and activity of the risen Lord, yet also in the perception of this Lord's absence, in communications between the risen Lord and believers and in the nature and scope of Christ's lordship. That this also reflects the Jewish God-relation pattern was confidently maintained precisely in those texts which are used by many to blur the distinctions between the one God of Israel and various human or intermediary figures (*1 En.* 37–71; Sir. 44–50 and the *L.A.E.*). In terms of the Christ-relation, very little of significance was found in the way the various intermediary figures were portrayed, or in the manner that certain humans and/or heavenly beings were worshipped. It was the material in the Similitudes, Sirach 44–50 and the *Life of Adam and Eve* that spoke of *the deity* (whether called YHWH, God, the Lord of Spirits, etc.) which corresponded, with remarkable consistency, to the Pauline Christ-relation pattern.

5) This Christ-relation is also expressed using the title κύριος. As noted above, one of Fee's most important contributions to the Pauline divine-Christology debate is his argument that Paul uses the replacement name for YHWH in many texts, namely κύριος, as a christological title, in such a manner that Christ is the κύριος = *Adonai* = YHWH. As the shape of the Pauline Christ-relation is the shape of the Jewish God-relation, if Fee is right, Paul's use of the title 'Lord', itself part of this dynamic of expressing the believer's relation to Christ, perhaps helped him generate conceptual space within which he could convey the significance of the relation between the risen Lord and believers.

In other words, because of Paul's deliberate link between God-language and certain Christ-relation elements, the use of the title κύριος, the relational monotheistic context with which Paul framed his rhetoric concerning the Christ-relation, and the important overlap of the general shape and contours of the Christ-relation which reflected the Jewish God-relation pattern, it can be argued that *the way Second Temple Judaism understood God as unique, through the God-relation pattern, was used, by Paul, to express the pattern of data concerning the Christ-relation.*

Fourth, while these two points together lead to the brink of a Pauline divine-Christology, before such conclusions are drawn the arguments proffered by Boers must be engaged. Boers argues that 'Paul does not develop the meaning of Christ into a configuration of ideas at the basis of his thought – a christology – because Christ continually achieves new meaning for him in changing situations'.[9] He argues that to write a Pauline Christology is merely a 'scholarly abstraction', 'constructive products of the scholars who engage in

---

[9] Boers, *Christ*, 4. Cf. also esp. 99.

such endeavors' and are thus not 'presentations of Paul's own christology'.[10] Hence he subtitles his work 'in place of a Christology'. This would imply, then, that to speak of Paul's divine-*Christology* is likewise merely a scholarly creation.

In response it must be disputed whether Christology can *only* be a scholarly construction and not an accurate presentation of 'Paul's own christology'. In order to challenge Boers' proposals and shed light on the developing argument as a whole, it is necessary to seek to understand the nature of Paul's epistemology.

Though there is no space in this thesis to undertake an independent study of Paul's epistemology, the results of two recent works (that of Ian Scott[11] and the collection of essays in Healy and Parry ed.[12]) concerning Pauline and biblical epistemology can be deployed, albeit with the necessary caveat that the relative strengths of their cases still need to be tested more thoroughly. With that qualification in mind, it is nevertheless striking that both studies conclude that Paul's 'way of knowing' was profoundly *relational*. Indeed, the collection of essays in the Healy and Parry volume proposes that a relational epistemology is either explicit or implicit in *all* of the biblical texts they examine (Deuteronomy, the Psalms, the Prophets, Wisdom literature, Luke–Acts, the Johannine literature, and Paul's letters). Scott's emphasis on 'story' in Paul's epistemology is likewise significant because his own study notes that the grand narrative is itself one 'of humanity's *relationship* with its Creator'.[13] As such the 'knowledge of God' in the OT is 'most often a passionate devotion to Yahweh'.[14] So in Paul, 'knowledge of God' involves, at its heart, 'a harmonious relationship with the Creator'.[15]

Mary Healy develops a relational emphasis in her recent study of Pauline epistemology. Having displayed the centrality of divine revelation in Paul's epistemology, she details how, for Paul, this revelation is 'self-disclosure' and 'personal encounter'. Thus 'those who accept the Spirit's revelation do not merely acknowledge *that* Christ is Lord and Savior, but come to know him *as* Lord and Savior by entering into a relationship with him'.[16] More specifically, she presses the argument to suggest that, for Paul, *knowledge can be expressed as relationship*.[17] Knowledge is to be understood in terms of participation and faith, matters that are best described with profoundly relational

---

[10] Ibid., 6.

[11] Ian W. Scott, *Epistemology*.

[12] Ibid; Robin Parry and Mary Healy, eds, *The Bible and Epistemology: Biblical Soundings on the Knowledge of God* (Milton Keynes: Paternoster, 2007).

[13] Ian W. Scott, *Epistemology*, 155, italics mine.

[14] Ibid., 147.

[15] Ibid., 150.

[16] Healy, "Knowledge," 140.

[17] Cf. the section title in Healy, "Knowledge," 142.

language.[18] This all means that Paul's way of knowing his own Christology, and thus his way of conceptualising and structuring it, if their arguments are accepted, would have been relational.[19]

To return to Boers' main argument, it need not be disputed that to speak of Paul's Christology (and hence *divine*-Christology) is in some sense a scholarly abstraction as the texts themselves do not use such language. As Deissmann maintained, when trying to 'understand this Christ of the apostle', at the beginning of the 20th century:

> The attempt is usually made under the heading, "the Christology" of St. Paul. But it would be more accurate, because more historical, to inquire concerning the apostle's "knowledge of Christ", or "experience of Christ", or "Christ as revealed to St. Paul". Anything that tends to petrify the fellowship with Christ, which was felt as the beginning so vividly, into a doctrine about Christ, is mischievous.[20]

Much seems proper here, yet the question is not whether abstraction is inevitable or necessarily mischievous, but whether it is appropriate. As Campbell writes, when drawing a distinction between personal and cognitive orientations in reading πιστ- words, a personal meaning 'does not exclude beliefs but suggests certain beliefs appropriate to a personal relationship' (cf. also n. 30 below).[21] In other words, to claim that Paul's understanding of Christ can be called a divine-Christology, is certainly to make a deduction. Yet this deduction or translation of Paul's understanding of Christ into a different manner of discourse, with different language, need not be merely an arbitrary extrapolation that does violence to the text. Rather, by analysing the Christ-*relation* in Paul, and by noting the Apostle's relational epistemology, one can claim, in light of the above points, that to speak of Paul's divine-Christology is still to present Paul's own conceptions, and in a mode that the Apostle likely employed. This is especially so, as has been repeatedly emphasised, because the Christ-relation data, analysed in chapter 5–8 above, is such that Paul would have likely recognised it as a pattern himself. Thus it can be claimed that to understand Paul's Christ-relation as a divine-Christology is to attempt to put a finger on the pulse of Paul's deepest theological convictions and yearnings, and not to impose alien and arbitrary structures. The same cannot be said, however, of those claims that speak of Paul's understanding of the Person-as-opposed-to-work of Christ.[22] As Wrede once wrote:

> *The religion of the apostle is theological through and through: his theology is his religion.* The idea that we can find in him a cold doctrine, to be grasped by the understanding, a doctrine which soars more or less beyond the reach of mere piety, is false; and equally false is

---

[18] Cf. Healy, "Knowledge," 145–56.

[19] Of course, the focus of this thesis on the relation between the risen Lord and believers is thus rendered all the more appropriate.

[20] Deissmann, *Paul*, 124.

[21] Campbell, *Deliverance*, 621.

[22] A problem relating to Fee's study, as noted above in chapter 3.

the idea that the piety of Paul can be described without mention of those *thoughts* in which he had apprehended Christ, his death and his resurrection.[23]

This thesis confirms Wrede's basic point, at least in terms of Paul's Christology. The Pauline Christ-relation is indeed christological through and through.

The opening chapters of this thesis presented a working definition of 'divine-Christology', one which places Christ, as Bauckham writes, 'on the divine side of the line which monotheism must draw between God and creatures'.[24] It remained provisional as it is difficult to define such a matter from the start, to perceive it as something external to the debate which must then be measured up to. But the definition adopted from Bauckham served a task: to identify the borders and the nature of the inquiry of this thesis. Yet this study arguably permits further precision. A Pauline divine-Christology is the Christ-relation expressed with the unique God-relational pattern of data by which Second Temple Judaism expressed the transcendent uniqueness of God. It is divine-Christology expressed as relationship.

In conclusion, on the basis of the way God's uniqueness was conceived and expressed in the literature of Second Temple Judaism, and in light of the pattern of Paul's Christ-relation data, a Pauline divine-Christology is the obvious and appropriate deduction. Not only did Paul seem consciously to express this Christ-relation in terms of Jewish relational monotheism (whether in specific arguments such as 1 Cor. 8–10, or in the general shape of his Christ-relation throughout his letters), but his likely relational epistemology speaks against the charge that this christological deduction is an inappropriate logical wringer. *The Christ-relation is Paul's divine-Christology expressed as relationship.*

3. Revisiting arguments used to deny a Pauline divine-Christology

In light of the proposals above, it is possible to return to the most important arguments employed against a Pauline divine-Christology, to ascertain their plausibility. In particular, this will facilitate an explanation as to why Paul's God- and Christ- relations do indeed evidence differences in details, a matter either glossed over by proponents of a divine-Christology, or unduly emphasised by others. For example, Dunn makes constant recourse to terminological distinctions between factors relating to God and Christ in terms of Paul's Christology.[25]

The first argument often used against a Pauline divine-Christology is the charge that alleged divine-christological snippets in Paul, such as Romans 9:5,

---

[23] Wrede, *Paul*, 76, italics his.

[24] Bauckham, "Apocalyptic," 335.

[25] Cf. various points in Dunn, *Worship?* e.g., 27–28.

1 Corinthians 8:6, 16:22, or the supposed 'worship' of Christ, are, as evidence, to quote Casey, 'sparse'. Likewise, Dunn speaks of Paul's christological 'reserve' and of the Apostle's *occasional* unconsidered statement that could speak for a divine-Christology. Chapters 5–8 of this thesis arguably lay such charges to rest. Paul's relational Christology, the shape and form of his divine-Christology, is expressed in almost every chapter of every letter. Paul's supposed christological 'reserve' is a myth.

Second, it has been claimed that devotion to Christ in Paul does not really amount to worship proper (e.g., Dunn, Schrage, Casey). Hurtado's response to this line of reasoning, to note the importance of the pattern of data which indicates the *cultic* worship of Christ, has, as noted above, failed to convince many. Had Hurtado focused on the more appropriate and larger pattern of data, the Christ-relation, perhaps the counterarguments of Casey and others would not have been necessary. Indeed, when this more appropriate, and broader, pattern is kept in mind it arguably does not matter whether specific 'worship' vocabulary is or is not found in Paul, or whether it can be shown to be specifically cultic. It is clear in verse after verse in Paul's letters that this Christ-relation overlapped with, and adopted as a pattern, the complex of interrelated themes, goals, practices etc. found in the Jewish God-relation. And seen from this perspective, those allegedly 'sparse' pieces of evidence, examined so ably by Hurtado, are indeed to be understood as Hurtado proposes: as indicating a divine-Christology. The present thesis, however, provides more substantial foundations for Hurtado's claims, as well as a different way of asserting them.

As noted above, some argue that Christ-devotion is best understood in light of worship and devotion offered to beings other than God, such as that given to Adam in the *Life of Adam and Eve*, the ancestors in Sirach 44–50, and the Son of Man in the Similitudes of Enoch. However, in the previous chapter it was shown that as a pattern the Christ-relation far more closely corresponds with the God-relation *in those texts*, and a thought-experiment sought to make the case clear: if Paul had only read these texts as he formulated his understanding of Christ's identity, it would have been patterned after God, not the various 'intermediary figures' in these texts.[26]

Third, it is often argued that divine-christological conclusions must be tempered – or in practice denied – by Paul's clear subordination language, which puts Christ subordinate to God.[27] The Father is Christ's 'God' (cf. Rom. 15:6;

---

[26] Although this conclusion was nuanced in terms of *1 En.* 37–71.

[27] Attempts to deny the clear subordinationist import of certain passages in Paul, such as offered in Fee, *Christology*, e.g. 113, 142–43, and Kevin Giles, *Jesus and the Father: Modern Evangelicals Reinvent the Doctrine of the Trinity* (Grand Rapids: Zondervan, 2006), e.g. 112–15, smack of the excessive employment of an 'apologetic' hermeneutic, and do not result in convincing exegesis, as maintained above in critique of Fee starting on p. 39.

2 Cor. 1:3; 11:31), Christ is the mediator, it is argued, not the ultimate goal,[28] etc. In the face of such language many have sought to express Paul's Christology in functional terms, claiming that it only later develops into an ontological divine-Christology in John's Gospel.[29] However, such proposals are misleading on a number of fronts.

3a) It needs to be remembered that John's Gospel was equally explicit about Christ's subordination. So why is it so easy to ascribe a divine-Christology to John yet not to Paul? If both Paul and John have evidence for divine-Christology and subordination language, why are they treated so differently? Though the answer has much to do with the various developmental schemes, in which a divine-Christology is supposed to have come later, there is arguably another more subtle yet important reason, the elucidation of which leads to the second point:

3b) Arguably, Paul's Christology, in light of subordination (and related) language, is partly denied divine status, as Bauckham defines it, because unlike John, Paul's affirmations of divine-Christology tend not to be as unambiguous at a propositional level. John has the 'I am' sayings, John 1:1, etc., and in this way the affirmative propositions are often seen to outweigh the subordination propositions (e.g., Jn. 14:28 'the Father is greater than I'). The snippets of Pauline divine-Christology (according to previous estimates), on the other hand, do not as clearly balance out the subordination texts. A crucial step is then taken by those denying a divine-Christology: priority is given to the theological propositions associated with the subordination language (which supposedly speak of ontology), which in practice outweigh the language supportive of a divine-Christology, especially that concerning Christ-devotion. Perhaps this is done because modern scholars tend to prefer static and intellectualised propositional statements in determining a theology, over the significance of a pattern of relationally imbued language that is not quite as easily domesticated and conceptually familiar as a bare proposition.[30] This comes to explicit expression in Dunn, for example, when he states that Paul's

---

[28] Schrage, *Unterwegs*, e.g. 158.

[29] Casey, *Prophet*, 133–35, 156–59.

[30] This, and the following, contrast of propositions with that which is relational is not meant to suggest Paul is against propositions themselves, as is manifestly not the case. His letters are full of them, with 'claims that things are such and such and so not their contradictories' (Colin E. Gunton, *A Brief Theology of Revelation* [London: T&T Clark, 1995], 13). Rather, the issue is how truth propositions were treated and understood. For the language employed in this section, cf. its usage in Healy, "Knowledge"; Ian W. Scott, *Epistemology*; together with the discussion on propositions and revelation in the Gunton book noted above.

mysticism refuses 'conceptual clarity'[31] and remains 'confusing'[32] when considered in theological terms.[33]

However, the breadth and nature of the data gathered in chapter 5–8 of this thesis show that Paul's Christ-relation language must be taken seriously, even if only because there is so much of it. But it should now be added that it was such a relational grasp of theology that Paul himself would have likely better appreciated. This can be claimed on the basis not only of a projected Pauline relational epistemology, but also in light of Paul's argumentation in 1 Corinthians 8:1–7, as detailed above in chapter 5. Paul's way of knowing God and Christ, and thus his way of expressing that knowledge, was to a great extent relational. Ironically, it would seem that the way some modern scholars have dismissed a Pauline divine-Christology, by emphasising Paul's subordination propositions over the wider pattern of Christ-relation language, puts them in the same epistemological camp as the Corinthian 'knowledgeable', whom Paul himself sought to correct on this matter (if Gäckle's thesis is accepted. Cf. chapter 5). In effect, Dunn and others have thus prioritised a kind of intellectualised thinking that was arguably less theologically determinative for Paul. They have promoted the logical possibilities of certain Pauline propositions over Paul's Christ-relation at the expense of misunderstanding him.

3c) To seek to dissolve the tension in Paul's thought, at this point, in favour of one aspect, the subordination side, is to underestimate how Paul could hold such language together precisely because his epistemology and form of expression regarding Christ were profoundly relational, not barely propositional, i.e., not merely about truth propositions that needed to be logically squared 'on paper', but a 'Christology' expressed through and known in a lifestyle of interaction with and loving commitment to the risen Lord. As argued above, the form and shape of Paul's divine-Christology was his Christ-relation. Healy has maintained that, because of the relational nature of Paul's epistemology, there is space for mystery and revelation in Paul's thought as even 'in the case of a human relationship, knowing another can never exhaust the mystery of the other'.[34] As such, this way of knowing could contain within itself subordination language; it was not a Christology determined by the logical possibilities of mere propositions, but precisely because it was relational, as Healy argues, it could embrace mystery, paradox and tension. Christ was subordinate to God yet was grasped in Paul's relational pattern of language in

---

[31] Dunn, *Theology*, 410.

[32] Ibid., 409.

[33] Cf. also Johnson's claim that the 'history of early Christianity has tended to be a history primarily of theological ideas or social institutions ... the language of religious experience appears as overly subjective and elusive to serve the cause of historical reconstruction' (Johnson, *Experience*, 12–13)

[34] Healy, "Knowledge," 154.

a manner which affirms a divine-Christology. So understood, the problem may well be ours, but it was not Paul's.

Fourth, Dunn objects to Capes' argument that Paul's use of OT YHWH texts in terms of Christ must lead to a divine-Christology. The lines of reasoning should allow, Dunn appeals, for more hermeneutical subtlety on Paul's part.[35] Arguably, Dunn has made a good point, at least if Capes' contention is taken as a stand-alone argument for the divinity of Christ. It was seen, for example, that the author(s) of the Similitudes of Enoch could apply YHWH or 'God' texts to its Son of Man figure. However, once Capes' argument is seen as part of the larger pattern of data, as examined here, the hermeneutical ambiguity, to which Dunn makes appeal, is clarified by the manner of discourse in which Paul employs such YHWH texts. This discourse, or wider pattern of data, means that the material analysed by Capes does indeed speak clearly for a divine-Christology, but only if this wider pattern is kept in mind.

Fifth, Schrage, among others, has forcefully made the claim that Paul's Christ is merely mediator. He is not 'goal' as only God is.[36] It appears that he considers the subordination statements as expressive of Paul's *theological* convictions, yet 1 Thessalonians 4:17 ('so we will be with the Lord forever') only shows that Paul does not offer, in his letters, a 'closed theological system', and that his texts were contingent to the situations he addressed.[37] However, the material analysed in chapter 6 shows that Paul's understanding of Christ, in relation to his goals, motives and aims, is more complex,[38] and Christ can indeed be considered Paul's goal and aim, and precisely so at the deeply existential and relational level of Paul's experience and thinking. It would seem that Schrage also promotes a type of theological knowledge that was actually less determiniative for Paul than that found in, as he cites, 1 Thessalonians 4:17.

Sixth, in response to Bauckham it has been argued that the texts of Second Temple Jewish literature do not support the categories by which he defines the 'unique transcendence' of God. This in turn means the supposed 'divine identity' of the risen Lord, in Paul, is undermined. However, the approach of this thesis shows that the 'unique transcendence' of God is preserved in texts even when Bauckham's rules are broken. What is more, and as detailed above, the general pattern of data in those texts, by which the uniqueness of God is actually preserved, corresponds with the pattern of language in Paul describing the Christ-relation. An inductive engagement with even the so-called 'problematic' apocryphal and pseudepigraphal texts, far from undermining the

---

[35] Dunn, *Theology*, 250 n.82.

[36] Schrage, *Unterwegs*, 170–71.

[37] Ibid., cf. 182–83.

[38] This is noticed too in Thüsing, *Per Christum*, though his analysis is limited to Rom., 1 Cor., 2 Cor. and Gal., hence misses *crucial* material in Phil., nor does he engage with the wider pattern of material as attempted here.

divine-Christology thesis here developed, indeed strengthens and supports it, as maintained in the previous chapter.

Seventh, as noted above, many understand Paul's Christology in functional, not ontological, terms.[39] As shall be discussed in the appendix, while a distinction between 'function' and 'ontology' may have made more sense in the 20th century when the concept of 'function' was popular in the field of meta-mathematics, the more recent employment of relational concepts, not only in meta-mathematics but also in physics, philosophy, social science, theology and anthropology, has opened a conceptual space not only to critique the functional/ontological distinctions of the previous century, but also to reengage with the relational mode of Christology and monotheism (and even epistemology) that one finds in Paul's letters.[40] Indeed, Paul's relational Christology, the shape of his divine-Christology, raises doubts that a functional/ontological distinction can serve in understanding Paul on his own terms (as far as this is possible). As the first part of this chapter has hopefully made clear, the divine-christological implications of Paul's relational Christology pushes the matter beyond a merely functional conception of the significance of Christ for Paul, but neither is it stated especially in terms of Christ's 'being' or 'essence', as in the later church creeds – even if the creeds can be fairly posited as a faithful 'translation' of the significance of Paul's Christ-relation.

Eighth, as noted above it has regularly been argued, in one way or another, that one cannot assert a Pauline divine-Christology in Paul as this would run against the restraining factor of Paul's monotheistic convictions (Casey, Dunn, Harvey). Indeed, this thesis has accepted a 'strict' monotheism. So how, at the same time, is a divine-Christology to be maintained without contradiction? As with the subordination argument above, this case against a Pauline divine-Christology is one that Paul would not likely understand. Only if Paul's monotheism is comprehended primarily as a set of theological propositions that cannot be conceptually blurred, will one struggle to accept the significance of Christ in Paul's faith. Ironically, it was possibly precisely such an understanding of monotheism that, if Gäckle's thesis is correct, Paul wrote against in 1 Corinthians 8. Because Paul's monotheism, as well as his Christology, was expressed as relationship, at least if this thesis is correct, then Paul likely did not feel the conceptual tension which modern scholars feel in light of their more propositional and cognitive epistemological categories and priorities. Arguably, a relational epistemology allows for both a real inclusion of Christ in, to use Bauckham's language, the 'divine identity', as well as an appreciation of the mystery and conceptual difficulties implied by such an inclusion. Paul's relational epistemology 'involves', so argues Healy, 'an element of trust and of self-surrender, committing oneself even while rec-

---

[39] E.g. Casey, *Prophet*, 133–35.
[40] Cf. Shults, *Christology*, which shall be discussed in more depth in the Appendix.

ognizing that one will never be able to mentally "grasp" or exhaustively comprehend the one who is known'.[41] So Paul's divine-Christology, relationally understood, does not annul his relational monotheism. Given the answer to the question of the nature of Paul's Jewish-style faith in God in chapters 4 and 5, one should rather say that they in fact belong together.

Ninth, and finally, as detailed above, Dunn finds one argument against a divine-Christology in Paul decisive. As Paul was persecuted, Dunn argues, by Jewish-Christian believers because of his position on Torah, *not* because of his Christology, his Christology could not, therefore, have been seen as a threat to these Jewish monotheists. Ergo, Paul's monotheism did not alter in shape and was not threatened by too high a Christology. In response to this, the argument of the previous paragraph is relevant. The christological changes were arguably not simply of the conceptually focused nature Dunn presupposes. Furthermore, that Paul's divine-Christology was expressed as relationship, means that it embraced not only his thinking but also his priorities and activities, passions and purposes. This perhaps helps to explain 'why objections to the Pauline missions were concentrated on *halakhah*'.[42] Put this way it can be seen that Paul's Christology and Paul's *halakhah* are two sides of the same coin. Against Casey, who maintains that objections to Paul were either *halakhah* or Christology, perhaps one could better say that Paul's relational Christology occasionally provoked criticism of his mission at the level of *halakhah*. Either way, it takes little imagination to see how Paul's understanding of *halakhah* was profoundly shaped and expressed through his understanding of the significance of Christ. Paul's Christology, relationally understood, cannot be hermeneutically sealed off from questions of *halakhah*.

Furthermore, Hurtado has maintained, contra Dunn, that 'there is evidence pointing to, and evidence from, the decades earlier than John, indicating sharp conflicts between Jewish Christians and other devout Jews over devotion to Christ'.[43] Hengel rightly notes that:

[A] small troop of simple, Aramaic-speaking disciples of Jesus from elsewhere, without a christological kerygma and armed with only the pious wisdom sayings of the Logia source, could hardly have provoked the ambitious Jerusalem Pharisee and scribe to intervene by force.[44]

That is, it could hardly provoke the persecution of the pre-Damascus Saul himself. Hurtado maintains that it was indeed Christology, understood in terms of the devotional practices of the earliest church, that probably evoked Saul's rage. Of course, even if Hurtado is wrong on this point, Dunn's argu-

---

[41] Parry and Healy, *Epistemology*, 144.

[42] Casey, *Prophet*, 138.

[43] Hurtado, "Opposition," 36 (a slightly edited version has been reprinted in Hurtado, *Earth*, 152–78). This thesis has since been affirmed in Bauckham, "Jerusalem," 76–77.

[44] M. Hengel and Anna Maria Schwemer, *Paul Between Damascus and Antioch: The Unknown Years* (London: SCM, 1997), 85.

ment remains an 'argument from silence'. It is based on what Dunn understands to be a *lack* of evidence, while the argument of this thesis is based upon clear Pauline data.

This is problematic enough, but one can go further, even if it is concluded that on this point Dunn is right and Hurtado wrong. Within the pagan cultures of the wider Mediterranean world of Paul's missions, is it not likely that Paul's Christ-relation would have looked like, in variously different ways, the manner in which the gods were treated? In a pagan context, does not the Christ-relation effectively place Christ on the level of divinity? For example, Paul contrasts the Lord and pagan gods in 1 Corinthians 10, he models prayer to this risen Lord, he speaks of the sovereign power and presence of this Christ over contingent events, he seeks this Lord for healing, he blesses with the grace of this Lord, his whole life is shaped by his fervent devotion to this Christ etc. These pagan converts to Christ would have previously prayed to the gods, sought them for healing, understood these gods as present and active yet in some ways absent, prized devotion to their gods etc.[45] Though this question is bigger than the space this paragraph can afford it, how would Paul's Christ-relation have been understood in such a pagan context, one which knew Jews strongly contrasted their God with the pagan gods? Surely Paul would have realised that his Christ-devotion would have looked a lot like Christ was understood as a god, and Paul would quickly explain, not merely a god but the world's one true Lord in contrast to the empty pagan deities (cf. Paul's argument in 1 Cor. 8–10; Gal. 4:8). Hengel draws attention to the religious language in Arabia and Syria (the place of Paul's formative missionary years) which included inscription to 'Zeus Kyrios' and asks: 'Does this not remind us of the twofold significance of Kyrios in Paul's terminology?'.[46] Acts explicitly depicts a scene where the pagan Athenians misunderstand Paul's proclamation to concern two gods, Jesus and Anastasis (Acts 17:8).[47]

With this in mind, why, then, did Paul not seek to contradict forcefully such potential and natural misunderstandings in his (largely ex-pagan filled) churches, if he was supposed to be 'reserved' about a divine-Christology? Yet there is no evidence that he did. One could justifiably contend that this argument from silence is indeed more appropriate than Dunn's given the geographical focus of Paul's missionary travels among the Gentiles. The 'problem' of the lack of evidence in our 'argument from silence' is further compounded by the fact that so much in his letters, especially as examined in chapters 5–8 above, would have easily provoked such misunderstanding. Of course, the relationship between Paul's Christology and its reception in his mission in the pagan world deserves much more attention. But arguably the point is clear

---

[45] Cf. Hengel and Schwemer, *Damascus*, 120–26. A more complete study of this theme would examine at least Cicero's *Nat. d.*

[46] Hengel and Schwemer, *Damascus*, 121.

[47] Cf. Hengel and Schwemer, *Damascus*, 124.

enough. For all of the above reasons, Dunn's argument from silence is not a decisive reason to reject a Pauline divine-Christology, at least one as detailed in this thesis.

4. Conclusion

While the divine-christological implications of this thesis are clear, are based on a vast amount of data and are strongly supported even in so-called problem texts such as Sirach 44–50, the Similitudes of Enoch and the *Life of Adam and Eve*, the usual rationale employed against a Pauline divine-Christology all fail to convince when the Christ-relation is the focus. Indeed, arguably it would be the exegetical resolve of King Canute-ian tenacity to attempt to stand against the tidal wave of evidence,[48] as has appeared on the horizon of this thesis, and do anything other than capitulate the point: from Paul's Christ-relation one should indeed deduce a Pauline divine-Christology.

---

[48] At the risk of spoiling the attempt at wit, Canute the Great (995–1035), once monarch of England, Denmark, and Norway, is now known as the king who creatively countered the sycophancy of his courtiers. While they sought to flatter the king by speaking of the Monarch's greatness and power, Canute called his servants to place his throne on the beach. There he sat as he tried to stop the waves of the sea merely through his authoritative command. Of course, the tide did not stop and the waves lapped around Canute's feet until his throne was covered by sea. Presumably the courtiers got the point.

Chapter 11

Paul's divine-Christology

1. A summary and conclusion

At the beginning of the last century Hermann Lüdemann dictated in one of his lectures to a young Karl Barth, the following thesis: 'The Christian knows through his religious consciousness ... The religious consciousness, being an empirical fact, is the small hole [*das Löchlein*] through which we can look into the transcendent'.[1] However, in Barth's pastoral career it soon became clear that *das Löchlein* was not wide enough. And so Barth forged one of the most significant works of theological literature of the 20th century, his commentary on Paul's letter to the Romans, in which he revolted against the attempt to squeeze Christianity through *das Löchlein* of religious consciousness. Instead of a squinted 'look into the transcendent', instead of a mining of the truth of God from the believer's pious religious feelings, Barth insisted that the proper starting point should be none other than *Dominus dixit*, the Lord has spoken! For Barth, all of a sudden the window to the panorama of God's truth was flung open. 'Within the Bible', he stated in a lecture in the church of his friend Thurneysen, 'there is a strange new world, the world of God'.[2] Arguably this escapade into the world of theological history has more than just a little relevance to the present study, albeit not without certain irony. This will become clear in the following as the proposals presented in this thesis are summarised.

In chapter 2, the overview of post-1970s scholarship suggested that the various scholarly approaches can be divided according to two questions: how does Paul's Jewish-style faith in God affect our understanding of his Christology? and where, if at all, is there evidence in the Pauline corpus for (or against) a divine-Christology? The analysis of various responses to these questions suggested that Fee, Bauckham and Hurtado are the prominent names among those affirming a Pauline divine-Christology.

While various criticisms of Fee's impressive *Pauline Christology* were marshalled, both Bauckham and Hurtado have also failed to convince many. So Chester takes issue with Bauckham's theological categories by which he

---

[1] Cf. Eberhard Busch, *Karl Barth: His Life from Letter and Autobiographical Texts*, trans. John Bowden (Philadelphia: Fortress, 1976), 46.

[2] Cited in John B. Webster, *Barth* (London: Continuum, 2000), 29.

determines the unique divine identity. In relation to the arguments of Hurtado, and his responses to certain critics, it was noted how important recourse to a pattern of evidence was for his case. Casey's claim that evidence for the worship of Christ, in Paul, is extremely sparse, or Fletcher-Louis' argument that beings other than God could be worshipped in Second Temple Judaism, were countered with the claim that the evidence of Christ-devotion in Paul presents a pattern of data, specifically one of cultic and communal devotion of the sort reserved only for God. However, it appears that this pattern has left some, like Dunn, unconvinced, who would still prefer to distinguish the idea of the full worship of Christ, in Paul, from what should rather be described as Christ's veneration. In other words, one need not necessarily draw, from Hurtado's pattern of data, a divine-Christology. At this point, and on the basis of the limited evidence in the Pauline corpus for or against specifically cultic worship, one may wonder if the argument has run aground due to shallow waters, unable to support such weighty cruise liners as the divine-Christology debate.

However, this thesis has maintained that Hurtado's pattern is insufficiently Pauline. The focus on the cultic worship of Christ, while important, is itself only a part of a larger pattern of data, namely the Christ-relation, one Paul himself would have recognised as a pattern.[3] Indeed, for Paul it is mainly the transformed lives of Christ-believers that could ever count as true spiritual worship (cf. Rom. 12.1). To make this case it was necessary to engage with the first of the questions isolated in the overview of scholarship in chapter 2, namely the question of Paul's Jewish faith in God and how it could relate to his Christology. It was provisionally argued that this faith can indeed be ɔescribed as monotheistic, that it understands the one God as uniquely transcendent. Yet the way this uniqueness is maintained is not simply through Bauckham's divine-identity categories or Hurtado's cultic worship alone, but rather through a pattern of language involving the relation between Israel / individual Israelites, on the one hand, and YHWH, on the other. Not only does this cohere with the relational emphasis of various OT theologies, but also the monotheism of Paul himself, not to mention that of a key text from which he draws at important points in his 'monotheistic' arguments (such as in 1 Cor. 8–10), namely Deuteronomy and specifically the *Shema*. God's transcendent uniqueness was expressed as relationship, it was about lives lived in loving commitment to the one true God over against the idols of the world.

---

[3] If Hurtado responds that his definition of devotion involves, in addition to "religious actions", also "beliefs" (see p.56 above), we would first suggest that "beliefs" is not a focused enough term to grasp the relevant issues as a pattern in Paul, something necessary if the (at least divine-christological) significance of Paul's language is to be properly grasped. Second, and perhaps more importantly, this is a suspicion arguably confirmed, despite Hurtado's centrally important contributions, by his omissions in his publications in dealing with devotion in the Pauline communities. We suggest that our engagement with Paul's letters highlights those omissions by grasping the scope of devotion and the appropriate interpretative pattern (the Christ-relation) in a way more faithful to Paul.

The fecundity and significance of these conclusions, while to a certain degree provisional, are however seen most starkly when kept in mind in terms of the second question above, namely, 'Where, if at all, is there evidence in the Pauline corpus for (or against) a divine-Christology?' An exegesis of 1 Corinthians 8–10 maintained that in an argument framed in terms of just such a relational monotheistic commitment to God over against idols, Paul, in this context, speaks principally of the relation between believers and, not God, but the risen Lord. What is more, he expresses this Christ-relation over against idols using the sort of language Second Temple Judaism employed to describe the relation between Israel and YHWH, in contrast to idolatry.

This suggested a more detailed exploration of the Christ-relation pattern in Paul, as undertaken in chapter 6. At various points it was seen that the relation between the risen Lord and believers was explicitly expressed, as in 1 Corinthians 8–10, with the language used to describe the relation between Israel and YHWH. The general shape of this Christ-relation was seen to involve:

– Paul's ultimate goals and motivations
– his explicit Christ-devotion language
– the passionate nature of this Christ-devotion
– the language Paul contrasted with this devotion
– the presence and activity of the risen Lord
– but also the absence of Christ, and thus the Lord's presence through the Spirit
– the communications between the risen Lord and believers
– and the various ways Christ was characterised and the depiction of the scope of his lordship.

All of this, it was argued, constituted the Pauline Christ-relation as a pattern of data Paul would recognise as such.

Armed with these conclusions it was necessary to turn to a number of texts to examine whether beings other than God were related to with the same sort of pattern of language as discovered in Paul to refer to the relation between the risen Lord and believers. As a test ground three texts were chosen, the *Life of Adam and Eve*, Sirach 44–50 and the Similitudes of Enoch – passages used by detractors of Hurtado and Bauckham to assert that beings other than God could be worshipped, and that blur Bauckham's divine-identity categories. However, precisely in these texts it was seen that the Pauline Christ-relation found very little correspondence with the language concerning 'worshipped' figures other than God (whether Adam in *L.A.E*, the praised ancestors in Sir., or the Son of Man in *1 En.*). Rather, the pattern of data concerning Paul's Christ-relation was, with remarkable consistency, reflected in the *God*-relation in these texts (whether the deity be called Lord of Spirits, YHWH or God). Furthermore, it was seen that God's transcendent uniqueness in these texts was maintained precisely through this relational pattern of data, which returns one to the 'relational monotheism' proposal in terms of the first question, noted above.

This led to the conclusion that the way Second Temple Judaism understood God as unique, namely through the God-relation pattern, was used by Paul to express the Christ-relation. Further, it seems that Paul often deployed this God-relation pattern to describe the Christ-relation quite deliberately (as in 1 Cor. 8–10), and he did this not atomistically, as if he were only using such God-language in terms of Christ occasionally.

Before drawing the conclusion that Paul's Christology is therefore divine, it was noted, in dialogue with Boers, that talk of any 'Christology' is always a matter of deduction, of speaking with language the texts do not use. But it was argued, drawing on recent work in the field of Paul's epistemology, that the deduction of a divine-Christology, as suggested here, coheres with the relational nature of Paul's knowing. On this basis it was maintained that the Pauline Christ-relation is a divine-Christology expressed as relationship. In light of this way of constructing and contending for a Pauline divine-Christology, the claims of Dunn, Casey and others who deny a Pauline divine-Christology were critically examined, and it was maintained that none of the arguments hitherto employed can carry weight. For example, Casey's claim that the evidence for a divine-Christology is 'sparse', or Dunn's notion that Paul's 'christological reserve' only slipped into a high Christology occasionally, are seen to crumble under the weight of data concerning the Pauline Christ-relation, Paul's divine-Christology.

This way of dealing with the data in terms of the divine-Christology debate arguably has certain strengths. To name a few: not only does it build on undeveloped lines of thought in Fee's work, but it constructively engages with the Christ-devotion emphasis in Hurtado, and the relational notion of identity in Bauckham. Furthermore, the approach here employed helps one to synergistically integrate the various arguments affirming a divine-Christology, overviewed in chapter 2, such that they discover further conceptual clarity. Of course, this manner of approaching Paul's Christology corresponds better with the phenomenon of Paul's letters, texts written not to detail an abstract theology but rather to instruct and encourage precisely the focus of this study, the Christ-relation. In approaching the debate in this way one can also arguably take the relational intuitions of Jewish monotheism more seriously. This approach also facilitates the handling of comparisons between texts (such as Paul and *1 En.*) as well as opening up exegetical insight into passages otherwise overlooked (as in, e.g., 1 Cor. 8–10; 2 Cor. 5:6–14)

In addition, the conclusion that the Christ-relation was Paul's way of expressing a divine-Christology can function as a vital link in the exploration of chronological matters. In response to the question of how early a Pauline divine-Christology can be traced, one can now look for the elements of this

Christ-relation, itself the shape of Paul's divine-Christology. That which is sought after to make the case either for or against a divine-Christology prior to his letters is thus increased beyond the limits of an analysis of merely the Damascus Christophany. Arguably such an approach would demonstrate that Paul's divine-Christology can be shown to date to the first months of his life in Christ, at least if his memory is to be trusted. But space sadly requires that this question be examined elsewhere.

Finally, this same conclusion, that the Christ-relation was Paul's way of expressing a divine-Christology, can also facilitate engagement with important modern theological concerns, such as how the 'Christ of faith' can relate to the 'Jesus of history'. Indeed, potentially fruitful engagement with this question, and other contemporary theological proposals, is commenced in the appendix.

To return to the opening excursion into Barth's theology, it has been argued that through an analysis of Paul's vehement and richly relational Christ-language, the 'window' is flung open and it is possible to see far more clearly the panorama of Paul's divine-Christology than was ever possible through *das Löchlein* of titular studies, Fee's 'exegetical method', Bauckham's divine identity or even Hurtado's 'beliefs and related religious actions', even if they were all, to a greater or lesser extent, looking in the right direction. The slight irony, of course – though it is indeed more apparent than real – is that the *Dominus dixit* of this thesis partly consisted of the religious 'feeling' orientation and soul's piety of Barth's liberal Schleiermacherian theological heritage that he so effectively overthrew.[4] Nonetheless, through an examination of the language that expresses the relation between the risen Lord and believers, it is possible at last, to echo the words Barth preached in Thurneysen's church, to behold 'a strange new world', the world of Paul's relational Christology, the world of his *divine* Christology.

---

[4] Shults has argued that a certain type of *relationality* exercised a regulative and constructive role in Schleiermacher's entire theological project (Shults, *Anthropology*, 97–116).

Paul's Christ-relation and modern theological discourse

1. Introduction

'"Problems" in modern Christological debates', so claims Anthony Thiselton, 'sometimes seem to reveal a deep chasm between the universe of discourse in which some New Testament specialists operate and that of many systematic theologians'.[1] This Appendix aims to cross this 'ugly broad ditch' by pointing out mutually enlightening lines of communication between the two mentioned disciplines. It does this as part of an argument focused, of course, on the New Testament, but in such a way that facilitates interdisciplinary dialogue. Indeed, this would seem to be very much in line with the nature of Paul's own letters which integrate scripture exegesis, pastoral response, theological discourse, social identity construction, and so on. 'Everyone specializes. No one integrates', proclaimed Ted Peters,[2] yet if one wants to remain faithful to the integrative dynamic of the Pauline material itself, it arguably suggests exactly the sort of dialogue, the absence of which Thiselton and Peters lament.[3]

The following argument will build on the result of chapter 8 above, in which it was argued that the Christ-relation was Paul's way of expressing what modern readers can call 'divine-christological' convictions. *Paul's Christ-relation is a divine-Christology*. When understood in this way, various bridges over the 'deep chasm' noted by Thiselton suggest themselves. Specifi-

---

[1] Thiselton, *Hermeneutics*, 376.

[2] Cited in Veli-Matti Kärkkäinen, *Christology: A Global Introduction* (Grand Rapids: Baker, 2003), 216.

[3] For further justification of this and related points, cf. Markus Bockmuehl, *Seeing the Word: Refocusing New Testament Study* (Grand Rapids: Baker Academic, 2006), who cogently argues that engagement with the Bible's theological *Wirkungsgeschichte* is an historically appropriate matter (pp. 101–19). Apart from his work are the many recent proposals which seek, in one way or another, to reengage biblical studies with explicit theological concerns (cf. e.g. Joel B. Green and Max Turner, eds, *Between Two Horizons: Spanning New Testament Studies and Systematic Theology* [Grand Rapids: Eerdmans, 2000]; N.T. Wright, *The New Testament and the People of God*, Christian Origins and the Question of God: Part I. [London: SPCK, 1992]; C. Marvin Pate, et al., *The Story of Israel: A Biblical Theology* [Leicester: Apollos, 2004]; etc. For a useful summary of these and other approaches, cf. James K. Mead, *Biblical Theology: Issues, Methods, and Themes* [London: Westminster John Knox Press, 2007]).

cally, the following arguments will attempt to shed light on the relationship between the 'Jesus of history' and the 'Christ of faith', they will critique a variety of arguably unhelpful distinctions imported into both systematic theological[4] and biblical study discourses, and at the same time will bring the Apostle's divine-Christology back into dialogue with the proposals of modern theologians and the contemporary church's communal life and concerns.

2. Negotiating the 'ugly broad ditch' between the 'Jesus of history' and the 'Christ of faith'

The words 'ugly broad ditch' used above of course refer to the now famous statement of G.E. Lessing (*'der garstige breite Graben'*), who contrasted 'accidental truths of history' with 'necessary truths of reason'. More generally, Kuschel has seen that this gulf gives rise to another more general one, that between 'the language of the New Testament and the language of dogmatics'.[5] Indeed, it is probably not an exaggeration to claim that the history of scholarly engagement with Christology can be plotted against the axes of history and theology, with some closer to the historical (e.g. Hegel, Strauss), others closer to the theological (e.g. Schleiermacher, Kähler).

This division is the foundation of a perennial problem confronted by NT experts and theologians alike, one that concerns the apparently uncomfortable space between their disciplines, namely between the 'Jesus of history' (conceived as a historical quest) and the 'Christ of faith' (conceived in terms of the church's developing reflection on Christ, especially in dogmatic terms). Many, in light of the surge of interest in the 'historical Jesus', are left wondering how the historical figure of Jesus relates to the church's creedal faith. And while Lessing's specific question may not be as central as it once was (namely, how one jumps from the accidental truths of history to the necessary truths of reason), an ugly broad ditch remains carved into the landscape of academic theology, not least in the division of its disciplines (between theology on the one hand, and biblical studies on the other). The essential question of the relationship between the Jesus who walked the shores of Galilee, and the developed theological formulations in the early Christian centuries, remains unsettled, not to mention the difference between the Jesus in the Gospels and Paul's risen Lord. So Grillmeier starts his multivolume study, *Christ in Christian Tradition*, by detailing 'the present situation' as concentrated on the 'historical Jesus' – 'Christ of faith' dichotomy.[6]

---

[4] For the meaning of 'systematic' theology as used here, cf. the discussion in Green and Turner, *Horizons*, 10–11.

[5] Cited in Thiselton, *Hermeneutics*, 397.

[6] Aloys Grillmeier, *From the Apostolic Age to Chalcedon (451)*, vol. 1 of *Christ in Christian Tradition*, 2d ed., trans. John Bowden (Atlanta: John Knox Press, 1975), 3.

Of course, some may want to deny that any significant development in Christology exists. But ultimately it must be accepted that the Jesus who said 'Why do you call me good? No one is good but God alone' (Mk. 10:18) is unlikely to have said in the next breath, that he is 'true God from true God'. There is a real conceptual, or at least hermeneutical, distance between the Palestinian Jew, Jesus, and 'a full-fledged doctrine of the Trinity, including [later] claims about intradivine persons, processions [and] relations'.[7] Furthermore, whether creedal statements are a faithful translation of biblical material from one context to another need not even be questioned because translations of concepts like this, from one 'symbolic universe' to another, by necessity involve development.[8] Some have attempted to deal with the church's developing Christology by prioritising either a historical or confessional stance. But one can ask whether a Christology 'from below' really manages to reach to the rich Trinitarian creeds of the early church. At the same time it must be asked whether a Christology 'from above' takes the history and teaching of Jesus seriously enough.[9] 'As George Caird used to say, Christianity appeals to history, and to history it must go'.[10] Indeed, 'Historical Jesus Questers' often seem to self-consciously model a flight from christological doctrine, while theologians often appear little interested in the developments of historical Jesus study. Notable exceptions can, of course, be mentioned,[11] and most recently the important contributions of Richard Bauckham deserve attention. In a study on the Gospels and eyewitness testimony he argues:

> Testimony ... is both the historically appropriate category for understanding what kind of history the Gospels are and the theologically appropriate category for understanding what kind of access Christian readers of the Gospels thereby have to Jesus and his history. It is the category that enables us to surmount the dichotomy between the so-called historical Jesus and the so-called Christ of faith.[12]

He ends his monograph with these words: 'It is in the Jesus of testimony that history and theology meet'.[13]

But is 'testimony' really where faith and history meet? Arguably more fundamental than testimony, and indeed its very basis, was a *relationship* with

---

[7] Catherine M. LaCugna, *God for Us: The Trinity and Christian Life* (New York: HarperSanFrancisco, 1991), 22.

[8] Cf. e.g. Jiang Tianmin, "Translation in Context," *Translation Journal* 10, no. 2 (April 2006) (accessed 19.12.2008)

[9] A point made in Wolfhart Pannenberg, *Jesus: God and Man*, trans. Lewis L. Wilkins and Duane A. Priebe (Philadelphia: Westminster Press, 1968), 17–18.

[10] N.T. Wright, "Jesus and the Identity of God," *ExAud* 14 (1998): 50.

[11] Thiselton, *Hermeneutics*, 407–13, notes James Dunn, N.T. Wright and Wolfhart Pannenberg.

[12] Richard J. Bauckham, *Jesus and the Eyewitnesses: The Gospels as Eyewitness Testimony* (Cambridge: Eerdmans, 2006), 473.

[13] Ibid., 508.

Jesus. This is evident, first, at a rather obvious level. The early disciples could testify to the historical Jesus because they existed in various kinds of relationship with Christ, some more intimate than others. Indeed, that there was a concern to testify to the Jesus who walked the shores of Galilee presupposes that this Jesus impacted people through relationships with them. 'To tell the story of Jesus', wrote historical Jesus scholar J.P. Meier, 'is to tell the story of his various relationships'.[14] Indeed, this was the foundational conviction for the third volume in his series on the historical Jesus. Dunn makes the point that Jesus tradition was always, from its first moment, the product of relationships with Jesus. He writes:

The traditions which lie behind the Gospels ... began from the various encounters between Jesus and those who by virtue of these encounters became disciples. The earliest traditions are the product of disciple-response.[15]

Likewise, Dale Allison recently argued that Jesus' personal identity cannot be isolated from his social identity, who he is in relationship with others. Jesus, he asserts, 'was always interacting with others, and their perceptions of him must constitute part of his identity'.[16] Jesus tradition is thus the product of various relationships with Jesus, and Jesus' identity is not neatly separable from these relationships. Interestingly, on the basis of Bauckham's own argument it should be noted that the one Gospel written by an eyewitness (at least according to Bauckham) is also the one which makes an especially intimate relationship of the eyewitness to Jesus most explicit.[17]

Relation to Jesus is not only generative of Jesus tradition, it is also intrinsic to and the motivation of the ongoing transmission and editing of that tradition, right up to its later form in the various Gospels. So Matthew begins his Gospel with the confession of faith, that the genealogy is that of Jesus the *Christ* (Mt. 1:1). Mark introduces his Gospel as 'The beginning of the good news of Jesus Christ' (Mk. 1:1). Luke writes his Gospel that Theophilus 'may know the truth concerning the things about which [he has] been instructed' (Lk. 1:4). As the Gospels were preserved, copied, read and re-read in the liturgical community gatherings of the early Christians, the implied readers of the Gospels were those seeking to establish or develop some kind of relationship with the risen Lord.[18] The Christ-relation was part of the motivation and goal in the continued preservation of use of the Jesus tradition.

---

[14] J. P. Meier, *A Marginal Jew: Rethinking the Historical Jesus. Vol. 3. Companions and Competitors* (New York: Doubleday, 2001), 2.

[15] James D.G. Dunn, *Jesus Remembered*, Christianity in the Making (Grand Rapids: Eerdmans, 2003), 128–29.

[16] Dale C. Allison Jr., *The Historical Christ and the Theological Jesus* (Cambridge: Eerdmans, 2009), 25.

[17] Cf. e.g. Bauckham, *Eyewitnesses*, 396–402.

[18] Cf. the erudite discussion in Bockmuehl, *Seeing*, 75–99.

This Christ-relation continued as a formative force in the development of creedal Christianity. The use of the language 'I/We believe' testifies to a continuing relational emphasis in the church's confession of Christ.[19] So Lash writes that the 'threefold confession in the [Apostle's] Creed declares our *present* relationship with God'.[20] Indeed, while the Christ-relation does not exhaustively constitute the actual christological ponderings of the developing tradition of the church through the centuries, one can, in light of these observations, suggest that the church's Christology be nevertheless partly understood in terms of the church's relation to Christ. Permeating throughout, then, from eyewitness testimony, through the church's reception of these texts, and up to their developing Christology, a Christ-relation was intrinsic and generative for each step. It is a more fundamental category than testimony.

In light of this, a new set of proposals emerge concerning Lessing's ditch. First, as the Christ-relation existed on both sides of the ditch, Christology, understood in terms of relation, *necessarily* straddles that ditch. Christology, understood in a Pauline way, cannot be mapped on the desolate landscape Lessing offers, with its focus on a cold ditch. It is a relation, and as such necessarily nullifies Lessing's dull geography as meaningless. Conceived in this way, there is no more an 'ugly broad ditch' between 'the Jesus of history' and the 'Christ of faith' than there is, to use an analogy, between a married couple's wedding ceremony, on the one hand, and the continued (and changing) development of that relationship, on the other. To dissolve the marriage relation into either a focus on something which essentially happened in the past, or into something which only happens in the present, is a meaningless – not to mention potentially divorce inducing – manoeuvre.

Second, while liberals have traditionally emphasised discontinuity, and conservatives continuity, between the Jesus of history and the Christ of Paul's faith,[21] Christology, understood as the church's Christ-relation, means that there is room for development, change and mystery. To quote Mary Healy in her essay on Paul's epistemology:

Even in the case of a human relationship, knowing another can never exhaust the mystery of the other ...: "persons we have come to know really well are often more mysterious to us than

---

[19] Nicholas Lash, *Believing Three Ways in One God: A Reading of the Apostles' Creed* (London: Notre Dame Press, 1993), 18–21.

[20] Ibid., 30, italics his.

[21] Cf. the summary of various proposals emphasising continuity and discontinuity in Eberhard Jüngel, *Paulus und Jesus: eine Untersuchung zur Präzisierung der Frage nach dem Ursprung der Christologie* (Tübingen: Mohr Siebeck, 1967), 5–16. Beyond this cf. the nature of the claims in David Wenham, *Paul: Follower of Jesus or Founder of Christianity?* (Grand Rapids: Eerdmans, 1995), 104–37; the debate in Bird and Crossley James G., *How Did Christianity Begin?*, Crossley emphasising discontinuity, Bird continuity; and the debate in N.T. Wright and Markus Borg, *The Meaning of Jesus: Two Visions* (London: SPCK, 1999), Borg emphasising discontinuity, Wright continuity.

others whom we know only superficially". Knowledge of another person ... thus involves a dialectic of mystery and intelligibility.[22]

A Christology understood in the way this thesis urges can thus account for, and even necessitate, both development and continuity in the church's faith in Christ, it allows for both mystery and truth claims.

The relational nature of Paul's divine-Christology language thus lends this discussion a constructive perspective. There is no need for an exclusive emphasis on either continuity, as if orthodox Christology was a *necessary* interpretation of the historical Jesus, or discontinuity, as if orthodox Christology was an *illegitimate* development from the same. Christology, grasped in the language of relationship, allows for, even necessitates, development and continuity, separation between earliest history and later faith, without assuming that an ugly ditch must exist between the two, anymore than a ditch exists between the vows at a wedding ceremony and a married couple's ongoing relationship. The Pauline Christ-relation suggests that it is not in testimony but in relationship with Christ that history and theology can meet and dialogue with one another. But to explore how that may look, it is necessary to engage with certain contemporary theological proposals.

3. Paul's relational divine-Christology and modern theological discourse

Moltmann wrote that the 'New Testament talks about God by proclaiming in narrative the relationships of the Father, the Son and the Spirit, which are relationships of fellowship and are *open to the world*'.[23] Elsewhere he writes of the significance of 'partnership, a mutual relationship, even about friendship between God and free man', and that '[w]ithout the social relation there can be no personality'.[24] Grenz speaks of the 'near consensus that *person* is a relational concept',[25] Lash claims, God *is* the relations he has,[26] Zizioulas states that 'without the concept of communion it would not be possible to speak of

---

[22] Healy, "Knowledge," 154.

[23] Jürgen Moltmann, *The Trinity and the Kingdom: The Doctrine of God* (Minneapolis: Fortress, 1981), 64, italics mine.

[24] Moltmann, *Trinity*, 144–45. Furthermore, not only are social scientists and psychotherapists increasingly understanding the 'self' as 'constituted in and through relationships' (F. LeRon Shults and Steven J. Sandage, *Transforming Spirituality: Integrating Theology and Psychology* [Grand Rapids: Baker, 2006], 25), but such language finds even more enthusiastic employment as these disciplines engage with theology (Shults and Sandage, *Transforming*, cf. 161–66, 221–33).

[25] Stanley J. Grenz, *The Social God and the Relational Self: A Trinitarian Theology of the Imago Dei* (Louisville: Westminster John Knox, 2001), 9, italics his.

[26] Cf. Lash, *Ways*, 32.

the being of God',[27] and LaCugna opines, 'God's way of being in relationship *with us* – which is God's personhood – is a perfect expression of God's being as God'.[28] This thesis enables a very different exploration of the exegetical and theological import of such claims. In so doing, the concrete outworking of the meeting between faith and history in the Christ-relation, described above, can be pursued. The following are clearly preliminary thoughts, and much more can be said. Suffice it for now to make a couple of points.

3.1. The mode of Paul's christological language

As has been noted in dialogue with Boers in chapter 10, to speak of a Pauline Christology is potentially problematic. However, a case for a Pauline divine-Christology was made on the basis of the pattern of data in Paul concerning the relation between the risen Lord and believers. In a way coherent with Paul's relational monotheism and epistemology, a deduced Pauline divine-Christology was expressed in his letters in terms of the relation between the risen Lord and believers. This Christ-relation was the primary mode of his divine-christological language.

With this in mind, there are a number of suggestive connection points with modern theological discourse that deserve brief exploration. First is the mode of Paul's Christology language and the late modern turn to relationality. A host of modern theologians have employed relational language to freshly artic-ulate the doctrine of God, with mixed results.[29] At this point it suffices to focus on the work of theologian LeRon Shults who, in a number of publica-tions, has ably detailed this shift.[30] Through examination of relationality in Locke, Hume, Kant and Hegel, he explains how the concept of relation came to the forefront, a development also reflected in the philosophy of logic, math-ematics and physics. Two examples:

Einstein's field equations for general special relativity ... are based on the use of functional relations. Quantum physics pressed philosophers of science even further, leading them to challenge the adequacy of substance/attribute predication theory to make sense of the entanglement phenomena discovered at the subatomic level. Here reality itself resists the abstraction associated with the category of "thing" (substance), and physicists increasingly

---

[27] J.D. Zizioulas, *Being as Communion: Studies in Personhood and the Church* (Crestwood, NY: St. Vladimir's Seminary Press, 1985), 17.

[28] LaCugna, *God*, 304–5, italics hers.

[29] Cf. Henry Jansen, *Relationality and the Concept of God* (Amsterdam: Rodopi, 1995) for an incisive analysis of a number of modern 'relational' proposals, with special focus on the works of Jürgen Moltmann and Wolfhart Pannenberg. Of course, the following theologians speak almost exclusively of the relation to 'God' rather than 'Christ'.

[30] Cf. Shults, *Anthropology*; Shults, *Reforming the Doctrine of God*; and now Shults, *Christology*.

appealed to inherently relational and dynamic modes of talking about what "happens between" and within the unpredictable flow of "interphenomena".[31]

This growing confidence in relationality contrasts with the demise of recourse to static substance. So in the field of evolutionary biology, he notes that '[t]he theory of evolution developed by Charles Darwin (1809–1882) challenged the notion of human nature as a substance that always remained the same'.[32] With such developments in mind he notes that '[m]any traditional depictions of the person, work and coming of Christ are shaped by assumptions about humanity and the world that no longer make sense in light of contemporary science'.[33] Traditional formulations of the doctrine of the incarnation presuppose certain philosophical commitments about sameness and difference – commitments, it should be noted, which have shaped the focus and concerns of New Testament scholars such as Fee with his concentration on the pre-existent nature of the 'Person' as opposed to 'work' of Christ. But Shults rightly points out:

> Why should we insist on expressing the doctrine of the incarnation in ways that are tied to ancient Greek or modern anthropological concepts of personhood, which focus on the sameness of hypostasized substances? Why not critically engage the relational and dynamic thought forms of contemporary anthropological discourse as we seek to articulate belief in the Word became flesh?[34]

So he attempts to show how this 'turn to relationality' opens fresh conceptual space in which to recapture relational biblical intuitions. Instead of detailing the incarnation in terms of static substance, he speaks of the need to develop a 'radically relational understanding of the identity of Jesus Christ'.[35] He adds that this reimagining of the formulation of christological expression is necessary as every generation of theologians must articulate 'the intuitions of the biblical tradition about the significance of Jesus Christ in a way that engages its own cultural context'.[36] Even if it is argued that a more relational emphasis is clear in the Fathers,[37] the point here is that a focus on relationality helps to engage biblical intuitions with modern concerns. Indeed, proponents of 'Radical Orthodoxy' (RO) have highlighted that a participatory ontology is not only faithful to pre-Scotus Christian theology, but is ultimately necessary to deliver contemporary life from the heresy of the so-called 'secular', and the various ills which are a consequence. It need only be added that the relational ontology indicated here is perhaps another way of expressing the concern to

---

[31] Shults, *Christology*, 7.

[32] Ibid., 29.

[33] Ibid., 1.

[34] Ibid., 34.

[35] Ibid., 23.

[36] Shults, *Christology*, 1. It could be maintained that a reengagement with Patristic, especially Capodocian, relational ontology is the necessary corrective (cf. Zizioulas, *Being*, 16–17).

[37] Cf. e.g. Zizioulas' analysis in Zizioulas, *Being*.

return to a participatory ontology, a suspicion confirmed by the RO tendency to use the term *methexis*. The use of a related word is found in verbal form in 1 Corinthians 10, right in the heartland of Paul's most profound exposition of the relation between the risen Lord and believers. Of course, many RO theologians use *methexis* in light of its Platonic heritage, but the overlap of terminology here is symptomatic of a deeper mutuality between Paul's relational intuitions and the concerns of RO.[38]

Paul's relational Christology, as explored in this thesis, can be brought into potentially fruitful dialogue with such concerns, ensuring the voice of canonical Scripture be heard in the developing discussions in fresh ways.

The second point concerns the link between revelation and relationship. Catherine LaCugna has maintained that trinitarian thought arose 'to express the idea that God's relationship to us in the economy originates in and is grounded in the eternal being of God'.[39] Indeed, to 'theorize about God as if God were *not* in relationship (*deus in se*), or to postulate God's nonrelationship with the world as the primordial truth about God's nature, is a fantasy about a God who does not exist'.[40] Thus the 'central preoccupation of the Christian doctrine of God' must then be 'the encounter between divine and human persons in the economy of redemption. Indeed, trinitarian theology is par excellence a theology of relationship'.[41] Further, 'God's existence is grasped in relationship to us; we do not know God "in Godself" or "by Godself'.[42] LaCugna makes her points in sharp polemic against the scholastic tendency to seal the relationality of God within the *intra*-trinitarian relations between Father, Son and Spirit.[43] On the contrary, she maintains, God's relationship to humans must be theologically accounted for in trinitarian theologising. Without necessarily accepting all of her arguments,[44] it is noteworthy that Paul's divine-Christology, as maintained in this thesis, was expressed as the relation between risen Lord and *believers*.

---

[38] On the use (and abuse?) of the term *methexis* in RO theology, cf. the masterful overview in James K.A. Smith, *Introducing Radical Orthodoxy: Mapping a Post-Secular Theology* (Grand Rapids: Baker Academic, 2004).

[39] LaCugna, *God*, 53.

[40] Ibid., 230.

[41] Ibid., 243.

[42] Ibid., 334.

[43] Ibid., Cf. e.g. 210, 215–16.

[44] For example, she claims that 'God's To-Be is To-Be-in-Relationship, and God's being-in-relationship-to-us *is* what God is' (LaCugna, *God*, 250). One can only speculate about Paul's response to such a proposition, but a text like Rom. 11:33–36 suggests that Paul would have preferred more ambivalence and hesitation about defining what God is without remainder. Cf. also the criticisms of LaCugna's position in Thomas Weinandy, *The Father's Spirit of Sonship: Reconceiving the Trinity* (Edinburgh: T&T Clark, 1995), 123–36.

Furthermore, T.F. Torrance, crediting Calvin with the insight, makes the same point in arguing that one cannot begin with a thing's 'essence' (*quid sit*) but rather with the thing 'as it discloses itself to us in relation (*quale sit*)'.[45] Likewise, John Zizioulas maintains that 'the being of God could only be known through personal relationships and personal love' on the alleged basis that St Athanasius 'approached the being of God through the experience of the ecclesial community'.[46] 'The being of God is a relational being', he notes, drawing the conclusion that 'without the concept of communion it would not be possible to speak of the being of God'.[47] While these potentially fruitful links with the mode of Paul's christological language can only be noted and not explored in this appendix, the question of the divinity of Christ and the appropriate epistemological access to this claim would appear, in Paul, to be firmly relational. Paul's divine-Christology is primarily a deduction from the relation between the risen Lord and believers and thus biblical material can now be more fruitfully brought into conversation with these theological concerns. Furthermore, these thoughts speak in favour of a Christology which starts from Paul's relation to Christ, rather than from one concerning Christ's essence apart from his relations, as effectively adopted, for example, in Fee.

At this point it is important to note that Paul's Christology was neither 'from above' or 'from below'. Indeed, Shults has already made the point that a Christology that takes the late modern turn to relationality seriously 'is no longer forced to choose between beginning "from below" or "from above". Neither of these is really possible'.[48] It is thus tempting to speak of christological discourse as best understood 'from the Christ-event' as a way of bypassing this potential dichotomy, because it is language (*Christusgeschehen*) which has now become an important part of both theological *and* New Testament discourse.[49] However, it needs to be remembered that Paul's language was generally dominated by the language of the relation between risen Lord and believers rather than that of 'event'. It is also to be noted that the language of the 'Christ-event' has often led to the expression of a functional Pauline divine-Christology, as opposed to an ontological one,[50]

---

[45] This summary of Torrance's argument is that of Shults, *Christology*, 134.

[46] Zizioulas, *Being*, 16.

[47] Ibid., 17.

[48] Shults, *Christology*, 9.

[49] The language of 'event', in terms of Paul, has also found expression in the field of modern continental philosophy where the Apostle has recently become fashionable. So Badiou writes that Jesus, for Paul, 'is the pure event' (Alain Badiou, trans., Ray Brassier, *Saint Paul: The Foundation of Universalism* [Stanford: Stanford University Press, 2003], 48).

[50] Cf. e.g. the Christology detailed under the section entitled 'The Christ Event' in Werner G. Kümmel, *The Theology of the New Testament: According to Its Major Witnesses, Jesus-Paul-John* (Nashville: Abingdon, 1973), 151–72. Note also the comments in Shults, *Christology*, 65.

arguably because the distinction between function and ontology made sense at a time when theological recourse to 'event' was becoming popular in German theology. However, the relationality that one finds in Paul, and in much late modern philosophy, suggests that the functional/ontological distinction is based on philosophical commitments discordant with Paul's relational intuitions.

To be noted is that Paul's Christ-relation involved recourse to public truths and events, yet it also involved a change in perspective that the new relation to Christ brought about. In the middle of a passage explaining the nature and motivations of his ministry, Paul writes that 'even though we once knew Christ from a human point of view (κατὰ σάρκα), we know him no longer in that way' (2 Cor. 5:16). The change in those included in this 'we' is associated with a developing relationship with Christ, and it brought about new insight into the event of Christ's death, and affirmation of Christ's resurrection, which was hardly, as Bultmann was forced to maintain because of his philosophical commitments, '*nothing other* than the rise of faith in the risen one ... not an objective event'.[51] In relation to Christ, Christology mixes history with the existential, 'from above' with 'from below'. Despite the worthy and especially German heritage which has made use of the language of the 'Christ-event', perhaps Paul's mode of christological formulation should counsel a stronger relational emphasis. Not 'from above', 'from below' or 'from the event', but *in relationship with Christ*.

Third, this same relational mode of expression in Paul means one must question preoccupation with the 'Person' of Christ, as if this must denote Christ, the *individual*, distinct from his relations. So Zizioulas argues that '[b]eing a person is fundamentally different from being an individual or a "personality", for a person cannot be imagined in himself but only within his relationships'.[52] Certainly such a line of reasoning would need careful nuancing, but there is an important point to engage with here.[53] The critique of Fee's analysis of Paul's Christology above, for example, shows Fee's emphasis lies on the substance of that Person, hence his unbalanced preoccupation with the question of pre-existence, with Christ's relations as more or less accidental to that Person. Just as Shults notes that 'substance categories' in traditional christological formulations lead to 'sometimes obscuring the importance of interpreting the *relation* of Jesus Christ to God, humanity and the cosmos',[54] so too, as maintained in chapter 3 above, Fee's lists of Christ's

---

[51] Cited in Thiselton, *Hermeneutics*, 381, italics his. Admittedly, this citation may be over-simplifying the more complex nature of Bultmann's argumentation.

[52] Zizioulas, *Being*, 105. For the distinction between the 'person' of Christ and the 'individual' Christ, cf. also pp. 164–65.

[53] At this point one should note a potentially fruitful dialogue between the relational content of Process Theology and Paul's Christ-relation.

[54] Shults, *Christology*, 7.

functions suppressed the relational import of the language. Arguably Fee has (unconsciously?) adopted an Aristotelian understanding of substance and relations against the grain both of late modernity[55] and, it can now be added, Paul's own relational intuitions. One can surely speak of the Person of Christ, as indeed Zizioulas does, but one must take care that the implicit philosophical assumptions imported into discussions do not betray the relational thrust of Paul's language. Shults correctly writes that '[u]nderstanding the relations in which a "thing" is embedded is necessary for understanding what it *is*'.[56] Likewise, understanding Paul's Christology means understanding his Christ-relation language.

Fourth, it was also seen that Paul's Christ-relation was very often the language of doxology, whether in the shape of Paul's Christ-shaped aims, goals and motivations, the variety of Christ-devotion expressions, or in the passionate nature of Christ-devotion. The mode of Paul's christological language was relational in a fundamentally doxological manner. With this in mind, Jürgen Moltmann notes that for the church Fathers 'knowing' meant not power or domination, but *wonder*.[57] Similarly, LaCugna argues that 'the form of language that best serves the mystery of divine-human communion is *theology in the mode of doxology*'.[58] Drawing on the liturgical theology of A. Kavanagh,[59] she notes that the 'language of praise is the primary language of Christian faith'. Further, secondary theology 'is reflection on primary theology, and raises questions of verification, systematic coherency, and applicability to a given situation'.[60] This distinction may be brought into dialogue with the distinction made in chapter 10 above, between the Christ-relation language in Paul and the secondary deduction of a Pauline divine-Christology.[61] One must however insist that Paul's doxological language not be reduced to corporate and liturgical settings. Paul's Christ-relation embraces the whole of life.

Further, LaCugna continues to claim that secondary theology 'must be doxological if it is to be theological'.[62] At this point one is reminded of the words of novelist Anita Mason: 'There is a kind of truth which, when it is

---

[55] Cf. e.g. the discussion in Shults, *Christology*, 25.

[56] Shults, *Christology*, 6.

[57] Moltmann, *Trinity*, 9.

[58] LaCugna, *God*, 15–16, italics hers.

[59] Ibid., 373 n.68.

[60] Ibid., 357.

[61] On the mutuality of the dialogue between exegesis and theology, cf. the stated purpose behind the new Two Horizons commentary series: to bring into conscious discussion both exegesis and modern systematic and practical theology 'in a dialogical and critical way that will not suppress either' (Green and Turner, *Horizons*, 3).

[62] LaCugna, *God*, 357.

said, becomes untrue'.[63] One could thus argue that the deduced Pauline divine-Christology fails on two fronts. It is not only insufficiently doxological but also attempts to say what should be left in the mode of relational data, the pattern of language concerning the Christ-relation. However, in defence of the christological deduction above in chapter 10, one should note that Paul's texts were collected and transmitted as part of a creedal community, one which unashamedly confessed the kind of christological deduction it has been insisted here is the appropriate conclusion to draw from Paul's Christ-relation language. The scriptures were part of a community which indeed attempted to speak its convictions. Indeed, these convictions were part of the church's doxological repertoire.

That said, the potential charge that the divine-Christology deduction above could be insufficiently doxological must be heeded. Paul's language, if separated from the creedal community of Christ-followers, becomes a mere theological fossil, thus betraying its very purpose and nature. Paul's divine-Christology, as understood in this thesis, could never be a 'free-floating' proposition or descriptive statement divorced from its mode of expression as the participatory and self-involved relation between the risen Lord and believers.[64] Hence it is necessary to turn, for reasons that shall become clear, to an analysis of the *scope* of Paul's language in dialogue with modern theological concerns in the following section.

3.2. The scope of Paul's christological language

It has been maintained that the *mode* of Paul's language, when his relational emphasis has been recaptured, brings him helpfully back into dialogue with the proposals of modern theological discourse. But more can be said in terms of the *scope* of Paul's christologically relevant language. While Pauline Christology has often been reduced to an analysis of the incarnation, and was consequently forced to obsess about the supposed pre-existence (or not) of Christ in this or that Pauline phrase (e.g. in 1 Cor, 8:6; Phil. 2:6–11 etc.),[65] Shults has noted that the turn to relationality facilitates appreciation of the relation between Jesus' *work and future* in terms of his Person. Philosophical commitments about time, causality and so on, he argues, have divided Christology unhelpfully from soteriology and eschatology. Hence his book on Christology incorporates extended discussion of the *parousia* and atonement, not to mention the albeit more limited reflections on Pneumatology, commu-

---

[63] Richard Hays cited these words during a NT seminar at Kings College, London, in December 2008, citing Rowan Williams (Rowan Williams, *Christ on Trial: How the Gospel Unsettles Our Judgement* [Grand Rapids: Eerdmans, 2003], 6), who himself cited Mason.

[64] For the language used in this sentence, cf. chapter 1, 'From Free-Floating "Problems" to Hermeneutical Questions from Life' in Thiselton, *Hermeneutics*, 3–18.

[65] Note the subtitle of Dunn, *Christology*: 'a New Testament inquiry into the origins of the doctrine of the incarnation'.

nal life, divine immanence and transcendence, among other themes.[66] Likewise, LaCugna has strongly emphasised the need to root trinitarian theology in communal and corporate life, worship and Pneumatology.[67] Zizioulas has also insisted that 'Pneumatology must be made *constitutive* of Christology'.[68]

With this in mind, it will be noticed that the approach of this thesis has also facilitated christological engagement with a scope of material normally excluded from examination of Paul's Christology. Thus the presence and absence of Christ,[69] certain eschatological themes, Christ-devotion, Pneumatology, Christ-related goals etc. have all been studied, themselves included in the larger pattern of relational data which, it was argued, Paul himself understood as a pattern. In other words, the identity of Christ has been approached with arguably more sensitivity to Paul's own concerns, less dominated by philosophical assumptions alien to the Pauline texts, and more attune to the variety of subjects relevant to his Christology.

Importantly, and engaging with the point made above about participatory and self-involved modes of expression, the centre point of Paul's rhetoric concerning the relation between the risen Lord and believers, namely 1 Corinthians 8–10 – the passage that launched the exegetical study above – is not only concerned about the relation between the risen Lord and believers in the context of the framing relational monotheistic concerns. The argument is also about the relation between the risen Lord and the *church*, not just individual Christians. LaCugna writes of her relational approach, noting that it is not 'a reversion to a "me and God" piety that bypasses the community. Indeed, both the experience of God and the emergence of personhood are ineluctably mediated by other persons'.[70] Likewise Paul states in 1 Corinthians 10:17: 'we who are many are one body, for we all partake of the one bread'. The Christ-relation was about the *community* of believers. Further, it was also seen that the 'necessary knowledge' (cf. 1 Cor. 8:1–3) was not theoretical abstraction but love for God. At various points elsewhere it was shown that the relation between the risen Lord was fundamentally about obedience, being ardent in spirit, serving the Lord (cf. e.g. Rom. 12:11 which, in context, relates to genuine love [12:9], mutual affection [12:10], contributing to the needs of the saints [12:13], hospitality to strangers [12:13], harmonious living with one another [12:15] etc.).

---

[66] Cf. the discussion in Shults, *Christology*, 13–14.

[67] LaCugna, *God.*

[68] Zizioulas, *Being*, 139.

[69] Christopher Schwöbel has noted the 'danger of emphazing God's relationship with the world at the expense of divine transcendence' (cited in Jansen, *Relationality*, 103). However, it is the relational approach explored in this thesis that enables examination of the christological significance of Christ's absence and activity in the world by the Spirit in a manner that more adequately accounts for theological language of God's transcendence.

[70] LaCugna, *God*, 290.

This all means that if the nature of the relation between the risen Lord and believers, in Paul, is taken seriously in the analysis of his understanding of the identity of Christ, Christology cannot be mere information, intellectual knowledge alone, even though it will surely include it. Paul's Christology cannot be expressed apart from the communal life of the church in relation to the risen Lord, to its faithfulness to Christ over the idolatry of the world (as in 1 Cor. 8–10). Paul's Christology is thus, in its warp and woof, about the way the church lives, loves and relates as a community, with each other and with its risen Lord. It is profoundly participatory and self-involved in both its mode of expression and in the scope of its concerns. Shults has argued that the 'study of Jesus Christ ought to have a reformative effect on contemporary life'.[71] Paul's Christology, as understood in this thesis, is precisely about reforming modes of living as Christians. To 'wrestle with the question of what to make of Jesus' is,[72] at least when the Pauline material is as inductively handled as possible, to wrestle with the question of how to live and love as a community of Christ-believers in the twenty-first century. The scope and mode of Paul's Christology means that it is thus fundamentally about our relationship with Jesus Christ today. This all suggests that it is thus in this relationship with Christ that not only theology and history meet, but also exegesis, ethics, epistemology and doxology.

---

[71] Shults, *Christology*, 1.
[72] Hurtado, *LJC*, 652–53.

Bibliography

Aasgaard, R. 2004. Brothers in brackets?: a plea for rethinking the use of "[]" in NA/UBS. *JSNT* 26(3):301–21.

Adams, E. 2000. *Constructing the world: a study in Paul's cosmological language.* Edinburgh: T&T Clark.

Aejmelaeus, L. 2000. *Schwachheit als Waffe: die Argumentation des Paulus im Tränenbrief (2. Kor. 10–13).* Göttingen: Vandenhoeck & Ruprecht.

Allison Jr., D. C. 2009. *The Historical Christ and the Theological Jesus.* Cambridge: Eerdmans.

Anderson, B. W. 1993[4]. *The Living World of the Old Testament.* Harlow, Essex: Longman.

Aune, D. 1972. *The cultic setting of realised eschatology in early christianity.* Leiden: Brill.

Bachmann, P. 1936[4]. *Der erste Brief des Paulus an die Korinther.* Leipzig: Deichert.

Back, F. 2002. *Verwandlung durch Offenbarung bei Paulus: eine religionsgeschichtlich-exegetische Untersuchung zu 2 Kor 2,14–4,6.* Tübingen: Mohr Siebeck.

Badiou, A., trans., Ray Brassier. 2003. *Saint Paul: The Foundation of Universalism.* Stanford: Stanford University Press.

Barker, M. 1992. *The Great Angel: A study of Israel's second God.* London: SPCK.

T: 1999. The High Priest and the worship of Jesus. In *The Jewish Roots of Christological Monotheism*, eds C. Newman, J. Davila, and G. Lewis, 93–111. Leiden: Brill.

Barnett, P. 1997. *The second epistle to the Corinthians.* Grand Rapids: Eerdmans.

Barrett, C. 1971[2]. *A Commentary in the First Epistle to the Corinthians.* London: Black.

–. 1973. *The Second Epistle to the Corinthians.* London: Black.

Bartchy, S. S. 1973. *Mallon chresai: First century slavery and the interpretation of 1 Corinthians 7:21.* Missoula, Mont.: SBL.

Barth, K. 2008. *Church Dogmatics.* London: Continuum.

Bassler, J. M. 1992. God in the NT. In *ABD*, 1049–55. New York: Doubleday.

Bauckham, R. J. 1981. The Worship of Jesus in Apocalyptic Christianity. *NTS* 27:322–41.

–. 1983. *Jude, 2 Peter.* Waco: Word.

–. 1990. *Jude and the Relatives of Jesus in the Early Church.* Edinburgh: T&T Clark.

–. 1992. The Worship of Jesus. In *ABD Vol 3.*, 812–19. London: Doubleday.

–. 1998. *God Crucified: Monotheism and Christology in the New Testament.* Carlisle: Paternoster.

–. 1998. The Worship of Jesus in Philippians 2:9–11. In *Where Christology Began: Essays on Philippians 2*, eds R. P. Martin and B. J. Dodd, 128–39. Louisville: Westminster John Knox.

–. 1999. *James: wisdom of James, disciple of Jesus the sage*. London: Routledge.
–. 1999. The Throne of God and the Worship of Jesus. In *The Jewish Roots of Christological Monotheism*, eds C. Newman, J. Davila, and G. Lewis, 43–69. Leiden: Brill.
–. 2004. Biblical theology and the problems of monotheism. In *Out of Egypt: biblical theology and biblical interpretation*, eds C. Bartholomew, M. Healy, K. Möller, and R. Parry, 187–232. Milton Keynes: Paternoster.
–. 2006. *Jesus and the eyewitnesses: the Gospels as eyewitness testimony*. Cambridge: Eerdmans.
–. 2007. James and the Jerusalem Community. In *Jewish Believers in Jesus*, eds O. Skarsaune and R. Hvalvik, 55–95. Peabody: Hendrickson.
–. 2008. *Jesus and the God of Israel*. Milton Keynes: Paternoster.
Becker, E.-M. 2002. *Schreiben und Verstehen: paulinische Briefhermeneutik im Zweiten Korintherbrief*. Tübingen: Francke.
Beentjes, P. 2002. God's Mercy: 'Racham' (pi.), 'Rachum', and 'Rachamim' in the Book of Ben Sira. In *Ben Sira's God: Proceedings of the International Ben Sira Conference*, ed. R. Egger-Wenzel, 101–17. Berlin: W. de Gruyter.
Bell, R. H. 1994. *Provoked to jealousy: the origin and purpose of the jealousy motif in Romans 9–11*. Tübingen: Mohr Siebeck.
Belleville, L. J. 1991. *Reflections of Glory. Paul's Polemical Use of the Moses-Doxa Tradition in 2 Corinthians 3.1–18*. Sheffield: JSOT Press.
Ben-Dov, J. 2007. Exegetical Notes on Cosmology in the Parables of Enoch. In *EMSM*, ed. G. Boccaccini, 143–50. Cambridge: Eerdmans.
Berger, K. 2002. *Paulus*. Munich: C. H. Beck.
–. 2003. *Identity and experience in the New Testament*. Minneapolis: Fortress.
Bird, M. F. 2007. *The Saving Righteousness of God: Studies on Paul, Justification and the New Perspective*. Milton Keynes: Paternoster.
Bird, M. F., and Crossley James G. 2008. *How did Christianity Begin? A believer and non-believer examine the evidence*. London: SPCK.
Black, M. 1985. *The book of Enoch or 1 Enoch: A new English edition with commentary and textual notes*. Leiden: Brill.
Boccaccini, G. 2007. Finding a Place for the Parables of Enoch within Second Temple Jewish Literature. In *EMSM*, ed. G. Boccaccini, 263–89. Cambridge: Eerdmans.
Bockmuehl, M. 1997. *The Epistle to the Philippians*. London: Black.
–. 2006. *Seeing the Word: refocusing New Testament study*. Grand Rapids: Baker Academic.
–. 2008. The Conversion of Desire in St. Paul's Hemeneutics. In *The Word Leaps the Gap: Essays on Scripture and Theology in Honor of Richard B. Hays*, eds J. R. Wagner, C. K. Rowe, and A. K. Grieb, 498–513. Cambridge: Eerdmans.
Boers, H. 2006. *Christ in the letters of Paul: in place of a christology*. Berlin: W. de Gruyter.
Bosman, H. 2004. The absence and presence of God in the book of Exodus a theological synthesis. *Scriptura* 85(1):1–13.
Bousset, W. 1970. *Kyrios Christos: Geschichte des Christusglaubens von den Anfängen des Christentums bis Irenaeus*. New York: Abingdon.
Börschel, R. 2001. *Die Konstruktion einer christlichen Identität: Paulus und die Gemeinde von Thessalonich in ihrer hellenistisch-römischen Umwelt*. Berlin: Philo.
Brown, R. E. 1994. *An introduction to New Testament Christology*. London: Chapman.

Brown, T. R. 2002. God and Men in Israel's History: God and Idol Worship in *Praise of the Fathers* (Sir 44–50). In *Ben Sira's God: Proceedings of the International Ben Sira Conference*, ed. R. Egger-Wenzel, 214–20. Berlin: W. de Gruyter.

Bruce, F. 1982. *1 & 2 Thessalonians*. Waco: Word.

Brueggemann, W. 1998. *Theology of the Old Testament: testimony, dispute, advocacy*. Minneapolis: Fortress.

Bultmann, R. 1933. *Glauben und Verstehen I*. Tübingen: Mohr Siebeck.

–. 1951. *Theology of the New Testament*. Trans. K. Grobel. New York: Scribner's.

–. 1952. *Theology of the New Testament*. London: SCM.

–. 1969. The Christology of the New Testament. In *Faith and Understanding I*. New York: Harper & Row.

–. 1976. *Der zweite Brief an die Korinther*. Göttingen: Vandenhoeck & Ruprecht.

Burnett, G. W. 2001. *Paul and the salvation of the individual*. Köln: Brill.

Burnett, J. S. 2005. The question of divine absence in Israelite and West Semitic religion. *CBQ* 67(2):215–35.

Busch, E. 1975. *Karl Barth: his life from letter and autobiographical texts*. Trans. J. Bowden. London: SCM.

Calvin, J. 1854. *The Epistles of Paul to the Galatians and Ephesians*. Trans. W. Pringle. Edinburgh: Calvin Translation Society.

–. 1960. *The institutes of the Christian religion*. Philadelphia: Westminster John Knox.

Campbell, D. A. 2005. *The quest for Paul's Gospel: a suggested strategy*. London: T&T Clark.

–. 2009. *The deliverance of God: an apocalyptic rereading of justification in Paul*. Grand Rapids, Mich.: Eerdmans.

Capes, D. B. 1992. *Old Testament Yahweh Texts in Paul's Christology*. Tübingen: Mohr Siebeck.

–. 2004. YHWH texts and monotheism in Paul's christology. In *Early Jewish and Christian monotheism*, eds L. T. Stuckenbruck and W. E. North, 120–37. London: T&T Clark.

Casey, M. 1991. *From Jewish Prophet to Gentile God: The Origins and Development of New Testament Christology*. Cambridge: James Clarke.

–. 1999. Monotheism, Worship and Christological Developments in the Pauline Churches. In *The Jewish Roots of Christological Monotheism*, eds C. Newman, J. Davila, and G. Lewis, 214–33. Leiden: Brill.

Charlesworth, J. H. 2007. Can We Discern the Composition Date of the Parables of Enoch. In *EMSM*, ed. G. Boccaccini, 450–68. Cambridge: Eerdmans.

------, ed. 1983. *The Old Testament Pseudepigrapha, 2 vols*. New York: Doubleday.

Chester, A. 1991. Jewish Messianic Expectations and Mediatorial Figures in Pauline Christology. In *Paulus und das antike Judentum*, eds. M. Hengel and U. Heckel, 17–89. Tübingen: Mohr Siebeck.

–. 2007. *Messiah and exaltation: Jewish messianic and visionary traditions and New Testament Christology*. Wissenschaftliche Untersuchungen zum Neuen Testament. Tübingen: Mohr Siebeck.

Chialà, S. 2007. The Son of Man: The Evolution of an Expression. In *EMSM*, ed. G. Boccaccini, 153–78. Cambridge: Eerdmans.

Churchill, T. W. R. 2008. *Divine Initiative and the Christology of the Damascus Road Encounter*. PhD thesis. Brunel University.

Collins, A. Y. 1999. The worship of Jesus and the Imperial Cult. In *The Jewish Roots of Christological Monotheism*, eds C. Newman, J. Davila, and G. Lewis, 234–57. Leiden: Brill.

–. 2007. The Secret Son of Man in the Parables of Enoch and the Gospel of Mark: A Response to Leslie Walck. In *EMSM*, ed. G. Boccaccini, 338–42. Cambridge: Eerdmans.

Collins, J. J. 2007. Enoch and the Son of Man: A Response to Sabino Chialà and Helge Kvanvig. In *EMSM*, ed. G. Boccaccini, 216–27. Cambridge: Eerdmans.

Collins, R. F. 1999. *First Corinthians*. Collegeville: Liturgical Press.

Conzelmann, H. 1969. *Der erste Brief an die Korinther*. Göttingen: Vandenhoeck & Ruprecht.

Corley, J. 2002. God as Merciful Father in Ben Sira and the New Testament. In *Ben Sira's God: Proceedings of the International Ben Sira Conference*, ed. R. Egger-Wenzel, 33–38. Berlin: W. de Gruyter.

Cotterell, P., and M. Turner. 1989. *Linguistics and Biblical Interpretation*. London: SPCK.

Cranfield, C. E. B. 2002[8]. *Romans 9–16*. Edinburgh: T&T Clark.

–. 2004[10]. *Romans 1–8*. Edinburgh: T&T Clark.

Crossley, J. G. 2010. *Reading the New Testament: Contemporary Approaches*. London: Routledge.

Cullmann, O. 1963[2]. *The Christology of the New Testament*. London: SCM.

Dahl, N. A. 1991. *Jesus the Christ: the historical origins of christological doctrine*. Minneapolis: Fortress.

Danker, F. W. 1989. *II Corinthians*. Minneapolis: Augsburg Publishing House.

Davila, J. 1999. Of Methodology, Monotheism and Metatron: Introductory Reflections on Divine Mediators and the Origins of the Worship of Jesus. In *The Jewish Roots of Christological Monotheism*, eds C. Newman, J. Davila, and G. Lewis, 3–18. Leiden: Brill.

–. 2005. The Old Testament Pseudepigrapha as Background to the New Testament. *ExpTim* 117(2):53–57.

–. 2005. *The provenance of the Pseudepigrapha: Jewish, Christian, or other?* Leiden: Brill.

Davis, C. J. 1996. *The name and way of the Lord: Old Testament themes, New Testament christology*. Sheffield: Sheffield Academic Press.

Deddo, G. W. 1999. *Karl Barth's theology of relations: trinitarian, christological, and human: towards an ethic of the family*. New York: Lang.

Deissmann, A. 1912. *Saint Paul: A Study in Social and Religious History*. London: Hodder & Stoughton.

Downing, F. 1998. *Cynics, Paul and the pauline churches. Cynics and christian origins II*. London: Routledge.

Droge, A. J., and J. D. Tabor. 1992. *A noble death: suicide and martyrdom among Christians and Jews in antiquity*. San Francisco: Harper.

du Toit, A. 2000. 'In Christ', 'in the Spirit' and Related Prepositional Phrases: Their Relevance for a Discussion on Pauline Mysticism. *Neot* 34(2):287–98.

Dunn, J. D. 1975. *Jesus and the Spirit*. London: SCM.

–. 1987. "A Light to the Gentiles": The Significance of the Damascus Road Christophany for Paul. In *The Glory of Christ in the New Testament: studies in Christology*, eds L. Hurst and N. Wright, 251–66. Oxford: Clarendon.

–. 1988. *Romans*. Waco: Word.

–. 1989[2]. *Christology in the Making: a New Testament inquiry into the origins of the doctrine of the incarnation*. London: SCM.

–. 1991. *The Partings of the Ways: between Christianity and Judaism and their significance for the character of Christianity*. London: SCM.

–. 1993. *The Epistle to the Galatians*. London: Black.

—. 1996. *The Epistles to the Colossians and to Philemon: A Commentary on the Greek Text*. Carlisle: Paternoster.

—. 1998. Christology as an aspect of theology. In *The Christ and the Spirit: Christology*, 377–87. Edinburgh: T&T Clark.

—. 1998. How controversial was Paul's christology? In *The Christ and the Spirit: Christology*, 212–28. Edinburgh: T&T Clark.

—. 1998. Pauline Christology: shaping the fundamental structures. In *The Christ and the Spirit: Christology*, 229–38. Edinburgh: T&T Clark.

—. 1998. *The Theology of Paul the Apostle*. Grand Rapids: Eerdmans.

—. 1998. Was Christianity a Monotheistic Faith from the Beginning? In *The Christ and the Spirit: Christology*, 315–44. Edinburgh: T&T Clark.

—. 1998. Why 'Incarnation'? A Review of Recent New Testament Scholarship. In *The Christ and the Spirit: Christology*. Edinburgh: T&T Clark.

—. 1998. 2 Corinthians 3:17. "The Lord Is the Spirit". In *The Christ and the Spirit: Christology*, 115–25. Edinburgh: T&T Clark.

—. 2003. *Jesus Remembered*. Christianity in the making. Grand Rapids: Eerdmans.

—. 2004. Review: The Spirit's Relation to the Risen Lord in Paul. *JTS* 55:283–86.

—. 2005. When was Jesus first worshipped? In dialogue with Larry Hurtado's *Lord Jesus Christ: devotion to Jesus in the earliest Christianity. ExpTim* 116(6):193–96.

—. 2010. *Did the first Christians worship Jesus?: the New Testament evidence*. London: SPCK.

Dupont, J. 1952. *ΣΥΝ ΧΡΙΣΤΩΙ: L'union avec le Christ suivant saint Paul*. Paris: Louvain.

Ebeling, G. 1963. *Word and faith*. Philadelphia: Fortress.

Eichrodt, W. 1961. *Theology of the Old Testament. Vol. 1*. Trans. J. A. Baker. Philadelphia: Westminster John Knox.

—. 1967. *Theology of the Old Testament. Vol. 2*. Trans. J. A. Baker. Philadelphia: Westminster John Knox.

Eisenbaum, P. 2009. *Paul was not a Christian: the original message of a misunderstood Apostle*. New York: HarperOne.

Eriksson, A. 1998. *Traditions as Rhetorical Proof: Pauline Argumentation in 1 Corinthians*. Stockholm: Almqvist & Wiksell.

Eskola, T. 2001. *Messiah and the throne: Jewish Merkabah mysticism and early christian exaltation discourse*. Tübingen: Mohr Siebeck.

Fatehi, M. 2000. *The Spirit's Relation to the Risen Lord in Paul: An Examination of its Christological Implications*. Tübingen: Mohr Siebeck.

Fee, G. D. 1987. *The First Epistle to the Corinthians*. Exeter: Paternoster.

—. 1994. *God's Empowering Presence: The Holy Spirit in the Letters of Paul*. Peabody: Hendrickson.

—. 2007. Paul's Use of Locative ἐν in Galatians: On Text and Meaning in Galatians 1.6; 1.16; 2.20; 3.11–12 and 3.26. In *The impartial God: essays in biblical studies in honour of Jouette M. Bassler*, ed. C. J. Roetzel and R. L. Foster, 170–85. Sheffield: Sheffield Phoenix Press.

—. 2007. *Pauline Christology: An Exegetical-Theological Study*. Peabody: Hendrickson.

—. 2009. *The First and Second Letters to the Thessalonians*. Grand Rapids: Eerdmans.

Feine, P. 1902. *Jesus Christus und Paulus*. Leipzig: Hinrichs.

Fitzgerald, J. T. 2003. Paul and Friendship. In *Paul in the Greco-Roman World: A Handbook*, ed. J. P. Sampley, 319–43. Harrisburg: Trinity Press International.

Fitzmyer, J. A. 2008. *First Corinthians*. AB. London: Yale University Press.
Fletcher-Louis, C. H. 1997. *Luke–Acts: Angels, Christology and Soteriology*. Tübingen: Mohr/Siebeck.
–. 1999. The Worship of Divine Humanity as God's Image and the Worship of Jesus. In *The Jewish Roots of Christological Monotheism*, eds C. Newman, J. Davila, and G. Lewis, 112–28. Leiden: Brill.
–. 2002. *All the glory of Adam: liturgical anthropology in the Dead Sea Scrolls*. Leiden: Brill.
–. 2004. Alexander the Great's worship of the High Priest. In *Early Jewish and Christian monotheism*, eds L. T. Stuckenbruck and W. E. North, 71–102. London: T&T Clark.
Fotopoulos, J. 2003. *Food offered to idols in Roman Corinth: a social-rhetorical reconsideration of 1 Corinthians 8:1–11:1*. Tübingen: Mohr Siebeck.
Fowl, S. E. 1988. *Engaging Scripture: A Model for Theological Interpretation*. Oxford: Blackwell.
–. 1990. *The Story of Christ in the Ethics of Paul*. Sheffield: JSOT Press.
–. 2005. *Philippians*. Cambridge: Eerdmans.
France, R. T. 1982. The worship of Jesus: A neglected factor in the christological debate. In *Christ the Lord: studies in Christology presented to Donald Guthrie*, ed. H. H. Rowdon, 17–36. Leicester: IVP.
Fredriksen, P. 1988. *From Jesus to Christ: the origins of the New Testament, images of Jesus*. New Haven: Yale University Press.
–. 2007. Mandatory Retirement: Ideas in the Study of Christian Origins Whose Time Has Come to Go. In *Israel's God and Rebecca's Children: Essays in Honor of Larry W. Hurtado and Alan F. Segal*, eds D. B. Capes, DeConick April D., Bond Helen K., and Miller Troy A., 25–38. Waco: Baylor.
Fretheim, T. E. 2005. *God and world in the Old Testament: a relational theology of creation*. Nashville: Abingdon.
Fröhlich, I. 2007. The Parables of Enoch and Qumran Literature. In *EMSM*, ed. G. Boccaccini, 343–51. Cambridge: Eerdmans.
Fuller, R. 1965. *The Foundations of New Testament Christology*. New York: Scribner's.
Furnish, V. P. 1984. *II Corinthians*. AB. New York: Doubleday.
Garland, D. E. 2003. *1 Corinthians*. Grand Rapids: Baker.
Gaventa, B. R., and R. B. Hays, eds. 2008. *Seeking the Identity of Jesus: A Pilgrimage*. Cambridge: Eerdmans.
Gäckle, V. 2005. *Die Starken und die Schwachen in Korinth und in Rom: Zu Herkunft und Funktion der Antithese in 1 Kor 8,1–11,1 und Röm 14,1–15,13*. Tübingen: Mohr Siebeck.
Geller, S. A. 2000. The God of the Covenant. In *One god or many?: concepts of divinity in the ancient world*, ed. B. N. Porter, 273–319. Chebeague, Me.: Casco Bay Assyriological Institute.
Gerhardsson, B. 1996. *The Shema in the New Testament: Deut 6:4–5 in significant passages*. Lund: Novapress.
Giblin, C. H. 1975. Three Monotheistic Texts in Paul. *CBQ* 37:527–47.
Gieschen, C. A. 1998. *Angelomorphic Christology: Antecedents and Early Evidence*. Leiden: Brill.
–. 2007. The Name of the Son of Man in the Parables of Enoch. In *EMSM*, ed. G. Boccaccini, 238–49. Cambridge: Eerdmans.
Giles, K. 2006. *Jesus and the Father: Modern Evangelicals Reinvent the Doctrine of the Trinity*. Grand Rapids: Zondervan.

Gnilka, J. 1968. *Der Philipperbrief / Der Philemonbrief*. Freiburg: Herder.

Goodwin, M. 2001. *Paul, apostle of the living God : kerygma and conversion in 2 Corinthians*. Harrisburg, Pa.: Trinity Press International.

Gorman, M. J. 2001. *Cruciformity: Paul's narrative spirituality of the cross*. Cambridge: Eerdmans.

–. 2009. *Inhabiting the Cruciform God: Kenosis, Justification, and Theosis in Paul's Narrative Soteriology*. Cambridge: Eerdmans.

Goshen-Gottstein, A. 2002. Ben Sira's Praise of the Fathers. In *Ben Sira's God: Proceedings of the International Ben Sira Conference*, ed. R. Egger-Wenzel, 235–67. Berlin: W. de Gruyter.

Grabbe, L. L. 2000. *Judaic religion in the Second Temple period*. London: Routledge.

–. 2007. The Parables of Enoch in Second Temple Jewish Society. In *EMSM*, ed. G. Boccaccini, 386–402. Cambridge: Eerdmans.

Gräbe, P. J. 2000. *The Power of God in Paul's Letters*. Tübingen: Mohr Siebeck.

Green, G. L. 2002. *The Letters to the Thessalonians*. Pillar New Testament Commentary. Leicester: Apollos.

Green, J. B., and M. Turner, eds. 2000. *Between two horizons: Spanning New Testament studies and systematic theology*. Grand Rapids: Eerdmans.

Grenz, S. J. 2001. *The social god and the relational self: a trinitarian theology of the Imago Dei*. Louisville: Westminster John Knox.

Grillmeier, A. 1975. *Christ in Christian tradition*. Vol. 1, *From the apostolic age to Chalcedon (451)*. Trans. J. Bowden. Atlanta: John Knox Press.

Gruber, M. M. 1998. *Herrlichkeit in Schwachheit: Eine Auslegung der Apologie des Zweiten Korintherbriefs 2 Kor 2,14–6,13*. FB. Würzburg: Echter.

Gunkel, H. 1888. *Die Wirkungen des heiligen Geistes nach der populären Anschauung der apostolischen Zeit und der Lehre des Apostels Paulus*. Göttingen: Vandenhoeck & Ruprecht.

Gunton, C. E. 1995. *A Brief Theology of Revelation*. London: T&T Clark.

Hafemann, S. J. 1995. *Paul, Moses, and the history of Israel: the letter / spirit contrast and the argument from scripture in 2 Corinthians 3*. Tübingen: Mohr Siebeck.

–. 2007. The Covenant Relationship. In *Central Themes in Biblical Theology: Mapping unity in diversity*, eds S. J. Hafemann, P. R. House, 20–65. Grand Rapids: Baker Academic.

Hahn, F. 1969. *The Titles of Jesus in Christology: Their History in Early Christianity*. New York: World Publishing.

Hannah, D. D. 2007. The Book of Noah, the Death of Herod the Great, and of the Date of the Parables of Enoch. In *EMSM*, ed. G. Boccaccini, 469–77. Cambridge: Eerdmans.

Harnack, A. 1990[4]. *Lehrbuch der Dogmengeschichte*. Tübingen: Mohr.

Harris, M. J. 1991. *Colossians & Philemon*. Grand Rapids: Eerdmans.

–. 1992. *Jesus as God: The New Testament Use of Theos in Reference to Jesus*. Grand Rapids: Baker.

–. 1999. *Slave of Christ: a new testament metaphor for total devotion to Christ*. Leicester: Apollos.

–. 2005. *The Second Epistle to the Corinthians: a commentary on the Greek text*. Milton Keynes: Paternoster.

Harrisville, R. A. 2006. Before πίστις Χριστοῦ: The Objective Genitive as Good Greek. *NovT* 48(4):233–41.

Harvey, A. 1982. *Jesus and the Constraints of History*. London: Duckworth.

Hawthorne, G. 1983. *Philippians*. Waco: Word.

Hayman, P. 1991. Monotheism—a misused word in jewish studies? *JJS* 42:1–15.

Hays, R. B. 1989. *Echoes of Scripture in the Letters of Paul*. New Haven: Yale University Press.

—. 1997. *First Corinthians*. Louisville: John Knox Press.

Head, P. M. 2004. The habits of New Testament copyists: singular readings in the early fragmentary papyri of John. *Bib* 85(3):399–408.

Healy, M. 2007. Knowledge of the Mystery: A Study of Pauline Epistemology. In *The Bible and Epistemology*, eds M. Healy, R. Parry, 134–57. Milton Keynes: Paternoster.

Heckel, U. 1993. *Kraft in Schwachheit: Untersuchungen zu 2. Kor 10–13*. Tübingen: Mohr Siebeck.

Heil, J. P. 2005. *The rhetorical role of Scripture in 1 Corinthians*. Leiden: Brill.

Heliso, D. 2007. *Pistis and the Righteous One: a study of Romans 1:17 against the background of scripture and Second Temple Jewish literature*. Tübingen: Mohr Siebeck.

Hengel, M. 1974. *Judaism and Hellenism: Studies in Their Encounter in Palestine During the Early Hellenistic Period*. London: SCM.

—. 1976. *The Son of God: The Origin of Christology and the History of Jewish-Hellenistic Religion*. London: SCM.

—. 1983. *Between Jesus and Paul: studies in the earliest history of Christianity*. London: SCM.

—. 1995. *Studies in early christology*. Edinburgh: T&T Clark.

Hengel, M., and A. M. Schwemer. 1997. *Paul between Damascus and Antioch: The Unknown Years*. London: SCM.

Henze, M. 2007. The Parables of Enoch in Second Temple Literature: A Response to Gabriele Boccaccini. In *EMSM*, ed. G. Boccaccini, 290–98. Cambridge: Eerdmans.

Hofius, O. 1997. "Einer ist Gott – Einer ist Herr". Erwägungen zu Struktur und Aussage des Bekenntnisses 1.Kor 8,6. In *Eschatologie und Schöpfung: Festschrift für Erich Gräßer zum siebzigsten Geburtstag*, eds M. Evang, E. Gräßer, H. Merklein, and M. Wolter, 95–108. Berlin: W. de Gruyter.

Horbury, W. 1998. *Jewish messianism and the cult of Christ*. London: SCM.

—. 2004. Jewish and Christian monotheism in the Herodian age. In *Early Jewish and Christian Monotheism*, eds L. T. Stuckenbruck and W. E. S. North, 16–44. London: T&T Clark.

—. 2005. Review of Hurtado's *Lord Jesus Christ*. *JTS* 59(2):531–39.

Horn, F. W. 1992. *Das Angeld des Geistes: Studien zur paulinischen Pneumatologie*. Göttingen: Vandenhoeck & Ruprecht.

Hurd, J. C. 1965. *The origin of 1 Corinthians*. London: SPCK.

Hurtado, L. W. 1979. New Testament christology: A critique of Bousset's influence. *TS* 40:306–17.

—. 1985. New Testament christology: retrospect and prospect. *Semeia* 30:15–27.

—. 1988. *One God, One Lord*. London: SCM.

—. 1993. Lord. In *DPL*, eds G. Hawthorne, R. Martin, and D. Reid, 560–69. Leicester: IVP.

—. 1993. Son of God. In *DPL*, eds G. Hawthorne, R. Martin, and D. Reid, 900–06. Leicester: IVP.

—. 1993. What do we mean by "First century Jewish monotheism"? *SBLSP*:348–68.

—. 1997. Philippians 2:6–11. In *Prayer from Alexander to Constantine: a critical anthology*, ed. M. Kiley, 235–39. London: Routledge.

–. 1998. First-Century Jewish Monotheism. *JSNT* 71:3–26.
–. 1998². *One God, One Lord.* Edinburgh: T&T Clark.
–. 1999. Pre-70 C.E. jewish opposition to Christ-devotion. *JTS* 50:35–58.
–. 2000. *At the origins of christian worship: The context and character of earliest christian devotion.* Grand Rapids: Eerdmans.
–. 2003. *Lord Jesus Christ: Devotion to Jesus in earliest christianity.* Grand Rapids: Eerdmans.
–. 2005. *How on earth did Jesus become a God?* Grand Rapids: Eerdmans.
–. 2010. *God in New Testament Theology.* Nashville: Abingdon Press.
Hübner, H. 1987. Paulusforschung seit 1945. Ein kritischer Literaturbericht. In *ANRW* II.25.4, 2649–2840.
Instone-Brewer, D. 2004. *Traditions of the Rabbis in the Era of the New Testament, Vol. 1.* Grand Rapids: Eerdmans.
Jansen, H. 1995. *Relationality and the concept of God.* Amsterdam: Rodopi.
Jewett, R. 2007. *Romans: a commentary.* Minneapolis: Fortress.
Johnson, L. T. 1998. *Religious experience in earliest Christianity: A missing dimension in New Testament studies.* Minneapolis: Fortress.
Jonge, M., de. 1988. *Christology in context. The earliest christian response to Jesus.* Philadelphia: Westminster John Knox.
Josephus, F. 2005. *Flavius Josephus: Judean Antiquities Books 5–7.* Trans. C. Begg, S. Mason and L. H. Feldman. Leiden: Brill.
Jüngel, E. 1967. *Paulus und Jesus: eine Untersuchung zur Präzisierung der Frage nach dem Ursprung der Christologie.* Tübingen: Mohr Siebeck.
Kärkkäinen, V.-M. 2003. *Christology: A Global Introduction.* Grand Rapids: Baker.
Käsemann, E. 1971. *Perspectives on Paul.* London: SCM.
–. 1980. *Commentary on Romans.* London: SCM.
Keck, L. 1986. Toward the Renewal of New Testament Christology. *NTS* 32:362–77.
Keener, C. S. 2005. *1–2 Corinthians.* Cambridge: Cambridge University Press.
Keesmaat, S. C. 1999. *Paul and his Story. (Re)Interpreting the Exodus Tradition.* Sheffield: Sheffield Academic Press.
Kim, B.-m. 2002. *Die paulinische Kollekte.* Tübingen: Francke.
Kim, S. 1984². *The Origin of Paul's Gospel.* Tübingen: Mohr Siebeck.
–. 2002. *Paul and the New Perspective: Second thoughts on the origin of Paul's gospel.* Grand Rapids: Eerdmans.
Kirk, J. R. D. 2008. *Unlocking Romans: Resurrection and the Justification of God.* Cambridge: Eerdmans.
Kleine, W. 2002. *Zwischen Furcht und Hoffnung: eine textlinguistische Untersuchung des Briefes 2 Kor 1–9 zur wechselseitigen Bedeutsamkeit der Beziehung von Apostel und Gemeinde.* Berlin: Philo.
Knibb, M. A. 2007. The Structure and Composition of the Parables of Enoch. In *EMSM*, ed. G. Boccaccini, 48–64. Cambridge: Eerdmans.
Koch, K. 2007. Questions regarding the so-Called Son of Man in the Parables of Enoch: A Response to Sabino Chialà and Helge Kvanvig. In *EMSM*, ed. G. Boccaccini, 228–37. Cambridge: Eerdmans.
Konradt, M. 2003. *Gericht und Gemeinde: eine Studie zur Bedeutung und Funktion von Gerichtsaussagen im Rahmen der paulinischen Ekklesiologie und Ethik im 1 Thess und 1 Kor.* Berlin: W. de Gruyter.
Koperski, V. 1996. *The knowledge of Christ Jesus my Lord: The high christology of Philippians 3:7–11.* Kampen, Netherlands: Kok Pharos.
Kramer, W. 1966. *Christ, Lord, Son of God.* London: SCM.

Kreitzer, L. 1987. *Jesus and God in Paul's Eschatology*. Sheffield: Sheffield Academic Press.

–. 1993. Body. In *DPL*, eds G. Hawthorne, R. Martin, and D. Reid, 71–76. Leicester: IVP.

–. 1993. Eschatology. In *DPL*, eds G. Hawthorne, R. Martin, and D. Reid, 253–69. Leicester: IVP.

Kuschnerus, B. 2002. *Die Gemeinde als Brief Christi: die kommunikative Funktion der Metapher bei Paulus am Beispiel von 2 Kor 2–5*. Göttingen: Vandenhoeck und Ruprecht.

Kümmel, W. G. 1973. *The New Testament: The history of the investigation of its problems*. London: SCM.

–. 1973. *The theology of the New Testament: according to its major witnesses, Jesus-Paul-John*. Nashville: Abingdon.

Kvanvig, H. S. 2007. The Son of Man in the Parables of Enoch. In *EMSM*, ed. G. Boccaccini, 179–215. Cambridge: Eerdmans.

LaCugna, C. M. 1991. *God for us: the Trinity and Christian life*. New York: HarperSanFrancisco.

Lambrecht, J. 1998. *Second Corinthians*. Collegeville: Liturgical Press.

Lash, N. 1993. *Believing three ways in one God: a reading of the Apostles' creed*. London: Notre Dame Press.

Lee, A. H. I. 2005. *From Messiah to preexistent son: Jesus' self-consciousness and early christian exegesis of messianic psalms*. Tübingen: Mohr Siebeck.

Leonhardt-Balzer, J. 2001. *Jewish worship in Philo of Alexandria*. Tübingen: Mohr Siebeck.

Leslau, W. 1987. *Comparative dictionary of Ge'ez: (classical Ethiopic); Ge'ez-Engl./Engl.-Ge'ez ; with an index of the Semitic roots*. Wiesbaden: Harrassowitz.

Liddon, H. 1875[7]. *The Divinity of our Lord and Saviour Jesus Christ. Eight lectures preached before the university of Oxford in 1866*. London: Rivingtons.

Liesen, J. 2002. "With all your heart": Praise in the Book of Ben Sira. In *Ben Sira's God: Proceedings of the International Ben Sira Conference*, ed. R. Egger-Wenzel, 199–220. Berlin: W. de Gruyter.

Lightfoot, J. B. 1869[3]. *St Paul's Epistle to the Galatians*. London: Macmillan.

–. 1893. *Biblical essays*. London: Macmillan.

Lincoln, A. 1981. *Paradise Now and Not Yet: Studies in the Role of the Heavenly Dimension in Paul's Thought with Special Reference to His Eschatology*. Cambridge: Cambridge University Press.

Lohse, E. 1996. *Paulus: eine Biographie*. München: Beck.

MacDonald, N. 2003. *Deuteronomy and the Meaning of "Monotheism"*. Tübingen: Mohr Siebeck.

Malherbe, A. J. 2000. *The letters to the Thessalonians*. AB. London: Doubleday.

Malina, B. J., and J. J. Pilch. 2006. *Social-science commentary on the letters of Paul*. Minneapolis: Fortress.

Marshall, I. 1976. *The Origins of New Testament Christology*. Leicester: IVP.

Martin, D. B. 1990. *Slavery as salvation: the metaphor of slavery in Pauline Christianity*. New Haven: Yale University Press.

Martin, R. 1986. *2 Corinthians*. Waco: Word.

–. 1993. Hymns, hymn fragments, songs, spiritual songs. In *DPL*, eds G. Hawthorne, R. Martin, and D. Reid, 419–23. Leicester: IVP.

Martyn, J. L. 1997. *Galatians: A New Translation with Introduction and Commentary*. AB. London: Doubleday.

Matera, F. J. 1999. *New Testament Christology*. Westminster: Louisville.

–. 2003. *II Corinthians: a commentary*. Louisville: Westminster John Knox.

Matlock, R. B. 2007. The Rhetoric of πίστις in Paul: Galatians 2.16, 3.22, Romans 3.22, and Philippians 3.9. *JSNT* 30(2):173–203.

McConville, J. G. 1993. *Grace in the End: A Study in Deuteronomic Theology*. Grand Rapids: Zondervan.

McGrath, A. E. 1994². *The making of modern German christology 1750–1990*. Leicester: Apollos.

McGrath, J. F. 2009. *The Only True God: Early Christian Monotheism in its Jewish Context*. Urbana: University of Illinois Press.

Mead, J. K. 2007. *Biblical Theology: Issues, Methods, and Themes*. London: Westminster John Knox Press.

Meier, J. P. 2001. *A Marginal Jew: Rethinking the historical Jesus. Vol. 3. Companions and competitors*. New York: Doubleday.

Meyer, B. F. 1979. *The Aims of Jesus*. London: SCM.

Minear, P. S. 1990. Singing and Suffering in Philippi. In *The conversation continues: studies in Paul & John*, ed. B. Gaventa and R. T. Fortna, 202–19. Nashville: Abingdon.

Mitchell, M. M. 1991. *Paul and the rhetoric of reconciliation: an exegetical investigation of the language and composition of 1 Corinthians*. Tübingen: Mohr Siebeck.

Moffatt, J. 1938. *The First Epistle of Paul to the Corinthians*. London: Hodder & Stoughton.

Moltmann, J. 1981. *The trinity and the kingdom: the doctrine of God*. Minneapolis: Fortress.

Moo, D. J. 1996. *The Epistle to the Romans*. Grand Rapids: Eerdmans.

–. 2005. The Christology of the Early Pauline Letters. In *Contours of Christology in the New Testament*, ed. R. N. Longenecker, 169–92. Grand Rapids: Eerdmans.

Morris, L. 1991. *The first and second Epistles to the Thessalonians*. Grand Rapids: Eerdmans.

Moule, C. 1977. *The Origin of Christology*. Cambridge: Cambridge University Press.

Moxnes, H. 1980. *Theology in conflict: studies in Paul's understanding of God in Romans*. Leiden: Brill.

Moyise, S., and M. J. J. Menken, eds. 2007. *Deuteronomy in the New Testament: The New Testament and the Scriptures of Israel*. London: T&T Clark.

Mulder, O. 2003. *Simon the High Priest in Sirach 50: an exegetical study of the significance of Simon the High Priest as climax to the Praise of the fathers in Ben Sira's concept of the history of Israel*. Leiden: Brill.

Murphy-O'Connor, J. 1976. Christological Anthropology in Phil., II, 6–11. *RB* 83:25–50.

–. 1978. *Becoming Human Together*. Dublin: Veritas Publications.

–. 1986. "Being at home in the body we are in exile from the Lord": (2 Cor. 5:6b). *RB* 93:214–21.

–. 1991. *The theology of the Second Letter to the Corinthians*. Cambridge: Cambridge University Press.

–. 1996. *Paul: A Critical Life*. Oxford: Oxford University Press.

–. 2003. The origins of Paul's christology: from Thessalonians to Galatians. In *Christian origins: worship, belief and society*, ed. K. J. O'Mahony, 113–42. London: Sheffield Academic Press.

Na, I. 2002. The Meaning of *KATOPTRIZOMENOI* in 2 Cor 3,18. *ED* 55(1):33–44.

Nanos, M. D. 2008. The *Polytheist* Identity of the 'Weak', And Paul's Strategy to 'Gain' Them: A New Reading of 1 Corinthians 8:1–11:1. In *Paul: Jew, Greek and Roman*, ed. S. E. Porter, 179–210. Leiden: Brill.

Neve, L. 1972. *The Spirit of God in the Old Testament*. Tokyo: Seibunsha.

Newman, C. C. 1992. *Paul's glory-christology: tradition and rhetoric*. Köln: Brill.

–. 1999. From (Wright's) Jesus to (the Church's) Christ: Can we get there from here? In *Jesus and the restoration of Israel. A critical assessment of N.T. Wright's* Jesus and the Victory of God, ed. C. C. Newman, 281–7. Carlisle: IVP.

Newman, C., J. Davila, and G. Lewis, eds. 1999. *The Jewish Roots of Christological Monotheism*. Leiden: Brill.

Neyrey, J. 2004. *Render to God: New Testament understandings of the divine*. Minneapolis: Fortress.

Nicholl, C. R. 2004. *From hope to despair in Thessalonica: Situating 1 and 2 Thessalonians*. Cambridge: Cambridge University Press.

Nicholson, S. B. 2007. Dynamic Oneness: The Significance and Flexibility of Paul's One-God Language. PhD thesis. Durham.

Nickelsburg, G. W. E., K. Baltzer, ed. 2001. *1 Enoch: a commentary on the book of 1 Enoch*. Minneapolis: Fortress.

Nickelsburg, G. W. 2007. Discerning the Structure(s) of the Enochic Book of Parables. In *EMSM*, ed. G. Boccaccini, 23–47. Cambridge: Eerdmans.

Nickelsburg, G. W., and J. C. VanderKam. 2004. *1 Enoch: A New Translation*. Minneapolis: Fortress.

North, J. L. 2004. Jesus and worship, God and sacrifice. In *Early Jewish and Christian monotheism*, eds L. T. Stuckenbruck and W. E. North, 186–202. London: T&T Clark.

Noth, M. 1981. *The deuteronomistic history*. Sheffield: JSOT Press.

O'Brien, P. 1991. *The Epistle to the Philippians*. Grand Rapids: Eerdmans.

O'Neill, J. 1995. *Who did Jesus think he was?* Leiden: Brill.

Oesterley, W. O. E. 1925. *The Jewish background of the Christian liturgy*. Oxford: Clarendon Press.

Olson, D. C. 2004. *Enoch: a new translation*. North Richland Hills, Tex.: BIBAL Press.

Orlov, A. A. 2005. *The Enoch-Metatron tradition*. Tübingen: Mohr Siebeck.

Ortlund Jr., R. C. 1996. *Whoredom: God's unfaithful wife in biblical theology*. Leicester: Apollos.

Ostmeyer, K.-H. 2006. *Kommunikation mit Gott und Christus: Sprache und Theologie des Gebetes im Neuen Testament*. Tübingen: Mohr Siebeck.

Pannenberg, W. 1968. *Jesus: God and man*. Trans. L. L. Wilkins and D. A. Priebe. Philadelphia: Westminster Press.

Parry, R., and M. Healy, eds. 2007. *The Bible and Epistemology: Biblical Soundings on the Knowledge of God*. Milton Keynes: Paternoster.

Pate, C. M. 2000. *Communities of the last days*. Leicester: Apollos.

–. 2000. *The reverse of the curse: Paul, wisdom, and the law*. Tübingen: Mohr Siebeck.

Pate, C. M., et al. 2004. *The story of Israel: a biblical theology*. Leicester: Apollos.

Pearsall, J., and W. R. Trumble, eds. 1995. *The Oxford English reference dictionary*. Oxford: Oxford University Press.

Perriman, A. 1989. Paul and the parousia: 1 Corinthians 15.50–7 and 2 Corinthians 5.1–5. *NTS* 35(4):512–21.

–. 2005. *The Coming of the Son of Man*. Milton Keynes: Paternoster.

–. 2007. *Re:Mission. Biblical Mission for a Post-Biblical Church*. Milton Keynes: Paternoster.

Peters, M. K. H. 1992. Septuagint. In *ABD*, 1093–1104. London: Doubleday.

Petry, S. 2007. *Die Entgrenzung JHWHs: Monolatrie, Bilderverbot und Monotheismus im Deuteronomium, in Deuterojesaja und im Ezechielbuch*. Tübingen: Mohr Siebeck.

Piovanelli, P. 2007. "A Testimony for the Kings and the Mighty Who Possess the Earth": The Thirst for Justice and Peace in the Parables of Enoch. In *EMSM*, ed. G. Boccaccini, 363–79. Cambridge: Eerdmans.

Piper, J. 1995. The Demonstration of the Righteousness of God in Romans 3.25, 26. In *The Pauline writings. A Sheffield Reader*, eds S. E. Porter and C. A. Evans, 175–202. Sheffield: Sheffield Academic Press.

Plevnik, J. 1997. *Paul and the Parousia*. Peabody: Hendrickson.

Popkes, W. 2004. 1 Kor 2,2 und die Anfänge der Christologie. *ZNW* 95:64–83.

Porter, S. 1990. Two Myths: Corporate Personality and Language/Mentality Determinism. *SJT* 43:289–307.

Powers, D. 2001. *Salvation through participation: An examination of the notion of believer's corporate unity with Christ in early christian soteriology*. Leuven: Peters.

Rabens, V. 2007. *The Holy Spirit and Religious-Ethical Life in Paul: The Transforming and Empowering Work of the Spirit in Paul's Ethics*. Brunel University: PhD thesis.

–. 2013². *The Holy Spirit and Ethics in Paul: Transformation and Empowering for Religious-Ethical Life*. WUNT II/283. Tübingen: Mohr Siebeck.

Räisänen, H. 1990. *Beyond New Testament Theology*. London: SCM.

Reumann, J. 2008. *Philippians: A New Translation with Introduction and Commentary*. AB. New Haven: Yale University Press.

Richard, E. 1988. *Jesus: One and Many. The Christological concept of New Testament authors*. Delaware: Michael Glazier.

–. 1995. *First and Second Thessalonians*. Minnesota: Liturgical Press.

Richardson, N. 1994. *Paul's Language about God*. Sheffield: Sheffield Academic Press.

Rissi, M. 1969. *Studien zum Zweiten Korintherbrief: der alte Bund, der Prediger, der Tod*. Zürich: Zwingli-Verl.

Royse, J. R. 2008. *Scribal habits in early Greek New Testament papyri*. Leiden: Brill.

Sacchi, P. 2007. The 2005 Camaldoli Seminar on the Parables of Enoch: Summary and Prospects for Future Research. In *EMSM*, ed. G. Boccaccini, 499–512. Cambridge: Eerdmans.

Sampley, J. P. 2002. The First Letter to the Corinthians. Introduction, commentary, and reflections. In *The New Interpreter's Bible*, ed. L. E. Keck, et al., 771–1003. Nashville: Abington.

Samra, J. G. 2006. *Being conformed to Christ in community: a study of maturity, maturation and the local church in the undisputed Pauline Epistles*. London: T&T Clark.

Sanders, E. 1977. *Paul and Palestinian Judaism: A Comparison of Patterns of Religion*. London: SCM.

Sandnes, K. O. 1991. *Paul – One of the Prophets?* Tübingen: Mohr.

–. 2002. *Belly and Body in the Pauline Epistles*. Cambridge: Cambridge University Press.

Schade, H.-H. 1984². *Apokalyptische Christologie bei Paulus: Studien zum Zusammenhang von Christologie und Eschatologie in den Paulusbriefen.* Göttingen: Vandenhoeck & Ruprecht.

Schlatter, A. 1977. *Die Theologie der Apostel.* Stuttgart: Calwer.

Schnabel, E. J. 1985. *Law and Wisdom from Ben Sira to Paul: a tradition historical enquiry into the relation of law, wisdom, and ethics.* Tübingen: Mohr Siebeck.

–. 2004. *Early Christian Mission Vol. 2: Paul and the early church.* Leicester: Apollos.

–. 2006. *Der erste Brief des Paulus an die Korinther.* Wuppertal: R. Brockhaus Verlag.

Schnelle, U. 2000. Heilsgegenwart. Christologische Hoheitstitel bei Paulus. In *Paulinische Christologie,* eds U. Schnelle, T. Söding, and M. Labahn, 178–93. Göttingen: Vandenhoeck & Ruprecht.

–. 2003. *Paulus: Leben und Denken.* Berlin: W. de Gruyter.

Scholtissek, K. 2000. 'Ihr seid ein Brief Christi' (2 Kor 3,3). Zur einer ekklesiologischen Metapher bei Paulus. *BZ* 44:183–205.

Schrage, W. 1991. *Der erste Brief an die Korinther (1).* Zürich: Benziger.

–. 1995. *Der erste Brief an die Korinther (2).* Zürich: Benziger.

–. 2001. *Der erste Brief an die Korinther (4).* Zürich: Benziger.

–. 2002. *Unterwegs zur Einzigkeit und Einheit Gottes: zum "Monotheismus" des Paulus und seiner alttestamentlich-frühjüdischen Tradition.* Neukirchen-Vluyn: Neukirchener Verlag.

Schreiner, T. R. 1998. *Romans.* Grand Rapids: Baker.

–. 2001. *Paul: Apostle of God's glory in Christ. A Pauline Theology.* Leicester: IVP.

Schröter, J. 1993. *Der versöhnte Versöhner: Paulus als unentbehrlicher Mittler im Heilsvorgang zwischen Gott und Gemeinde nach 2 Kor 2,14–7,4.* Tübingen: Francke.

Schweitzer, A. 1968. *The mysticism of Paul the apostle.* Trans. B. D. Montgomery, William. New York: Seabury Press.

Scott, I. W. 2006. *Implicit epistemology in the Letters of Paul: story, experience and the spirit.* Tübingen: Mohr Siebeck.

Scott, J. M. 1993. Restoration of Israel. In *DPL,* eds G. Hawthorne, R. Martin, and D. Reid, 796–805. Leicester: IVP.

–. 1998. *2 Corinthians.* Peabody: Hendrickson.

Segal, A. F. 1977. *Two Powers in Heaven: Early rabbinic reports about christianity and gnosticism.* Leiden: Brill.

–. 1980. Heavenly ascent in hellenistic judaism, early Christianity and their environment. In *ANRW II.23/2,* 1333–94.

–. 1990. *Paul the Convert: The Apostolate and Apostasy of Saul the Pharisee.* London: Yale University Press.

Seifrid, M. A. 1993. In Christ. In *DPL,* eds G. Hawthorne, R. Martin, and D. Reid, 433–36. Leicester: IVP.

–. 2000. *Christ, our righteousness: Paul's theology of justification.* Leicester: Apollos.

Sheriffs, D. 1996. *The friendship of the Lord: an Old Testament spirituality.* Carlisle: Paternoster.

Shults, F. L. 2003. *Reforming theological anthropology: after the philosophical turn to relationality.* Grand Rapids: Eerdmans.

–. 2005. *Reforming the doctrine of God.* Grand Rapids: Eerdmans.

–. 2008. *Christology and Science.* Aldershot: Ashgate.

Shults, F. L., and S. J. Sandage. 2006. *Transforming spirituality: integrating theology and psychology*. Grand Rapids: Baker.

Siegert, F. 1985. *Argumentation bei Paulus: gezeigt an Röm 9–11.*. Tübingen: Mohr.

Silva, M. 1993. Old Testament in Paul. In *DPL*, eds G. Hawthorne, R. Martin, and D. Reid, 630–42. Leicester: IVP.

—. 2005. *Philippians*. Grand Rapids: Baker.

Smit, J. F. M. 2000. *"About the idol offerings": rhetoric, social context, and theology of Paul's discourse in First Corinthians 8:1–11:1*. Leuven: Peeters.

Smith, I. K. 2006. *Heavenly Perspective: A Study of the Apostle Paul's Response to a Jewish Mystical Movement at Colossae*. London: T&T Clark.

Smith, J. K. 2004. *Introducing Radical Orthodoxy: Mapping a Post-secular Theology*. Grand Rapids: Baker Academic.

Söding, T. 2003. Ekklesia und Koinonia: Grundbegriffe paulinischer Ekklesiologie. *Catholica* 57(2):107–23.

Sparks, H. F. D., ed. 1984. *The Apocryphal Old Testament*. Oxford: Clarendon Press.

Stanley, D. M. 1973. *Boasting in the Lord: the phenomenon of prayer in Saint Paul*. New York: Paulist.

Steenburg, D. 1990. The Worship of Adam and Christ as the Image of God. *JSNT* 39:95–109.

Stegman, T. 2005. *The character of Jesus: the linchpin to Paul's argument in 2 Corinthians*. Roma: Ed. Pontif. Ist. Biblico.

Stone, M. E. 2007. Enoch's Date in Limbo; or, Some Considerations on David Suter's Analysis of the Book of Parables. In *EMSM*, ed. G. Boccaccini, 444–49. Cambridge: Eerdmans.

Strachan, R. H. 1935. *The Second Epistle of Paul to the Corinthians*. London: Hodder & Stoughton.

Stuckenbruck, L. T. 1995. *Angel veneration and christology: A study in early judaism and in the christology of the Apocalypse of John*. Tübingen: Mohr Siebeck.

—. 2004. 'Angels' and 'God': Exploring the limits of early Jewish monotheism. In *Early Jewish and Christian monotheism*, eds L. T. Stuckenbruck and W. E. North, 45–70. London: T&T Clark.

—. 2007. The Parables of Enoch according to George Nickelsburg and Michael Knibb: A Summary and Discussion of Some Remaining Questions. In *EMSM*, ed. G. Boccaccini, 65–71. Cambridge: Eerdmans.

Stuhlmacher, P. 1986. *Vom Verstehen des Neuen Testaments: eine Hermeneutik*. Göttingen: Vandenhoeck & Ruprecht.

—. 1994. *Paul's Letter to the Romans*. Edinburgh: T&T Clark.

Sumney, J. L. 2007. *Philippians: A Greek Student's Intermediate Reader*. Peabody: Hendrickson.

Suter, D. W. 2007. Enoch in Sheol: Updating the Dating of the Book of Parables. In *EMSM*, ed. G. Boccaccini, 415–43. Cambridge: Eerdmans.

Tate, M. E. 1990. *Psalms 51–100*. Waco: Word.

Theißen, G. 2007. *Erleben und Verhalten der ersten Christen: Eine Psychologie des Urchristentums*. München: Gütersloher Verlagshaus.

Thiselton, A. C. 1995. New Testament interpretation in historical perspective. In *Hearing the New testament. Strategies for interpretation*, ed. J. B. Green, 10–36. Carlisle: Paternoster.

–. 1997. Human Being, Relationality, and Time in Hebrews, 1 Corinthians, And Western Traditions. *ExAud* 13:76–95.

–. 2000. *The First Epistle to the Corinthians. A commentary on the Greek text.* Carlisle: Paternoster/Eerdmans.

–. 2007. *The Hermeneutics of Doctrine.* Cambridge: Eerdmans.

Thomas, D. W., ed. 1958. *Documents from Old Testament times: translated with introductions and notes by members of the Society for Old Testament Study.* London: Nelson.

Thrall, M. E. 2004. *The Second Epistle to the Corinthians Vol. 1.* London: T&T Clark.

–. 2004. *The Second Epistle to the Corinthians Vol. 2.* London: T&T Clark.

Thurston, B. B., and J. Ryan. 2005. *Philippians and Philemon.* Collegeville: Liturgical Press.

Thüsing, W. 1969. *Per Christum in Deum: Studien zum Verhältnis von Christozentrik und Theozentrik in den paulinischen Hauptbriefen.* Münster: Aschendorff.

Tianmin, J. 2006. Translation in Context. *Translation Journal* 10(2), April.

Tigchelaar, E. J. 2007. Remarks on Transmission and Traditions in the Parables of Enoch: A Response to James VanderKam. In *EMSM*, ed. G. Boccaccini, 100–109. Cambridge: Eerdmans.

Tuckett, C. 2001. *Christology and the New Testament: Jesus and his earliest followers.* Edinburgh: Edinburgh University Press.

Turner, M. 1994. The Spirit of Christ and 'Divine' Christology. In *Jesus of Nazareth: Lord and Christ. Essays on the Historical Jesus and New Testament Christology*, eds J. B. Green and M. Turner, 413–36. Carlisle: Paternoster.

–. 1999. *The Holy Spirit and spiritual gifts: Then and now.* Carlisle: Paternoster.

–. 2003. 'Trinitarian' pneumatology in the New Testament? – towards an explanation of the worship of Jesus. *AsTJ* 58(1):167–86.

Ulrichs, K. F. 2007. *Christusglaube: Studien zum Syntagma pistis Christou und zum paulinischen Verständnis von Glaube und Rechtfertigung.* Tübingen: Mohr Siebeck.

VanderKam, J. C. 1995. *Enoch: A man for all generations.* Columbia: University of South Carolina Press.

–. 2007. The Book of Parables within the Enoch Tradition. In *EMSM*, ed. G. Boccaccini, 81–99. Cambridge: Eerdmans.

Vollenweider, S. 2002. *Horizonte neutestamentlicher Christologie: Studien zu Paulus und zur früchristlichen Theologie.* Tübingen: Mohr Siebeck.

von Rad, G. 1975. *Old Testament Theology. Volume 1.* London: SCM.

Voorwinde, S. 2005. Ἀγαπάω and Φιλέω – Is there a difference? *RTR* 64(2):76–90.

Vos, G. 1953. *The Pauline eschatology.* Grand Rapids: Eerdmans.

Vriezen, T. C. 1970. *An outline of Old Testament theology.* Revised edition no. 2. Newton, Massachusetts: Charles T. Branford Company.

Waaler, E. 2008. *The Shema and the First Commandment in First Corinthians: an intertextual approach to Paul's re-reading of deuteronomy.* Tübingen: Mohr Siebeck.

Waddell, J. A. 2010. *The Messiah in the Parables of Enoch and the Letters of Paul: A Comparative Analysis.* University of Michigan: Phd Thesis.

Wainwright, A. 1962. *The Trinity in the New Testament.* London: SPCK.

Walck, L. W. 2007. The Son of Man in the Parables of Enoch and the Gospels. In *EMSM*, ed. G. Boccaccini, 299–337. Cambridge: Eerdmans.

Wanamaker, C. 1990. *The Epistles to the Thessalonians.* Carlisle: Paternoster.

Warfield, B. B. 1974. *The Lord of Glory: a study of the designations of our Lord in the New Testament with especial reference to his deity*. Grand Rapids: Baker.

Waters, G. P. 2006. *The end of Deuteronomy in the Epistles of Paul*. Tübingen: Mohr Siebeck.

Watson, F. 2004. *Paul and the hermeneutics of faith*. London: T&T Clark.

Watts, J. D. W. 1987. *Isaiah 34–66*. Waco: Word.

Webster, J. B. 2000. *Barth*. London: Continuum.

Webster, J. 2003. *Holy Scripture: a dogmatic sketch*. Current issues in theology, vol. 1. Cambridge: Cambridge University Press.

Wedderburn, A. 1985. Some Observations on Paul's use of the Phrases 'in Christ' and 'with Christ'. *JSNT* 25:83–97.

Weinandy, T. 1995. *The Father's Spirit of Sonship: Reconceiving the Trinity*. Edinburgh: T&T Clark.

Wendland, H.-D. 1972[13]. *Die Briefe an die Korinther*. Göttingen: Vandenhoeck & Ruprecht.

Wenham, D. 1995. *Paul: follower of Jesus or founder of Christianity?* Grand Rapids: Eerdmans.

Williams, R. 2003. *Christ on trial: how the Gospel unsettles our judgement*. Grand Rapids: Eerdmans.

Willis, W. L. 1983. *Idol meat in Corinth : the Pauline argument in 1 Corinthians 8 and 10*. Chico, Calif.: Scholars Press.

Windisch, H. 1914. *Die göttliche Weisheit der Juden und die paulinische Christologie*. Leipzig: Hinrich.

–. 1924. *Der zweite Korintherbrief*. Göttingen: Vandenhoeck & Ruprecht.

Witherington, B., III. 1992. *Jesus, Paul, and the end of the world: a comparative study in New Testament eschatology*. Downers Grove: IVP.

–. 1994. *Friendship and finances in Philippi: the letter of Paul to the Philippians*. Valley Forge, Pa: Trinity Press International.

–. 1995. *Conflict and community in Corinth: a socio-rhetorical commentary on 1 and 2 Corinthians*. Grand Rapids: Eerdmans.

–. 2006. *1 and 2 Thessalonians: a socio-rhetorical commentary*. Grand Rapids: Eerdmans.

Witherington, B., III, and D. Hyatt. 2004. *Paul's Letter to the Romans: a socio-rhetorical commentary*. Grand Rapids: Eerdmans.

Wolff, C. 1989. *Der zweite Brief des Paulus an die Korinther*. Berlin: Evangelische Verlagsanstalt.

Woyke, J. 2005. *Götter, "Götzen", Götterbilder: Aspekte einer paulinischen "Theologie der Religionen"*. Berlin: W. de Gruyter.

–. 2007. Das Bekenntnis zum einzig allwirksamen Gott und Herrn und die Dämonisierung von Fremdkulten: Monolatrischer und polylatrischer Monotheismus in 1. Korinther 8 und 10. In *Gruppenreligionen im römischen Reich. Sozialformen, Grenzziehungen und Leistungen*, ed. J. Rüpke, 87–112. Tübingen: Mohr Siebeck.

Wrede, W. 2001. *Paul*. Trans. E. Lummis. Eugene, OR: Wipf & Stock.

Wright, B. G. 2007. The Structure of the Parables of Enoch: A Response to George Nickelsburg and Michael Knibb. In *EMSM*, ed. G. Boccaccini, 72–78. Cambridge: Eerdmans.

Wright, N. 1991. *The climax of the covenant: Christ and the law in Pauline theology*. Edinburgh: T&T Clark.

–. 1992. *The New Testament and the People of God*. Christian Origins and the Question of God: Part I. London: SPCK.

–. 1996. *Jesus and the Victory of God.* London: SPCK.

–. 1998. Jesus and the Identity of God. *ExAud* 14:42–56.

–. 2002. The Letter to the Romans. Introduction, commentary, and reflections. In *The New Interpreter's Bible*, ed. L. E. Keck, et al., 393–770. Nashville: Abington.

–. 2003. *The resurrection of the son of God.* London: SPCK.

–. 2005. *Paul: Fresh Perspectives.* London: SPCK.

Wright, N., and M. Borg. 1999. *The Meaning of Jesus: Two Visions.* London: SPCK.

Wright, T. 2009. *Justification: God's Plan and Paul's Vision.* London: SPCK.

Wyse, J. A. 2005. Loving God as an act of obedience: The Shema in context. In *Take this Word to Heart: The Shema in Torah and Gospel*, ed. P. B. Yoder, 11–51. Elkhart, Ind.: Institute of Mennonite Studies.

Yeo, K.-K. 1995. *Rhetorical interaction in 1 Corinthians 8 and 10: a formal analysis with preliminary suggestions for a Chinese, cross-cultural hermeneutic.* Leiden: Brill.

Yonge, C. D. 1995[3]. *The works of Philo.* Peabody: Hendrickson.

Zeilinger, F. 1992. *Krieg und Friede in Korinth: Kommentar zum 2. Korintherbrief des Apostels Paulus. Band 1: Der Kampfbrief, Der Versöhnungsbrief, Der Bettelbrief.* Köln: Böhlau.

–. 1997. *Krieg und Friede in Korinth: Kommentar zum 2. Korintherbrief des Apostels Paulus. Band 2: Die Apologie.* Köln: Böhlau.

Ziesler, J. 1990[2]. *Pauline Christianity.* Oxford: OUP.

Zizioulas, J. 1985. *Being as Communion: studies in personhood and the church.* Crestwood, NY: St. Vladimir's Seminary Press.

Zmijewski, J. 1978. *Der Stil der paulinischen "Narrenrede": Analyse der Sprachgestaltung in 2 Kor 11,1–12,10 als Beitrag zur Methodik von Stiluntersuchungen neutestamentlicher Texte.* Köln: Hanstein.

Zuntz, G. 1953. *The text of the epistles: a disquisition upon the Corpus Paulinum.* London: British Academy.

Index of Ancient Sources

1. Hebrew Bible and Septuagint

2. New Testament

4:11	131, 178	*Hebrews*		
4:13–5:11	112, 156, *168*	9:18	100	
4:13–18	*112*, 157	9:20	100	
4:14	151	10:29	100	
4:15–18	112	12:24	100	
4:16	164, 209, 227	13:20	100	
4:17–18	162, 163, 179, 186,			
	190, 193, 207, 221	*James*		
4:17	111, 112, 129, 157,	1:2	110	
	177, 186, 248	1:14–15	*121*	
4:18	112	2:1	227	
5:1–11	157			
5:9–10	162	*1 Peter*		
5:9	*168*	1:6–8	110	
5:10–11	163, 179, 186, 190,	1:8	*193*	
	193, 207, 221	2:17	*193*	
5:10	112, 129, 157, 177			
5:11	112	*2 Peter*		
5:16	132	2:4	226	
5:17	132			
5:23	155, 157, 238	*1 John*		
5:28	143, 154, 170, 179	2:15	*193*	
2 Thessalonians		*Jude*		
1:17	164	6	226	
3:3	171	14–15	227	
3:18	143			
		Revelation		
1 Timothy		13:8	208	
1:14	143	22:20	166	

3. Apocrypha and Pseudepigrapha

1 Esdras		9:4	*166*
4:20	116	16:1	*166*
6:33	*166*		
		1 Maccabees	
Esther		3:3–9	230
13:17	110	14:4–15	230
Judith		*2 Maccabees*	
2:28–3:2	216	2:22	173
6:21	*166*	3:15	*166*
8:17	*166*	3:22	*166*

4. Other Early Jewish Sources

Index of Modern Authors

Index of Subjects

(Author appears in footnotes when number is italicised)

Abraham 171, 215

Achaicus 155

Adam 8, 26, 27, 172, 173, 196, 201, 202, 205, 206, 232, 234, 240, 245, 255

Adonai 44

America 13

Anastasis 251

angel(s), angelology 20, 21-22, 73, 126, 127, 197, 202, 203, 207, 210, 225, 226, 228

apocrypha(l) 68, 197, 248

Arabia 251

Aramaic 14, 44, 188, 194, 223, 250

Asia 114

Athanasius 267

Athenians 251

Azazel 210

Ben Sira *199*

Cairo Genizah *15,*

Calvin, John *11*, 109, 267

Canute the Great 252

Christ-devotion esp. 113-137

Christian(s) 8, *28*, 70, 112, 126, 132, 133, 134, 135, 162, 165, 177, 179, 183, 189, 204, 215, 226, 236

– community 4, 14, 134, 152, *254*, 261, 267, 270, 271, 272

– life, living 4, 48, *56*, 113, 118, 131, 272

Christianity

– early 1, 5, 16, 18, 28, 29, 30, 31, 52, *56*, *64*, 122, 127, 197, 198, 201, 206,

223, 230, 234, *247*, 249, 250, 259, 260, 261, 262

church 4, 9, 12, 28, 30, 93, 97, *104*, 106, 108, 114, 123, 140, 178, 214, 237, 272

Cicero *89*, *251*

Clement of Alexandria 78

Colossians, book of *228*

Corinth 96, 116, 131, 150, 151, 159, 178

Corinthian correspondence 51, *101*, 138, 145, 155

Corinthians, believers 82, 83, 88, 89, 91, 94–97, 101, 102, 103, 107, 123, 125, 136, 138, 140, 141, 145, 150, *151*, 154, 156, 158, 159, 169, 175, 177, 194, 238

Corinthians, First book of 45, 51, 77, 114, 138, 139, 141, 176, 178, 181, 191, 194, 236, *248*

Corinthians, Second book of 51, 107, 142, 143, 144, 148, 161, 173, 176, 181, 185, 186, *248*

covenant 66, 67, 70, 81, 84, 97, 98–99, 100, 102, 104, 148, 191, 192, 193

creation 19, 27, 38, 39, 67, 71, 136, 148, 165, 175, 202, 223, 240, 242

curse 52, 98, 136, 190, 191, 192, 193, 218

Daniel, book of 157

David 94

death 106, 107, 109, 110, *112*, 119, 133, 136, 154, 161, 162, 163, 172, 175, 176, 177, 185, 192